The Biographical Process

Religion and Reason 11

Method and Theory
in the Study and Interpretation of Religion

MOUTON · THE HAGUE · PARIS

The Biographical Process

Studies in the History and Psychology of Religion

Edited by

FRANK E. REYNOLDS and DONALD CAPPS

MOUTON · THE HAGUE · PARIS

ISBN: 90-279-7522-1

Jacket design by Jurriaan Schrofer

Printed in Hungary

Preface

In the spring of 1971 the process which has culminated in the present collection of essays began in the coffee shop at the Divinity School of the University of Chicago. The two editors became engaged in a conversation which soon turned to the courses they were planning for the following year. In discussing Reynolds' course on 'Sacred Biography' in the History of Religions field and Capps' course on 'Psychohistorical Approaches to the Study of Religious Leaders' in the field of Religion and Psychological Studies, it became clear that while the two projected offerings had quite different foci, there were several areas of common interest. It was soon decided that a juxtaposition of the approaches represented by the two courses might be a fruitful undertaking, and that the courses should be replaced by a joint seminar wherein the areas of overlap and common interest could be explored.

As the planning for the seminar proceeded we learned that several of our colleagues in the Divinity School and in other areas of the University were working on biographically oriented projects, using materials and methods having much in common with our own. Consequently the conception of the seminar was revised and expanded, and these colleagues were invited to contribute papers and to participate in the discussions. Their responses were extremely positive and it was soon apparent that the seminar should be expanded from a one-term to a two-term endeavor. The first of these seminars was held in the spring of 1972, and the second in the winter of 1973.[1]

While these seminars were in progress we became increasingly aware that the kinds of scholarly approaches to the study and practice of biography being exemplified and refined in the seminar context were being pursued by a number of scholars in other university settings. Given the extent and quality of related research both within the seminar and beyond, we decided that the publication of a number of these research projects in a single collection would be useful. The present volume is the fruition of that decision.[2]

Without the cooperation and good will of our contributors, this volume would not have been possible. Our profound thanks goes to them. We were also the beneficiaries of an excellent editorial assistant in Judith Van Herik. In edited volumes of this nature, it is often the editorial assistant whose attention to matters both large and small insures the coherence of the final product. There is a fine line between editor and editorial assistant, and we are aware that this line has been transgressed innumerable times in the preparation of the manuscript. Ms. Van Herik merits special mention for giving the volume shape commensurate with its substance. Mr. Gary Alexander gave unstintingly of his time in completing the final typescript copy of the manuscript, as did Ms. Regina Clifford who took responsibility for the difficult task of proof-reading the text and for preparing the index of proper names.

We are indebted to our colleague, Professor Mircea Eliade, for his helpful critical reading of our introductory essay. It is the stronger for his patient and thoughtful guidance. Joseph M. Kitagawa, Dean of the Divinity School, University of Chicago, demonstrated his personal interest in the project both by contributing an essay to the volume and by making available generous monetary subsidies for editorial purposes. Finally, we are deeply thankful to Professor Jacques Waardenburg, general editor of the Mouton Press 'Religion and Reason' series, for his eminently trustworthy counsel throughout the conception and eventual accomplishment of our task. Our thanks, also, to Walter Capps for informing Professor Waardenburg of our seminar in biography. Needless to say, we and our contributors take appropriate responsibility for the contents of the volume.

Frank E. Reynolds
University of Chicago

Donald Capps
University of North Carolina at Charlotte

NOTES

1. A number of scholars who were not able to contribute formal papers made presentations in the seminars and contributed their perspectives to the discussion. Among these were Robert Grant (Eusebius' biography of Origen), Charles Long (W. E. B. DuBois), Bernard McGinn (Joachim of Fiore), Alan Miller (Japanese holy men), Fazlur Rahman (Ibn Taymiya), Jonathan Z. Smith (Appolonias of Tyana), Karl Weintraub (development of biography in the West), Jay Wilcoxen (Jeremiah), Susanne

H. Rudolph (the diary of Amar Singh), and John Woods (Shah Isma'il, of the Safavi dynasty in Iran). We wish to express our thanks to all of these persons, and to the many other students and faculty members who participated in the seminars as well.

2. Of the sixteen items in the collection, nine were presented in some form in the seminar content. The remaining seven were contributed by scholars who did not participate directly in the seminar sessions.

Contents

BIBLIOGRAPHY

Introduction

A random survey of the various authors who have contributed to this collection, and of the essays themselves, might well leave the impression of radical diversity rather than common orientation and purpose. The authors represent several disciplines, including history of religion and religious literature, religion and psychological studies, and anthropology. In terms of cultural content and geographical focus their subjects range from a tribe of non-literate headhunters in the Philippines, to the 'great traditions' of India, to 'popular' culture in America. Chronologically, they extend from ancient times to the contemporary period. However, in spite of this diversity there are common concerns which permeate the collection and give a distinctive flavor to the whole.

When the seminars began,[1] the editors self-consciously chose to avoid premature methodological closure. We decided to draw into the discussion those scholars whose biographical projects seemed interesting to us, and seemed to have some significant point of contact with our own projects. However, as the discussions proceeded and as our own reflections became more focused, it became clear that an implicit principle of selection was operative and that most if not all of those involved in the project shared a basic methodological concern. Despite the great diversity of personal approaches, disciplinary perspectives, and primary materials, our attention turned, more directly and explicitly, to the mythohistoric character of biographical traditions and biographical writing. We were reminded time and again of the common assumption of participants in the project that biographical traditions and writing, by their very nature, involved an intricate interweaving of the 'mythic' and 'historical' elements.

The recognition that mythic and historic factors interact in biographical traditions is certainly not in itself new. In fact, each of the three major disciplines which were represented has produced a considerable body of research and interpretation which bears directly on this problem. Since these bodies of research have provided the scholarly context for our own attempts to further the biographical enterprise, brief discussions of these scholarly traditions will serve as useful introductions to the collection of papers. The three major disciplines represented here are the history of religions, the anthropology of religion and the psychology of religion. While the project has had the effect of enticing each of the editors from his own chosen area of expertise into that of the other, and while the discussion which follows has involved collaboration from beginning to end, this discussion reflects the areas of specialty of each of the editors. However, in what follows, the interweaving of myth and history provides the unitive theme for our discussion of major studies in the three related disciplines.

1. Sacred biography and critical biography: The biographical process in the history of religions

Any discussion of the history of religions' contribution to the study of biography as we conceive it here must begin with myth and history as fundamental categories in the history of religions. The writings of Mircea Eliade on this theme have become classics in the field. Moreover, Eliade's discussions of the relation of myth and history are frequently accompanied by specific references to mythical and historical personages. For example, in *Myths, Dreams and Mysteries*, Eliade describes the religious man's view of his myths as the expression of 'absolute truth, because it narrates a *sacred* history ... which provides the pattern for human behavior'. Then, immediately following this more general statement on the nature of myth, Eliade focuses on the person of Christ, noticing that Christ is not a 'mythical' but a 'historical' personage, but that nonetheless 'the religious experience of the Christian is based upon an imitation of the Christ as an *exemplary pattern*'.[2] Numerous examples of general statements about 'myth and history' followed by 'biographical' illustrations can be found throughout Eliade's work. His suggestion that myth provides the exemplary pattern to be actualized in human history is central to our own view of biography as the complex interweaving of myth and history. Myth and history are not discontinuous, in this view, but manifest a complex interaction.

Among historians of religion who have dealt more specifically with biographic traditions, two styles of research have been pursued with particular intensity. On the one hand, many scholars have explored the structure and significance of the classical biographical texts and traditions within their own areas of specialization. On the other hand, other scholars have employed text-critical and other religio-historical methods to study the lives of religious individuals.

As we consider the work of the former group, we find that historians of religion who study classic biographical traditions are especially attracted to 'sacred' biographies. 'Sacred biography' refers to those accounts written by followers or devotees of a founder or religious savior. Such documents are an extraordinary form of biography because they both recount the process through which a new religious ideal is established and, at the same time, participate in that process.

Precisely because the sacred biography participates in the establishment of a new religious vision, authors of such sacred biographies are forced to make difficult decisions. Determining which biographical facts belong to the emerging image is a critical issue and, where two or more sacred biographies of the same biographical subject are extant, marked differences of judgment among the early followers are apparent. Indeed, two major divisions within sacred biography can often be discerned, namely, those biographies which 'humanize' the biographical subject by including episodes which reflect his common humanity, and those which 'spiritualize' the subject by expunging references to his human weakness, mental lapses, signs of occasional cruelty, and so on. The central issue here is the relation of biographical fact to the emerging mythical ideal. Given that the mythical ideal remains somewhat fluid at the time the sacred biography is written or compiled, the selection of biographical material is an extremely vexing problem. A single reported episode may have a constitutive effect on the resulting mythical ideal.

That the sacred biographer is understood to confront such problems implies that he is quite self-conscious about the nature of his task and of the problems involved in the inclusion or omission of materials. Such self-consciousness may seem surprising, since this form of 'sacred biography' represents the earliest biographical effort in a religious tradition. Nonetheless, this kind of awareness is very apparent. However, what is less prominent is a self-consciousness regarding the 'fit' between the actual life of the subject and the biographer's rendering of it. The sacred biographer is not primarily concerned to provide a narrative portrait or 'likeness' of the subject. Establishing the mythical ideal, or what might better be called the biographic image, takes precedence over a simple chronicling of biographical facts. Very often this biographic image is established by directing attention to a few key events in the life of the subject including, in most cases, his birth, his religious quest and its denouement, and his death. On the other hand, given the sacred biographer's concern with establishing the mythical ideal, he often finds it necessary to fill gaps in the subject's life which the less 'devoted' biographer might simply recognize and pass over. Stories of an apocryphal nature may be supplied to fill gaps left by a relatively inaccessible or uneventful childhood. Or, in the interests of the mythic intention of the narrative, years otherwise left unrecorded may be filled with episodes drawn from another period of the subject's life. Or finally, experiences of other members of the religious community may be attributed to the life of the founder or savior – only, however, when such attribution will enhance the claim for his personification of a new image of man.[3]

In short, the study of the sacred biographies of founders and saviors within the history of religions has raised fundamental issues concerning the genesis and formative development of the religious symbols and images which have been the basic constitutive elements of many of the great world religions, and of many lesser traditions as well. Moreover, such studies have provided material for the kind of comparative study of religious symbols and processes which historians of religion have traditionally seen as their higher goal. Unfortunately, however, the possibilities inherent in this kind of comparative study have thus far remained largely unexploited.[4]

Among other forms of sacred biography which historians of religion have confronted, the lives of saints, mystic prophets, kings and other charismatic religious figures have received the greatest attention. Though these several kinds of sacred biography, or more specifically, hagiography, have much in common with the sacred biographies of religious founders and saviors, there is an important difference. Whereas sacred biographies of founders and saviors primarily intend to depict a distinctively new religious image or ideal, those which chronicle lives of lesser religious figures present their subject as one who has realized, perhaps in a distinctive way, an image, ideal, or attainment already recognized by his religious community. In this kind of sacred biography slight attention may be given to chronological rendering of the life. More typically, the narrative is organized to emphasize the virtues or attainments manifested in the subject's life. For example, in the Chinese context, hagiographies of various monarchs are organized to highlight the virtues (or, in some cases which are a kind of mirror image of hagiography, the vices) associated with the subject and with his position in the history of his dynasty. Similarly, in the Buddhist tradition biographies of the various disciples of the Buddha are organized to highlight the particular virtue, attainment or vice which that disciple exemplified in classic form. Thus, Sāriputta is presented as a paragon of wisdom, Moggallāna as preeminent in the possession of magical power, Ānanda as the prime exemplar of compassion, and Devadatta as the embodiment of evil. In the Christian tradition, too, there are numerous accounts of lives of saints which are organized topically, with the acts of the subject recounted in terms of virtues such as 'charity' or 'honor'.[5]

In addition to sacred biographies of religious founders and hagiographies of lesser religious figures, sacred biographies of a more modern type have also appeared in the history of religions. For example, there have been numerous more or less confessional biographies of Western religious leaders and, more recently, of Eastern religious figures as well. Unlike the more traditional hagiographic writings, such confessional biographies tend to create a narrative portrait or likeness of the subject. They often organize his life story in terms of chronology, developmental patterns, and the process of self-realization. However, since the religious biographies written in these more contemporary styles have lost many of the qualities evident in traditional sacred biographies and hagiographies, historians of religion have tended to leave their interpretation to others. Nonetheless, it is quite possible that insights and sensitivities gained through the study of earlier forms of religious biography could be usefully applied to these more modern types of texts. It may be possible to discover the basic mythic or religious patterns which underly all, or at least some, of these texts. And it certainly would be possible to highlight a variety of symbolic, paradigmatic, and stereotypical elements which have not yet received the attention they deserve.[6]

Alongside their studies of classic biographical traditions, historians of religion have undertaken a second style of research, the creation of their own biographical reconstructions. Employing text-critical and other religio-historical methods, they have sought to penetrate behind various traditions of sacred biography and hagiography in order to develop 'historical' accounts of the lives of innovators and leaders. And further, they have traced the sources and development of various figures' religious experiences and creativity, and have interpreted their quality and religio-historical significance.

In many cases, particulary in studies of lives of great religious founders, the difficulties of the former, historical biographical, task have proved so immense that relatively little work of the latter type has been possible. Perhaps the classic example of this situation is to be found in the traditions of New Testament scholarship concerning the figure of Jesus. During the late nineteenth and early twentieth centuries, a series of spirited efforts were made to cut through the 'myths' of the New Testament accounts of Jesus' life to establish a core of historically verifiable facts and episodes around which a truly historical biography could be reconstructed. However, during the decades following the publication of William Wrede's *Das Messiasgeheimnis in den Evangelien* (1901)[7] the basic methodological foundations of this endeavor were devastated by a long line of so-called 'form' or 'redaction' critics who demonstrated that the presuppositions concerning the historical intentions of the Gospels on which the 'quest for the historical Jesus' had been based were erroneous, and that whereas Gospel studies could tell us a great deal about the traditions of the early Church they could provide little or no significant data concerning the life of Jesus. In recent years the question has been reopened by a number of scholars who accept the basic principles of form and redaction criticism, but who are now engaged in an effort to forge still more sophisticated methods through which they hope to establish the historicity of a few key episodes in Jesus' career. Nevertheless, even the most optimistic participants in this 'new quest' recognize that the hard information which can be generated by such methods is minimal indeed.[8]

Outside the Christian context, the fates of biographical researches into the actual lives of great religious founders have varied. In the case of Mohammed more adequate source material has been available and important biographical studies have resulted, including an older classic by Tor Andrae and a more recent two volume study by W. Montgomery Watt.[9] And in 1949 an important study of the life of Mani was included in Henri Puech's *Le manichéisme: son fondateur, sa doctine.*[10] However, most quests for historical figures behind traditional accounts of lives of great religious founders have followed the pattern of the quest for the historical Jesus; generally, the methods have been less refined and the results have been equally limited.[11]

With a few notable exceptions (e.g., the work of Andrae and Watt on Mohammed) the most interesting and lasting work done by those historians of religion concerned with the lives of founders has grown out of the study of their sacred biographies, whereas the scholars who have done the most important biographical reconstructions have concentrated on figures whose historical lives can be more easily documented. These latter scholars have also had to face the problems posed by the mytho-historic character of their data, including not only any traditional biographies which have been available, but also such items as eye-witness accounts, personal documents and other autobiographic materials. But because their documentation has usually been richer, more historically reliable and more varied, they have faced more manageable historiographic problems; and because the historiographic problems have been more manageable they have been able to treat issues which transcend the single question of historicity. They have been able to use historical critical methods to establish a defensible framework of fact and sequence, and then to work within that framework to develop a creative religio-historical interpretation which highlights the sources of the particular religious experience of the individual, the process through which it developed, the forms through which it was expressed, its significance in the immediate religious context, and (in some instances) its significance in the general history of religions.

Unfortunately no major figure within the discipline has yet spelled out in any detail the procedures and implications of this specifically religio-historical style of biographical scholarship. However, some indications can be gleaned from the various biographical studies which historians of religions have published over the years. For example, Mahasaru Anesaki, the great Japanese historian of religions who wrote in the early decades of the twentieth century, has contributed a fascinating although perhaps overly confessional biography of Nichiren in which he adroitly synthesizes two seemingly contradictory themes. Anesaki's narrative traces the historical and developmental process through which Nichiren came to realize and implement his religious vocation, and at the same time he emphasizes that Nichiren's life was lived, often quite self-consciously, 'in thorough-going conformity to, or emulation of, Buddha's deeds and work'.[12] Shortly after Anesaki published his work, Louis Massignon came forth with a classic study of al-Hallāj. Massignon interprets the life of the great Muslim mystic and martyr by the dual means of reconstructing a 'silhouette' of the historical life (Volume I) and of exploring the impact of his unique religious experience, thought and example in subsequent Islamic history (Volume II).[13] More recently, R. J. Zwi Werblowski published an impressive biographical study of Joseph Karo, which focuses on the development and continuing coexistence of the mystical (Kabbalah) and legal (Halakhah) aspects of Karo's religious experience and activities, and concludes with a discussion of the way these two distinctive modes of experience and action coexisted, not only in Karo's own life but also within the broader context of Rabbinic Judaism.[14] While we do not intend to present these three studies as either ideal or typical representatives of religio-historical biography, they do illustrate the historian of religion's concern to be historical in such a way that the specifically religious dimensions of his subject are brought into sharp relief. Perhaps equally important, each of these three studies suggests a specific insight or emphasis which has contributed to our own methodological reflections.

2. Cultural models and life histories: The biographical process in the anthropology of religion

Like the studies of biography developed in the history of religions, those carried out in the field of anthropology may be roughly classified into two groups. First, some anthropologists have adopted what we call the 'cultural models' approach which is concerned with 'life models' which express the culture's understanding of the ideal or essential man. Insofar as this approach includes historical as well as mythical personages, it emphasizes not the individuality of these personages, but their role in generating and/or personifying the life model. Secondly, other anthropological interpreters have used an approach which aims to record the 'life history' of an individual in the society under investigation (usually a non-literate or village society), and then to analyze it in the context of the prevailing culture. This view emphasizes the individuality or personality of the biographical subject ('individuality' and 'personality' are often used interchangeably in this literature). When it considers 'external' influences on the formation of the personality, it tends to stress cultural as opposed to hereditary factors.[15]

The recent anthropological interest in biographical materials was first stimulated by the work of Paul Radin in the 1920s, and particularly by Radin's influential biography of a Winnebago Indian, *Crashing Thunder*. According to Radin, the primary purpose of the research which culminated in his publication of *Crashing Thunder* was 'not to obtain autobiographical details about some definite personage, but to have some representative, middle aged individual of moderate ability describe his life in relation to the social group in which he had grown up'.[16] Hence, Radin inaugurated the 'life models' approach in anthropology. At the same time, however, Radin has been recognized by the proponents of the 'life history' school as that anthropologist who first devoted serious study to biographical materials, and he has therefore been recognized by this school as *its* intellectual founder as well. Hence, Radin's work made possible the two biographical approaches which have characterized anthropological research to date. Once the issue of biography was addressed, some would follow his own explicit intention, and would concentrate their attention on the 'life model' which expressed a given culture's understanding of the representative, if not, in the strict sense, the 'ideal' man. Others would follow Radin's encouragements to concentrate on biographical materials *per se*, and would use such materials to deal with the questions of 'individual variability' and the 'idiosyncratic component' in individual lives, and to explore the relationship between 'personality' and 'culture'.[17]

As indicated, the 'cultural models' approach to biographical research in anthropology is illustrated by Paul Radin's *Crashing Thunder*. However, there have been various applications of this basic methodological emphasis in the decades following the publication of Radin's book. The conception which underlies much of this research – the belief that, in many of the non-literate societies studied by anthropologists there is a more or less direct, one-to-one relationship between the cultural model and the individual life – has received support from various anthropological sources. Thus, in discussing Australian aborigines, W.E.H. Stanner suggests that these so-called 'primitive' people understood life as a 'one-possibility thing' which admitted little basis of variation. One fails to find among these aborigines those sentiments of tragedy or self-pity 'which develop only if life presents real alternatives, or if it denies an alternative that one feels should be there'.[18] The British anthropologist, Gregory Bateson, provides a specific example of life understood as a 'one-possibility thing'. A young Iatmul, aged seventeen, on being asked to describe his life, started with birth, went through childhood, adolescence, manhood and his advanced years, without indicating any awareness of his actual age. What the young man described was the prescribed course of his life, the life of a man in a specific culture.[19] Much evidence, then, supports the view that at least in some cultures there is no clear differentiation between the life of the individual and the life model of the culture. This is not to say that Radin believed this to be true of Winnebago society, but it does mean that a biography which merely assumed, without investigating the basis for the assumption of a differentiation between the individual life and the life model of the culture would, in the cases cited, miss a critical element of the community's own view of life as a 'one-possibility thing'.

However, it is clear that Radin's approach in *Crashing Thunder* was not based on considerations of the Winnebago's own view of this matter, but was rather a narrative device intended to shed light on the culture. As John Dollard put it, *Crashing Thunder* provides 'an inside view of the Winnebago culture rather than ... a careful analysis of a human life'.[20] More recently, this narrative device has been used by Clifford Geertz in his comparison of two Islamic leaders. As Geertz writes: 'These men are metaphors. Whatever they originally were or did as actual persons has long since been dissolved into an image of what Indonesians or Moroccans regard to be true spirituality.'[21]

Since Radin's pioneering work, other anthropologists have not only applied but have also significantly extended the 'cultural models' approach. For example, some scholars have addressed the fact that in most cultures more than one life model is represented as worthy of emulation. Alternative life models are recognized. Again, an example is provided by Bateson in his studies of the Iatmul.[22] Bateson points to a series of myths (which are ordinarily the original source of life models) in which two brothers are contrasted, the elder being a man of discretion and the younger being a man of violence. The younger is the great hero of the society, but it is also he who, in fits of temper, set fire to the original mythological ceremonial house and killed his sister's son. According to Bateson, the violent man was most admired among the Iatmul, but at the same time they believed he could not be trusted with the society's secret lore. For, in erudite debate, he might blurt out some important aspect of that tradition. Such traditions were therefore entrusted to the man of discretion whose balance and caution enabled him to keep esoteric discussion more or less systematic. In short, the violent man figuratively 'sets fire' to the tradition while the man of discretion preserves it. On the other hand, the violent man is assertive and resists intimidation, and this refusal to be cowed was a highly valued trait in Iatmul society. The point, of course, is that two life styles were valued in Iatmul society and both were supported by the primal myths of the society.[23]

There are other variants of the extension of the cultural model view of biography. Presumably, the alternative life models of the Iatmul were indigenous to the society. But among American Indians, a problem is presented by the impact of non-Indian models on the society as a result of outside cultural influences. Don Handelman's biographical study of Henry Rupert, the last shaman among the Washo Indians of western Nevada and eastern California, describes an individual forced to choose between the traditional Washo model and the Christian model inculcated in the Indian School supervised by the United States Army.[24] According to Handelman, Rupert resisted the Christian model, appealing to certain exemplary forebears who were also Washo shamans as the rationale for this resistance. But, significantly, Rupert did not as successfully resist a Hindu man whom he had taken on as a spiritual helper. Through a dream, Rupert came to realize that, contrary to the advice of two Indian women, he should recognize that Hindus and Indians do the same work and should therefore become partners. In Handelman's view, this acceptance of the cultural model of Hinduism (as refracted through his young spirit helper) led Rupert to synthesize new and traditional alternatives to create a model having greater coherence than a synthesis of Indian and Christian cultural models could possibly have effected. Rupert also seems to have recognized the deficiency of traditional Indian models for coping with the influence of white Christianity, while Hinduism offered an additive which, when joined with Washo tradition, would presumably compete successfully against Christianity. Hence, Handelman's study offers an alternative view of the 'cultural model' approach in biography by recognizing a conflict of two or more life models. In addition, it suggests a synthesis of two models, one of which is involved in the fundamental conflict.

Still another alternative within the cultural model approach to biography has been developed with great penetration by Kenelm Burridge in his study of two messianic leaders of twentieth century Cargo Cults in New Guinea.[25] Like Bateson, Burridge refers to the 'primal myths' which provide the basis of life models, especially the models of leadership. And, again like Bateson, Burridge shows that the four myths which comprise the primal myth provide three fundamental alternative life models, each of which is presented as native reaction to the Europeans who control most of the island's wealth. These alternatives include an acceptance of the status quo, an attempt to force Europeans to cooperate with their black neighbors, and an ethic of self-help in the face of European non-cooperation. In addition to these alternatives as presented in the myths, Burridge recognizes a fourth possibility by which, neglecting the myths altogether or interpreting them in a single willful sweep without regard to their detail, the Tangu try to rid themselves of Europeans and start afresh. The fourth alternative, while reflecting the deep anger of the Tangu toward Europeans, is not strictly consistent with what Burridge calls the 'myth-dream' as expressed in the primal myth.

This formulation of alternatives becomes of direct biographical importance when Burridge focuses on the lives of the two messianic leaders, Mambu and Yali. Mambu and Yali, each in his own way, adopted the fourth alternative of ignoring the myth and hence the life models advocated in the 'primal myth'. Needless to say, Mambu and Yali were unsuccessful in driving the Europeans out and both were eventually imprisoned. However, the Tangu did not allow the 'historical', Mambu and Yali the last word; rather, 'myth-dream' came into play and the lives of both Mambu and Yali were retrospectively altered so that both leaders were portrayed as successful in forcing the Europeans *to cooperate* with native New Guineans. As Burridge observes, they now represent the 'new man' whose 'purpose is to remove white men from the amoral dominance they have currently assumed'.[26] The myth-dream draws both Mambu and Yali back under the aegis of the primal myth, where they now personify the 'cultural model' of mutual cooperation between natives and Europeans. However, this model is precisely the one which has little historical basis and is thus an 'ideal model' whose reality is not historical but mythical.

With Burridge's *Mambu* the anthropological study of 'cultural models' has come a great distance from Radin's *Crashing Thunder*. While the relation of an individual life to a cultural model is still its dominant concern, more recent work has significantly complicated the issue. On the one hand, a number of 'cultural models' grow out of a single set of primal myths. On the other hand, the relation of life to model is made the more complex when the New Guineans themselves introduce a myth-history distinction. The 'historical' leaders (Mambu and Yali) respond to one cultural model (not explicitly approved by the myth) while the 'mythical' leaders respond to another. By tracing the historical life and its subsequent mythicization, the biographer succeeds in capturing the 'unresolved tension' experienced both by the leaders (the biographical subjects) and by the society as a whole.[27]

As noted above, the 'life history' approach to biography contrasts with the cultural models approach in that it stresses the individuality or personality of a member of a society. Scholars using the life history approach frequently select community leaders as biographical subjects. In a leader, the anthropologist finds immediate support for the argument for 'individual variations' in the life structures of members of a given society. As Clyde Kluckhohn, author of the seminal study, *The Use of Personal Documents in Anthropology*, writes: "Without invoking any exaggerated 'great man theory of culture', it may be submitted that the source of the history of various societies was unmistakably different because at a crucial period there 'just happened' to be a leader of unusual capacity or foresight." Kluckhohn cites as an example of this critical difference the role of Juan Pistola as leader of the Uaqui village of Pascua.[28] Some twenty years earlier, Robert H. Lowie made the same point when he noted that 'it was natural for older writers to make the assumption still current among educated laymen, that on primitive levels no individuality can assert itself sufficiently to rise definitely above the rank and file and impress its own stamp upon the whole community'. As an example of such individuality, Lowie cites the case of Medicine Crow of the Wovoka Indians. However, from the point of view of later 'life history' proponents, this example is unfortunate, for the commonplace personality of Medicine Crow leads Lowie to conclude that historical circumstances 'lent a purely accidental halo' to one of 'the least interesting and powerful of [Indian] personalities'.[29] Nonetheless, these anthropologists' interest in unique leaders has had the effect of drawing attention to the dynamic, historical character of even supposed 'non-historical' preliterate societies.[30]

Of course, the life-history school has not restricted itself to consideration of leaders. For, in addition, it has developed numerous studies based on the personal documents of non-leader figures, also with the intention of demonstrating individual variations. In some cases, a topical approach has been employed, segregating life history materials under topics such as widowhood and divorce, inheritance, adolescence and adulthood, the tribal code, etc.[31] And, more recently, the work of Oscar Lewis has drawn attention to what we might call the 'collective biography' of families. His *Children of Sanchez* is a classic example of family life history. Nor has the emphasis on 'individual variations', or the 'idiosyncratic component' (to use Kluckhohn and Mowrer's phrase) led anthropologists to adopt an extreme view of the potential influence of individuals in the transformation of societies and cultures. Rather, what distinguishes the life-history school is not its emphasis on individuality *per se*, but on the question of the relative weight which ought to be given to individuality and culture.[32] Thus, as Kluckhohn, commenting on Leo Simmons' extremely important life-history of the Hopi Indian *Sun Chief*, points out, the real issue is 'how much is culture pattern and how much is true individual history'. In setting this out as his primary problem, the life-history proponent is required, within the limits of his material, to take a historical-critical view of the life. This means paying careful attention both to the psychological dynamics of human growth and development and to the cultural setting in which this individual was socialized.[33]

The implications of this historical-critical methodology for anthropological biography are perhaps best seen in former Harvard University anthropologist Alfred M. Tozzler's essay, 'Biography and Biology', published in Clyde Kluckhohn and Henry A. Murray's *Personality in Nature, Society, and Culture*. While not intended as a seminal article for the life-history approach to biography, this article clearly demonstrates the desire of culture-and-personality theorists to use historical-critical methods in penetrating behind biographical myth. Tozzler's argument is directed against those biographers who employ notions of hereditary influence to account for personality characteristics. And he is perhaps especially critical of the efforts of biographers to adduce the influence of 'racial strains' which presumably account for fundamental personality conflicts in the subject. We can hardly criticize Tozzler's analysis of the various heredity fallacies employed in biography. However, a fundamental myth-history issue is at stake here, and Tozzler himself uncovers it when he concludes: "From the days of Alexander the Great, who Plutarch 'allowed as certain' was a descendent of Hercules, to the most modern of writers, the *biographical pattern* has remained fixed. The biologist has done little to alter this model, and an anthropologist ventures to step in and suggest a more careful scrutiny of scientific facts in writing of the lives of the great and the near-great."[34] Tozzler's concern is to separate the 'biographical pattern' prompted by traditional heredity views from the authentic biographical task, and to do so in the name of science. Thus, the fundamental biographical issue that lies behind the culture-heredity debate is the problem of biography as mythical construct. The 'cultural models' approach takes such constructs very seriously, but frequently at the expense of neglecting individual variation. Conversely, the 'life history' approach lays heavy emphasis on the historical life, but neglects the role of myth as providing cultural models which continue to influence the lives of individuals. Obviously, this problem requires much more attention than anthropologists of religion currently accord it.

Finally, one other related problem also remains insufficiently explored by either the 'cultural models' or the 'life history' approach. This is the possibility of biographical patterns which transcend specific cultures and their traditions. As Claude Lévi-Strauss suggests in his review of Simmons' *Sun Chief*, there is basis for the view that through biography the alien character of other cultures is immediately transcended; the grounds for this view of biography invite the possibility of biographical images of a more universal sort. Lévi-Strauss writes: 'The function of primitive biographies is to provide a psychological expression of cultural phenomena. This psychological expression – because it is psychological – is immediately accessible to any human being, even to one who belongs to a quite different cultural surrounding. The systematic study of a culture, on the other hand, is always a description of that culture from the outside.'[35] His view suggests that biography plumbs those forms of life which transcend cultural boundaries. To our mind, this is a fundamental issue which the anthropological study of biography needs to address, perhaps by centering attention on trans-cultural biographical patterns. It is also an issue which, as Lévi-Strauss suggests when he bases his argument for a universal biographical pattern on the supposition of a psychological sub-stratum common to all cultures, leads us directly into the psychological study of the biographical process.[36]

3. Hero myths and men of genius: The biographical process in the psychology of religion

When we turn to the psychology of religion, we encounter a scholarly tradition in which the study of biography has played an important role both in the development of theory and in the empirical work of the discipline. Those theoretical and empirical contributions of biography to the psychology of religion have been made under the aegis of two distinct emphases: the psychoanalytic study of the hero myths which persist in formal biography, and the interests of 'academic' pschologists in men of genius. However, the latter emphasis has not fared well in recent years, and many of its concerns have been taken up by psychohistorians identified with the psychoanalytic school.

The study of hero myths was a prominent interest of Freudian psychologists from the very earliest years of the psychoanalytic movement.[37] An essential element in their interest in hero myths was the early psychoanalysts' efforts to discover the 'biographical pattern' behind myths, legends, and folklore. If such mythology manifests a biographical pattern to which all mythical heroes conform, and if this pattern could be shown to be universal in its scope, then this pattern or aspects of the pattern might appear in historical lives as well. In *The Myth of the Birth of the Hero*, Otto Rank believes that he has isolated such a pattern.[38] It includes the following events: (1) the hero is the child of distinguished parents; (2) his origin is preceded by difficulties, such as the continence, prolonged barrenness or secret intercourse of the parents; (3) during or before the pregnancy, there is a prophecy cautioning against his birth and usually threatening danger to the father or father-surrogate; (4) he is surrendered to the water, then saved by animals or lowly people and suckled by a female animal or a humble woman; (5) after he grows up, he finds his parents, takes his revenge but is acknowledged as heir; and (6) he finally achieves rank and honors.

Rank contends that this pattern is exemplified in the biographies of Sargon Moses, Oedipus, Gilgamesh, Jesus, Siegfried, Lohengrin and a host of other mythic and historical personages. And he considers this search for the biographical pattern an exercise in 'myth interpretation' which requires an ability to distinguish the essential aspects of the biographical pattern from 'crude variations from the prototype'. Since this pattern is rooted in the human psyche, Rank claims that it constitutes a universal pattern. That the list of figures above makes an extremely broad cultural sweep suggests some basis for this view.

More recently, Joseph Campbell has carried forward Rank's interests in the universal biographical pattern, or what he calls the 'monomyth'.[39] Campbell's biographical pattern is based on the pilgrimage of the hero, that 'one composite adventure ... of a number of the world's symbolic carriers of the destiny of Everyman'. The adventure itself consists of three great stages, the separation or departure, the trials and victories of initiation, and the return. There are innumerable individual differences within the general pattern. Some myths enlarge on one or two aspects of the cycle, others string together a number of independent cycles into a single series, and still others condense two or more episodes into a single episode. For example, in the second, initiatory stage, Campbell includes such episodes as the meeting with the goddess, woman as the temptress, atonement with the father, etc. As an interpretive procedure, this recognition of subthemes in the overall biographical pattern allows Campbell to take seriously the 'crude variations' which Rank dismissed. And, by recognizing variations within the pattern, Campbell is also able to discern historical development in the versions of the monomyth. On investigation, the variations reveal a long range development in the versions of the pattern. This development is exemplified in such processes as a god outgrown immediately becoming a life-destroying demon.

While Campbell's stress on the historical development of variations within the pattern is his most important contribution to our present discussion, we should also note his emphasis on the 'social function of the hero'. The hero finds himself in a world suffering from 'a symbolical deficiency' and, through the biographical pattern of separation, initiation and eventual return, the hero 'brings back from his adventure the means for the regeneration of his society as a whole'.[40] (In fairy tales the hero achieves a domestic rather than, as in the case of myths, a societal triumph.) With a rather different emphasis, this theme of the social function of the hero also figures in the work of a third psychoanalytic student of biography, Ernst Kris.

Moving closer to biography proper, but still within the realm of folklore and myth, Kris makes further refinements in the notion of the 'biographical pattern'. Observing that Freud was inclined to center his attention on the attitudes of individual biographers, Kris proposes a different emphasis, i.e., the psychoanalytic study of biography as a literary category with a social function.[41] More specifically, he addresses himself to biographical patterns in medieval and Renaissance biographies of artists. The pattern which he discerns in these early biographies includes such events as the child's chance encounter with a highly regarded artist who recognizes the boy's miraculous talent, the youth's early striving for artistic expression, and his competition with other contemporary artists in demonstrating his greater ability to paint visual illusions. In his discussion of this pattern, which is admittedly not as detailed as the patterns which Rank and Campbell recognize in traditional hero myths, Kris nonetheless anticipates Campbell by centering on the historical development implicit in the overall biographical pattern. Specifically, Renaissance biographies of artists alter the theme of the princely origin of the abandoned infant (as emphasized by Rank) through their emphasis on the divine origin of genius. This alteration indicates an historical development within the biographical pattern.

Moving beyond Rank and Campbell, Kris also notices a connection between the biographical pattern in medieval and Renaissance biographies of artists, and the mythical ideal reflected in the preeminent 'sacred biography' in the religious culture. In an apocryphal gospel of Jesus, the Lord is portrayed as sculpting clay birds into which he thereupon breathed life. According to Kris, Jesus himself is the mythical ideal behind the biographical pattern of the medieval and Renaissance artist. Kris thus recognizes historical development within the biographical pattern, and he also takes note of the historical connection between the biographical pattern and an exemplary figure as portrayed in a sacred biography.

Finally, Kris emphasizes the social function of the biographical pattern. As we have seen, Campbell recognizes the hero's social function within the myth itself. Kris does not reject this view, any more than he rejects Freud's attention to the attitudes of the biographers. But, in addition, Kris recognizes the social function, or the exemplary role, of the biographical pattern itself. This social function of the pattern, which he calls 'enacted biography', is based on the fact that, once the biographical pattern becomes known, younger would-be artists begin self-consciously to pattern their lives according to the biographical model. Thus, the pattern becomes constitutive of human life and not merely its consequence. However, as the pattern becomes constitutive, it also undergoes changes. In some cases, the pattern assumes new depth as new life-events are added and old ones reinterpreted or discarded. In other cases, the pattern is trivialized with melodramatic events being substituted for genuinely dramatic events in the original pattern. One such melodramatic event in later forms of the biographical pattern of artists' lives is the suicide of the artist because he discovers he has omitted the horse-shoes from an equestrian statue. Hence, in some later accretions, much of the deeper subtlety of the earlier pattern may be obscured and the more encompassing 'events' are replaced by 'episodes' which are not always related thematically to the overall pattern.

However, Kris' major point is not the decline of the pattern itself, though this is extremely important to the student of biography. Rather, his primary concern is to show that the biographical pattern is an effective means of transmitting the life of an exemplary type, in this case, the artist, to succeeding generations. He writes, 'One gains sometimes the impression that the actual behavior of one or another of the famous artists of the time has been used as a prototype, frozen into a formula which is being handed down as such to succeeding generations.'[42] And, related to this issue of the transmission of the model is the question of its reception. Here Kris suggests that there are particular times in history, especially when the natural succession of generations has broken down, when 'the boundary between the individual and tradition grows hazy and identification with the ancestor decides the nature and direction of the individual's existence.'[43] In such times, the phenomenon of 'enacted biography' comes to prominence. However, at no time is it entirely without influence.

In short, Kris addresses the same general concerns as Rank and Campbell but he makes a number of important refinements. Unlike Rank, whose interest in the unalterability of the pattern (hence, its universality) caused him to believe that possible transformations of the pattern are merely 'crude variations', Kris joins Campbell in recognizing historical development as the pattern itself remains intact. But he surpasses Campbell in suggesting that in this historical development, new patterns may emerge out of older patterns. We have seen one example of this in the case of biographical patterns of the artist.[44] Too, in showing that the theme of princely origin is replaced by the theme of the divine origin of genius, Kris not only indicates how one pattern may emerge from another but also how two patterns might become synthesized. As he puts it, 'We are in a position to narrow the gap between the legend of the discovery of talent and the myth of the birth of the hero.'[45] And finally, Kris emphasizes the reciprocity between the biographical pattern and a specific audience. The pattern influences the lives of social groups – e.g., artist 'types' – as they 'enact' it, and this enactment in turn leads to alterations in the biographical pattern. Hence, Kris recognizes a social dimension in the historical evolution of biographical patterns.

We turn next to the second major trend of biographical concern within psychological studies, namely, the interest of 'academic' psychologists in the man of genius. This interest can be traced to two nineteenth century psychologists, Galton and Lombroso. Galton's classic study, *Hereditary Genius*, which is based on an analysis of eminent British families, argued for a high degree of inherited talent among men of genius. This study prompted a spate of scientific studies of the problem of genius, including Cattell's studies of eminent men, Castle's study of eminent women and Terman's use of intelligence testing in his *Genetic Studies of Genius*. Unlike the emphasis of the Galton school on the role of inheritance in genius, Lombroso emphasized the relation of 'genius and madness', contending that the popular view of the relation between genius and mental aberration has much basis in fact. The Lombroso view was developed and modified by Ernst Kretschmer in the 1920s with his lectures on the psychology of men of genius. These two trends in the psychology of genius were well established by the 1920s and 1930s but, by the 1940s and 1950s the biographical slant of much of the earlier literature was supplanted by studies in the measurement of intelligence and creativity. The biographical approach did not die out entirely; however, the focus of the remaining interest in biography now shifted to the study of 'personal documents' as a basis of psychologists' collaboration with anthropologists in their 'life-history' studies.

Ernst Kretschmer is a pivotal figure in the psychology of men of genius.[46] Perhaps more than any other academic psychologist, he was very much aware that he approached biographical issues from a historical-critical point of view. Unlike the Freudians, he had little patience with 'mythical' biography. His statement to this effect deserves quotation: 'The personalities which form the material of our research have been selected in the first place according to the purely external criterion of fame – that fame which attaches itself to tangible personal creations: Literary or scientific works, works of art, inventions, concrete historical documents, etc. *The legendary, archaic-*

mythological sort of fame which still constitutes the core of the medieval traditions clinging to saints and heroes is, on the other hand, of little or no use for systematic inquiries into the nature of genius.'[47] Kretschmer goes on to say that the medieval traditions have 'no interest for the living personality itself.' In contrast, 'We find the modern conception of genius bound strongly to individuality, however much it may oscillate from time to time back to the archaic saint and hero apotheosis.'[48] Here, Kretschmer clearly betrays his bias in favor of non-mythological conceptions of biography, especially such conceptions which root genius in the living personality itself.

For his own study of men of genius, Kretschmer sought a method appropriate to this modern conception of genius. The criteria which he adopted to study such men clearly demonstrate his attention to historical-critical methods. For example, he argued that the basis for determining who qualifies as a 'man of genius' is 'the relative permanence of the reputation'. However, he warned that in 'a critical, historical atmosphere' as opposed to 'mythological circles', the permanence of reputation will be judged not on the basis of 'a happy conjunction of social circumstances or from the stupefying effect of a blatant, psychopathic singularity of person', but on the basis of real achievement as reflected in sustained artistic work, the transformation of political institutions, a lifetime of scientific achievement, etc.[49] The important point is Kretschmer's belief that the mythological view of genius emphasizes the social accident, while the historical-critical view makes judgments based on the real attainments of the living personality. Hence, the historical-critical view of biography is consistent with the emerging science of personality which seeks to capture the living individual.

When Kretschmer moves to the psychology of genius proper, his most significant contribution lies in his emphasis on 'spiritual periodicity' in the flowering of individual genius. On the assumption that no form of mental or spiritual activity, especially the creative force of genius, flows evenly and constantly through the whole course of life, Kretschmer directs his analysis of lives to the problem of 'spiritual periodicity', i.e., to the pattern of creative energy in an individual life. Following Goethe's own observation that 'the man of genius experiences a repetition of adolescence', he isolates a series of such 'repetitions' in Goethe's life, occurring roughly seven years apart and each culminating in artistic achievement. Now, not every life of genius involves a regular pattern of the repetition of artistic achievement. In some lives the artistic achievement comes early, in others it comes late. But the critical biographical point is that the notion of 'spiritual periodicity' is a concept of biographical pattern and Kretschmer himself uses the term 'pattern' to describe it. However, here the pattern is not the product of a traditional myth or the life of an exemplary figure. Rather, in consonance with the modern conception of individuality, the pattern is idiosyncratic to the individual himself.

On the other hand, there is an interesting twist in Kretschmer's discussion of spiritual periodicity, one which begins to suggest the recovery of the mythological dimension of biography which he so vehemently denounces. For, in the end, he concludes that it is precisely the man of genius who is least in control of his own life pattern. While the normal individual of strong mental constitution is relatively impervious to the fluctuations of the 'cosmos' (seasonal changes and the like) and to his own bodily resonances, the genius is considerably affected by these natural and bodily rhythms. If he is unusually sensitive to the social world around him, he is also uniquely responsive to the natural and physical world as well. This may mean, therefore, that 'the biographical pattern' is actually less 'individualistic' in the life of the genius and that his life, therefore, marks the beginning of a reaffirmation of more traditional structures.

A more explicit fusion of the modern concept of individuality and traditional structures (based on cosmological and biological processes) is provided by Erik Erikson. While he is formally a psychoanalyst, Erikson's studies, *Young Man Luther* and *Gandhi's Truth*, bear certain similarities to academic psychology's studies of men of genius.[50] Like Kretschmer, he emphasizes the study of individual lives with attention to the historical-critical view of biography. Too, he emphasizes his interest in capturing his subjects' 'genius' – in each case, their 'religious genius'. At the same time, Erikson is conscious of standing in the psychoanalytic tradition in that his interpretations of individual lives employ psychoanalytic concepts. In this, he follows a tradition in psychoanalysis (one which we consider less important to biographical study than the mythical hero tradition developed above) which treats historical lives as 'case studies'. (Precursors of Erikson's work include Freud's study of Leonardo Da Vinci, Edward Hitschmann's shorter studies of Brahms and Swedenborg, L. Pierce Clark's study of Abraham Lincoln and a host of others.) It is not inaccurate to say that Erikson stands in this tradition; certainly, he uses psychoanalytic notions throughout his studies of Luther and Gandhi. On the other hand, to view these books as merely 'case studies' is to miss their larger significance for the psychological study of biography. For, at the very least, Erikson's work reflects Kretschmer's concerns with both the problem of genius and the matter of spiritual perodicity, and his notion of the life cycle is especially important as a major contribution to efforts to chart *patterns* of spiritual periodicity. And, on the other hand, his emphasis on the life cycle, with its basis in modern notions of individuality, leads Erikson eventually to address the problem of myth – thus recovering aspects of the myth of the hero approach to biography. Erikson's contribution to the psychological study of biography is therefore that of synthesizing the hero myth and the man of genius approaches. This accomplishment requires further elucidation.

As noted, the key to Erikson's achievement is his notion of the life cycle. With its central focus on the problem of identity, the life cycle theory is especially responsive to the modern concept of individuality. However, the life cycle theory is also definitely rooted in patterns of biological rhythm and is at least attentive to larger 'cosmic' rhythms. Even more important is the simple fact that the theory of an eight stage life cycle resonates with traditional biographical patterns. Thus, Erikson notes that Shakespeare developed a seven stage life cycle whose structure is not unlike his own, and suggests that Shakespeare's formulation is rooted solidly in the Christian tradition.[51] But his life cycle theory is also related to a non-Western traditional biographical pattern in his study of Gandhi.

In an introductory chapter to *Gandhi's Truth*, Erikson gives an account of a seminar held in Ahmedabad for the purpose of discussing his life cycle theory. More specifically, the seminar focused on the relation of Hindu life stages to Erikson's life cycle. Erikson indicates that he did not resist attempts to correlate the two biographical patterns, recognizing that his life-stages, for all their seemingly scientific aura, harbored a 'mythological trend' of their own. Hence, he acknowledges that his own life cycle schema was as suspect to the modern sceptic in the seminar as was the Hindu schema. He writes: 'A group of otherwise well-trained individuals when confronted with religious world-images never quite knows whether to consider the existence of such remnants of magic thinking the result of meaningless habituation or an irrational systematization. And yet, a pragmatic world-view which shuns all concepts of the cycle of generations can cause widespread disorientation. In such a dilemma, one cannot help admiring the ideational and ceremonial consistency of the older world-images.'[52] Erikson here does not claim that his life cycle scheme qualifies as a 'religious world-image'. But he does recognize that it articulates similar religious meanings. And this recognition is especially evident in his use of both life-stage schemas – the Hindu dharmic structure and his own life cycle theory – to provide the *pattern* which structures the biography as a whole. While the Hindu stages are especially prominent in chapter headings – that is, at the formal structural level – the Eriksonian life cycle stages operate more prominently at the level of biographical narrative. Nonetheless, there is a structural fusion of the Hindu and the Eriksonian life cycle schemas.

This fusion enables Erikson to claim that he brings to the traditional interpretation of the events in Gandhi's life 'a new awareness'. Take, for example, his interpretation of Gandhi's first appearance as a lawyer in the section which he entitles, 'Arjuna in the Court of Small Claims'. On the one hand, Gandhi's experience here is reminiscent of the event recounted in the Bhagavad-Gita when Arjuna shrinks from engaging in battle. (This event would seem to fit within the apprentice or *antevasin* stage in the Hindu life cycle and within the *identity* stage in Erikson's cycle.) It is interesting to note that Arjuna's reluctance to fight was not simply due to fright, but to the fact that he would be involved in fighting against members of his own family. We seem to have a parallel here to Gandhi's decision to begin his work in India in his own home town. But the basic issue which the Arjuna event poses is that Gandhi seems vaguely aware that the incident in the court of small claims – his inability to plead his case – fits the Arjuna event. Erikson points out, for example, that Gandhi used language taken from the Bhagavad-gita when describing a similar experience in England. So on the one hand, we have Gandhi reflecting a traditional biographical pattern in this event in the court of small claims. But on the other hand, Erikson wants to infuse this traditional event with new awarenesses – the awarenesses which he senses Gandhi has brought to this event and which have thereby transformed it. Erikson notes that Gandhi was smitten in the drabness of a court of 'small claims' – as if to suggest that his future style of leadership would involve seeking out 'the smallest and most local situations as a great soul's proper battleground'. He would stake his leadership on 'small claims' which had much larger moral and legal implications. Perhaps this is the way that the modern lawyer transforms the biographical pattern exemplified in the life of the ancient warrior.

In the foregoing example, the traditional biographical pattern remains essentially unchanged; the Arjuna event simply assumes new meaning as Gandhi infuses it with new awarenesses. However, there is another element in the process of the evolution of biographical patterns which Erikson also touches upon in his study of Gandhi. At times, Erikson recognizes not simply the transformation of traditional events but also the inclusion of new events into existing patterns. In response to queries, Erikson says that the train episode in South Africa would best qualify as marking Gandhi's identity crisis. It is therefore possible that an event of this nature, especially given modern man's preoccupation with identity as a problem which his increased sense of individuality poses, may be incorporated into the traditional biograhical patterns. The fact that Gandhi's life-events have been preserved in mural form in the Birla house in Delhi (a memorial shrine to Gandhi) would indicate that some infusion of his life into more traditional patterns is inevitable.[53]

Finally, any adequate consideration of Erikson's use of biographical patterns in *Gandhi's Truth* would need to recognize Erikson's own accomplishment, namely, the fusion of his life cycle schema with the more traditional Hindu model. He appears to seek this kind of fusion of biographical patterns because he recognizes that Gandhi himself represented the infusion of traditional life-structures with 'modern' understandings. Erikson and Gandhi, the one in his psychological work and the other in his political activity, share this common understanding of their tasks. This is perhaps most dramatically evident in Erikson's famous letter to Gandhi. This letter, which concludes the householder or intimacy-isolation stage of Erikson's narrative, seems to want to inform Gandhi that it was in matters of intimacy that he failed to infuse the traditional Hindu pattern with 'new awarenesses'. On the other hand, this letter also suggests that Erikson is acknowledging his difficulty with his own intimacy-isolation responses to Gandhi. He wonders aloud whether he should address Gandhi with a 'personal word'. But then we ask, is this not precisely the dilemma which the writer of self-consciously *religious* biography has to face at some point in his narrative? He needs to ask himself, and at the same time inform his reader, whether the subject of his biography is to be taken as exemplary. Is his subject's life worthy of being emulated, as the basis for future biographical enactments? If Erikson finally concludes that Gandhi's *personal* standards are in some instances too high and too low (Erikson is very conscious of the importance of middle-range dignity), nonetheless, Gandhi's 'truth' – his embodiment of *satyagraha* – is not only understood to be worthy of emulation, but also in some senses as necessary to the survival of mankind. Erikson's authorial intrusion in his letter to Gandhi also points to the fact that the neutrality of the historian employing the historical-critical approach to biography is not appropriate to religious biography as exemplified by *Gandhi's Truth*, for the religious biographer cannot remain neutral as to whether his subject is to be taken as an exemplary model. Finally, then, Erikson's effort to infuse traditional life-models with new awarenesses means that his own identity as biographer is not unlike that of the sacred biographer concerned with the creation and continuing enactment of a new religious ideal.[54]

The foregoing discussion of Erikson's approach to biography indicates that, like Campbell and Kris, he also attends to problems of 'variation' within and the evolution of the biographical pattern. However, he does so not only in the sense that the 'contents' of the various historical-religious traditions are found to be compatible with the biographical pattern, but also in the sense that the historical 'actuality' of the biographical subject is not ignored. Concerning the life of the biographical subject, Erikson (like Kretschmer) is not simply interested in biographical 'facts' but in the biographical structure peculiar to the life of this individual. As biographer, he discerns the unique life pattern of this individual by attempting to isolate 'recurring themes' which eventually yield a single dominant 'unitary theme' in that pattern. The source materials for these 'themes' may be biographical (historical) events or, as in the case of Luther's fit in the choir, apocryphal or mythical 'events'. Regarding the latter, Erikson describes his briefer studies of Hitler and Gorky as studies of the 'legends' of childhood, as if to underscore his appreciation of the mythical dimensions of the life pattern itself.[55] As the Gorky study demonstrates, it was precisely this childhood shrouded in legend which yielded the 'theme' which Erikson considered fundamental to the Gorky life pattern. For, like all Russian children, Gorky was wrapped in tight swaddling clothes in his infancy, and when these physical strictures are contrasted with the enormous geographical expanses of Russia, the essential elements of a personal theme emerge: the paradoxical sense of being suffocated in a world of limitless horizons.[56]

In short, Erikson's psychological approach to biography moves on two related levels. There is the level of *biographical pattern* with the eight-stage life cycle bearing marked affinities to traditional religious biographical patterns. On the other hand, there is the level of *life pattern* with its recurring personal themes. In the terms of our myth-history distinction, it is clear that both levels may manifest mythical and historical elements simultaneously. The *biographical* pattern is primarily a mythical construct which opens itself to the historical 'variations' of traditional images of man, while the *life* pattern is essentially historico-biographical, but mythical 'contents' (including apocryphal events, the subject's own heroic self-consciousness, his identifications with ancestors, etc.) are admitted as evidence in the discernment of recurring themes. Finally, then, the life cycle theory and its profound implications mark Erikson as one who is neither content merely to affirm the modern concept of individuality and the historical-critical method it has spawned, nor simply to recapitulate traditional biographical patterns. Rather, accepting the former as a necessary fact of life, he seeks, in the words of Kris, to 'realize the old ideals of biographers in a new form'.

4. Biographical images and individual lives: A new line of demarcation

As we have moved through our brief survey of the traditions of biographical research which have developed in the disciplines of history of religions, anthropology and psychology, certain important differences between the respective approaches have become obvious. Not only have we discerned differences determined by the particular religio-historical, culturally oriented, and psychological methods, but we have also noted related differences in the kinds of subjects chosen for study. However, in addition to these differences, there is an important division which cuts directly across the lines established by these academically defined areas of specialization. Our survey of the three fields of study has suggested that in each of the three there has been one important strand of scholarship focused on what might appropriately be called biographical images. In the history of religions this first pole of biographical studies is represented primarily by the interpreters of sacred biographies and hagiographies. In the field of anthropology it is represented by those scholars who have sought to identify and clarify biographically relevant cultural paradigms, models, and patterns of ethnic identity; and in psychology it is represented by the psychoanalytically oriented scholars who have focused on mythic patterns. It is also clear from our review of the literature that an alternative style of scholarship has developed within each of the three disciplines which has stressed the structure and dynamics of individual lives.

By describing this cross-disciplinary division in terms of the distinction between the study of biographical images and the study of individual lives, we are indicating that it confronts us with still another transformation of the basic myth-history issue. To be sure, many of those who have studied biographical images have taken some account of the fact that such images have both a mythic and an historical aspect. And many who have concentrated on the study of individual lives have recognized that these lives have been constituted by an intricate interweaving of mythic, paradigmatic, and historical elements. However, without denying that the more sensitive scholars on each side of the division have been concerned with both myth and history, it is clear that those who have been concerned with biographic images have been primarily oriented toward myth, whereas whose who have been basically engaged in the study of individual lives have been oriented toward history.

In the various disciplinary contexts there have been a few scholars who have recognized the need to move beyond this division between myth-oriented and history-oriented studies, and to explore the dynamics of the interaction between the two. For example, in the history of religions context Mircea Eliade has noted the existence of 'a very general human tendency ... to hold up one life history as a paradigm and turn an historical personage into an archetype'.[57] Eliade instances the life of Goethe who, he reports, sought to imitate in his own life the behavior of the gods and mythical heroes and, at the same time, sought to mold his career so that it could become a biographical pattern normative for others and therefore constitutive of future human activities.[58] In the field of anthropology we have already noted Kenelm Burridge's study of the Melanesian Cargo Cult tradition, which brilliantly analyzes the complex interaction between the primal 'myth-dream' of the Tangu natives and the individual lives of local prophetic figures. And in the field of psychology we have made reference to the work of Ernst Kris in which he discusses the lives of individual artists as 'enactments' of pre-existing biographical patterns, and the fact that these individual lives have sometimes come to exert a compelling paradigmatic impact on the self-conceptions and lives of their successors. We have also seen how Erik Erikson understood Gandhi both as 'enacter' of pre-existing patterns and as paradigmatic individual.

As we have reflected on the basic thrust of the papers in the present collection we have become convinced that the kind of myth-history issue which has been posed in such different ways by Eliade, Burridge, and the psychologists, Kris and Erikson, constitutes a pervasive theme which links the various essays into a coherent whole. In some cases the question is raised explicitly, while in others it is simply implicit in the selection and treatment of materials. In some cases only one phase of the interaction is considered, whereas in others the full sweep of the movement from image to life to image comes within the author's ken. However, despite these significant variations in the styles and emphases of the various contributors, the myth-history issue is never completely lost from view.

Having dentified this issue as basic, we have organized our essays accordingly. We have ignored the more traditional lines of demarcation established by the au thors' disciplinary specializations and by the religious or cultural contexts from which they have drawn their material. Rather, we have placed the papers in groups distinguished by the phase of the central myth-history interplay which they have singled out for special consideration. Part I includes those essays in which the primary focus is on biographical images. Part II includes those essays which are primarily concerned with the way in which biographical images have provided structure and dynamism in the self-conceptions and lives of individual men. Part III includes those papers which evidence a primary concern with the individual lives of religious innovators. And Part IV includes those papers which explore the ways in which individual lives have become transformed into biographical images of religious and cultural significance.

Taken separately, each paper in the present collection is intended by its author to contribute to the work of his own discipline, and to the study of a specific religious or cultural tradition. As editors, we believe that in each case the objective has been achieved. But, at the same time, we hope that when the various studies are seen as a whole they may further stimulate a new style of inter-disciplinary research which will strive to develop more adequate understandings of the continuing interaction between biographical images and individual lives – an interaction which we have chosen to call 'the biographical process'.

Notes

1. See *Preface*.
2. Mircea Eliade, *Myths, Dreams and Mysteries*, trans. Philip Moiret (New York: Harper Torchbooks, 1967), p. 30.
3. These and related issues are given particular attention in the essays by Reynolds and Waugh, *infra.*
4. Some preliminary efforts have been made in this area; see, for example, Henri de Lubac's *Aspects of Buddhism*, trans. G. Lamb (New York: Sheed and Ward, 1954). However, in order to be successfully implemented, this kind of task requires a greater breadth of knowledge and a higher degree of methodological sophistication than has thus far been brought to bear.
5. The character and development of hagiographic lives are dealt with in various ways in the contributions by Lorenzen, Dimock, La Fleur and Foard, *infra.*
6. Some suggestions relevant to both of these points are provided in Capps' articles on Newman and Lincoln, *infra.*
7. Göttingen: (Vandenhoeck & Ruprecht); trans. by J. C. G. Greig as *The Messianic Secret* (Cambridge: J. Clarke, 1971).
8. It is perhaps worth noting that a well know historian of religions has recently attempted to reconstruct a more interpretive biography of Jesus [Samuel G. F. Brandon, *Jesus and the Zealots* (Manchester: Manchester University Press, 1967)]. But, from a scholarly viewpoint his methods are dubious and his arguments far from convincing.
9. Tor Andrae, *Mohammed, the Man and his Faith* (New York: Scribner, 1936); William Montgomery Watt, *Muhammed at Mecca* and *Muhammed at Medina* (Oxford: Clarendon Press, 1953 and 1956), abr. as *Muhammed: Prophet and Statesman* (London: Oxford University Press, 1961).
10. Paris: Civilizations du Sud (SAEP), 1949.
11. For a survey of some of the basic work which had been done in gleaning historical biographical data concerning various religious founders see Geo Widengren, Prolegomena to *Historia Religionum: Handbook for the History of Religions*, ed. Widengren and Class J. Bleeker (Leiden: E. J. Brill, 1969). For a more detailed and updated discussion of the search for data concerning the life of the Buddha see Reynolds, *infra.*
12. Masaharu Anesaki, *Nichiren, the Buddhist Prophet* (Cambridge: Harvard University Press, 1916), p. 133. Another important study of a Japanese figure is Joseph Kitaga-

wa's analysis of Kūkai, the founder of the Shingon sect, *Kō-bō-Daishi and Shingon Buddhism* (University of Chicago: unpublished doctoral dissertation, 1951). Some of the highlights of this research and of Kitagawa's subsequent reflections on Kūkai and his role in the history Japanese religion can be gleaned from his article in the present collection.

13. Louis Massignon, *Akhbar al-Hallāj* (Paris: J. Vrin, 1957). For another excellent work on an Islamic figure, see Henry Corbin, *Creative Imagination in the Sufism of Ibn' Arabi*, trans. Ralph Manheim (Princeton: Princeton University Press, 1969).
14. R. J. Zwi Werblowski, *Joseph Karo, Lawyer and Mystic* (London: Oxford University Press, 1962).
15. The distinction between the two groups is discussed from a slightly different perspective by Renato Rosaldo in his article on Tukbaw, *infra.*
16. Paul Radin, *Crashing Thunder: The Autobiography of a Winnebago Indian* (University of California). Pub. in *American Archeology and Ethnology*, vol. 16 (1920), p. 384. Later pub. New York: D. Appleton and Co., 1926.
17. For the history of the biographical interest as it has developed in anthropology, the major source is Clyde Kluckhohn's *The Use of Personal Documents in Anthropology* (New York: Social Science Research Council, Bulletin 55, 1945), pp. 79–113. For a discussion which follows the development into the 1960's see Lewis L. Langness, *The Life History in Anthropological Science* (New York: Holt, Rinehart and Winston, 1965).
18. W. A. Lessa and E. Z. Vogt, eds., *Readings in Comparative Religion: An Anthropological Approach* (Evanston, Ill.: Row, Peterson, 1958), p. 520.
19. From a seminar discussion reported by Ernst Kris, *Psychoanalytic Explorations in Art* (New York: International Universities Press, Inc., 1952), pp. 64–84.
20. John Dollard, *Criteria for the Life History* (New Haven: Yale University Press, 1935), p. 260.
21. Clifford Geertz, *Islam Observed: Religious Development in Morocco and Indonesia* (New Haven: Yale University Press, 1968), pp. 25–35.
22. Gregory Bateson, *Naven* (Stanford: Stanford University Press, 1958), pp. 160–163.
23. The existence of the two alternative life models need not necessarily contradict the example of the Iatmul youth who described the life pattern of the Iatmul. Since the description itself is not reported, we do not know whether the youth described a life pattern in sufficiently general terms that it applied to both the violent and discreet man, or whether he described the life model of only one or the other. Even if the latter, this does not obviate the fact that the youth considered his life preestablished and admitting of essentially no personal variation.
24. Don Handelman, 'The Development of a Washo Shaman', *Ethnology*, vol. 6, No. 4 (October, 1967), pp. 444–464.
25. Kenelm Burridge, *Mambu: A Melanesian Millenium* (London: Methuen & Co., Ltd., 1960). See also his *New Heaven and New Earth* (New York: Schocken, 1969).
26. Burridge, *Mambu*, p. 206.
27. A creative application of the cultural models approach to very different materials is

Victor Turner's essay on Thomas Becket, *infra.* See also his 'Hidalgo: History as Social Drama' in Victor Turner, *Dramas, Fields, and Metaphors: Symbolic Action in Human Society* (Ithaca and London: Cornell University Press, 1974). Still another way of extending this style of anthropological biography is illustrated in Obeyesekere's essay Anagārika Dharmapala, *infra.*

28. Clyde Kluckhohn, *The Use of Personal Documents*, pp. 140–141.
29. Robert H. Lowie, *Primitive Religion* (New York: Boni and Liveright, 1924), pp. 247–257.
30. For an important collection of autobiographical material collected from Siberian shamans see *Schamanengeschichter aus Siberian und Russian ubersetzt und eingeleitet*, by Adolf Friedrich and George Buddous (originally compiled by Ksenofontov) (München–Planegg: Otto Wilhelm Barth-Verlag GMBH, 1955).
31. Siegfried F. Nadel, *The Nuba: An Anthropological Study of the Hill Tribes in Kordofan* (London: Oxford University Press, 1947).
32. For comments on some forms of this emphasis see Rosaldo, *infra.*
33. Clyde Kluckhohn, *The Use of Personal Documents*, p. 98. Indicative of the sorts of historical-critical problems the life-history proponents face is that cited by Kluckhohn when he warns of the danger of ascribing a certain personality trait to an 'accident' in the biographical subject's life that in fact he shares with all other persons in his community. Simmons' book is *Sun Chief, The Autobiography of a Hopi Indian* (New Haven: Yale University Press, 1942).
34. Alfred M. Tozzler, 'Biography and Biology' in C. Kluckhohn and H. Murray, eds., *Personality in Nature, Society and Culture* (New York: Alfred A. Knopf, 1948), pp. 144–157.
35. Claude Lévi-Strauss, *Social Research*, vol. 10 (1943), pp. 515–517.
36. For some comments directly relevant to this issue, see Rosaldo, *infra.*
37. For the purposes of this introduction, we are considering the Jungian school of depth psychology under the general heading of psychoanalytic interest in biography. Jung's most accessible contribution to the problems addressed herein is his work in collaboration with C. Kerényi, *Essays on a Science of Mythology* (Princeton: Princeton University Press, 1959).
38. Ed. Philip Freund (New York: Vintage Books, 1959), p. 65. For a similar effort to isolate a heroic pattern see Lord Raglan, *The Hero: A Study in Tradition, Myth and Drama* (New York: Oxford University Press, 1937), pp. 179–180. The Jungian study by Maud Bodkin, *Archetypal Patterns in Poetry* (London: Oxford University Press, 1934) also includes sections on the myth of the hero.
39. Joseph Campbell, *The Hero with a Thousand Faces* (Princeton: Princeton University Press Bollingen Series, 1949), pp. 36 ff.
40. *Ibid.*, pp. 37–38.
41. Ernst Kris, *Psychoanalytic Explorations in Art.*
42. *Ibid.*, p. 80.
43. *Ibid.*, p. 83.

44. For the discussion of the relationship between the lives of two creative writers and the establishment of a new pattern or variant see Homans' essay, *infra*.
45. Kris, *Psychoanalytic Explorations in Art*, p. 74.
46. Ernst Kretschmer, *The Psychology of Men of Genius*, trans. R. B. Cattell (London: Kegan Paul, Trench, Trubner & Company, Ltd., 1931).
47. *Ibid.*, p. 14. Our italics.
48. *Ibid.*, p. xiv.
49. *Ibid.*, p. xvi.
50. Erik H. Erikson, *Young Man Luther* (New York: W. W. Norton, 1958); *Gandhi's Truth: On the Origins of Militant Nonviolence* (New York: W. W. Norton, 1969).
51. Erikson has reference to Shakespeare's seven ages of man. See *As You Like It*, Act II, sc. vii.
52. Erik H. Erikson, *Gandhi's Truth: On the Origins of Militant Nonviolence*, pp. 39–41.
53. Joanne Punzo Waghorne, a student in our seminar on biography, pointed out that Bhimrao Ramji Ambedkar, one of Gandhi's rivals, structured his biography of the Buddha in such a way that it incorporated many parallels to his own life history. See his *The Buddha and His Dhamma*, (Ahmednagar: People's Education Society, 1957). The essay on John Henry Newman by Capps in the present collection focuses on a similar self-conscious identification with a traditional biographical pattern in Newman's studies of lives of early Christian saints.
54. See the discussion of sacred biography in the history of religions section of this introductory essay.
55. Erik H. Erikson, 'The Legend of Hitler's Childhood'; 'The Legend of Maxim Gorky's Youth'. In *Childhood and Society*, 2nd rev. ed. (New York: W. W. Norton, 1963), pp. 326–328; 359–402.
56. Here Erikson draws on G. Gorer's controversial swaddling hypothesis. See G. Gorer and J. Rickman, *The People of Great Russia* (London: Cresset Press, 1949). For studies which utilize aspects of the kind of approach taken by Erikson see the essays by Obeyesekere and Klass, *infra*.
57. Mircea Eliade, *Myths, Dreams and Mysteries* (New York: Harper Torchbooks, 1967), p. 32.
58. Reynolds has also pointed to the need for historians of religion to undertake the study of the relationship between biographical images and individual lives. See his paper entitled 'Erikson and the History of Religions: Some Possibilities for Future Research' delivered at a symposium held in honor of Erikson at the Institute of Religious Studies at the University of California at Santa Barbara, February, 1972. This paper will be published in the proceedings of the symposium, which is being edited by Walter H. Capps, Donald Capps and Gerald Bradford, entitled *Encounter with Erikson* (Missoula, Montana: Scholar's Press, 1975).

PART I

Essays in Sacred Biography

FRANK E. REYNOLDS

1

The Many Lives of Buddha

A Study of Sacred Biography and Theravāda Tradition

Buddha and the Buddhologists

Within the entire history of religions there is no sacred biography which has had a wider dissemination or made a greater impact than that which recounts the life of the Buddha.[1] This sacred biography is among the earliest about which we have any knowledge, and is also what Joachim Wach could have called a 'classical example' of the genre.[2] Both because of its importance in the history of Buddhism, and because of the continuing fascination which it has exerted outside the specifically Buddhist world, this biography has been the object of a considerable body of modern scholarship.

Western interest in the person and career of the Buddha began long before the modern period, and has had a variety of expressions. Within the first centuries of the Christian era references to the Buddha figure occur in Western literature, notably in the fourth century Acts of Archelaus, and in the work of St. Jerome who probably derived his comments from those which appeared in the Acts.[3] In the eighth century an account of the Buddha known as the story of 'Barlaam and Josaphat' (in the account, Barlaam is a hermit who converts Josaphat, whose story has been shown to be that of the Buddha) appeared in the Eastern Christian context, and by the fourteenth century the two figures had become recognized saints of the Western church.[4] A number of early European travellers to East and South Asia such as Marco Polo and Robert Knox mention the Buddha in the context of their comments on the forms of the Buddhist tradition which they encountered; and a more adequate account, based on selected translations from the Pali canon, is given by Simon de le Loubère in his very insightful *Descriptions du Royaume de Siam*.[5] During the nineteenth century, as Western contacts with the Buddhist world increased, the interest in the figure of the Buddha grew rapidly and was expressed through the publication of translations of various Indian, Burmese, Thai, Tibetan and Chinese versions of the sacred biography, through the publication of popular romanticized renderings such as the famous work of Edwin Arnold entitled *The Light of Asia*, and through the gradual development of a body of serious philological and historical scholarship. In the twentieth century this interest has expanded rapidly and has been expressed through the publication of new and different versions of the sacred biography, through creative literary reformulations such as Herman Hesse's *Siddhartha*, and through the further investigations of historians and other interpreters of the textual and literary history of the Buddhist tradition.

Among the modern Buddhologists who inaugurated the scholarly study of the Buddha biographies serious differences of style and interpretation are evident.[6] During the late nineteenth and early twentieth centuries the field was largely divided between a group of myth-oriented scholars such as Émile Senart, Heinrich Kern and Ananda Coomaraswamy on the one hand, and a group of more historically oriented philologists such as Herman Oldenberg and T.W. and C.A.F. Rhys-Davids on the other. Among the myth-oriented interpreters the emphasis was placed on the study of the Sanskrit sources and on the importance of those elements in the sacred biography which pointed in the direction of solar mythology; for these scholars the historical Buddha was, at most, a reformer who provided the occasion for the historicization of the solar myth. In contrast, among those who took the second position, the emphasis was placed on the Pali Theravāda texts and on those elements in the Pali tradition which they could use to reconstruct what they considered to be the actual historical life of the Buddha. From the perspective of these scholars the mythic elements (and in some cases other elements as well) were considered to be later addenda to the true historical memory, addenda which represented a degeneration of the tradition which it was the responsibility of critical scholarship to identify and to discount.[7]

More recently, however, Buddhologists have come to recognize the inadequacy of both the purely mythic and the historical, essentially rationalistic, modes of interpretation, and have reached a rather widely shared consensus concerning a number of basic methodological issues. First, there is now a common recognition that the study of any aspect of the most ancient forms of Buddhism requires a careful comparison and analysis of sources which have been preserved in a variety of traditions, including those which have come down to us not only in both Pali and Sanskrit, but in other Asian languages as well. Secondly, most scholars presently working in the field are convinced of the existence and importance of the historical Gotama Buddha; but at the same time they are painfully aware that the available texts provide us with very little authentic information concerning the details of his life. Beyond this, there is a widespread consensus that the most crucial problems which are amenable to future investigation cluster around the identification of the various levels or stages in the development of the biographical tradition, the question of the structure of the various biographical fragments and texts, and the role which these fragments and texts have played within the broader tradition.

Strong intimations of these principles which inform the contemporary approach to the study of the sacred biography and its development were already present in E. J. Thomas' *The Life of the Buddha as Legend and History* which was first published in 1927 and remained an authoritative treatment for almost two decades.[8] However, in the late 1940s three important works were published which carried the discussion well beyond the position established by Thomas. In 1944 and 1948 Ernst Waldschmidt published the first and second sections of an important comparative and critical study of the Mahāparinibbāna Sutta, a Sutta which deals with the final days of the Buddha's life and its immediate aftermath.[9] Shortly thereafter Etienne Lamotte contributed an important article in which he clearly demonstrated the inaccessibility of any extensive information concerning the historical life of the Buddha, and made considerable progress in delineating the various stages in the development of the sacred biography.[10] Then in 1949 Alfred Foucher published his *La Vie du Bouddha d'après les textes et monuments de l'Inde* which, as the title suggests, brought new kinds of materials into the discussion. Foucher's work, which attempts to reconstruct the sacred biography as it existed in India around the beginning of the Christian era, remains today the single most adequate introduction to the early biographical tradition.[11]

During the 1950s two more important studies appeared which defended radically diverging views of the development of the sacred biography. In 1956 Erich Frauwallner published a monograph entitled *The Earliest Vinaya and the Beginnings of Buddhist Literature*. In this work he ingeniously utilized text-critical methods to argue that some 100 years after the Buddha's death an unknown Buddhist author compiled an extensive literary text which he called the Old Skandhaka and which contained, among other things, an extended segment of the sacred biography of the Buddha.[12] However, several years later Etienne Lamotte, in his classic *Histoire du Bouddhisme Indien des origines à l'ère Śaka*, pointed out the weakness in Frauwallner's case and extended his own arguments in favor of a more gradual development of various biographical cycles and their later synthesis into a series of more complete sacred biographies.[13] Finally, in the period since 1960 the major new contributions have been made by the French Buddhologist André Bareau. Bareau has written an important article in which he traces 'La légende de la jeunesse du Bouddha dans les Vinayapiṭaka anciens', a full length book in which he seeks to discern the development of the portions of the sacred biography which deal with the Enlightenment and the events surrounding it, and a short but interesting essay on 'The Superhuman Personality of the Buddha and Its Symbolism in the Mahāparinirvāṇasūtra of the Dharmaguptaka'.[14]

In the discussion which follows I will rely heavily on the studies of these earlier Buddhologists, and especially on the careful work of reconstruction which has been carried forward by Lamotte and Bareau. However, my treatment of the subject will be both more limited and at the same time more extended than theirs. It will be more limited because I will focus primarily on the Theravāda tradition, making reference to other traditions only when it is helpful in illuminating the developments which have taken place in the Theravāda context.[15] But, on the other hand, it will be more extended since I will trace the development forward into the more recent phases of Theravāda history.[16]

First, I will trace the process through which the early Buddhist community expressed and conveyed the meaning which it perceived in the person and message of its founder through the gradual development of narrative cycles concerning his previous lives, the various phases of his life as Gotama, and the fate of his relics. Secondly, I will discuss the two major types of more complete and integrated Buddha biographies which appeared within the Theravāda tradition toward the middle of the 5th millenium A.D., and continued to develop up to the beginning of the modern period. Finally, I will devote a few concluding remarks to the new trends which have emerged in the Theravāda account of the Buddha's life during the 19th and 20th centuries.

THE EARLY TRADITION: 5TH CENTURY B. C. – 5TH CENTURY A. D.

The difficulties involved in discussions of the development of any aspect of early Buddhism are vividly illustrated by the lack of certainty concerning even such a basic matter as the dates of the birth and death of the Founder. Different Buddhist traditions affirm different dates, the external evidence is slight and problematic, and modern scholars have ventured diverging opinions. However, among recent interpreters there is a widespread concensus that circa 650 B.C. is the earliest date which can reasonably be affirmed for his birth, while circa 483 B.C. (some say 477) is the latest date which can reasonably be affirmed for his death. Since the texts agree that the Buddha lived a long life of circa 80 years, and since the later dates seem the most probable, we can tentatively assume that the Buddha lived between 567 and 483 B.C.[17]

A second crucial chronological guidepost for the discussion of early Buddhist history is provided by the reign of King Asoka, the famous Indian monarch who was converted to Buddhism and sponsored the spread of the faith in India and in neighboring areas, including Ceylon and possibly even Southeast Asia. Though this reign, which extended from circa 274 to circa 236 B.C., is significant for a variety of reasons, its importance here is our knowledge that before Asoka's death certain major Buddhist schools had established separate traditions. Thus we can reasonably assume that scriptural passages which have been preserved in very similar form in those diverging schools represent a tradition which had developed within the first two and a half centuries of Buddhist history.

Finally, two other chronological guideposts enable us to make rough distinctions between the different strata of the tradition within the specifically Theravāda Pali context. First, we know that the canonical scriptures were written in basically their present form in Ceylon in the first century B.C. And we know further that the major Pali commentaries, which include the first more complete Buddha biographies to appear within this particular tradition, were given their present form during the fifth century A.D., almost a millenium after the death of the Founder.

Given this general historical framework, it is possible to reconstruct, at least in broad outline, the development of the major elements in the formation of the sacred biography, and to trace the major phases in the process which led to the appearance of the first more complete biographical texts. In order to facilitate this task I will distinguish four major segments of the biography and consider each in turn. The first of these segments is constituted by the Jātaka tales which are the stories of events in the Buddha's previous lives; the second, by the accounts of the Buddha's genealogy, birth and youth; the third, by the accounts of his Enlightenment and the early phases of his ministry; and the fourth by the accounts of the final months of this life, his Great Decease, and the distribution and subsequent fate of his relics. Though the inclusion of all of these narratives implies a very broad conception of the meaning of biography, all are integrally involved in the traditional Buddhist accounts of the Buddha and his career.

Strange as it may seem at first glance, it is not improbable that the first items of the sacred biography to appear within the Buddhist tradition were the Jātaka stories which recount events in the previous lives of the Founder.[18] In fact, it is quite possible that such stories were told by the Buddha himself to illustrate a point or to drive home a moral.[19] But whether the Buddha himself actually initiated the Jātaka tradition, it is well established that during the pre-Asokan period one of the nine (according to the Theravāda tradition) or twelve (according to the Sanskrit traditions) segments into which the normative tradition was then divided consisted specifically of Jātaka stories.[20] From much artistic and iconographic evidence, we know that in the centuries immediately following Asoka's reign the Jātaka stories enjoyed great popularity, and we can point to two relatively late texts in the Pali canon which are devoted primarily to the relation of Jātakas. The Buddhavamsa relates the stories of the future Gotama Buddha's encounters with twenty-four previous Buddhas. The Cariyāpiṭaka, which is somewhat more extensive, contains thirty-five stories including a series of ten in which the future Buddha acquires the great perfections which lead directly to Buddhahood.

In the post-canonical tradition of the Theravādins the Jātaka tradition culminated with the appearance of the Jātaka Commentary in Ceylon in the fifth century A.D.[21] In this massive collection some 547 stories are brought together, including some in which the future Buddha appears as an animal hero, some in which he appears as a divine figure, and some in which he appears as a hero in the world of men. Some of the stories are very short, while others are quite extended literary creations which played an important role in the history of literature and the dramatic arts in the various Theravāda countries. Some are highly folkloric and free from any specific Buddhist piety or moralism (they seem to be folktales which have been made into Jātakas simply by identifying the leading character with the Buddha and other characters with members of the Buddha's family, his disciples, his archetypal enemy, Devadatta, etc.). But others, like the story of the Buddha's penultimate birth as King Vessantara, have an obvious Buddhist coloring and have become popular and effective vehicles for the inculcation of specifically Buddhist virtues. Finally, even after the tradition was stabilized by the appearance of the Jātaka Commentary, new Jātaka stories were added to the tradition. For example, in Indochina a whole new set of tales was adapted from the local folklore and came to be recognized as Jātakas.[22]

Unlike the Jātaka tradition, which appears to be rooted in the preaching of the Buddha himself, the stories which recount the genealogy of Gotama, his birth, and the events of his youth have no place in the earliest sections of the scriptural tradition. There are, to be sure, early and historically reliable references which identify the Buddha's birthplace as the Sākyan tribal center of Kapilavatthu, which is located in the foothills of the Himalyas in what is now southern Nepal. Similar references, which also seem to be historically reliable, refer to the Buddha's birth into a khattiya or noble family, and provide some incidental information such as the name of his father (Suddhodana) and that of his son (Rāhula). However, the rich narrative accounts which have served as sources for many of the modern, supposedly 'historical', accounts of this phase of the Buddha's life represent a relatively late development.

Within the Pali scriptural tradition the only text in which the richer traditions concerning the Buddha's birth and youth play a crucial role – the Mahāpadāna Sutta – seems to be rooted in a tradition which was gaining acceptance during the Asokan period, but probably did not receive its canonical form until a slightly later date.[23] This Sutta recounts the main events in the life of a previous Buddha named Vipassī, and concludes by affirming that these events were repeated in the life of each subsequent Buddha up to, and including, Gotama. It is significant that in this Sutta, which is extolled in the Commentaries as the 'King of Suttas', one half of the narrative is devoted to the birth and youth of the Buddha, including his descent from the Tusita heaven where he resided before his final birth, the earthquake and miraculous light which accompanied his descent and, then months later, his birth. The Sutta continues by describing a series of events through which the Buddha's future destiny as either a Cakkavattin (Great Wheel-Rolling or Universal Monarch) or a Buddha (an Enlightened One or Universal Teacher) is revealed and a number of childhood events through which his extraordinary qualities and greatness are made manifest. Its descriptions highlight the luxurious surroundings which the Buddha enjoyed throughout his youth. It then tells of the Buddha's encounter with an aged man, a sick man, a corpse, and a wandering mendicant, and recounts the story of the 'Great Departure', including both the Buddha's renunciation of household life and his acceptance of the vocation of a wandering mendicant.

In the period following the Asokan era, Kapilavatthu became an important pilgrimage site. Although pilgrimages to the site of the Buddha's birth were probably taken prior to Asoka's time, their popularity grew as a result of his influence and was perhaps especially enhanced by his own journey to Kapilavatthu. Thus the traditions concerning the Buddha's family, birth and youth developed very rapidly. In the Sanskrit traditions and in the lay oriented and non-sectarian iconographic traditions, accounts of the Buddha's royal genealogy and new elaborations involving signs, miracles and portents indicative of the Buddha's greatness in relation to both gods and men soon produced a rich and complex cycle of Buddha lore. Even in the Theravāda tradition, where resistance to incorporation of new elements was certainly greater than in any other Buddhist school about which we have knowledge, the Kapilavatthu cycle assumed very significant proportions. For example, the Theravādins gradually accepted a royal genealogy which traced the Buddha's ancestry from the 'first king' of mythical times, through a long series of the most illustrious royal ancestors, down to Suddhodana and his Queen Mahāmāyā, and thence to the Buddha himself. They incorporated greatly embroidered versions of the Buddha's descent from the Tusita heaven, a number of stories associated with his mother and her premature death, and a variety of intriguing episodes in which the Buddha's future greatness is signified. For example, they incorporated a highly symbolic account of an incident at a ploughing festival in which the shadow of the tree under which the infant prince was meditating remained immobile as the sun proceeded through its course.

During this period the Theravādins also accepted a number of highly colorful episodes which further dramatized the spiritual crisis which provoked the Buddha's Great Renunciation, including the famous account of the Buddha's revulsion when he viewed the disheveled bodies of the dancing girls of his harem after they had fallen asleep. They also included within their biographical tradition a variety of memorable episodes which punctuated the Buddha's Great Departure from Kapilavatthu, including the story of his flight to the city walls on the back of a great mythical horse named Kanthaka. Another such episode is the Buddha's encounter with Māra in which this deity, who represents the power of desire and therefore of evil, makes a final attempt to entice the Great Being to reconsider his decision to renounce the world and to accept instead the role of a Cakkavattin or Universal Monarch.

This process of incorporating new elements into the narrative of the Buddha's ancestry, birth and youth continued into the fifth century A.D. when an orthodox version of the cycle became clearly formulated; however, even after this time some freedom was exercised by those who retold the story, and some local variants were developed in the various areas where the Theravāda tradition became established.[24]

Both the logic of the situation and the results of modern text-critical scholarship suggest that, of all the aspects of the Buddha's final life as Gotama, the Enlightenment and the earliest events of the Buddha's ministry were of the greatest interest to the monks who compiled, molded, and transmitted the tradition. In the Pali canon there are a variety of references to occasions and events in the Buddha's career from the time of his Great Departure from Kapilavatthu on through the most important phases of his ministry. However, in spite of the fact that many of these references in both the Sutta and Vinaya Piṭakas (the two oldest segments of the canon) reflect actual historical episodes, it is impossible to reconstruct anything like a complete narrative which can claim historical authenticity. Nonetheless, the particularly serious interest which the early compilers showed in the Enlightenment and the events immediately preceding and following it makes it possible to discern something of the process through which the accounts of this crucial phase of the Buddha's career developed, even in the pre-Asokan period.

Within the Pali canon there are four Sutta which relate the Enlightenment and the events surrounding it which appear to have been firmly established in the tradition within two centuries of the Founder's death. In addition, there is a somewhat later account which forms the Introduction to the Mahāvagga section of the Vinaya Piṭaka which was firmly established in the tradition by the time of King Asoka. In the two earliest Sutta, the Bhayabherava and the Dvedhāvitakka, three episodes are described including, in both cases, the Buddha's attainment of the four exalted states of meditational experience (the four jhānas) and the three forms of saving knowledge (the three abhiñña).[25] In the two somewhat later Sutta, the Ariyapariyesana and the Mahāsaccaka, the tradition has been supplemented by stories which were probably related at the pilgrimage site at Uruvelā where, according to the tradition, the Enlightenment had taken place in a grove under the famous Bo tree.[26] For example, these two somewhat later Sutta recount additional episodes which occurred prior to the Buddha's Enlightenment (e.g., his unfruitful apprenticeships to the famous teachers Ālāra Kālāma and Uddaka-Rāmaputta) and some which occurred immediately following the Great Attainment (e.g., the Buddha's hesitation before deciding to preach the Dhamma, and the conversion and ordination of five disciples who had been his companions during an earlier phase of his spiritual quest). Finally, the Vinaya narrative shows even more vividly the impact of the traditions which emerged in the pilgrimage sites at Uruvelā and at nearby Benares (and perhaps at Rājagaha as well). It shows the influence, too, of the kind of royal and mythic ethos which was evident in the roughly contemporary Mahāpadāna Sutta, and it witnesses to the tendency to extend the narrative to include more events in the early phase of the Buddha's ministry. In this account of the Enlightenment some forty-three separate episodes are narrated. These include the highly significant preaching of the First Sermon in the Deer Park at Benares by virtue of which the newly enlightened Buddha, like a great Cakkavatti king, 'sets in motion the Wheel of Dhamma' (this act, which establishes the 'Kingdom of Righteousness' is one which is associated with all Buddhas in the Mahāpadāna Sutta). They also include the conversion and ordination of Yasa and his companions at Benares, the equally important conversion and ordination of Kassapa and his Brahman followers at Uruvelā, and the conversion and ordination of the two great disciples, Sāriputta and Moggallāna, at Rājagaha.[27]

In the post-Asokan period the pilgrimage sites at Uruvelā, the Deer Park at Benares, and Rājagaha enjoyed increasing popularity. These pilgrimage centers provided, along with an increased emphasis on the royal and mythic qualities of the Buddha, an atmosphere in which the Enlightenment narrative incorporated many more new elements. Once again the Theravādins, in comparison to the Sanskrit schools and the lay oriented iconographic tradition, adapted rather slowly and maintained rather strict doctrinal restraints. Nevertheless the Theravāda community gradually accepted a number of new episodes into the narration both of the events which led up to the Enlightenment and of its immediate sequel. Among the former one of the most important is an account of the radically ascetic spiritual experiments which the Buddha undertook immediately following his unfruitful apprenticeships with Ālāra Kālāma and Uddaka-Rāmaputta. Others are an account of the offering of a peasant girl named Sujātā who mistook the meditating Buddha for a tree deity whom she had been in the habit of worshipping, and an account of the appearance of the great Wisdom Throne, symbolically situated at the center of the universe, on which the Buddha seated himself and attained his goal. Perhaps most important of all, there is a highly dramatic and colorful description of the Buddha's great battle against Māra and his hosts, in which the Master triumphed by calling the Earth to witness to the great deeds of compassion which he had performed in his penultimate life as King Vessantara. Among the new episodes absorbed into the accounts of the period immediately following the Enlightenment are an account of a week which the Buddha spent in a house of gems created by the angels during which he thought through the entire Abhidhamma (the third segment of the Pali canon which, from an historical point of view, is a definitely post-Asokan text). There is also the report of the Buddha's gift of a hair relic to the merchants Tapassu and Bhalluka who, according to the text, proceeded to build a stupa in their own city and to place the relics within it. There is, further, a much expanded and dramatized account of an episode in which the Buddha successfully resisted the efforts of the three devious and sensuous daughters of Māra (craving, discontent and lust) to break his serenity and to arouse his passion.[28]

Also during the same post-Asokan period, accounts of the events of the Buddha's ministry were being extensively elaborated in the broader Buddhist tradition, and many of these developments were incorporated by the Theravādins. The proliferation of the pilgrimage sites, and the emphasis which came to be placed on the miraculous powers of the Buddha, contributed to the appearance of colorful and dramatic accounts of a number of key events. For example, the Theravādins came to include in their biographical tradition the story of the great miracle at Kapilavatthu which the Buddha performed in order to humble his Sākyan relatives who had refused to show him appropriate deference, and the story of the similar miracle which he performed at Sāvatthi in order to confound the heretics. To cite just two further examples, they incorporated the story of the Buddha's ascent to the Tāvatimsa heaven where he preached the Dhamma to his mother (according to the tradition it was preached in the form of the Abhidhamma), as well as a series of episodes involving encounters between the Buddha and Devadatta, his cousin and archetypal enemy, who caused a schism in the order and on several occasions sought to take the Buddha's life. At the same time the concern of many local Buddhist communities to relate the Buddha to their own topography and traditions led to the incorporation of accounts of a rather different kind. For example, by the fifth centiry A.D. the Theravāda tradition in Ceylon had generated an account of three important visits which the Buddha had made to the island kingdom. During these visits he prepared the way for later historical developments and, at the same time, consecrated a number of sites which later became the major pilgrimage centers for Sinhalese Buddhists.[29] Finally, the Theravādins during this period made considerable progress in organizing the events of that ministry into a consistent chronological sequence. By the fifth century they had developed a rather full narrative account of the first year following the Enlightenment, and a much sketchier account of the first half of the ministry.[30]

When we turn our attention from the accounts of the Buddha's Enlightenment and ministry to those of his final journey and his death, we immediately confront one of the very few canonical narratives which covers an extended series of events in the Founder's career. This text, which is the very famous Mahāparinibbāna Sutta, was certainly composed in the pre-Asokan period on the basis of the memories of the Buddha's disciples, supplemented by traditions which gradually emerged at various pilgrimage centers including the one at the death site at Kusinārā.[31] It relates the Buddha's decision to undertake a journey from Rājagaha, where he was staying at the time, and the events which occurred during his journey from that city to Vesāli, where he made his famous prediction that in three months his life would come to an end. (The great significance which is attached to this prediction is signaled in the text by the fact that it is specified as one of those very special events, such as the descent from the Tusita heaven, the miraculous birth, the Enlightenment, and the Parinibbāna itself, which occurs in the life of all

Buddhas and is accompanied by a great quaking of the earth.)[32] It then proceeds to describe the trip from Vesāli to Kusinārā and the events which took place during the last weeks of the Buddha's earthly career.

The Mahāparinibbāna account of the final events which occurred in Kusināra includes a discourse in which the Buddha instructs his monastic followers to leave the arrangements for his funeral to laymen. In this discourse he specifically affirms that these rites will be the kind which have traditionally been reserved for a Cakkavatti king, and he also affirms that a stupa shall be erected at the four crossroads. The narrative goes on to report a discourse in which the Buddha consoles his disciples by telling them that despite its small size and unkempt appearance, the village where he is to die is an appropriate place for such a great event, since in the distant past it was the capital of a great Cakkavatti king named Mahāsudassana.[33] The Sutta proceeds to relate the stories of the Great Decease itself and of a dispute among the neighboring kings concerning the distribution of the relics and the compromise suggested and arranged by a Brahmin named Doṇa. The text then concludes with two lists which tell of the fate of the relics. The first list, which is held by the Pali commentaries to be an addition made at a Council held during the reign of King Asoka, mentions eight relics which were taken by eight neighboring kings and deposited in their respective capitals, the measuring bowl used to divide them which was placed in a stupa by Doṇa, and the ashes taken by the ancestors of the Moriyas (the dynasty of Asoka) and placed in a stupa in their own kingdom. The second list, attributed by the same Pali commentaries to the 'elders of Ceylon', mentions eight relics including seven which were kept in India and one which was taken away to the land of the Nāga kings, and refers specifically to four tooth relics, one which was worshipped by the gods and one which was kept in Gandhāra. It goes on to report another discourse which was kept by the Kāliṅgas in South India, and one which was revered by the Nāga kings.[34]

In contrast to the gradual, but still definite and quite obvious development in the Theravāda stories concerning the Buddha's previous lives and the early portions of his life as Gotama, the ancient canonical narrative of the Buddha's last journey from Rājagaha and his death at Kusinārā was not extensively elaborated. However, the tradition established in the concluding segment of the Mahāparinibbāna Sutta was vastly extended through a rich plethora of stories which recount the adventures and powers of the Buddha's relics. In the Sinhalese context, where it was explicitly stated that those who beheld the relics also beheld the Conqueror, the traditions concerning the relics and related stupas and images grew rapidly, were incorporated into the local chronicles, and were eventually given expression in a variety of independent texts. Two well-known examples are the Thūpavaṃsa, which provided an account of many stupas including the renowned Mahā Thūpa at Anurādhapura, and the Dhātuvaṃsa, which recounted the history of the Tooth Relic which ultimately became the palladium of the Sinhalese monarchy.[35] In still later times parallel traditions came to the fore in each of the various Theravāda areas of Southeast Asia. A case in point is the Chronicle of the Emerald Buddha which recounts the adventures of the relic-filled image which ultimately became the palladium of the present Chakri dynasty in Thailand.

Autonomous biographies and the biographical chronicles

As we have pursued our study of the earlier stages in the development of the Theravāda version of the Buddha biography it has been necessary to recognize that for approximately nine centuries after the death of the Buddha the various segments and cycles of biographical material emerged and developed in various ways, and that at least at the literary level of the tradition they were kept quite separate from one another. It is also important to keep in mind that the early texts which describe various limited segments of the Buddha's career have been preserved in the canon and the commentaries, and that these texts, along with later materials which deal with similarly restricted series of episodes (notably the stories of relics, stupas, and images), have continued to perform important and often quite specific functions in the context of Theravāda religion and Theravāda societies. However, in order to deal adequately with the later stages in the development of the Theravāda biographical tradition, it is necessary to take account of the fact that in the fifth century A.D. the Theravādins began to compile biographical accounts which brought together and synthesized many of the previously segmented narratives.

In examining these later and more complete accounts it will be helpful to distinguish two types of biographical texts which have had an important impact and role in the history of the Theravāda community. The first type includes those accounts which are sacred biographies in the more traditional and limited sense, and includes many texts compiled in various Theravāda countries and in various historical periods. Certainly the earliest and most famous account of this kind is found in the Niddānakathā (the introduction to the fifth century Jātaka Commentary) which traces the Buddha's career from the time of his previous birth as Sumedha when he made his original vow to attain Buddhahood, to the time when Gotama, in the year following his Enlightenment, took up residence in the famous Jetavana monastery in the city of Vesāli (it was here, according to the main body of the commentary, that the Jātakas were preached). However the most developed, complete, and literarily appealing of the accounts of this first type is the Pathamasambodhikaṭha, written by H.R.H. Paramanuchitchinorot who served as the Sanghrājā (the highest ecclesiastical officer) of the Thai Monastic Order in the mid-nineteenth century. The second type, on the other hand, includes those rather differently structured accounts which can appropriately be called biographical chronicles. The earliest and most famous example of a Theravāda chronicle which possesses some biographical elements is the fifth century Sinhalese Mahāvaṃsa. However, the integration of biography and chronicle becomes more fully developed in the later tradition, and is perhaps best illustrated in the sixteenth century Thai text known as The Sheaf of Garlands of the Epochs of the Conqueror.

Unlike the somewhat similar Sanskrit texts which preceded and followed it, the Niddānakathā is a rather conservative and restrained text.[36] With the exception of an important and obvious increase in the dramatic quality of the narrative, and the addition of a number of colorful and suggestive but doctrinally neutral incidents, the Niddānakathā account remains basically faithful to the canonical testimony. However, in the process of weaving an extended and continuous narrative the author presents a fully developed story of the life of Gotama with a structure directly parallel to that of the life stories of other great heroes which appeared at about this time in India, and in other parts of the world as well.[37] And what is more, the account achieves a remarkable synthesis of the motifs which were evident in the various segments of canonical material. First, the narrative preserves and conveys the canonical sense of the historical figure around whom first the oral, and later the written, tradition took form. Secondly, the story maintains and conveys the canonical emphasis on those aspects of the Buddha's career which led to his achievement as the Great Ascetic. In the account of the Buddha's previous lives which begins the Niddānakathā text, the Buddha's perfection of the virtues of renunciation is highlighted. In the stories of the spiritual quest which preceded the Enlightenment a prominent place is given to his Great Depature from Kapilavatthu and the household life, to his apprenticeship to two of the great ascetic teachers of his day, and to his own experiments with the most severe forms of ascetic practice. And most important of all, the Enlightenment itself is vividly portrayed as an event in which the Buddha transcends the achievements of the traditional ascetics and attains a goal which is beyond anything they had experienced – namely the realization of Omniscience. Thirdly, the author of the Niddānakathā both maintains and highlights the canonical emphasis on the royal dimensions of the Buddha's attainment. In his recounting of the previous lives the perfection of the royal virtues of goodness and compassion is very much to the fore, and in his account of the Buddha's ancestry the royal element is emphasized. In the narration of the Buddha's career from his descent from the Tusita heaven to the Enlightenment there are continuous references to those qualities, manifestations, and episodes which reveal that he has become a Mahāpurusa (Great Being) who embodies all the charisma and virtues which the Indian tradition had come to associate with the figure of the ideal Cakkavatti king. And above all, in the account of the Great Departure, the Enlightenment, and the events which immediately followed the Enlightenment, the author vividly portrays the process through which the Buddha transcends the vocation appropriate for a Great Universal Monarch, and achieves the higher sovereignty of Wisdom and the higher vocation of a Buddha or Universal Teacher. Finally, it is crucially important that the author succeeds in fusing the human, ascetic and royal themes so that they become absolutely inseparable and interdependent.

Although the Niddānakathā account remained a standard for all subsequent Theravāda Buddha biographies of the same type, the development of the tradition continued, both in Ceylon and in the Theravāda countries of Southeast Asia. In various texts new episodes which had been included in other commentaries were incorporated into the narrative of the events which occurred during the early period of the Buddha's ministry up to the point at which he took up his residence at Vesāli. And in many cases the narrative was extended to include subsequent events of the Buddha's career (again, most of these incidents had already been recounted in one of the older commentaries).

As we have suggested, the tradition of sacred biographies of the Niddānakathā type was brought to perhaps its fullest development in the Thai account called the Pathamasambodhikaṭha.[38] In this biography, which covers some 500 pages in Thai script and is considered a classic of Thai literature, the events in the previous lives of the Buddha, his genealogy, and his life as Gotama are extensively elaborated and many episodes which are not included in the Niddānakathā are recounted. To give only three examples, the Thai text tells the story of the Buddha's prediction that the monk Ajita will become the future Buddha Metteyya, it tells of the Buddha's ascent to the Tāvitimsa heaven in order to preach the Dhamma to his mother, and it incorporates a series of stories dealing with the Buddha's encounters with Devadatta. Moreover the story is extended to include an account drawn from the Buddhavamsa Commentary of the places where the Buddha spent the rain retreats during the second halt of his ministry, as well as the account of the events of the final phase of the Buddha's life which had been preserved in the Mahāparinibbāna Sutta.

Perhaps more surprisingly, the text also includes a series of fascinating stories concerning the Buddha's relics. The story of the distribution of the relics is recounted, as is the story of their collection and burial in a single spot where they were later discovered by King Asoka. The Sangharājā then recounts Asoka's great celebration in honor of the relics, the attempt of Māra to disrupt it, the resistance which was offered by the great monk Upagupta, and the final humiliation of Māra as well as his vow to attain Buddhahood. (This story has close associations with the early Sanskrit tradition and incorporates elements which seem to be related to myths and practices which were indigenous to Southeast Asia.)[39] And what is more, the Sangharājā concludes his account by describing five stages in the inevitable decline of the religion, a process which will be culminated by the coming together of the relics at the sight of the Enlightenment under the Bo Tree, and their subsequent disappearance.[40] According to the text it is this event which is the real culmination of the sacred biography; the Buddha, it affirms, attained his first or *kilesa-Nibbāna* (the cessation of the defilements) at the time of his Enlightenment, and his second or *khandha-Nibbāna* (cessation of the mental and bodily agregates) at the time of his Great Decease – however his final or *dhātu-Nibbāna* will only come to pass at that somewhat indefinite future time when the five stages in the decline of the religion have been completed, and nothing further remains to be accomplished.[41]

Though the 'biographical chronicles' share a great deal with texts such as the Niddānakathā and thus Pathamasambodhikaṭha, they differ in a number of very important respects. In the case of the Mahāvaṃsa and other early chronicles of the same type, the biographical element is somewhat attenuated, but it is nevertheless clearly present.[42] Like those of the still earlier Dīpavaṃsa which covers much of the same 'historical' material as does the Mahāvaṃsa, the opening chapters of the latter are explicit biographical accounts. In the first chapter the author of the chronical provides a biographical sketch which traces the high points of the Buddha's career from the time of his original vow through those events in his ministry which are of special relevance to the author's particular purpose. These events, which provide the focus for the biographical narrative, are the Buddha's three visits to Ceylon. These three visits prefigure three basic developments which the text subsequently relates in more historical fashion – namely the 'civilizing' of Ceylon, its 'pacification', and its conversion to Buddhism by Asoka's missionary son (Mahinda) during the reign of King Devānampiyatissa. The second chapter continues the biographical pattern by tracing the royal or physical genealogy of the Buddha from Mahāsammata, the first king of the race, to the Buddha himself, and then proceeds to a second account of the Buddha's life as Gotama. In this second account special attention is given to the relationship between the Buddha and King Bimbisāra, a relationship which provides a normative paradigm for the interaction between the Sangha and the later secular rulers in India and Ceylon, which constitutes the dominant theme in the remaining chapters of the chronicle. Finally, it is worth noting that though the biographical implications are not emphasized, these later chapters of the Mahāvaṃsa are filled with references to the travels, presence, and power of the relics, and even recount how, on several occasions, the Sinhalese kings performed great rituals in which the relics were invested with sovereignty over the kingdom.

Again, as in the case of the biographical tradition initiated by the Niddānakatha, the tradition of biographical chronicles launched by the Mahavaṃsa gradually developed during the course of Theravāda history in Ceylon and Southeast Asia. Thus in many later chronicles the specifically biographical content was greatly expanded, and the biographical structure became more obvious and pervasive. As the title vividly indicates, the sixteenth century Thai text known as the Jinakālamālipakaraṇam or Sheaf of Garlands of the Epochs of the Conqueror, is a classic case in point.[43] This text, written by a monk named Ratanapañña in order to justify the preeminence of the Sinhalese sect in the northern kingdom of Lanna Thai and to glorify the local rulers who had come to support it, devotes nine chapters (a quarter of the total narrative) to the story of the Buddha up to and including the distribution of his relics. These chapters begin by recounting a number of the Buddha's lives previous to his birth as Sumedha, starting with one in which he saves his mother from drowning in the great ocean. They go on to recount the vow which he made in his life as Sumedha, to tell many of the other traditional Jātaka stories, and to recite his royal or physical genealogy. In the subsequent account of the Buddha's life as Gotama the Jinakālamāli includes many more of the traditional episodes than did the Mahāvaṃsa, but like the Mahāvaṃsa, it gives special emphasis to events which set the stage for the future development of the religion in Ceylon. The three visits are fully described, and in addition, the story of the Buddha's Great Decease (not included in the Mahāvaṃsa account) is dominated by his request to Indra to protect the religion in Ceylon, and by five final resolutions of will which deal with the establishment of the Bodhi tree and the relics in the island kingdom. Perhaps even more significant than this expansion of obviously biographical material, the account of the subsequent periods in the history of Buddhism in India, Ceylon and Thailand not only incorporates a wide variety of accounts of relics, stupas, and images, but also explicitly recognizes these various periods as 'epochs of the life of the Conqueror'. Moreover, in the Jinakālamāli just as in the Pathamasambodhikaṭha, it is clearly implied that there are further 'epochs of the Conqueror' which have not yet come to pass.

The Buddha biography and recent Theravāda religion

In any attempt to discuss the Buddha biography and its role in modern Theravāda religion it is important, first, to note that the Theravādins have for the most part retained the traditional accounts, and secondly, to emphasize that these traditional accounts continue to function in most of the same ways that they have functioned in the past. The Jātaka stories continue to be used to illustrate the meaning of the Dhamma at the level of practical action. Texts such as the Dhammapada Commentary and the Commentary on the Maṇgala Sutta, which depend heavily on Jātaka stories to illustrate basic religious principles, continue to play an important role in contemporary monastic education in various Theravāda areas. And – to cite just one further example – the recitation of the Mahāvessantara, which is certainly the most widely renowned of the Jātakas, still is a central element in important ritual celebrations, particularly in Thailand.[44] At another level various episodes in the Buddha's historical life as Gotama are still used to lend authority to the Sutta and Vinaya segments with which they are associated, and to provide background and content for important cultic celebrations. On the one hand they justify and give substance to such celebrations as the Vesākha Pūjā which commemorates the Buddha's birth, his Enlightenment, and his Parinibbāna. On the other hand they provide models for ceremonies such as the entrance of young men into the Sangha which, in many areas, involves a reenactment of the classical story of the Buddha's Great Departure from Kapilavatthu.[45] The traditional accounts of the relics, stupas and images also continue to perform important functions, particularly in the sphere of civic and popular religion. For example, the story of the gift of the Buddha's relic to Tapassu and Bhalluka, and their construction of a stupa to house it, still serves as a legitimizing etiology for the veneration of stupas; the stories of the Tooth Relic still serve to legitimize the very active life and institutions associated with the Temple of the Tooth in the old Sinhalese capital of Kandy; and the story of Upagupta's encounter with Māra which appears in the later Thai biographies is basic to important contemporary rituals in various Theravāda areas of Southeast Asia.[46] In addition, these traditional biographical fragments and the more complete and integrated accounts of the Buddha's life continue to express and to transmit a sense of the ascetic and royal greatness and charisma of the Founder, and to support his continuing role as one of the Three Jewels (the Buddha, the Dhamma, and the Sangha) in which all Buddhists 'take refuge'.

Nevertheless, it is also true that alongside the forms of the biography which have been inherited from the past, new emphases have been developed among the urban elites which in recent years have become an important factor in each of the major Theravāda countries.[47] On the more negative side, the modernist reformers who have expressed and influenced the orientation of this newly emerging segment of the community have engaged in the kind of process which in the West has sometimes been called 'demythologizing'. For example, the Jātaka stories have been deemphasized, and where references have been made to jātakas they have been treated almost exclusively as moral fables; the fantastic or miraculous elements in the Buddha's life have been passed over or given a purely 'symbolic' interpretation and significance; and the stories of the relics and images have been ignored or, in some cases, subjected to a radical historicization. On the more positive side, the modernist reformers have presented the Buddha as the teacher of a rationalistic or 'scientific' ethical system and, in still more recent times, have portrayed him as a social reformer who devoted himself to the struggle against caste and ecclesiastical decadence, who was committed to the cause of democracy and, in some cases, socialism, and whose preeminent concern was the general well-being of the society. To be sure, the Theravādins have not yet produced a full scale modernist biography such as Dr. Ambedker's *Buddha and His Dhamma* (in fact, the Indian leader's book was not particularly well received in the Theravāda world); however the conception of the Buddha as a great harbinger of reformist ideals has been reflected in practically all 'modern Buddhist' writings, and represents and understanding of the Founder's career and meaning which is held by a significant number of contemporary Theravāda leaders.[48]

Thus in the modern world, just as in the earlier periods of Theravāda history, the sacred biography of the Founder is being appropriated from the past at the same time that it is being reinterpreted in relation to contemporary attitudes and experiences. So long as this process continues we may affirm, along with the authors of the Pathamasambodhikaṭha and the Jinakalāmāli, that there are, in fact, further 'epochs of the life of the Conqueror' which have not yet come to pass.

NOTES

1. Though we refer here to *the* sacred biography there were, as we shall see, a number of different versions which narrated the story in rather different ways.
2. 'The Concept of the *Classical* in the Study of Religion' in *Types of Religious Experience Christian and Non-Christian* (Chicago: University of Chicago Press, 1951), pp. 48–60.
3. For a fuller discussion of the early Western interest see the Introduction to Edward J. Thomas, *The Life of Buddha as Legend and History* (London: Kegan Paul, Trench, Trubner and Co., 1927).
4. For a fuller treatment see the Introduction to T. W. Rhys-Davids, tr., *Buddhist Birth Stories* (Boston: Houghton and Mifflin, 1880), pp. XXXVI–XLI.
5. This book is available in an English translation, *The Kingdom of Siam* (Kuala Lumpur: Oxford University Press, 1969).
6. For an excellent survey of this development as it relates to one problem see Guy Welbon, *The Buddhist Nirvana and Its Western Interpreters* (Chicago: University of Chicago Press, 1968).
7. A very concise but accurate summary of the two schools of intepretation, which discusses their style of dealing with various aspects of early Buddhism, can be found in Edward Conze's essay on 'Recent Progress in Buddhist Studies' in his *Thirty Years of Buddhist Studies* (Columbia, South Carolina: University of South Carolina Press, 1968).
8. Edward J. Thomas, *The Life of the Buddha as Legend and History*.
9. *Die Überlieferung vom Lebensende des Buddha* (2 parts; *Abhandlungen der Akademie der Wissenschaften in Göttingen*, Philologisch-Historische Klasse, 3rd series, nos. 29 and 30: Akademie der Wissenschaften, 1944, 1948).
10. 'La légende du Bouddha', *Revue de l'historie des religions*, Vol. 134 (1947), pp. 37–71.
11. This book is available in an abridged translation by Simone Boas, *The Life of the Buddha according to the Ancient Texts and Monuments of India* (Middletown, Connecticut: Wesleyan University Press, 1963).
12. Serie Orientale Roma, VIII; Rome: Istituto Italiano per il Medio ed Estremo Oriente, 1956.
13. Institut Orientaliste; Louvain: University of Louvain, 1958.
14. The article on the legend of the Buddha's youth appears in *Oriens Extremus*, Vol. 9, No. 1 (February, 1962), pp. 6–33. The book referred to is *Recherches sur la Biographie du Bouddha dans les Sūtrapitaka et les Vinayapitaka anciens: de la Quête de l'éveil a la conversion de Śāriputra et de Maudgālyayana* (Vol. 53; Publications of the Ecole Francais d'Extrême-Orient; Paris: Ecole Francaise d'Extrême-Orient, 1963). The essay on the superhuman personality of the Buddha appears in Kitagawa and Long, eds., *Myths and Symbols: Essays in Honor of Mircea Eliade* (Chicago: University of Chicago Press, 1969).
15. As the following discussion will demonstrate, I have made the decision to focus on the Theravāda tradition not because I assume that its scriptures are necessarily more

ancient or authoritative than those of other early Buddhist schools. Rather, I have made this choice because of my interest in the Theravāda tradition as one which, while having roots in the very early period of Buddhist history, has maintained its continuity through the medieval period, and on into modern times.

16. Because the paper is focused on the Theravāda tradition I will use Pali transliterations except in cases where the discussion refers specifically to Sanskrit material.
17. One very interesting discussion of the subject is by Andrè Bareau in 'La date du Nirvāna', *Journal Asiatique* (1953), pp. 27–62.
18. There have been few good scholarly works on the Jātaka tradition. One of the few reasonably adequate and comprehensive treatments can be found in Alfred Foucher, *Les vies antèrieures du Bouddha d'après les textes et les monuments de l'Inde* (Publications du Musèe Guimet, Biblioteque de diffusion, t. 61; Paris; Presses Universitaires de France, 1955).
19. The ability to remember all of his previous lives was the first of the three forms of higher knowledge which, according to the tradition, the Buddha achieved in the process of his Enlightenment.
20. For a discussion of these early divisions the of canonical material see Lamotte, *Historie du Bouddhisme Indien*, pp. 157–160.
21. See E. W. Cowell, ed., *Jātaka; or Stories of the Buddha's Former Birth*, 6 vols. (Cambridge: Cambridge University Press, 1895, 1907, 1913, and reprinted in 3 vols., 1969).
22. For a discussion of this set of stories see Schweisguth, *Etude sur la littérature Siamoise* (Libraire d'Amèrique et d'Orient; Paris: Adrien Maissonneuve, 1951), p. 96 and *passim*.
23. The Sutta itself is found in T. W. and C. A. F. Rhys-Davids, tr., *Dialogues of the Buddha* (*Dīgha Nikāya, Part 2*), (*Sacred Books of the Buddhists*, No. 3; London: Oxford University Press, 1910), pp. 1–41. An important comparative study of the various versions of the text, which provides the basic data for dating its appearance and development in the tradition has been published by Ernst Waldschmidt, *Das Mahāvadānasūtra* (1952, No. 8; *Abhandlungen der Deutschen Akademie der Wissênschaften zu Berlin:* Akademie der Wissenschaften, 1953).
24. This orthodox version is found in the famous Niddānakathā which forms the Introduction to the Jātaka Commentary. See Rhys-Davids, *Buddhist Birth Stories*, pp. 58–59.
25. Lord Chalmers, tr., *Further Dialogues of the Buddha (Majjhima Nikāya*, Part 1), *(S.B.B.*, No. 5; London: Oxford University Press, 1926), pp. 12–17 and 79–81.
26. *Ibid.*, pp. 113–124 and 170–179. Unlike the other three Sutta mentioned, the Mahāsaccaka has no direct counterparts in other extant traditions; however its close similarity to the other three strongly suggests that it, also, was a very ancient text.
27. Isaline B. Homer, tr., *Book of the Discipline*, Part IV (*S.B.B.* 14; London: Luzac, 1951), pp. 1–57.
28. For the full narrative see the Niddankatha account in Rhys-Davids, *Birth Stories*, pp. 89–118.
29. Wilhelm Geiger, tr., Mahāvaṃsa (Tr. S. No. 3; P.T.S.: London, 1912), pp. 3–9. In

later centuries similar stories of Buddha visits developed in various Theravāda countries in Southeast Asia. For some examples see Camille, Notton, tr., *Annales du Siam*, Part I (Paris: Charles Lavanzelli, 1926).

30. The more detailed account of the first year is found in the Niddānakathā, pp. 118–152. The more sketchy account of the first twenty years is contained in Buddhadatta's untranslated commentary on the Buddhavamsa. It should be noted that though Buddhadatta's framework has been adopted by subsequent biographers, both Buddhist and Western [for a Buddhist example, see The Sheaf of Garlands of the Epochs of the Conqueror (Tr. S., No. 36; P.T.S.; London: Luzac, 1968), p. 47], it is based on quite late commentarial sources and has little claim to historical authenticity.
31. T. W. and C. A. F. Rhys-Davids, trs., *Further Dialogues (Digha Nikāya*, Part 2), pp. 71–191.
32. For insight into the significance which this prediction had for some later Buddhists, see William LaFleur's article on 'The Death and the Lives of the Poet-Monk Saigyō' in the present volume.
33. This discourse served as the basis for a full length Sutta which was given a place in the Dīgha Nikāya immediately following the Mahāparinibbāna Sutta.
34. For a discussion of the text and commentaries see Thomas, *The Life of the Buddha as Legend and History*, pp. 158–159.
35. The reference to the equivalence between beholding the relics and beholding the Buddha is made in the Mahāvaṃsa, tr. Geiger, p. 116.
36. Rhys-Davids, *Birth Stories*, pp. 1–133.
37. For a discussion of this structure in relation to the Buddha biography see Joseph Campbell, *The Masks of God: Oriental Mythology* (New York: Viking Press, 1962), pp. 252–255.
38. H. R. H. Paramanuchitchinorot, Pathamasambodhikaṭha (Bangkok: Ministry of Education, 1962).
39. For a discussion of the story and its background see Stanley J. Tambiah, *Buddhism and Spirit Cults in Northeastern Thailand* (Cambridge: Cambridge University Press, 1970), p. 169.
40. This is a common Theravāda tradition. For a Sinhalese variant see Richard Gombrich, *Precept and Practice: Traditional Buddhism in the Rural Highlands of Ceylon* (Oxford: Clarendon Press, 1971), p. 287.
41. The doctrine of the three Nibbānas is presented in non-biographical Theravāda texts as well. See, for example, Trai Phum Phra Ruang (The Three Worlds According to King Ruang) (Bangkok: Teacher's Association, 1964), p. 313.
42. Geiger, tr., Mahāvaṃsa.
43. Jayawickrama, tr., The Sheaf of Garlands of the Epoch of the Conqueror.
44. For a discussion and analysis of such a ritual celebration and the recitation of the Mahavessantara (known locally as Mahachad or Great Life), see Tambiah, *Buddhism and Spirit Cults*, pp. 160–175, esp. pp. 165–166. In this context it is worth noting that a major Thai movie which recounts the story of Vessantara has recently been produced and is presently (late 1973) enjoying considerable popularity throughout the country.

45. For a futher example see the discussion of royal funerals as, in large part, a reenactment of the funeral of the Buddha in Adhemard Leclere, *La Crémation et les Rites Funéraires au Cambodge* (Hanoi: F. H. Schneider, 1907).
46. An excellent discussion of the ritual and institutions associated with the Tooth Relic with particular emphasis on the contemporary period is contained in H. L. Seneviratane, 'The Natural History of a Buddhist Liturgy' (Unpublished Doctoral Dissertation: University of Rochester, 1972). A short but insightful treatment of a Thai festival in which the story of Upagupta and Māra is basic to major segments of the ritual is contained in Tambiah, *Buddhism and Spirit Cults*, pp. 160–175 and 300–309.
47. An interesting discussion of the urban elite in Ceylon can be found in Gananath Obeyesekere, 'Religious Symbolism and Political Change in Ceylon' in G. Obeyesekere, Frank E. Reynolds and Bardwell L. Smith (ed.), *The Two Wheels of Dhamma: Essays on the Theravada Tradition in India and Ceylon*, AAR Studies in Religion no. 3 (Chambersburg, Pa.: American Academy of Religion, 1972).
48. For a nineteenth century example of the reformist attitude see Henry Alabaster, *The Wheel of the Law* (London: Trubner, 1971), Part I. For a more recent example see D. C. Vijayavardhana, *Dharma-Vijaya, Triumph of Righteousness, or the Revolt in the Temple* (Colombo: Sinha Publications, 1953).

EARLE WAUGH

2

Following the Beloved

Muhammad as Model in the Ṣūfī Tradition

The composite nature of our information concerning Muhammad has been recognized by specialists for some time; Tor Andrae in *Die Person Muhammeds in Lehre und Glauben seiner Gemeinde* (Stockholm, 1918) traced the prophet's image in legends, theology, mysticism and sectarianism, while Widengren, in *The Ascension of the Apostle and the Heavenly Book* (Uppsala, 1950) and *Muhammad, the Apostle of God and His Ascension* (Uppsala, 1955) analyzed the material on the prophet through the long-standing Middle Eastern categories of 'Apostle' and 'Ascension'. As with most founders of religious groups, the 'historical' aspects of Muhammad's life are filtered through the attitudes and longings of those associated with him and the interpretation of his life has to take the milieu of the sources into account. Hence the best approach to the subject may be to identify and trace clusters of traditions which provide the schemata for understanding the Prophet. These clusters have their own emphases, and, without claiming completeness, we could identify several crucial groupings: Muhammad, the Legislator-Prophet with a normative role being Muhammad in the Medinese community; Muhammad, the Prophet-Leader of a specifically 'called' community (in which the Prophet gathers up and fulfills notions from the Semitic prophetic tradition); Muhammad, the revealer, in which the prophetic message, not the man, becomes the focal point of concern; Muhammad, the 'sacred presence', in which the avataristic elements (to use Schuon's word[1]) are stressed; and Muhammad, the spiritual guide, in which the intuitive and ascetic dimensions are fundamental. In the history of Islam, these have interacted and expanded, but each has retained its own flavor, and it would be instructive to examine each. My purpose here is to consider some important aspects of the last group, i.e., what I have called Muhammad, the spiritual guide.

Dimensions of Muhammad's spiritual ancestry

It seems clear that Muhammad understood himself to stand in the illustrious tradition of Semitic prophets;[2] it is less obvious that he fulfilled the role of mystic. Yet the developing Ṣūfī movement regarded him as the trailblazer into the secrets of God. How did this materialize?

The response most readily available is that the Ṣūfī vision was grafted onto the Prophet as ascetic interests became more prevalent, especially under influence of converted Christian Monks and hermits. But while this may have played an important role, it appears to violate Muslim evaluations of Muhammad's own rich personality, as well as the conviction that right from the beginning Islamic mysticism depended upon spiritual insights of the Prophet. It is more rewarding to see certain themes from the life of the religious leader lending themselves to mystical interpretation in a creative and probably unconscious manner, so that ancient spiritual meanings could interact with motifs from Mohammad's experience, enriching and diversifying the composite picture of the Prophet. In this manner, Muhammad could become the model for the Ṣūfī of a sacred enterprise embracing all men regardless of their doctrinal convictions regarding Islam.

A good example of this expansion is that of the mi'rāj-legends, those religiously significant stories of Muhammad's journey to heaven to receive special guidance for the community. Whatever Muhammad's original experience, the legends indicate him to be of such superior character that he could converse directly with God by ascending to heaven in person. Such a motif was a key element in the ideology of the ancient practitioners of shamanic religion.[3] Through interaction with paradigms reminiscent of this archaic mystical group, the Prophet's ancestry was extended in a direction consonant with the new religious requirements of the Muslim asceticism and mysticism. In the following section we will examine some aspects of these paradigms as they unfold in the myth concerning Muhammad. In our final section we will briefly sketch how the composite picture of the Prophet was then adopted as a model for the pursuit of God.

INITIATION

Horovitz noted some time ago that there were similarities between the opening of Muhammad's breast and the legend of Zarathustra;[4] Birkeland devoted a full length study to the theme of the opening of the breast legend in the early sources.[5] Al-Bukhārī's collection records the following:

"I was one night sleeping at Mecca in the house of Umm Hani, Daughter of Abū Talib and a sister of ʿAlī, when Gabriel came to me. He opened my chest on the side of the heart, washed it with the water of Zamzam in a golden basin, filled it with wisdom and mercy and put it back in its place."[6]

In the sixteenth century version of al-Ghaiṭī, the purification includes Michael, as well as other differences:

"Then Gabriel said to Michael: 'Bring me a basin of Zamzam water that I may purify his heart and set his breast at ease.' Then he drew out his heart, which he bathed three times, thus removing everything noxious that was in it, while Michael came and went with the three basins full of Zamzam water. Then he brought a golden basin filled with wisdom, knowledge, assurance and Islam. Then he closed up (his breast) and sealed him between the shoulders with the seal of prophecy."[7]

Some held that Muhammad's purification was accomplished in childhood. According to Ṭabarī, when Muhammad was small, perhaps three to six, three men descended from heaven, took him and laid him on the ground. They held a basin and a gold knife. One made an incision in his chest and then washed his intestines; another reached to his heart, opened it, and removed a black spot; the third arranged all in place and sealed the Prophet with a sign.[8] Another remarkable version, whose evidence indicates it is very old, perhaps predating the above examples,[9] replaces the men or angels with birds:[10] While Muhammad is tending the lambs of Banū Saʿd, his milk-brother left him to fetch some provisions. Muhammad was approached by two white birds, 'like eagles'. The one said to the other: 'Is it he?' The latter answered: 'Yes'.

"Then they went forward, came up to me, seized me, and threw me down on the neck and split my belly. Then they took out my heart and split it and took out of it two dark clots of blood. Then one of them said to his fellow: 'Bring me some water of snow!' Then they cleansed my interior (gaufī) with it. Afterwards he said: 'Bring me some cold water!' Then they closed my heart with it. Afterwards he said: 'Bring me the sakīna!' Then they sowed it in my heart. Afterwards one of them said to his fellow: 'Sew him up!' Then he sewed him up and sealed him with the seal of prophethood."

Ascension

There are striking similarities between this legend and the complex usually associated with shamanic practice. The candidate may be asleep or in a trance;[11] he is then 'killed' by the appropriate religious representative, usually his tutelary spirit, and his breast is opened and the heart or other vital organs is removed and cleansed.[12] In place of the evil found there, some sacred quality is inserted into the initiate, which gives him extraordinary powers and insight.[13] The candidate is sealed without a sign of his operation, but the nature of his experience is known and he is regarded in a strange light, and perhaps set apart.[14]

Some have argued that the ascent to heaven itself is an initiation; Shrieke, Bevan and Horovitz regard it so,[15] and Birkeland holds that the ascension was an initiation into divine secrets, but not into the prophethood. The miʿrāj, in his view, was only of initiatory significance among 'heterodox' groups and then only before the form of the miʿrāj and the problems outlined by it had become settled by the ijmāʿ.[16] It is however, less important whether the ascent was or was not an initiation into prophethood, as it is to see the *form* in which Muhammad's experience was expressed. Spiritual achievement was conceived in ascensional terms, rather than, for example, in term of enlightenment or incarnation.[17]

The miʿrāj theme began unpretentiously in Sūrah 17: 1

"Glory be to Him, who carried His servant from the Holy Mosque to the Further Mosque the precincts of which We have blessed, that We might show him some of our signs. He is All-Hearing, the All-Seeing."[18]

Soon thereafter it became popular with story tellers and itinerant preachers who expanded it to accommodate the growing need for pious lore about the Prophet; in one of the most popular versions, the scenario emerges as follows:

"Muhammad is awakened by Gabriel, escorted to Burāq, the sacred horse, for the ride to Jerusalem. There he leads prophets, holy men and angels in prayer. Gabriel and the Prophet then ascend to heaven; while on the way, he visits the several levels of heaven, each presided over by a dignitary from the Biblical or cultic past and then investigates hell. When he reaches the Lotus tree of the Boundary,[29] Gabriel can go no further, because it is the most holy ground, and Muhammad proceeds on his own. He meets with God, during which time various signs are disclosed to him and the prescription of five prayers per day established. He then returns to earth."[20]

The ascension was uniquely Muhammad's achievement, and the subtle distinction between the speciality of Muhammad and his revelatory role in the community must be held in perspective, if the mystical development is to grow from him. Such a distinction appears in Sūrah 17: 90–93:

"They say: We will not put faith in thee till thou cause rivers to gush forth from the earth for us;
Or thou have a garden of date-palms and grapes, and cause rivers to gush forth therein abundantly;
Or thou cause the heaven to fall upon us piecemeal, as thou hast pretended, or bring Allah and the angels as a warrant;
(Or) Thou have a house of gold; or *thou ascend up into heaven, and even then we will put no faith in thine ascension till thou bring down for us a book that we can read.* Say: My Lord be glorified! Am I naught save a mortal messenger?"[21]

The point of his critics was that even though he might ascend to heaven like holy men before him, they would not believe him until he brought back a complete book, i.e., not the piecemeal book he was claiming to reveal. This point is made clear in Sūrah 25: 34: "The unbelievers say, 'Why has the Koran not been sent down upon him all at once?'" From the standpoint of his critics, there could be no sense to a trip to heaven as a proof of Muhammad's mission, since they disbelieved the nature of revelation from him, and he never claimed to have the total revelation. At any rate, Gabriel was the source of the revelations as Muhammad received them:[22]

Say: "Whosever is an enemy to Gabriel –
he it was that brought it down upon thy heart
by the leave of God, confirming what was before it,
and for a guidance and good tidings to the believers." (Sūrah II: 91)

One verse in the Qur'ān appears to recreate the scene of Muhammad receiving the revelation from above:

> "This is naught but a revelation revealed, taught him by one terrible in power, very strong; he stood poised, being on the higher horizon,
> Then drew near and suspended hung, two bows'-length away, or nearer, then revealed to his servant that he revealed.[23]
> His heart lies not of what he saw;
> What, will you dispute with him what he sees?
> Indeed, he saw him another time by the Lote-Tree of the Boundary nigh which is the Garden of the Refuge,
> When there covered the Lote-Tree that which covered;
> his eye swerved not, nor swept astray.
> Indeed, he saw one of the greatest signs of his Lord." (103: 4–17)

The import of the selection appears to be that Muhammad *saw*, that is, he had a personal illuminating glimpse of something or someone, which he regarded as 'one of the greatest signs of his Lord'. The focus is not, then, upon the reception of the Qur'ān, or even of the number of times to pray supposedly given at that moment, but on the unveiling of the being of God for the Prophet. It seems evident that Muhammad knew full well that his ascending to heaven would not convince his detractors of his calling, hence the main intention could not have been to impress anyone with his spiritual accomplishment. This is borne out by the fact that in Sūrah 99: 91 the revelation through the instrumentality of Gabriel was regarded as normative by the Prophet.

This is not to say that the ascension did not have repercussions for his prophetic calling. Immediately after Muhammad reported his journey, the interpretations centered on this crucial area. The rather sarcastic, 'What do you think of your friend now, Abū Bakr?'[24] is clearly designed to throw Muhammad's career into disrepute. Ibn Isḥāq reveals the quandary the scholar felt when faced with material purporting to tell of the isrā'-mi'rāj:

"The matter of the place (or time ... masrā) of the journey and what is said about it is a searching test and a matter of God's power and authority wherein is a lesson for the intelligent; and guidance and mercy and strengthening to those who believe. It was certainly an act of God by which He took him by night in what way He pleased to show him His signs which he willed him to see so that he witnessed His mighty sovereignty and power by which He does what He wills to do."[25]

No one ever seemed to doubt that Muhammad had experienced an ascension, but it was hotly debated whether it had been in the body, in dream or vision, and what significance could be placed upon the occurrences within the mi'rāj.[26] In the developing theological circles, the ascension was regarded as initiation into divine secrets, viz., 'And He revealed to me secrets that I am not allowed to communicate to you;'[27] and, 'And I reveal to you the Lord of all the books, which is the guarantor of them, the Qur'ān, which We have parcelled out ... Thereafter He communicated to me after these words what is not allowed to me to repeat to you.'[28] Others regarded it as a test of whether the hearers really believed in Muhammad or not.[29] Still others regarded it as an expression of God's power and sovereignty,[30] and to others the whole story was allegorical.[31] The doctrinal results, then, followed from the presuppositions brought to the material; those who focused on the inner life and sought mystical dimensions in the Prophet's life regarded this as an example for spiritual attainment, and perceived something normative in the Prophet's spiritual life that set him apart as a guide.

If the personal experience of the Prophet elevated him to a novel position above and beyond that of ordinary men,[32] the symbolisms of his ascent are strongly reminiscent of those used by the ancient shamanic tradition. For example, the elevation to heaven was accomplished by various means in the legends. One of the most obvious is the ladder.

"Then Gabriel, on whom be peace, conducted me to Sakhra and there was a ladder, which reached to the Sakhra in the clouds of heaven. I was thrust onto this most beautiful of ladders, with rungs of gold, silver, emeralds and rubies."[33]

Or, in al-Ghaiṭī's version:

"Then they brought in the ladder on which the spirits of mortals mount up (to the heavens). Nothing so beautiful has ever been seen by (Allah's) creatures. It has one ascent of silver and one of gold. It comes from the (celestial) garden (called) Firdaus, and is set with pearls. To its right are angels and to its left are angels."[34]

The Qur'aníc term *ma'arij* may be a borrowing of the Ethiopic *ma'areg*, hence in Sūrah 70: 3–4 God is called *Dhū'l-ma'arij* or 'Lord of the Stairways'; the phrase 'Lord of the Stairways' has its origin in the Ethiopic *Book of Jubilees* (27: 21).[35] Horovitz thinks there may have been direct influence from Jewish mystics upon Muhammad, suggested by the Prophet's apparent familiarity with writings such as the *Books of Enoch*, *The Ascension of Isaiah* and the *Baruch* apocalypses, and other evidence such as the stairs motif in Jacob's ladder, etc.[36] The ladder itself is found in other places in the Qur'ān expressed in the word *sullam*, which is of Hebrew origin (e.g., Sūrah 6: 35, 52: 38).[37] Altmann notes that Jewish mystics were those who were reputed 'to have a ladder in the house',[38] and he generally supports Horovitz's views.

However, there are additional antecedents of ascension and flight among religious and political figures of surrounding peoples: the religious reformer Tansar of the fourth and early fifth century, A.D., among the Sasanians was reported to have won back the pure religion by going up to heaven and then down to hell.[39] Flights were popularly ascribed to political figures, if we can judge from the stories of the flight of Alexander.[40] There are several possible sources of the motif, so a single source need not be regarded as exhaustive; furthermore, the implication that Muhammad deliberately formulated his religious views on the model of any particular group is unsatisfactory in the light of his revelations as a whole, and raises the question of why more substantive elements were not emulated.[41]

While the religious functions of the ladder are extremely diverse a few of the more important are: the means of initiation into the shamanic career,[42] the instrument of ascent employed by the shaman in ecstasy,[43] the way upward for departing souls,[44] and a symbol of the cosmic structure.[45] If the other methods of elevating Muhammad to heaven are considered, i.e., the large bird,[46] Burāq the winged horse,[47] the rising tree that lofts him to the other world,[48] and the presence of Gabriel,[49] we see the dominance of those themes morphologically similar to those found in a shamanic complex. This association of ascension and elevation by upward steps, as we shall explore below, plays a significant role in the Ṣūfī tradition.

The geography of the journey

It is impossible in our limited space to discuss the richness and diversity that characterize the sacred geography of the journey. Several motifs could be examined at length, including the nature of the holy place from which the journey begins,[50] the mountains and rivers which must be forded,[51] the trials that must be passed,[52] and the sacred locations along the way.[53] Muslim sensitivities embellished the glories of heaven,[54] and the ancient religious personages who served as keepers of the various levels of heaven held lengthy conversations with Muhammad.[55] Many of the miʿrāj-legends contain vivid portrayals of the Prophet's visit to hell; he comes as a kind of tourist, and is only sustained during the gross experience by the presence and guidance of Gabriel.[56]

The outer limits of heaven are defined by the *Sidrat al-Muntahā*, the famed Lotus tree of the Boundary.[57] The tree enjoyed fantastic descriptions, including the detail that a cavalier riding at full gallop could not cross its shadow in seventy years,[58] and the assertion that its fruit was the size of large water jars, its leaves the size of elephant ears, etc.[59] In al-Ghaiṭi's version, the two rivers of Paradise and the two rivers of earth (the Nile and Euphrates) flow from beneath it.[60] But what is important for us is the fact that this tree is the dividing line between the presence of God and heaven as such; Gabriel cannot proceed beyond it, since he would be destroyed by the light of God. It is the precinct of God Himself.[61]

The colloquy with God

The final theme reminiscent of the ancient shamanic complex is the colloquy with God;[62] admittedly, some versions of the miʿrāj do not include this meeting, and a great deal of controversy surrounded the issue of whether Muhammad could have seen and talked with God.[63] But devotional and religious meanings outweighed the theological problems, and by al-Ghaiṭī's time the speech appears as a statement covering all elements previously considered to have been given the Prophet:

"Then Allah – glorified and exalted be He – said:'But you have I taken as (my) beloved one. . . . 'And I have sent you to mankind as a whole, (to be) a bringer of good tidings and a warner. I have expanded for you your breast removed from you your burden, and exalted for you your reputation, so that no longer shall I be mentioned (by men) but you will be mentioned with me. I have made your community the best community that has appeared among mankind, made it a (mediating) middle community, making them the former and the latter peoples. Moreover, I have so arranged it that your people cannot have a sermon without bearing witness that you are My servant and My Apostle. I have appointed among your community some whose hearts will be their gospels. You have I made the first Prophet to be created, the last to be sent (on his mission), and the first to be discharged (at judgement). To you have I given the Seven Mathānī, which I gave to no previous people. Also I gave you the concluding verses of the Sura of the Cow, from a Treasury beneath the Throne, which I gave to no previous Prophet. To you have I given al-Kauthir, and I have given you eight portions, viz., Islam, the Hijra, Holy War, almsgiving, fasting (during) Ramaḍān, the (task of) enjoining that which is proper and forbidding that which is improper, and on the day when I created the heavens and the earth I laid as an incumbent duty on you and on your community fifty prayer times, so see that you observe them, both you and your community'."[64]

It is widely held among the colloquy versions that Muhammad returned to God at Moses' insistence to have the prayers reduced to five. In one such selection, God placed His hand on the Prophet's chest, and gave him supernatural vision to view heaven and earth at the same time. The author appears to have been of Ishrāqī persuasion,[65] which might account for the dominance of light imagery, but even so the important point is that Muhammad made personal and direct contact with God, and that the spiritual values imparted during the meeting had ramifications for both Muhammad and the community.[66]

The ascension of Abū Yazīd al-Bistāmi: Internalizing Muhammad's Miʿrāj

One of the most evident areas of miʿrāj development took place among the Ṣūfīs. Muhammad was more than a figure of popular devotion for this movement; certain aspects of his life became archetypal in achieving union with God.[67] Where popular and folk writers concentrated on the glories of heaven, the awe displayed before the Prophet, or the terrors and anguish of hell, the Ṣūfī saw the mi'rāj as a spiritual achievement, and Muhammad the exemplary figure in the pursuit of union with God. This application is dramatically stated by Abū Yazīd al-Bisṭāmī, the first known Ṣūfī to use the theme for mystical purposes:

"And I saw that my spirit was borne to the heavens. It looked at nothing and gave no heed, though Paradise and Hell were displayed to it, for it was freed of phenomena and veils. Then I became a bird, whose body was of Oneness and whose wings were of Everlastingness, and I continued to fly in the air of the absolute, until I passed into the sphere of Purification and gazed upon the field of Eternity and beheld there the tree of Oneness. When I looked I myself was all of those. I cried: 'O Lord, with my egoism I cannot attain to Thee and I cannot escape from my selfhood. What am I to do?' God spake: 'O Abū Yazid, thou must win release from thy thou-ness by following my Beloved (i.e. Muhammad). Smear thine eyes with the dust of his feet and follow him continually'."[68]

Of the many areas where Muhammad is viewed as normative in the relationship with God, the ascension was of particular significance: the unique position of Muhammad as Seal of the Prophets[69] meant that he was the archetypal model for man's movement toward the sacred; as a man, he embodied everything that was associated with human existence,including being the recipient of God's love;[70] as the beloved of God, he was elevated to a state of miraculous closeness, a state transcending the natural capabilities of humanity;[71] as the experiencer of the mi'rāj, he became the symbol for God's desire to bring the mystical initiate into a state of ecstasy and revelation.[72] Because of this interwoven complex of meanings, the ascension became the Ṣūfī model for following Muhammad into intimate relationship with God. It is, then, instructive to examine the progression of images in the text concerning Abū Yazīd.

The ascent begins in this manner:

"I dreamed[73] that I ascended to the heavens; and when I came to the nearest heaven, lo, I saw a green bird; and it unfolded one of its wings and mounted me thereon and flew with me till at last it reached the ranks of the angels who stand with burning feet on the shore, glorifying God at morn and eve."[74]

While the Ṣūfī's ascent is explicitly a 'quest of God', he seeks a more authentic state of being and a more vivid quality of experience than normal. Hence the author states: 'Whoever wishes to know his (i.e., Abū Yazīd's) perfection and eminence, let them look at his Dream and Vision, which is truer in meaning and nearer to real knowledge than the waking state of others.'[75] The images of this experience provide greater reality than that ascribed to physical phenomena: the ascent expresses first an elevating which raises him to heaven, and then a 'flying' which is associated with a bird. The first implies a particular orientation in the psychic life, an orientation not distinguished from his relation to the universe during the normal state; the second provides a plastic image of the transcending quality of the experience.

The medium he uses is purely descriptive, much along the same lines as the legends of Muhammad's mi'rāj, but it contains an implicit rejection of the normal mode of perception (i. e.,' 'It looked at nothing and gave heed ... for it was freed of phenomena and veils.') Moreover those aspects of Muhammed's ascension which had attracted the interest of pious believers, such as depictions of heaven and hell, were obviated by the new perspectives of the religious experience: the myth of the Prophet's ascension was retained as a model but existential truths contained in the experience were immediate and personally vital.

The priority of the new dimension immediately becomes evident:

"And God knew my true will to seek him, and lo, I saw an angel who stretched forth his hand and lifted me towards him. Then I dreamed that I ascended to the Sixth Heaven;[76] and there I saw the longing angels, who came to me and greeted me and confided in me of their longings; and I confided in them of some of the flutterings of my inmost heart."[77]

Once the break was made with the normal state by the 'flying' with the bird, his transcending did not take the form of a journey out of himself, but an exploration within, a movement described in terms of arriving at another level of heaven, but in reality, an explication of his inner motives and desires. In contradistinction to the legendary depictions in Muhammad's mi'rāj, the various levels are not richly and sensuously portrayed. Instead the notion of 'heavens' is retained in its barest form, and homologized into the maqām (stages) and hāl (stations) of the inner man's progress to fanā' (passing away into God).[78] Where Muḥammad had swept on from heaven to heaven because of his prophethood, the Ṣūfī is elevated on the grounds of veracity to the inner vision. His 'being' is constantly tested by the most subtle attractions; even the angels tempt him to discard the model of the Prophet by offering him intimacies only available to saints and prophets. But it is the loyalty to the truth which all believers held concerning the miʿrāj, that is, that it led to special communion with God, which continually assisted him in rejecting these temptations. Hence the shape of his inner experience is cast by an internalization of the mythic pattern, interpreted through existential categories and, in turn, making new kinds of demands.

This new state of being can only be expressed in religious terms by shifting the image of himself to one comprehensible but impossible in normal human conditions:

"And when God knew my true will to seek Him, He changed me into a bird, and every feather of my wings was farther than from the east to the west, a thousand thousand times. And I ceased not from flying in the worlds of Malakūt and Jabarūt[79] and transversing realm after realm and veils after veils and field after field and seas after seas and curtains after curtains untli ... the Cherubim and the Bearers of the Throne and all others whom God had created in heaven and earth – seemed less than a mustard-seed betwixt heaven and earth to the flight of my inmost heart in its quest of God."

The image is concrete and experiencable at the most phenomenal level; it is not mystical or ethereal in itself, and it gets its power from the tension between the assumptions built into being bird-like and being human. Being a bird opens the possibilities for man to reject his normal limitations, to operate according to laws and directives unseen and unknown by ordinary systems of knowledge, and to participate in a mode of being which can only be intuitively grasped. The Ṣūfī 'flying' was the image of the overwhelming nature of the experience in God; he understood his inner being to be wafted along into that unique and fulfilling state of *fanā'*, a state which he held Muhammad had experienced in his ascension.

This state is difficult to interpret, since Ṣūfī theorists disagreed about what identity the mystic had when in union with God.[80] A follower of Abū Yazīd describes it this way:

"My state of annihilation, accompanying me, was replaced by the emergence of godhead, until He took me through Him, that is to say, not Him through me, until He achieved a union which is, without a hint of aught else, that Union which gives no sign of any created work when such oblivion is met with. Afterwards (I walked) on the carpet of the Essence of Truth, hence I was asked: 'At what are you aiming, while this is Abū Yazīd?' I was then taken to a green garden. I said, 'O! That is Abū Yazīd!' He said, 'This place is Abū Yazīd's; but Abū Yazīd is searching for his self but will not find it'."[81]

Three aspects stand out: (1) the subject-object model of description is invalidated ('I . . . came to a place where my sight left me . . .') yet the entire passage retains an eyewitness flavor; (2) the normal states of personal identity and self-consciousness are replaced by a consciousness of God-ness ('no sign of any created work'); and (3) this state is the most authentic state (i.e., 'The Essence of Truth'). The prophetic mi'rāj is peripheral: What had been a colloquy between God and Muhammad in the ascension legends becomes a completely transforming experience for which terms of phenomenal derivation are insufficient. This is dramatically signified by the calling into question of the last and most impervious distinction in Muslim religious language – that between God and man.[82]

Abū Yazīd's miʿrāj is a fascinating example of the archetypal role the figure of Muhammad played in the Ṣūfī tradition. The ascension itself diversified its meaning: Hujwīrī says the term denotes proximity *(qurb)* to God. Distinguishing between the ascension of prophets and that of saint he notes: 'When a saint is enraptured and intoxicated he is withdrawn from himself by means of a spiritual ladder and brought near to God; as soon as he returns to the state of sobriety all those evidences have taken shape in his mind and he has gained knowledge of them.'[83] Hence a *muquarrab* is literally 'one who is brought near', and Ṣūfīs generally considered this to designate the highest class of saints. Later, Ibn al-Farīd was to insist on three stages in the experience of Oneness, with the miʿrāj the third and highest.[84]

Another dimension is added to the meaning by the Ṣūfīs when great import is placed upon the spatializing aspects of the ascension, that is, the various sacred places of the miʿrāj become solidified into stages of prayer:

"The ascension had three stages: (1) from the Masjid al-Harām to the Masjid al-Aqsā; (2) then to the Lote-tree of the Boundary; (3) and thence to the space of two bowlengths, or nearer. Similarly, prayer has for us three stages: (1) the preparatory stance; (2) kneeling; (3) and then prostration, which is the ultimate proximity. As God has said: 'Prostrate yourself and draw near'."[85]

Finally, in the writings of Ibn 'Arabī, we see the working out of the figure of Muhammad and the ascension in a different manner. Ibn ʿArabī held that participation in the miʿrāj of the spirit instituted the saint into the lineage of the prophets; by virtue of having followed the Beloved in this way, the initiate himself became a prophet.[86] He became a prophet not by action nor character but by gnosis, and it was through gnosis that he participated in the reality of Muhammad.[87] Muhammad was the seal of the Prophets in his historical existence, but he was also the creative rational principle in the Universe.[88] This reality of Muhammad is manifested through the prophets and saints, and their reality is united in this principle, hence for the saint, one comes to know God through himself: 'By knowing Him, I give Him being'.[89]

"The believer praises the God who is his form of belief and with whom he has connected himself. He praises none but himself, for his God is made by himself, and to praise the work is to praise the maker of it: Its excellence or perfection belongs to its maker. For this reason he blames the beliefs of others, which he would not do, if he were just. Beyond doubt, the worshiper of this particular God shows ignorance when he criticizes others on account of their beliefs. If he understood the saying of Junayd, 'The colour of the water is the colour of the vessel containing it', he would not interfere with the beliefs of others, but would perceive God in every form and in every belief. He has opinion, not knowledge: therefore God said, 'I am in My servant's opinion of Me', i.e., 'I do not manifest Myself to him save in the form of his belief.' God is absolute or restricted, as He pleases; and the God who is contained by anything, for He is the being of all things and the being of Himself, and a thing is not said either to contain itself or not to contain itself."[90]

Where al-Ḥallāj had suggested that God had a human and divine nature (nāsūt and lāhūt) united in one being, so that in mystical union man could become unified with God,[91] Ibn ʿArabī held that the mystic was already an attribute of God, so there could be no 'union' with God. What happened then in mystical union with God? So long as it could be given form, it was the idealized form of one's 'celestial pole'. Somewhat oversimplified, it might be stated: Gather all the thoughts about yourself together, picking those which seem to be your superior spiritual qualities, combine them with those notions that you have about your real self and perhaps what you hope you are, and then note that this composite image is not only real for *you*, but has ultimate dimensions. The attraction this composite image has for you comes from the fact that it is not only you but an archetype, a form of complete significance in the scheme of things, and you must bring this form to reality by attaining that image in your life. The journey to *this* reality, for Ibn 'Arabī, is your prophethood and your mi'rāj.[92]

MUHAMMAD, THE SPIRITUAL GUIDE

We are now better able to appreciate the religious complexity of Muhammad in the Ṣūfī tradition. He is, like Jesus or the Buddha, larger than any modular designation, but some very striking characteristics appear.

It is of prime importance that the spiritual meaning of Muhammad became the norm around which mystical experience was ordered; the results of this phenomenon moved in two directions. The first was that the Prophet accrued and expressed symbols and images reminiscent of the ancient shamanic heritage; naturally, there is no direct relationship between the archaic complex and Muhammad at a historical or literal level. But the values caught up in understanding his spiritual pilgrimage were defined by those which had functioned in that ancient ecstatic milieu, and, from this viewpoint, we can glimpse meanings more rich and variegated than we may have imagined. In some ways, then, Muhammad became a spiritual guide whose roots reached to the depths of human religiosity.

The second was the 'internalization' of Muhammad at the psychological and religious level. Motivation to re-enact the mi'rāj could not derive basically from Muhammad as a prophet or as a legislator; rather it was because he was the very image of man, with all the weaknesses and strengths thus entailed, responding to the call of God and acknowledging the inner directions that God's guidance afforded. Muhammad's exemplary achievement made possible the elaboration of a kingdom of the heart for *all* individuals; henceforth, all men could be confident that God and man touched at the most intimate area of existence.

This presupposition undergirded the homologizing of the Muhammad-figure and the inner life of the Sūfī. Not only could he follow his beloved into the secrets of God, but now he could also recover and relive the richness of Muhammad in a wholly spiritual domain. The data we have indicates that he worked this out through a spatialization of the inner experience into levels of attainment, each with its own potential for expansion and elaboration, modelled on the elevations of Muhammad during the mi'rāj, or through the multivalent facets of intoxication, ecstasy and love which are everywhere present in Muslim mystical writings and were charged with the task of explicating the Ṣūfīs' 'colloquy' with God.

To this must be added the diversity in applying the model. Within the spiritual development of Ṣūfism we can see several nuances, ranging from the technique of training the inner man according to the form suggested by the mi'rāj, to defining the contents of inner experience so man could work through it to transcendence, to a more sophisticated plateau, where it operates as the motivaton for re-enacting the archetype Muhammad and experiencing the full expanse of his inner life as one's own.

Finally there is the *telos* of the Prophet-figure; solitary, explorative, moving among the most sacred designations of human experience with the grace and ease that comes from being chosen, Muhammad instilled into the Ṣūfī tradition a unique perception of mystical vigor. Centuries later, Muhammad Iqbal, searching for an idiom to translate his conception of *Man*, reached back to that potent source:

In my heart's empire, see
How he rides . . .[93]

Notes

1. Frithjof Schuon, *Comprendre l'Islam* (Paris: Gallimard, 1961), p. 119.
2. E. g., Sūrah 3: 60–65, 75–85.
3. See Mircea Eliade, *Shamanism: Archaic Techniques of Ecstasy*, tr. Willard Trask (New York: Bollingen Foundation, 1964), p. 377. For a thorough examination of the shamanic aspects of Prophet before the establishing of the Ummah, see Charles Wendell, 'The Pre-Islamic Period of Sirāt al-Nabī', *Muslim World*, LXII (1971), pp. 12–41.
4. J. Horovitz, 'Muhammad's Himmelfahrt'. *Der Islam*, IX–XI (1918–1921), pp. 159ff.
5. Harris Birkeland, *The Legend of the Opening of Muhammad's Breast* (Oslo: I kommisjon has J. Dywood, 1955), p. 31.
6. Muhammad ibn Isma'ī al-Bukhārī, *al-Ṣaḥiḥ*, V (Cairo: Dar Wamzaba' al-Sha'b, 196?), p. 66.
7. 'The Story of the Night Journey and the Ascension', trans. A. Jeffrey, *Reader on Islam* The Hague:(Mouton and Co., 1962), p. 621. Notice that the purification initiated Muhammad into his prophetic career.

8. Abū Ja'far al-Tabarī, *Annales quos scripsit Abul-Jafar Mohammed ibn Djarir at-Tabari*, ed. N. J. de Goeje, X (Leiden: E. J. Brill, 1879–90, pp. 95f.
9. See Birkeland, *The Legend of the Opening*, p. 56.
10. Ibn Hanbal, *Musnad*, III (Cairo: Dar al-Ma'āref, 1949), pp. 76 f. Selection is translated in Birkeland, *The Legend of the Opening*, p. 56. It is even more intriguing that this version is found in Ibn Hanbal, who certainly would not have included it if he had not held it reliable.
11. This trance-like state is dramatically expressed in the Mi'rāj-Nāma, variously attributed to Avicenna and Suhrawardī [See H. Corbin, *Avicenna and the Visionary Recital*, trans. W. Trask (New York: Pantheon Books, Inc., for the Bollingen Foundation, 1960), p. 166]. 'One night I lay asleep in my house. It was a night in which there were thunder and lightning. No living beings could be heard, no bird journeyed. No one was *awake*, whereas I was not asleep; I dwelt between waking and sleep' (Corbin, *Avicenna*, p. 171). The hypnotic sleep is a rite of passage found in the initiation ceremonies of many secret societies (see Eliade, *Shamanism*, p. 64). The version, admitted much later than Muhammad's initiation as expressed in the hadīth, points out the affinity Muslim mystical expression had for these ancient motifs.
12. The role of the tutelary spirit is discussed in D. Schroder, 'Zur Struktur des Schamanismus', *Anthropos*, I (1955), pp. 849–881, especially pp. 863f. The motif of opening and removing is widely found: See, for example, K. Rasmussen, *Intellectual Culture of the Igaulik Eskimos*, trans. W. Worster (Copenhagen: Gyldeadal, 1931), p. 112.
13. In the Muslim versions a quality is placed in Muhammad, not in a sacred stone as in shamanic ceremonies, but the intentionality of the action is the same: the imparting of a trans-human characteristic to the initiate.
14. A fascinating statement of these powers as conceived among the Eskimos is the following: '... it is as if the house in which he is, suddenly rises; he sees far ahead of him, through mountains, exactly as if the earth were one great plain, and his eyes could reach to the ends of the earth. Nothing is hidden from him any longer; not only can he see things far, far away, but he can also discover souls, stolen souls, which are either kept concealed in far strange lands or have been taken up or down to the Land of the Dead.' Rasmussen, *Intellectual Culture of the Igaulik Eskimos*, p. 113. This strange power to see is also found in the hadīth on the isra', viz., 'al-Hasan said that he was lifted up so he could see the apostle speaking as he told Abū Bakr what Jerusalem was lake.' Ibn Isḥaq, *The Life of Muhammed*, trans. A. Guilaume (London: Oxford University Press, 1955), p. 183.
15. See B. Schrieke, 'Die Himmelsreise Muhammeds', *Der Islam*, VI (1916), p. 12; A. A. Bevan, 'Muhammad's Ascension to Heaven', *Studien zur Semitischen Philologie und Religionsgeschichte: Julius Wellhausen zum siebzigsten Geburtstag*, ed. K. Marti (Berlin: Giessen, 1914), pp. 49ff; Horowitz, *op. cit.*, pp. 167 ff. G. Widengren follows those writers in regarding the intentionality of the phenomenon to be initiation [*Muhammad, the Apostle and his Ascension* (Uppsala: 1955), p. 56].
16. Birkeland, *op. cit.*, pp. 58 ff.
17. The acceptance of such a structure imposed certain limits and shapes on the way

spirituality would be understood, as well as on conceptions of degrees of spirituality, etc.

18. All quotations in this study are from A. J. Arberry, *The Koran Interpreted* (New York: The Macmillan Co., 1956) unless otherwise indicated. The phrase 'from the Holy Mosque to the Further Mosque' is translated as 'from the Inviolable Place of Worship to the Far Distant Place of Worship' by Pickthall; see *The Meaning of the Glorious Koran*, trans. M. Pickthall (New York: The New American Library, 1962). The first is the mosque at Mecca, the second the mosque in Jerusalem, or sometimes considered to be the heavenly mosque above Jerusalem. A. Guillaume ['Where was al-Masjid al-Aqsa', *al-Andulus*, XVII (1953), pp. 323–336] argues that the Further Mosque was neither in Jerusalem nor heaven, but a local mosque about 15 miles northeast of Mecca on the pilgrim road leading to Iraq. M. Plesser ['Muhammad's Clandestine 'Umra ...', *Rivista Degli Studi Orientali*, XXXII (1957), pp. 525–530] rejects this view, claiming that the questionable implications of such a thesis far outweigh the scant evidence for it.
19. I. e., the *Sidrat al-Muntahā*, the sacred tree marking the limits of heaven from the precints of God.
20. The record of the ascension is originally traced back to Anas b. Mālik who did not die earlier than 70–80 A. H.; therefore the legend of the ascension must have been established by the end of the first century A. H. See Birkeland, *The Legend of the Opening*, p. 31, for sources. As elaboration of details began, the community concensus decided what was legitimate and illicit, and each time it was retold, elements from former mi'rāj-stories were woven into the new legend. Asin Palacios, *Islam and the Divine Comedy*, abridged and trans. H. Sunderland (London: Frank Cass and Co. Ltd., 1926) re-creates several of these stories. This version is based on al-Ghaiṭī, (d. 982/1547) who was an Egyptian belonging to the Shafī'ite *madhhab*.
21. Following Pickthall, *The Meaning of the Glorious Koran;* the italics are mine. That section shows that ascending to heaven is regarded as completely outside the capability of a man (just as creating was so considered in the previous sentence) and that his may be subject to deception; they required a complete book like other prophets before Muhammad.
22. R. Bell, *Introduction to the Qur'ān* (Edinburgh: University of Edinburgh Press, 1953), p. 31: 'Tradition is unanimous on the point that it was Gabriel who was the agent of revelation.'
23. Usually understood as Gabriel, according to R. Blachere, *Le Coran* (Paris: Presses Universitaire de la France, 1960), p. 5 and pp. 83–84. However, both Ibn 'Abbas and Anas b. Mālik said it was God who drew near, Ṭabarī, *Annales*, XXVII, p. 26.
24. Most of them said, 'By God, this is a plain absurdity! A caravan takes a month to go to Syria and a month to return and can Muhammad do the return journey in one night?' Many Muslism gave up their faith; some went to Abū Bakr and said, 'What do you think of your friend now Abū Bakr? He alleges that he went to Jerusalem last night and prayed there and came back to Mecca.' Ibn Isḥaq, *The Life of Muhammad*, p. 183.

25. *Ibid.*, p. 181.
26. For example, the Mu'tazilites rejected the literal sense: see Abū'l Mu'īn al-Nasafī, *Bahr al-Kalām fi 'Ilm al-Tawhīd*, trans. A. Jeffery, *Reader on Islam*, pp. 423f; other thought it was a literal journey, as in Taftāzānī's commentary, *A Commentary on the Creed of Islam*, trans. Earl E. Elder (New York: Columbia University Press, 1950), pp. 136–137. 'A'isha objected that Muhammad had never seen God literally, calling that 'the greatest lie ever forged against God' according to Ṭabarī, *Tafsīr*, XXVII, p. 30.
27. Ṭabarī, Tafsir, XXVII, pp. 26 f.
28. as-Suyūṭī, *Kitāb al-la'ālī al-muasmu'ah*, 1, 75, quoted in Widengren, *Muhammad, The Apostle of God*, p. 106.
29. I. e., Ibn Isḥāq, *The Life of Muhammad*, p. 183.
30. As in Ibn Isḥāq, *The Life of Muhammad*, the quote above.
31. E. g., the *Ikhwān al-Safā;* see A. Altmann, 'The Ladder of Ascension', *Studies in Mysticism and Religion Presented to G. C. Scholem*, ed. E. Urbach, R. J. Zwi Werblowsky, and Ch. Wirszubski (Jerusalem: Mahnes Press, Hebrew University, 1967), pp. 4 f.
32. There is a wide range of 'extra'-ordinary aspects of Muhammad: the initiatory experience set him apart, his poetic ability which was assumed to be jinn-inspired, his revelations and the attendant physical phenomena, etc. Yet Muhammad claimed he was no more than a mortal man called to bring a message.
33. Ibn 'Abbās, *al-Isrā' w-al-Mi'rāj* (Cairo: Muhammad 'Ali Sabī and Sons, 1959), p. 7.
34. al-Ghaiṭī, 'The Story of the Night Journey', p. 627. Note the strong similarity between the souls of the dead mounting up in death and the ladder motif: A. Coomaraswamy, 'Svayamatrnna: Janua Coeli', *Zalmoxis*, II (1939), p. 47.
35. Horovitz, 'Muhammad's Himmelfahrt', pp. 159 f.
36. *Ibid.*, p. 165.
37. *Ibid.*, p. 159.
38. Altmann, 'The Ladder of Ascension', pp. 2n 5, 7, 8.
39. See Ernst Herzfeld, *Archeological History of Iran* (London: H. Milford of the Oxford University Press, 1935), pp. 100 f.
40. On the flight of Alexander see *The Pseudo-callisthenes*, II, 39 in Howard R. Patch, *The Other World According to Descriptions in Medieval Literature* (Cambridge: Harvard University Press, 1951), p. 24, n. 58.
41. For a fine discussion of the 'origins' problem see F. Rosenthal's introduction to C. C. Torrey's *The Jewish Foundation of Islam*, 2nd ed. (New York: KJAV Publishing House, Inc., 1967).
42. See J. Partanen, *A Description of Buriat Shamanism* (Helsinki: Porvo, 1941–42), p. 19, sec. 10–15.
43. Eliade, *Shamanism*, pp. 487 ff.
44. Note the plates of funerary ladders in E. A. Budge, *The Egyptian Heaven and Hell*, II, 3 vols. (London: Kegan Paul, Trench, Trubner, and Co., Ltd., 1905), pp. 159 f.
45. E. g., Albrecht Dieterich, *Eine Mithrasliturgie* (Leipzig and Berlin: B. C. Teubner, 1910), p. 183.

46. See E. Cerulli, *Il Libro della Scalle e la questione delle fonti Arabo spagnole Divina Comedia* (Vatican City: Biblioteca Apostolica Vaticana, 1949), p. 42.
47. Muslim, *Jami'a al-Ṣaḥīḥ*, on the margin of *Qastalānī's Irshād al-Sarī*, I (Egypt: Bulaq, 1304–5 A. H.), p. 114.
48. al-Bukhari, *al-Ṣaḥīḥ*, V, pp. 66 f.
49. Ṭabarī, *Tafsir*, XXVII, pp. 26 f.
50. Jerusalem was regarded as the navel of the earth; see Ḥamdhāni's quotation in Asin Palacios, *Islam and the Divine Comedy*, p. 144. Note also A. J. Wensinck, *The Ideas of the Western Semites Concerning the Navel of the Earth* (Amsterdam: Noord-hollansche uitgenersmoatschappij, 1916), p. 15.
51. D. Perron, 'Le Mirādj', *Revue de Paris*, XXIII (October, 1854), p. 238.
52. Ibn Ishāq, *Life of Muhammad*, p. 182, records the test of the vessels of milk, wine, and water. Muhammad chose the milk and Gabriel commended him for his choice.
53. E. g., the Bait al-Ma'mūr, the counterpart to the earthly Ka'ba, Perron, 'Le Mirādj', pp. 89 ff.
54. *Ibid.*
55. E. g., al-Ghaiṭī, 'The Story of the Night Journey', pp. 630–631.
56. *Ibid.*, p.628.
57. Sūrah 53: 14; al-Ghaiṭī, 'The Story of the Ascension', p. 632.
58. D. Perron, 'Le Mirādj', pp. 89–90.
59. *Ibid.*
60. al-Ghaiṭī, 'The Story of the Night Journey', p. 633.
61. See Asin Palacios, *Islam and the Divine Comedy*, pp. 13–14.
62. In the shamanic scenarios, the journey ends with receiving some indications from the god relative to the community's affairs, see K. Rasmussen, 'A Shaman's Journey to, the Sea Spirit', in *Reader in Comparative Religion*, ed. W. Lessa and E. Vogt, 2nd ed. (New York: Row, Peterson and Co., 1965), p. 421.
63. For a sketch of the problem see A. J. Arberry, 'The Divine Colloquy in Islam', Bulletin, *John Rylands Library*, XXXIX (1956), pp. 18–21.
64. al-Ghaiṭī, 'The Story of the Night Journey', pp. 634–635.
65. In the tenth century, this version was attributed to 'Abd al-Rabīhī al-Maysāra. For a version of the eighth and early ninth century see Asin Palacios, *Islam and the Divine Comedy*, p. 24.
66. There are, of course, dramatic differences between the shamanic complex and the journeys of Muhammad: Muhammad does not practice this ascension as a 'technique' in the manner found among shamans; for the most part, the Muslim stories stress an unaware Muhammad being summoned to God, hence the mi'rāj is not a religious ritual in the same sense; Gabriel bears little resemblance to the helper figures of the shaman stories; Muslim legends place more emphasis on the sacred topography than appears present in shamanic sources, etc. But the differences point out the milieu, rather than arguing that the entire symbol system has no relevance.
67. For example, the mi'rāj lasted as a modelling motif from the time of Abū Yazīd al-Bisṭāmī (d. 261/875) to Ibn Qadib al-Bān (d. circa 1040/1630). As a devotional theme,

it still has significance; see Jan Knappert, 'Utenzi wa Miiraji', *Afrika und Übersee*, XLVIII (1965), pp. 241–274.

68. A. J. Arberry, *Sufism* (London: George Allen and Unwin, 1950), pp. 54–55. Arberry argues that the model for Abū Yazīd's ascension was Jesus and not Muhammad ('The Divine Colloquy', pp. 30–33); this could only be so if the early Sūfīs made a distinction between the ascension of the Prophet into the state of intoxication and the elevation of Jesus into nearness to the Beloved. I suspect, if they were distinguished, that the two soon merged into the figure of Muhammad.
69. I. e., the last of the prophets: Sūrah 29: 45–50; 30: 55–60.
70. This made possible the subtleties of meaning in the Sūrahs 73 and 74 of 'enmantled' and 'enwrapped', and the Ṣūfī use of love imagery.
71. The elevation and flying of the Ṣūfīs took them even beyond the angels: al-Kharaqānī, a famous Ṣūfī, said: "I ascended at noon to the Throne, to circle it, and I encircled it a thousand times; then I saw round it people who were still of little value in my eyes. I said: 'Who are you, and what is this laggardliness in your circling?' They said: 'We are angels created of light and this is our nature beyond which we cannot pass.' They then said: 'Who are you and what is this speed in your circling?' I said: 'I am a man compact of light and fire and this speed comes from the light of longing'." Quoted in Q. al-Sāmarrā'ī, *The Theme of Ascension in Mystical Writings* (Baghdad: The National Printing and Publishing Co., 1970), p. 193.
72. See al-Sarrāj, *Kitāb al-Luma' fi'l-Taṣawwuf*, ed. R. A. Nicholson, Gibb Memorial Series, XXII (London: Luzac and Co., Ltd., 1963), pp. 427–429.
73. It is explicitly stated to be a dream here; it is not in another source: Farīd ad-Dīn 'Aṭṭar, *Tadhkirat al-Awliya* (Memoirs of the Saints), ed. R. A. Nicholson, I (London: G. Bell and Sons, Ltd., 1905–07), pp. 172–176.
74. R. A. Nicholson, 'An Early Arabic Version of the Mi'rāj of Abū Yazīd al-Bisṭāmī', *Islamica*, II (1927), p. 409.
75. *Ibid.*
76. Muslims accepted the sevenfold structure of heaven in common with the other religious groups in the Middle East.
77. Nicholson, 'An Early Arabic Version', p. 412.
78. On the *maqām* and *hāl* see Arberry, *Sufism*, p. 75, and al-Sarrāj, Kitāb *al-Luma'*, pp. 42–71.
79. Two mystical countries said to adjoin Mount Qaf. Their inhabitants did not know the existence of Adam or Iblis and had no sexual distinctions, see E. I.: *Kaf*.
80. Abū Yazīd was exiled from his city for such brash statements as 'I am God; why do you not worship me', or 'Look to my Majesty and Purity'. The technical problems of the union of man and God as expressed in intoxication led some to reject it (Junaīd), while others saw sobriety as the 'perfection of the state of the intoxicated man': Hujwīrī, *The Kashf al-Mahjūb*, p. 186.
81. Quoted in al-Sāmarrā'ī, *The Theme of Ascension*, pp. 194–195.
82. If God is closer to man than his own neck-vein (Sūrah 50: 15) how can one distinguish one's individuality from the experience he has of God? See R. A. Nicholson, *The Idea*

of Personality in Sufism (Cambridge: Cambridge University Press, 1923), pp. 41 f.
83. Hujwīrī, *The Kashf al-Mahjūb*, p. 239.
84. R. A. Nicholson, *Studies in Islamic Mysticism* (Cambridge: Cambridge University Press, 1921; reprint 1967), pp. 230n., 326, 327; p. 239, n. 454.
85. Abū 'Alī al-Daqqāq quoted in al-Sāmarrā'ī, *The Theme of Ascension*, pp. 187–188.
86. For discussion of this motif, see Corbin, *Avicenna*, pp. 165–178, and Corbin, *The Creative Imagination of Ibn 'Arabi* (Princeton: Princeton University Press, 1969), pp. 120, 288.
87. Arberry, *Sufism*, pp. 100 ff.
88. *Ibid.*
89. Ibn 'Arabī. *Fuṣūs*, I, 282, in Nicholson, *Studies*, p. 159.
90. *Ibid.*
91. Louis Massignon, *La Passion d'al-Hallāj*, I (Paris: Geuthner, 1922), pp. 520 f.
92. The wealth of detail makes if difficult to leave this discussion at this point. In addition, other mi'rāj depictions could have been discussed, e. g., that ascension attributed to Avicenna (see Corbin, *Avicenna*, pp. 165 ff.) or Suhrawardī's [See *œvres philosophiques et mystiques de Sohrawardi*, ed. H. Corbin, II (Teheran: Institut Franco-Iranienne, 1952), pp. 296 f].
93. M. Iqbal, *Zabūr-i 'Ajam*, I, 31, in Arberry, *Sufism*, p. 133.

DAVID N. LORENZEN 3

The Life of Śaṅkarācārya

Hagiography, whether mostly myth or mostly history, stands at the center of the major world religions. Without the lives of Jesus, Gautama, Mohammad, and Kṛṣṇa and Rāma these religions are virtually inconceivable. Once we divert our attention to more minor figures, however, we find a surprising dearth of scholarly interest in saints and their hagiographies or in hagiology as a general phenomenon. Saints seem to have suffered the same neglect that Victor Turner has recently noted with regard to pilgrimages. Religious leaders and 'engaged' scholars have been silenced by their ambivalence or embarrassment and anthropologists by their concentration, until recently, on phenomena of a more local and secular character. Both hagiography and pilgrimage serve as a half-way house or link between Redfield's Little and Great Traditions in which neither group of scholars has felt entirely comfortable.[1]

With regard to India we must exclude from such a concept of hagiography both the lives of the founding fathers of Jainism and Buddhism and of the major incarnations of Viṣṇu. Whatever their original character these are now thoroughly integrated within their respective Great Traditions. The hagiographies we refer to are primarily those of historical figures such as Śaṅkara, Rāmānuja, Kabīr, and Caitanya who were founders of sectarian movements or in some way important religious innovators. These texts seem to reflect a response to the needs and demands of popular religious taste as well as efforts from above to disseminate on a popular level a more learned tradition.

What scholarly interest has been expressed in these hagiographies has come mostly from historians and students of mythology. In general the former have limited their enquiry to extracting the 'historical' aspects of the texts. In most cases this approach reduces an extensive literature to a short paragraph or two. Students of mythology for their part have mostly preferred to work with literature less tainted by historical reality.

The quest for the historical Śaṅkarācārya will not carry us very far.

Even his dates are uncertain though scholars until recently have accepted as most probable the years 788–820 A.D.[2] The facts we can accept with confidence are that he was born in a Brāhman family from the Kerala region but left home at an early age to become a wandering ascetic *(saṃnyāsin);* that he became a student of a teacher named Govinda, a pupil of Gauḍapāda; that he wrote various philosophical and devotional works including commentaries on the Upaniṣads, Bhagavad Gītā, and Brahmasūtra; and that he travelled throughout India with his own disciples defeating rival theologians. It is probable though not at all certain that his father was named Śivaguru and was a Yajurvedin Brāhman of the Taittirīya branch; that his father died while he was still a young child; that he later performed the funeral rites of his widowed mother over the objections of his kinsmen; that one of his most important debating triumphs was his victory over a man named Maṇḍana Miśra, a mīmāṃsā follower of Kumārila; that his most important disciples were named Ānandagiri, Padmapāda (Sanandana), Sureśvara (doubtfully identified with Maṇḍana Miśra and Visvarūpa), Hastāmalaka, and Toṭakācārya; that he established various religious centers especially at Śṛṅgerī in the South, at Purī in the East, Dvārakā in the West, and Badarikāśrama in the North; and that he died at a young age, thirty-two according to most accounts, at either Badarikāṣrama, Kāñeī or somewhere in Kerala.

By Indian standards this is quite a lot to know about an author of the period, but considering the extensive hagiography dedicated to Śaṅkara it is pitifully little. To make matters worse we know only the broad outlines of the religious, political, economic and social background. Further scholarship may fill some of the gaps, but it seems unlikely that a historical study comparable, for instance, to S.G.F. Brandon's on the relation between Jesus and the Zealots will be done for Śaṅkara.

There remain, however, historical problems worthy of further discussion. Hagiography is a nearly universal phenomenon whose existence in any specific context does not require recourse to theories of historical borrowing, even, as we shall see, in the case of the remarkably similar life stories of saints and heroes from different cultures. Nonetheless it is valid to ask what the factors were which led to its appearance within the religions of India and how, once the hagiographical tradition was established, the lives of various saints influenced each other and evolved in the course of time.

In Vedic religion hagiography does not seem to have played any important role. Neither in the Vedas themselves, the Brāhamaṇas, nor the Upaniṣads is there evidence that the life histories of either human saints or the gods were regarded with special interest. The first important hagiographies for which evidence survives are those of the Buddha, Mahāvīra and Kṛṣṇa. In the former two cases it is probable that the actual historical persons died in the earlier half of the fifth century B.C. How soon afterward their life stories became significant in the religious movements they founded is not certain. In the sculpture of the stupas of Bhārhut and Sānchī dating from about the second or first centuries B.C. appear scenes not only of the life of the Buddha, Gautama, but also of his former lives. The sources for these former lives, which were later codified in the *Jātakas*, were popular folktales. The central character was simply identified with the Buddha in a former life and a Buddhist moral added. In this way a large body of hagiographical literature was created almost at a single stroke. In Jainism the lives of the twenty-four *tirthakaras* including Mahāvīra occupy an analogous position and probably developed at about the same time.

The earliest Hindu god to be given a real hagiology is apparently Kṛṣṇa. The dates in his case are even more inexact but we fortunately have a new discovery of two coins of an Indo-Greek king of Taxila which clearly show on one side the figure of Kṛṣṇa and on the other his plough-carrying brother Saṅkarṣaṇa. This king ruled in about 200 B.C.[3] The coins strongly suggest that the hagiography of Kṛṣṇa was already well developed, at least orally, by that date, and they strengthen the more enthusiastic interpretations of the references found in Pāṇini, Megasthenes, the Besnagar inscription of Heliodoros, and the *Mahābhāsya* of Patañjali.[4]

Evidently, hagiography first became important in India sometime between about 500 and 200 B.C., a period marked by the most important social, political and religious changes until the industrial revolution. The old Aryan tribal society was demolished together with much of its religious foundation, and on its ashes arose new territorial kingdoms with important urban centers, new social institutions, and new religious movements. At their inception the principal new movements – Buddhism, Jainism, Ājīvikism, the Upaniṣadic Hinduism – were basically elitist in character with a message directed at free-thinking Brāhmans, aristocrats, and educated merchants. The 'heresies', Buddhism in particular, soon gained considerable strength and political support. The result was a competition for popular support between the heresies, Upaniṣadic Hinduism, and the still important though weakened traditional sacrificial cult, a competition which lasted until the virtual disappearance of Buddhism from India.[5] One of the most important weapons in the struggle, we suggest, was the elaboration of hagiographies which appealed to the emotions of the general populace and also served as a medium through which popular beliefs, gods and heroes could enter the various great traditions.

The relative lack of scholarly interest in Śaṅkara hagiography is reflected in the lack of published texts. At present it is in fact unclear how extensive the literature is. The best secondary work is Baldev Upādhyāy's Śrī Śaṅkarācārya in Hindī. Uphādhyāy lists some twenty-two Sanskrit hagiographies by various authors.[6] My own search for references to such texts has added another dozen or so titles. Unfortunately only four or five of the texts are available in printed form. Most important are the *Śaṅkaradigvijaya* ascribed to Mādhava, alias Vidyāraṇya,[7] the *Śaṅkaravijaya* of Vyāsācala,[8] and the *Śaṅkaravijaya* of Ānandagiri, alias Anantānandagiri.[9] The secondary literature is equally slim. Apart from the introductions to the published texts and Upādhyāy's already mentioned work there exists only a number of rather short summaries of Śaṅkara's life and one or two important articles.[10] Of particular value is an appendix to Upādhyāy's edition and translation of Mādhava's *Śaṅkaradigvijaya* in which he summarizes several of the texts which remain unpublished.

Mādhava's text is without doubt the most important of the hagiographies and is considered authoritative by most of Śaṅkara's present day followers. In the light of Upādhyāy's arguments it seems probable that the author belongs to the latter half of the seventeenth or first half of the eighteenth century and is not the same as the famous fourteenth century Vijayanagar *rājaguru* Mādhava Vidyāraṇya who he apparently claims to be.[11] It is difficult, in any case, to accept even a later Mādhava as the real author of the text which seems rather a compilation of earlier material, probably from a variety of sources. Although Upādhyāy accepts a later Mādhava as the author he notes that the first twenty-five verses of chapter twelve are taken from the *Śaṅkarābhyudaya* of Rājacūḍāmaṇi.[12] A large number of Mādhava's verses are also found in Vyāsācala's *Śaṅkaravijaya*. The secondary title of Mādhava's work, the *Saṅkṣepa-Śaṅkaravijaya* or *Concise Śaṅkaravijaya*, gives another clue to its composite character. Most importantly, the text is marked by abrupt breaks and transitions in the narrative which coincide with breaks in the style of the verses. Often these breaks also coincide with the beginning or end of a series of verses found in Vyāsācala. One rather curious example occurs in chapter eleven of Mādhava's text where of fifty-nine verses written in the related meters Indravajrā, Upendravajrā and Upajāti slightly more than half are rhymed. None of these rhymed verses is found in Vyāsācala's text but over a third of the non-rhymed ones are. The most logical conclusion is that Mādhava borrowed these non-rhymed verses from Vyāsācala (or possibly a common source) and the rhymed ones from another, rhymed source. Also significant is the fact that of the several short series of verses written in Drutavilambita meter in this and other chapters of Mādhava's text virtually all are also found in Vyāsācala, while in the case of other meters there are no mutual verses. Further research in the unpublished hagiographies will presumably reveal more such borrowings.

In the remainder of this essay I will discuss the life of Śaṅkara as presented in these texts, with primary emphasis on Mādhava's *Śaṅkaradigvijaya*, paying particular attention to the role played by religious devotion (*bhakti*) and to the related comparison made between Śaivism and Vaiṣṇavism.

In his own philosophical works Śaṅkara asserts that the only real path to salvation is the path of wisdom leading to a deep realization of the identity of the individual soul (ātman) with the impersonal ground of being (*brahman*) and of the illusory nature of the multiplex physical world. For the ordinary man in the world devotion is a valuable propaedeutic to raising himself to a higher level but it cannot in itself produce liberation. A personal god (*īśvara*) does exist, but only as an imperfect perception of *brahman* as equivalent to the physical universe or endowed with its qualities (*saguṇa-brahman*). There is no clear indication in these works of any special preference for either Viṣṇu or Śiva. Most scholars have followed the hagiographies in assuming that Śaṅkara was a Śaivite although Paul Hacker has recently argued, not altogether convincingly, on the basis of Sankara's philosophical works, that he was a Vaiṣṇava.[13]

The many devotional hymns attributed to Śaṅkara give a quite different picture.[14] These texts express and advocate impassioned devotion to a variety of specific gods and goddesses. Although a majority of the more important hymns praise either Śiva or his consort, many hymns are dedicated to other gods including Viṣṇu. A logical conflict between these devotional hymns and the philosophical works is avoided in so far as the former never quite claim that devotion leads directly to salvation, but the contrast between the two remains difficult to reconcile. The best explanation we can offer is to relate the composition of the devotional texts to the previously mentioned competition between Buddhism and Hinduism and to the desire of both to gain popular support. Śaṅkara's metaphysical system, like those of the Buddhists from which it is partly derived, is too complex to provide religious consolation to the common man. The addition or inclusion of devotionalism was evidently undertaken both out of an altruistic concern for the religious needs of the laity and a practical concern for the continued existence of the monastic organization set up to preserve that doctrine.

The hagiographies dedicated to Śaṅkara are basically Śaivite in character. Firstly, Śaṅkara himself is regarded as an incarnation of the god Śiva. Secondly and more interestingly, the story of Śaṅkara's childhood and youth reveals a conscious or semi-conscious design by his followers to appropriate and refashion the stories of Kṛṣṇa's boyhood and to associate Vaiṣṇavism with an inferior level of spiritual development. It is necessary to note, however, that this Śaivite devotionalism does not imply acceptance of any and all types of Śaivism. For the authors of the hagiographies as for Śaṅkara himself sectarian movements were judged primarily on their theological and ritual compatability with Śaṅkara's doctrine and not simply on which god was held in highest esteem. Many of Śaṅkara's most important opponent were in fact Śaivites. Some like the Pāśupatas were objectionable for their philosophical beliefs and others, like the Kāpālikas, primarily for their rejection of ritual orthodoxy *(varnāsrama-dharma)*.

The motive and process of Śiva's incarnation as Śaṅkara will be best illustrated by a brief summary of the story as presented by Mādhava. The story begins with a relation of the heavenly background of the incarnation:

"In heaven the minor gods came to Śiva to complain that on earth Viṣṇu had entered the body of the Buddha and was leading men astray: 'Like the night with darkness, the earth is full of Buddhists who rely on the *āgamas* composed by him. They corrupt (orthodox) doctrine, despise *brahman* and reject the customs of class and stage of life *(varṇāśrama-dharma)*'."

"In addition to the Buddhists, who seem to be the gods' chief concern, they also complain against the false doctrines and customs propagated by 'heretics devoted to the *āgamas* of Śiva and Viṣṇu', by Kāpālikas who worship Bhairava with offerings of human heads, and other proponents of 'thorny paths'. They then beg Śiva to incarnate himself on earth and 'establish the path of *śruti*'. Śiva consents saying: 'Becoming incarnate on earth in human form I will fulfill your desire'. He then prophesies that as the Brāhman Śaṅkara he will establish true dharma by composing a definitive commentary on the *Brahmasūtra* and spread its message throughout India with the help of four great disciples. Meanwhile other gods were to become incarnate on earth to prepare the path for him. Most importantly, the gods Viṣṇu and Śeṣa were to become the *munis* Saṃkarṣaṅa and Patañjali who would establish the *upāstiyoga-kaṇḍa*, i.e. the path of devotion and Yoga. The *karma-kāṇḍa* or path of Vedic rites would be established by Śiva's own son Skanda as Kumārila Bhaṭṭa and by the god Brahmā as his disciple Maṇḍana Miśra. The establishment of these two paths would prepare men for the jhāna-kāṇḍa or path of knowlege of Śaṅkara. The god Indra would become incarnate as a king named Sudhanvan, the future protector of Śaṅkara. Other gods would become incarnate as his future disciples and other worthy Brāhmans."

The second chapter of Mādhava's text transfers the scene to earth:

"On the bank of the Pūrṇā River in Kerala, Śiva became manifest in the form of a *liṅga*. A certain Rājaśekhara, whom the commentator and other texts identify as the king of the region, built a temple over it. Near this temple in an *agrahāra* named Kālaṭi lived a Brāhman named Vidyādhirāja. He had a son named Śivaguru who was devoted to his Vedic studies and wished to become an ascetic. Vidyādhirāja insisted that his son become a householder first, and Śivaguru was married to Satī, the daughter of another Brāhman named Maghapaṇḍita. The couple lived together happily for many years, but had no male heir. Finally, they offered prayers and fierce penances to the god Śiva in order that he might grant them a son. Eventually Śiva granted them a boon. In a dream the god offered Śivaguru a choice of one omniscient but short-lived son or many long-lived but ordinary sons. Śivaguru chose the former and on that auspicious day the power of Śiva *(śaiva-tejas)* entered Śivaguru's food and 'the deer-eyed (Satī) conceived the embryo of Śiva'. While pregnant she experienced various auspicious dreams and eventually gave birth, without any pain, to her marvellous son. At his birth many natural wonders occurred. Hostile animals became friends, trees and plants blossomed out of season, rivers turned clear, and flowers rained down from heaven. Since the child had been born by the grace of Śiva, Śivaguru named him Śaṅkara. Astrologers predicted his future greatness and his body displayed a supernatural lustre and auspicious marks such as those of Śiva's third eye and trident. Thus, when 'heaven had become inaccessible and salvation was exceedingly difficult to attain . . ., Śiva descended on earth in bodily form'."

In this story we find much thematic similarity with the classic accounts of the births of the *avatāras* of Viṣṇu such as Kṛṣṇa. Much in fact resembles the birth myths of other supernatural heroes from various parts of the ancient world. The psychoanalyst Otto Rank, writing in 1914, compared several myths of the birth of such heroes and extracted a 'standard saga' of their life. Apropos of the hero's birth and infancy he wrote:

"The hero is the child of most distinguished parents, usually the son of a king. His origin is preceded by difficulties, such as continence, or prolonged barrenness, or secret intercourse of the parents due to external prohibitions or obstacles. During or before pregnancy, there is a prophecy, in the form of a dream or oracle, cautioning against his birth, and usually threatening danger to the father (or his representative). As a rule, he is surrendered to the water, in a box. He is then saved by animals, or by lowly people (shepherds), and is suckled by a female animal or by a humble woman."[15]

Most striking is the almost exact correspondence of this 'saga' to the birth of Kṛṣṇa, particularly in view of the fact that the Kṛṣṇa story was not one of Rank's examples. There are also, however, several obvious parallels with the birth of Śaṅkara. The two major deviations are the lack of a conflict with a father figure such as Kaṃsa and the absence of an abandonment and adoption by other more humble parents such as Nanda and Yasodā. The rejection by or of one's parents implied in the abandonment is nonetheless, in a somewhat different form, the major theme in Śaṅkara's childhood as well, as we shall see. In Śaṅkara's case, briefly to anticipate our argument, the conflict between parent and child-hero is expressed as, or is an example of the opposing loyalties of the duty to parents and ancestors to preserve the family *(gṛhastāśrama-dharma)* and the duty or right to renounce family concerns and seek one's personal salvation *(saṃnyāsa-dharma)*.

An important aspect of the theory of incarnations or *avatāras*, and of the Buddhas and Tīrthakaras as well, is that the god or supernatural person manifests himself on earth in periods when heresy and evil are triumphing and true religion and morality need to be rescued from the depths to which they have fallen. The avatāra, Buddha or Tīrthakara, is the renewer who rescues man and earth from encroaching chaos and reestablishes the cosmic order. In the famous formulation of the *Bhagavad Gītā* (IV. 6–7), Kṛṣṇa says to Arjuna:

"Though (I am) unborn, and My self (is) imperishable, though (I am) the Lord of all creatures, yet establishing Myself in My own nature, I come into (empiric) being through My power (māyā) . . . Whenever there is a decline of righteousness and rise of unrighteousness, O Bharata (Arjuna), then I send forth (create incarnate) Myself."[16]

Although the avatāra theory relates primarily to Vaiṣṇavism, it is not exclusive to it. Already in Gupta times we find Kauṇḍinya, the commentator on the *Pāśupatasūtra*, claiming that the reputed author of those *sūtras*, the ascetic Lakulīśa (c. 125 A.D.?), was an incarnation of Śiva.[17] The fact that Lakulīśa, like Śaṅkara, had four main disciples suggests the possibility of direct influence. By medieval times almost every famous sage or saint was regarded as the full or partial incarnation of one god or other, a degeneration of the avatāra doctrine seen in full flower in the Śaṅkara hagiographies.

The 'rise of unrighteousness' which Śiva as Śaṅkara sets out to eradicate is represented by the various theological and sectarian opponents he defeats in the course of his Tours of Victory *(digvijayas)*. Some of these opponents, such as the *mīmāmsā* theologians Kumārila Bhaṭṭa and Maṇḍana Miśra are treated quite respectfully since they revere the Vedas and, according to the texts, have helped rid the country of the heretical Buddhists. Other groups, such as the Kāpālikas, are dealt with more harshly.[18] The itineraries of the Tours of Victory and the identity of Śaṅkara's opponents vary widely in the different hagiographies, but the most important seems to be that described in chapter fifteen of Mādhava's text.[19] Śaṅkara first meets and defeats some Śāktas in Rāmeśvaram (vss. 1–3); then some tantric worshippers of Bhagavatī in Kāñcī (vss. 4–5); the Kāpālika Krakaca in Karṇāta (vss. 8–28); the Śaivite dualist Nīlakaṇṭha and his disciple Haradatta in Gokarṇa on the west coast (vss. 29–72);[20] some Vaiṣṇava Pāñcarātras in Dvārakā (vss. 73–75); the *bhedābheda vedāntin* Bhaṭṭa Bhāskara in Ujjain (vss. 76–140); some Jains among the Bāhlikas or Bactrians (vss. 141–155); a Śākta named Abhinavagupta in Kāmarūpa or Assam (vss. 158–160);[21] and finally some not clearly identifiable philosophers in Bengal (vss. 161–162). What is striking in this list is the almost complete lack of Vaiṣṇava opponents. The only ones that appear, the Dvārakā Pāñcarātras, are disposed of in three verses. One possible explanation is that the South, the region with which Mādhava and his sources seem best acquainted, was in fact dominated by Śaivites in their time and probably as far back as Śaṅkara's time as well. The general dominance of Śaivism in the South from a comparatively early period is, of course, an accepted fact, but Vaiṣṇavism also had some strength there, particularly in parts of Tamilnad, and it is curious that Vaiṣṇava sects receive so little mention.

The conflict between the Śaivite bias of the hagiographies and Vaiṣṇavism is instead surreptitiously introduced through the implied comparison of the childhoods of Śaṅkara and Kṛṣṇa, and through the association of Vaiṣṇavism with the life of the householder or *gṛhasthāśrama-dharma* and Śaivism with the life of the ascetic or *saṃnyāsāśrama-dharma*. On the side of Vaiṣṇavism and the *dharma* of the householder stand Śaṅkara's mother, worship of Viṣṇu, family obligation, water and sea-monsters, caves, and yogic trance. With Śaivism and the *dharma* of the ascetic stand Śaṅkara himself as the avatāra of Śiva, renunciation and abandonment of family, homeless wandering, worship of Śiva, and *mukti* or complete enlightenment itself.

To understand better the sociological and psychological basis of this dialectic a variety of theoretical models suggest themselves. Wendy O'Flaherty in her valuable article, "Asceticism and Sexuality in the Mythology of Śiva",[22] has identified the tension between ascetic renunciation and sensual gratification as the foundation of most Śaivite mythology. It is possible to interpret the life of Śaṅkara as simply another expression of this basic conflict, but this only transfers the question of *why* such a theme to Śiva. A more intriguing experiment would be to try to assimilate the conflict to Georges Dumézil's sociological and historical theory of the tripartite 'ideology' of the Indo-Europeans. In this case one might relate Kṛṣṇa and Balarāma to Dumézil's third 'function', i.e., natural fecundity and agriculture; Śaṅkara's protector King Sudhanvan, the incarnate Indra, and perhaps the disciple Padmapāda converted into the fierce Man-lion, to the second, warrior function; and Śaṅkara himself, possibly with his disciples and the god Śiva himself, to the third, religious sovereignty function. On the whole, however, the logical and historical difficulties in squeezing the Śaṅkara story into Dumézil's theoretical frame seem too great to consider this approach seriously.

Most useful, I think, to explain the thematic conflict of the hagiographies is the sociological analysis of Louis Dumont as put forward in his well-known article, "World Renunciation in Indian Religions".[23] Very crudely summarized, Dumont contrasts the lack of substance or individuality of the Indian 'man-in-the-world', the man caught in the web of traditional religious law and caste society, with the freedom and individuality of the ascetic who renounces this society and becomes an 'individual-outside-the-world'. The personal identity of the ordinary householder is defined only through the great web of family and caste relationships. The peculiarity of the Indian situation is that in order to acquire the individuality which this man-in-the-world feels is lacking, he feels constrained to reject the material world and seek an 'other world' which in fact entails the extinction of his own purely human identity. Although there exists, according to Dumont, a dialectic by which the world view and social institutions of the man-in-the-world are pervaded by those of the renouncer and vice versa, both the renouncer and the man-in-the-world remain true and significant as ideal types. One criticism which nonetheless can be leveled against Dumont is that he underestimates the extent to which an 'in-the-world' ethic pervades the vocation of the renouncer in the form of his loving concern for his fellow men and his efforts to lead them to salvation.[24] In the Śaṅkara hagiographies, although the conflict between the *dharmas* of the householder and ascetic is obviously central, Śaṅkara's altruistic concern both for his fellow man in general and his mother in particular is emphasized throughout.

To see how this dialectic between the renouncer and the householder is developed in the hagiographies we will return to a review of the story as given by Mādhava.[25] The fourth chapter takes Śaṅkara up to his sixth or seventh year.

"In his first year Śaṅkara mastered his mother tongue and learned to read letters. In his second he could read and was able to intuitively understand recited Sanskrit texts. By his third year he was reciting the Vedas, teaching his fellow students and defeating in debate adults. Sometime in his third year his father died. After Śaṅkara had been consecrated for a full year, his mother, with the aid of her kinsmen, had him invested with the sacred thread. This took place in his fifth year. By this time he had mastered everything his teacher could teach him including the Vedas and their six auxiliary subjects, analytical philosophy (*ānvīkṣikī*), Sāṃkhya, Yoga and Mīmāṃsā. He had also intuitively grasped the truth of *advaita*."

"One day he entered the house of a poor Brahman couple to beg alms. The pious wife of the Brāhman lamented that she had nothing to give him and had thus caused to be in vain her present life. All she could find to offer him was a single *āmalaka* fruit. Impressed by her sincerity, Śaṅkara interceded with Laksmī, the wife of Viṣṇu, and she filled the house with *āmalakas* of solid gold."

Śaṅkara's precocity is, of course, perfectly natural for the incarnation of a great god. The death of his father, a worshipper of Śiva, leaves him with only his mother, who favors Viṣṇu, to represent the ties of parental affection and duty. The miracle he performs with the aid of Lakṣmī does not seem to have any specific Kṛṣṇaite parallel but is noteworthy in that as a child he invokes the aid of a Vaiṣṇava deity and that the blessing conferred is one of simple material prosperity of a household.

In his fifth chapter Mādhava relates how the young scholar requests and eventually receives his mother's reluctant permission to become a wandering ascetic (*saṅnyāsin*), takes a man named Govindanātha as his first instructor in *advaita* Vedānta, and then travels to the holy city of Varanasi on the Gaṅgā.

One of Śaṅkara's first exploits is to bring the river Pūrṇā near to his own house to save his aged mother the necessity of walking so far to bathe. This incident has a definite Kṛṣṇaite parallel in the episode in which Balarāma, the brother of Kṛṣṇa and either co-incarnation of Viṣṇu or incarnation of the cosmic serpent Śeṣa, drags the river Yāmunā from its bed. In the *Viṣṇu Purana* version (V. 25), the drunken Balarāma orders the river to come to him so that he can bathe. When the river refuses Balarāma drags her about with his ploughshare. The differences between the two stories, here as elsewhere, redound to Śaṅkara's credit. Śaṅkara does not act out of a drunken whim but to aid his poor mother. He changes the river's course not by violence but by convincing it to move of its own accord with flattering verses of praise. Another important feature of this episode is the association of Śaṅkara's mother with the river and water, but it will be better to postpone our discussion of this until we have seen some of the other ways in which the theme of water enters the story.

Sometime after Śaṅkara relocates the river, the king of Kerala arrives to pay homage to the young sage and to present him with a magnificent elephant, gold and other gifts. Śaṅkara refuses the king's munificence since worldly pleasures only distract from the pursuit of learning and salvation. In

Kṛṣṇaite myth the ruling king of Mathurā, Kaṃsa, is the enemy of Kṛṣṇa and instead of sending gifts he dispatches a host of demons to kill the young cowherd, including one in the form of a mighty elephant.

Since Śaṅkara has already completed his studies, his mother and kinsmen begin searching for a suitable bride for him to marry. Like his deadfather before him Śaṅkara desires instead to go directly from the stage of celibate student to that of celibate ascetic. Meanwhile a group of famous sages arrives to pay respect to Śaṇkara, as, in the *Bhāgavata Purāṇa* (X. 84), a similar contingent of sages arrives to pay homage to the young Kṛṣṇa. The spokesman of the sages who visit Śaṅkara, Agastya, foretells the child's early death, a prediction which, from Śaṅkara's point of view, makes his renunciation all the more urgent. When Śaṅkara openly requests that his mother allow him to become an ascetic, however, she refuses with the complaint that this would leave her with no one to protect her, perform her funeral ceremony, and make the necessary offerings to their ancestors. Śaṅkara agrees to delay his decision. Then one day as he enters the river to bathe his foot is seized by a crocodile (*makara*). He calls his mother and tells her that the crocodile will release him only if she agrees to his renunciation. His poor mother has no choice but to consent. Even so she extracts a promise that he will perform her funeral rites. Just before Śaṅkara departs he hears the disembodied voice of Kṛṣṇa who pleads that Śaṅkara save the Kṛṣṇa idol in the nearby temple which was being attacked by the newly moved river Pūrṇā. Śaṅkara easily lifts the heavy idol and puts it on higher ground. Finally, having received the blessings of both his mother and Kṛṣṇa, he sets out, 'his heart set on Kṛṣṇa', in search of a guru.

In this sequence we can see clearly the thematic conflict between the *dharmas* of the householder and the ascetic as well as the association of Kṛṣṇa (and hence Vaiṣṇavism) with the former. Although Śaṅkara proves his superiority to Kṛṣṇa by saving the idol of that god, he nonetheless departs meditating on the same god. At this stage of his career Śaṅkara still has not broken completely either with his past or with his dependence upon others. When he reaches the banks of another river, the Narmadā, he encounters the sage Govindanātha, or He Whose Lord is Govinda (Kṛṣṇa), and chooses him as his guru. This Govindanātha is none other than an incarnation of the great *yogin* and grammarian Patañjali,[26] who is in turn an incarnation of the cosmic serpent Śeṣa whom we have already met as Kṛṣṇa's elder brother Balarāma.

When Śaṅkara arrives at Govindanātha's hermitage the sage is sitting meditating in his subterranean cave. When Śaṅkara praises him he wakes from his yogic trance and asks: "Who (or What) are you?" Śaṅkara replies with a verse demonstrating his intuitive grasp of *advaita* Vedānta. Govinda acknowledges the superiority of Śaṅkara as the incarnation of Śiva but agrees to accept him as a pupil in order to preserve the tradition of transmission of *advaita* doctrine.

This episode resembles in some respects the curious encounter between Kṛṣṇa and King Mucukunda. In the *Viṣṇu Purana* version (V. 23), Kṛṣṇa is pursued by a Yavana king and cunningly leads him to a cave where Mucukunda has lain asleep for many years. The Yavana kicks the sleeping figure thinking it to be Kṛṣṇa and is burnt to ashes by the supernatural power of Mucukunda's fiery glance. Mucukunda then asks Kṛṣṇa: "Who are you"? Kṛṣṇa replies that he is the son of the Yādava Vasudeva and Mucukunda then recognizes him as the incarnation of Viṣṇu.

Mādhava's text next relates how one day during the rainy season, while Govindanātha sits in yogic trance in his cave, the river Narmadā begins to flood and threatens to drown him. Śaṅkara grabs his own begging bowl, consecrates it with a *mantra*, and places it at the entrance to the cave. All the waters are magically absorbed in the bowl and Govindanātha, like the Kṛṣṇa image before him, is saved from the river's destructive waters. This incident has a parallel in Kṛṣṇaite myth in the story of Kṛṣṇa saving the cowherds of Gokula from the angered god of rain, Indra, by raising up the mountain Govardhana to protect them. Many scholars have interpreted this incident as reflecting the rejection of the religion of the old Vedic pantheon. Given the many correspondences between the myths and legends of Kṛṣṇa and Śaṅkara, it is reasonable to conclude that the Śaivite hagiographers have in part a similar intention to prove the the superiority of Śiva to Viṣṇu and to elevate Śaṅkara, the avatāra of Śiva, to a level of popularity equal to that of Kṛṣṇa. The very emphasis on Śaṅkara's childhood, a theme continued in the hagiographies of later saints such as Kabīr, is an indication of Kṛṣṇaite influence and of an attempt to counteract or take advantage of the natural appeal of the myths of the cowherd god.

An aspect of the story we have left to one side is the role played by rivers and water. At each stage in his development Śaṅkara has one or more encounters with a river which presents an obstacle or danger which he masters.[27]

In India, as in most world mythologies including psychoanalysis, rivers and water are also female goddesses. Although rivers and river goddesses are generally beneficial and auspicious, they can also become powerful sources of danger and destruction. In part this simply reflects the facts of nature. In addition, however, water has acquired symbolic characteristics beyond its purely natural associations. Water can represent the life of the unconscious, life before evolution of the names and forms of creation, a regression to a primal unity, a return to the womb of nature, the peace of death itself.

A graphic Hindu myth of this ambivalence is that of the churning of the ocean by the gods and demons at the beginning of creation. Their object was to secure the ambrosia of immortality, but before this came to the surface a great many other magical substances arose including the cosmic poison which Śiva swallowed to save the universe. Śiva's relation to water is thus hostile from the very beginning. Śiva is a god of the mountains, of ascetic heat and yogic power, the god who burns to dust the god of love, a god of sublimation and not regression. Viṣṇu, on the other hand, is more at home in the watery element. He rests in the cosmic waters on the world serpent Śeṣa who is in fact part of himself. As Kṛṣṇa his amorous sport with the cowherd girls takes place near and in the water of the sacred Yāmunā. The goddess Yāmunā, however, is also the sister of the god of death while the beneficent Śeṣa has an evil counterpart in Kāliya, the cruel serpent in the Yāmunā whom Kṛṣṇa defeats and banishes to the ocean. Kāliya and Śeṣa may be said to represent two aspects of what H. Zimmer has called 'the giant serpent power of the world abyss', the 'ever threatening counter-current, antagonistic to the trend of evolution, which periodically halts, engulfs and takes back what has already been given form'.[28]

In the story of Śaṅkara, the regressive feminine quality of the river Pūrṇā is emphasized by its association with his mother. Śaṅkara first brings it near to their house for her, then, when he wishes to abandon her, he is trapped in the same river by the *makara*, an animal which also graces the banner of the god of love. Śaṅkara is released only after he has obtained his mother's consent to his renunciation. River, mother, crocodile and the Kṛṣṇa idol he saves are all forces striving to keep him in the bosom of the family as dutiful son, husband and father. For Śaṅkara the continuity of family life is a form of death; in renunciation he finds the freedom and individuality the householder lacks. Here again we find another curious contrast and parallel with the life of Kṛṣṇa. From this point of view the life styles of both Śaṅkara and the young Kṛṣṇa are attempts to evade the anonymity of the Indian man-in-the-world and win personal freedom and individuality: one through ascetic renunciation, the other through adulterous sexual license, both paths being negations of traditional society.

Govindanātha lives along the banks of the Narmadā. As a goddess this river is the wife of Purukutsa into whose body Viṣṇu entered to aid the Nāgas or Serpents against the subterranean Gandharvas. The goddess herself has the form of a Nāga. As we have noted, Govindanātha is an incarnation of the cosmic serpent, Śeṣa. While he remains with his Vaiṣṇava preceptor he remains still in an incomplete and dependent stage of his development. He finally breaks this dependence when he collects in his bowl the flood which threatens to drown his teacher as he sits in yogic trance in his subterranean cave. The images of the flood, trance, and cave are, like the river and water serpents, associated with regression and dependence. Śaṅkara's begging bowl, on the other hand, is the badge of the homeless ascetic and as such is the means to his release. When all the waters of the flood have been absorbed in this bowl and the dark clouds of the rainy season have left the sky, Govindanātha instructs Śaṅkara to travel on alone to Varanasi, the city of Śiva on the Gaṅgā, to preach *advaita* and compose the texts which would establish its supremacy for all time.[29]

This brings Śaṅkara to his third and most important river, the Gaṅgā. This most holy of rivers, the very wife of Śiva, is said to spring from the toe of Viṣṇu but was first brought to earth by the sage Bhagīratha to bathe the ashes of the sons of Sagara. To lessen the great impact of her waters, Śiva caused her to fall to earth through his own matted locks. In order to enter Varanasi Śaṅkara has to cross this river. He dives into the water and is carried off by the swift current to the other side where he emerges glistening in the moonlight "like an image of Śiva carved in moonstone". In this episode the principal motif is precisely the crossing to the other shore, a universal symbol for a decisive turning point in a person's life. In India this image is important not only in Hinduism but also in Jainism, whose chief saints are known as Tīrthakaras or Ford-makers, and in Buddhism where enlightenment is traditionally described as a passage to the other shore.[30] When Śaṅkara crosses the Gaṅgā he abandons the life of a student as he had earlier abandoned that of son and potential householder. Likewise he abandons his varied associations with Vaiṣṇavism and immediately goes to pay homage to the feet of Viśveśvara, the form of Śiva who is the patron deity of Varanasi.

A final episode which draws together perfectly the thematic contrast between, on the one hand, the *dharma* of the householder and Vaiṣṇavism and, on the other, the *dharma* of the ascetic and Śaivism is the death of Śaṅkara's mother. In Mādhava's account (XIV. 29–55), Śaṅkara learns through his yogic power that his mother is ill and he levitates himself to her side. She then requests that he honor his promise to perform her funeral rites and cause her to reach to heavenly worlds (*punya-lokān*) by the path prescribed in the sacred texts. Śaṅkara first imparts to her instruction about the unqualified Absolute (*nirguna-brahman*). This she rejects as being too difficult to understand. Next he recites for her a hymn to Śiva entitled 'Śiva-bhujaṅga'. The pleased god sends his messengers to guide her soul, but when she sees that they bear the marks of Śiva's trident and bow she refuses to leave with them. Śaṅkara then recites a hymn to Viṣṇu-Kṛṣṇa who sends his own messengers whom Śaṅkara's mother accepts. They take her to the highest heaven (*paraṃ padam*) by the ancient path of the souls who do not return.[31]

In order to perform the funeral rites Śaṅkara calls his kinsmen and requests that they give him some sacred fire. They refuse, claiming that he has no authority (*adhikāra*) to perform the ceremony since he cut himself off from the rights and duties of persons in caste society when he abandoned his sacred thread and became an ascetic. Although their objection is legally correct, Śaṅkara curses them to be forever prohibited from the study of the Veda, to live near cremation grounds, and to be unacceptable as donors of alms to ascetics. Śaṅkara kindles his own fire and performs the ceremony alone.

In this episode the relative status of metaphysical wisdom, worship of Śiva, and worship of Viṣṇu is clearly established. No theologically and ritually acceptable mode of worship is rejected but each is suitable to persons of different character and levels of understanding. Those ready for final liberation meditate on the unqualified brahman; those of somewhat lesser spiritual achievement worship Śiva; and those still lower on the scale worship Viṣṇu and his avatāras. Even for these, however, it is possible to enter on the path of liberation and after death dwell in the Brahma-worlds. The conflict between the ascetic Śaṅkara and his householder kinsmen is yet another microcosm of the conflict between the ascetic individual-outside-the-world and the householder man-in-the-world. A curious aspect of the episode is the technical illegality of Śaṅkara's performance of his mother's funeral. This suggests firstly that the event is historically true, but it may also be intepreted metaphorically as an attempt on Śaṅkara's part to establish some kind of a compromise, or *modus vivendi*, between the modes of life of the ascetic and the householder, which thus reinforces the similar accommodation implicit in the idea of different but complementary modes of worship. The kinsmen's rejection of Śaṅkara's request results in the curse which leaves them not only forever cut off from the first step of the path of salvation, but with reduced prestige within hierarchical caste society as well.

To sum up, we have seen how Śaṅkara's hagiography presents the famous theologian as an incarnation of the god Śiva. Like Śaṅkara himself, however, the texts regard metaphysics as more important than the choice of object of devotion and feel free to portray Śaṅkara as an opponent of non-advaita Śaivite sects. The rivalry between Śaivism and Vaiṣṇavism is nonetheless essential since it is used to display and develop the basic thematic contrast between the life orientations of the renouncing ascetic and the householder. This is expressed in a variety of ways, but particularly in terms of a comparison between the life of Kṛṣṇa, the avatāra of Viṣṇu, and that of Śaṅkara, the avatāra of Śiva. The best theoretical model for understanding the underlying dialectic of the contrast, we have suggested, is Louis Dumont's analysis of the basic tension in the Indian world view between the desire for and fear of human freedom and individuality, between the ascetic who is an individual-outside-the-world and the insubstantial man-in-the-world of caste society.

ACKNOWLEDGMENTS

I would like to thank the members of the workshop of the Conference on Religion in South India (Philadelphia, May 1973) and of the Seminar on Contemporary Asia (Mexico City, June 1973) for the comments they have offered on preliminary drafts of this paper.

NOTES

1. See Victor Turner, 'The Center Out There: A Pilgrim's Goal', *History of Religions*, XII (1973), pp. 208–209.
2. A somewhat earlier date proposed by Hajime Nakamura has had increasing acceptance. See Sengaku Mayeda, 'The Authenticity of the Bhagavadgītābhāsya Ascribed to Śaṅkara', *Wiener Zeitschrift für die Kunde Süd- und Ost-Asiens*, IX (1965), p. 155.
3. This information was obtained from Professor J. Filliozat in May 1973.
4. In a letter dated 18 September 1973 Dr. W. O'Flaherty has pointed out to me that as far as literary evidence is concerned the first developed birth of the hero myth in India is that of Skanda which is recounted in some detail in the *Mahābhārata*. Although this myth contains several of the basic archetypical motifs of the birth of the hero it is much less of a hagiography than the story of Kṛṣṇa. The actual historical precedence between the two is uncertain.
5. This condensed analysis, based mostly on the work of Weber, is now generally accepted. The history of the subsequent evolution of these hagiographies and their mutual interaction is beyond the scope of this essay though we will return to a rather detailed account of the relations between the hagiographies of Kṛṣṇa and Śaṅkara.
6. 2nd ed. (Allahabad: Hindustani Ekeḍemī, 1963), pp. 11–12.
7. Ed. with Dhanapatisūri's *Diṇḍima* commentary (Poona: Anandāsram Press, 1915); ed. with Hindi translation by Baldev Upādhyāy, 2nd. ed. (Hardwār: Mahant Mahādevnāth, 1967); and an earlier edition unavailable to me ed., as *Saṅksepa-śaṅkaravijaya*, by Kesnalāla Govindarāma Devāsrayi (Bombay: 1899).
8. Ed. E. T. Chandrasekharan (Madras: Superintendent Government Press, 1954).
9. Ed. J. Tarkapanchana, 'Biblioteca Indica' (Calcutta: Baptist Mission Press, 1868) and a new edition by Thiru N. Veeshinathan (Madras University of Madras, 1971).
10. Probably the best easily available summary in English is T. M. P. Mahadevan, *Sankaracharya* (New Delhi: National Book Trust, 1968). Another such work is *Sri Sankara Vijayam* (Madras: Ganesh & Co., n.d.). I have published Spanish translations of chapters III and V of Mādhava's text with introductions in *Estudios Orientales* (Mexico], VI (1971), pp. 86–99 and VII (1972), pp. 335–358. It is quite possible that I have overlooked useful work in other Indian languages. See also Kashinath Trimbak Telang, 'The Śaṅkaravijaya of Ānandagiri', *Indian Antiquary*, V (1876), pp. 287–293; and H. H. Wilson, *Religious Sects of the Hindus*, first published in 1828–32 (Varanasi: Indological Book House, 1972); and C. N. Krishnasamy Aiyar, *Sri Sankaracharya*. 3rd ed. (Madras: G. A. Natesan & Co., n.d.).
11. See Śrī Śaṅkarācārya, pp. 14–16. I formerly accepted the attribution to Mādhava Vidyāranya.
12. *Ibid*., 0. 15.
13. Paul Hacker, 'Relations of Early Advaitins to Vaisnavism', *Wiener Zeitschrift für die Kunde Süd- und Ost-Asiens* IX (1965), pp. 147–154.
14. It is by no means clear which if any of the devotional hymns were actually composed

by Śaṅkara. For present purposes it is mostly sufficient that they have been accepted by his followers as authoritative.

15. *The Myth of the Birth of the Hero*, ed. P. Freund (New York: Vintage Books, 1959), p. 65.
16. Trans. S. Radhakrishnan, 2nd ed. (London: George Allen & Unwin, 1949).
17. Pāśupatasūtra ed, R. A. Sastri (Trivandrum: University of Travancore, 1940), pp. 3–4.
18. The encounters between Śaṅkara and the Kāpālikas Ugrabhairava of Śrīparvata, Krakaca of Karṇāta, and Unmattabhairava of Ujjayīni are discussed in more detail in my *The Kāpālikas and Kalāmukhas* (Berkeley: University of California Press, 1972), pp. 31–48. It is somewhat odd that this sect, which was never very influential, is portrayed as one of Saṅkara's most assiduous opponents. Apparently it was used as a convenient stalking horse, objectionable for both theological and ritual reasons, for other more moderate Śaivite sects.
19. Ānandagiri, for instance, arranges the opponents into sects on the basis of the god they chiefly worshipped. This arrangement seems rather artificial and one doubts whether some of the sects listed really existed.
20. The sectarian affiliation of Nīlakaṇṭha and Haradatta is not certain. It is possible that they are intended to represent Pāśupatas or Śaiva Siddhāntins. The Pāśupata *Gaṇakārikā* was written by a Haradatta who is possibly the one mentioned here. Śaṅkara himself attacks the sect at considerable length in his *Brahmasūtra* commentary (II. 2. 37).
21. It is possible that Mādhava is erroneously referring to the Kashmiri Śaivite of the Pratyabhijñā school who lived c. 1000 A. D.
22. *History of Religions*, VIII (1969), pp. 330–337, and IX (1969), pp. 1–41. Although sexuality does not play a central role in the life of Śaṅkara, a popular episode found in several of the hagiographies tells how Saṅkara finds himself at a loss when challenged to debate on the science of love by Sarasvatī or Ubhayabhāratī, the wife of Maṇḍana Miśra. In order to acquire the necessary expertise without breaking his ascetic vows, Śaṅkara temporarily incarnates himself in the dead body of King Amaruka and educates himself with the ladies of the king's harem.
23. Of the several published versions of this essay, I have used that found in *Contributions to Indian Sociology*, No. III, ed. Louis Dumont and D. Pocock (The Hague–Paris: Mouton, 1960), pp. 33–63.
24. This criticism was forcefully argued at the above noted 1973 workshop of the Conference on Religion in South India by Professor J. Filliozat. Another point worth mentioning is that for all the real originality of Dumont's formulation it is based on the traditional Indian distinction between the *saṃyāsin* and the *gṛhastha*. The central role of the predilection toward renunciation and 'life-rejection' in Indian religions was earlier recognized by A. Schweitzer and M. Weber, both of whom Dumont acknowledges in a footnote (*ibid.*, p. 44).
25. Some of the ideas which follow I have presented in different form in *Estudio Orientales*, VII (1972), pp. 335–358.

26. Mādhava's text identifies what most modern scholars consider to have been two different sages by this name.
27. In this regard Dr. W. O'Flaherty, in her letter of 18 September 1973, has pointed out to me that there exist similar episodes in puranic mythology which relate to Śiva. For example, in the *Brahma-purāṇa* 35. 31–60 Śiva is grabbed by a water demon. In general Dr. O'Flaherty feels that I should have paid more attention to the Saivite archetypes for the episodes in the life of Śaṅkara.
28. *Myths and Symbols in Indian Art and Civilization* (New York: Pantheon Books, 1946), p. 78.
29. Another encounter between Śaṅkara and a flood occurs in a story found in the late Sanskrit Bhaktamālā of Candradatta (Bombay: Srī Veṅkatosvara Steam Press, saṃvat 1983, 1926). According to this work (sarga 29 verses 24–53) Śaṅkara met somewhere in Marwar a Jain theologian and magician who created an illusion of a great flood and then of a boat in which to save himself. When the Jain got in the boat Śaṅkara by his own magic power *(māyā)* caused the boat to rise into the sky and then destroyed the whole illusion. The Jain was killed as he fell back to the dry land.
30. Some particularly striking examples of this image are found in E. Dimock's article, 'Rabindranath Tagore – The Greatest of the Bāuls of Bengal', reprinted in *South and Southeast Asia*, ed. John A. Harrison (Tucson: The University of Arizona Press, 1972), pp. 143–146. The examples are taken from Tagore and some of the Bāul poets, particularly Lālan Phakir.
31. A complete description of this famous soul journey is found in *Bṛhadāraṇyaka Upaniṣad* Vi. 2. 15.

EDWARD C. DIMOCK

4

Religious Biography in India: The 'Nectar of the Acts' of Caitanya

A good deal has been written regarding traditional Indian attitudes toward time, and the effect of those attitudes on literature as well as written history. If, for example, the creation of an attitude of depersonalized esthetic pleasure, in which all secular consciousness is suspended, is the aim of literature, as it is according to one school of thought,[1] the Western notion of linear development of plot is meaningless. Or, if it is true that the classical Indian idea is that time is cyclical, certain categories of literature are no longer possible, among them historical biography; for human personality is irrelevant in the working out of the repeated patterns of the cosmic order. This is not to say that there has been no concern with the lives of great individuals. Aśvaghoṣa wrote his life of the Buddha, the *Buddhacarita*, in perhaps the lst century B.C., and there has been a steady stream of writings on the lives of such individuals – one is reluctant to call them 'men' in this context – ever since. For the paradigm is divinely established, and periodically reenacted, as Kṛṣṇa says in *Bhagavad-gitā* IV, 7–8, 'in age after age'. So the question itself becomes circular: if the life of an individual has cosmic significance, its particularities are unimportant, and if the particularities are important, the life is not worth writing.

In regard to the life of the Bengali Vaiṣṇava[2] saint Caitanya (1486–1535) we are more than usually fortunate. For the traditional views of the most orthodox 'biography', the *Caitanya-caritāmṛta* of Kṛṣṇadāsa Kvarāja, written about eighty years after Caitanya's death, are sometimes balanced by the more earthy observations of texts such as the *Caitanyamaṅgala* of Jayānanda, anathema to the pious. The paradigm, for example, forbids mention of the subject's death; Jayānanda, interested in particulars, tells us that Caitanya injured his foot in a spate of frenzied dancing, and, after suffering for six days, died from an infection of it. The presence of Jayānanda and other texts not yet censored out of existence by orthodoxy obviously suggests that exceptions must be made to the above general statements about historical biography. But the fact that they are considered heretical by the dominant orthodoxy also suggest the more widely accepted texts, it states its own program.

As its name suggests, it is not with the acts *(carita)* but with the 'nectar of the acts' *(caritāmrta)* that it is concerned. Caitanya walked the earth and interacted with other men. Kṛṣṇadāsa is not constrained to detail the interaction; he is constrained by its meaning. When Caitanya is asked why, when he is himself the full godhead, he goes about patiently preaching and converting people, he replies that he must act in a social way, for if he revealed his true form, as Kṛṣṇa does to Arjuna in the *Gitā*, people would be terrified and not turn to him for the right reasons.

It is possible, then, to be very brief about the facts of Caitanya's life as Kṛṣṇadāsa outlines them, despite the fact that his text covers 30,000 lines. Caitanya was born, auspiciously, one full moon night in the town of Navadvīpa, in the district of Nadīyā in present-day West Bengal. True to the paradigm, the birth was accompanied by the usual wonderful signs: his father dreamt that something luminous had entered into his body and thence into the body of his wife. The child Visvambhara (Kṛṣṇa-Caitanya was his religious name) had all the marks of Kṛṣṇa on his body; and, like Kṛṣṇa, was a mischievous child. About Caitanya's boyhood and youth, Kṛṣṇadāsa does allow himself some particulars, for he tells us that Caitanya studied Sanskrit grammar in a traditional school, a *tol*, run by a scholar called Gaṇgādāsa But even within this probably accurate statement, there is what seems to be hyperbole, for Kṛṣṇadāsa together with other biographers insists on Caitanyas great skill as scholar, rhetorician, poet, and philosopher, when there is nothing really to indicate this. Caitanya has in fact left no writing except eight Sanskrit verses, devotional in nature, and demonstrating no exceptional poetic skill. In any case, Caitanya married young, but his bride died of snakebite (she was 'bitten by the serpent of separation') while Caitanya was on a trip to East Bengal. On his return, he married a second time, and opened a Sanskrit *tol* of his own. Then, when he was about twenty-two, he went to Gayā to peform there the funeral obsequies for his father. What happened there is a mystery. He returned to Navadvīpa God-maddened, and proceeded to organize and lead the *kirtana* – singing of devotional hymns and dancing – every night for the next two years. At the end of that time he took initiation in an ascetic order. He wanted to go to live at Vṛndāvana, the place of his beloved Kṛṣṇa, but gave in to his mother's pleas and went instead to live at Puri in Orissa, a place easier of access from Bengal. He stayed in Puri only eighteen days on this first trip, before leaving on a two year pilgrimage that was to take him to the southern tip of India, up the west coast to Maharashtra, and across the sub-continent back to Puri.

No details of this pilgrimage are known,[3] but it seems that about this time another turning-point in Caitanya's life occurred. The *Caitanya-caritāmṛta* text tells us that it was on the banks of the Godavari, in present-day Andhra, that he met Rāmānanda Rāy. Rāmānanda was a high official in the court of Rājā Pratāparudra of Orissa; he was a learned man and a poet and, it seems, a Tāntric Vaiṣṇava.[4] The conversation between the two, as reported in the *Caitanya-caritāmṛta*, centered on the place of the love between Rādhā and Kṛṣṇa in the Vaiṣṇava scheme. Rāmānanda pointed out to Caitanya the latter's true nature as both Rādhā and Kṛṣṇa in a single body: he saw Caitanya's golden complexion (that of Rādhā) as overlaying his blue-colored form (that of Kṛṣṇa); Caitanya then

"smiling, showed him his true form – Rasarājā [i.e., Kṛṣṇa] and Mahabhāva [i.e., Rādhā], these two as one form; and seeing it Rāmānanda fainted in pure joy. He could not hold his body upright, and he fell to the earth." (II: i: 233–234).

From this time on, Rādhā manifested herself more and more in Caitanya's person, until in the pain of separation from Kṛṣṇa, she took him over completely, and he became irrevocably withdrawn from the ordinary world of men – mad, or so it seemed to human sight.

For he was certainly mad, whether this be interpreted as the divine madness of the holy fool, the random madness of the child, or, as one modern historian claims, as epilepsy. He was literally pulled apart by his passion for Kṛṣṇa, by the tension of living in the world of men when his true life was in Vṛndāvana:

"His body was unconscious, and there was no breath in his nostrils. His arms and legs were each three hands long; the joints of his bones were separated, and over the joints there was only skin." (III: 14: 59 ff.)

Increasingly withdrawn, Caitanya remained in Puri for the rest of his life, except for two pilgrimages. The first, an attempt to visit Vṛndāvana, was aborted in Bengal. On the second he did succeed in reaching Vṛndāvana but was so distracted by the sights of the place of his beloved Kṛṣṇa that his companions felt it imperative to get him away before he did himself bodily harm. He returned to Puri and remained there for the last eighteen years of his life.

The manner of his death is a mystery. The *Caitanya-caritāmṛta* does not comment on it. Other texts say that he was absorbed into the image of Jagannāth, since he and that great god are one. Still others say that he was drowned, or, in Jayānanda, that he died of an injury. And this is literally almost all the biographical fact that can be gleaned from Kṛṣṇadasa's long text.

For Kṛṣṇadāsa, this type of fact was not important. There was little point in treating overt detail, for true significance lies in meaning, which only devotees can comprehend. Kṛṣṇadāsa writes:

"The līlā of Caitanya is sweet, and profound as the sea. People do not understand it; only steadfast devotees can understand. Have faith and listen to the actions of Caitanya; do not engage in argument, for in such argument is adversity." (III: 2: 168–169).

And the truth is that Caitanya is Kṛṣṇa.

Kṛṣṇadāsa's training was at the hands of the theologians who shaped the doctrine of the Vaiṣṇava movement, the six Gosvāmins of Vṛndāvana.[5] These Gosvāmins were perceptive as well as learned men, and their teachings are sometimes original and sometimes adaptations of pecularities of Vaiṣṇava belief to more traditional teachings. Thus they accept the doctrine of revelation, of *sabda*, 'word', and say that the *Bhāgavatapurāṇa*, the basic text which tells of Kṛṣṇa and the Gopīs in the tenth book, is that revelation. What that text describes as having happened at Vṛndāvana did literally happen, and furthermore, it is in capsule form what is happening eternally in the Vṛndāvana. What the *Bhāgavata* describes is simultaneously finite and infinite; the relationship is not one of reality and reflection for both are fully real. This means of course that Kṛṣṇa appears in time, in the *Bhāgavata* revelation which is also outside time. And since the revelation is outside time, it can occur again and again, and does so, not as parallel events but as exact and complete duplications.

The theory goes still further. As Kṛṣṇa is the ultimate reality, all that is around him in the *Bhāgavata* idyll – the cows and trees, the cowherds and cowherd girls, the river and meadows – is also in the ultimate sense reality. Thus, when the reality of the *Bhāgavata* is duplicated, it is duplicated totally. When Caitanya is brought to a picnic on the banks of the Ganges, he and his companions know that the river is not the Ganges, but the Yamunā of Vṛndāvana, and that the picnic is that enjoyed by Kṛṣṇa and his friends. The *Caitanya-caritāmṛta* text is clear: they do not imagine this to be Kṛṣṇa's picnic, they do not perceive it to be so, they know it (III: 6). And when Caitanya runs into a garden in Puri, he knows it to be a meadow in Vṛndāvana. Although others may see only the overt manifestation, his madness allows him to operate at the level of truth, unconfused by the overt level of apparent reality.

Elements of overt reality are superimpositions which hide the true reality from all but devotees. One looks at an image of the child Kṛṣṇa holding the stolen butter; this is only the imposed form, and in the image are contained not only Kṛṣṇa the child, but Kṛṣṇa the lover, Kṛṣṇa the high god, and all the other aspects of Kṛṣṇa. Caitanya the man looks and acts like a social being (at least in the days of his lucidity), but his true nature is of an order of reality unaffected by men or by society. He whose eyes can strip away mere appearance can see the truth: Caitanya is Kṛṣṇa, and all that surrounds Caitanya is Vṛndāvana.

There are two other connected aspects of this idea: that of *avatāra* and that of the dual nature of Caitanya as not only Kṛṣṇa but Rādhā as well. The term *avatāra* is usually translated as 'incarnation'; in the Vaiṣṇava context that is incorrect, for as we have seen, the flesh is also the spirit. The power of the godhead is infinite, and therefore nothing can diminish it. Thus each time the godhead appears on earth, it is with the full power of the godhead, while the essential godhead remains fully powerful. Each *avatāra* of Kṛṣṇa, then, is fully Kṛṣṇa, not a 'part' of Kṛṣṇa, or even an aspect of him. Further, such *avatāras*, being outside time and space, can appear in infinite number at the same moment of earthly time, or singly, widely spaced in earthly time, or in any other combination, none of the appearances in any way differing in essence, though perhaps differing in form, from one another or from the source. Caitanya, then, is Caitanya in overt form, Kṛṣṇa (and Rādhā) in covert form, and Kṛṣṇa in essence.

It is on the question of the dual essence that the Gosvāmins, and thus Kṛṣṇadāsa, are truthly athletic. The argument is this. Since all of Vṛndāvana of the *Bhāgavata* is an extension of Kṛṣṇa himself, the Gopīs also belong to his essence. Yet the text says that the Gopīs were in love with Kṛṣṇa, and such a love relationship implies at least two parts. Thus the Gopīs (and, by extension, Rādhā, the Gopī par excellence) must be both the same and not the same as Kṛṣṇa. Kṛṣṇa, the essence of whose nature is to love and be loved, separated Rādhā from himself in order that the love relationship could take place. But Kṛṣṇa could not appreciate fully the depth and extent of Rādhā's love and at the same time his own. So he recombined the parts, both still fully individual but bound up in one, the person of Caitanya. Only then could he fully taste the combined joys of two and of one.

All of this, more than the facts of Caitanya's life, is what really concerns Kṛṣṇadāsa. Devotee that he was, he too was trying to see beneath overt appearances, to describe the true divine nature of Caitanya, to see Vṛndāvana in all that surrounded him. He might not always understand all that he sees. He is mortal, and if he speaks truth, it is because Caitanya speaks through him: "For I am an insignificant creature, and write only by the grace of Caitanya" (III:3:257). As true devotee, loving Kṛṣṇa and therefore loved in return, he is in a state of grace, in almost the Christian sense of that term. In this state what he says is true, whether he himself understands it fully or not.

His critics are quick to point out that in his text Kṛṣṇadāsa makes such flagrant errors as deputing people to go to Vṛndāvana to meet the Gosvāmins before he had deputed the Gosvāmins themselves to go there. Such criticism is correct but dreary; chronology had no meaning for Kṛṣṇadāsa, for time itself had no meaning. Caitanya was not imitating Kṛṣṇa as Christians imitate Christ, but was following his nature as Kṛṣṇa; the results were inevitable. Kṛṣṇadāsa was revealing the truth, and in the context of truth the details of the form of revelation are true as well: if people are bothered by time sequence, they have not understood the revelation.

For his writing is an act of devotion. Some critics are faintly troubled by what seems to be a dichotomy between the careful and highly wrought qualities of English Metaphysical poetry and the devotional attitude of the poets. It does seem that puns and intellectually subtle turns of phrase are vaguely out of place in devotional verse, which should be somehow personal, highly charged, and immediate. The reaction of such critics to the *Caitanya-caritāmṛta* as poetry would be similar. Kṛṣṇadāsa, scholar that he was and trained by scholars, takes depressing delight in splitting Sanskrit scholastic hairs in sixty-four different ways; his verse, written in a variety of Sanskritic meters, is often heavy; his language is somber and careful, his thoughts involved and seemingly impersonal. But having said this, it is necessary to turn immediately to the opinion of the best and most recent editor of the text, Rādhāgovinda Nāth, who calls the book

"an unprecedented and special jewel even in the wealth of Bengali literature; I do not know that there is anywhere a combination so beautiful and sensitive of philosophical discussion and poetry."[6]

This suggests that a reexamination of the work from the esthetic point of view of the Vaiṣṇava would be in order.

Caitanya-caritamṛta III: 5: 88–118 is a passage which it might be well to quote in full.

"There was a brahman of eastern Bengal who had written a drama on the actions of Prabhu [i.e., Caitanya], and he brought it so that Prabhu could hear it. He was acquainted with Bhagavān-āçārya, and meeting him there, he took up residence in his house. He read the drama first to him, and many Vaiṣṇavas were there with him to listen. And all praised it, saying that the drama was the greatest and best, and all thought that he should have Mahāprabhu [i.e., Caitanya] hear it. Now, whoever had written a song or a verse or a book brought it first for Svarūpa to hear; and if it received Svarūpa's approval, then it was read to Prabhu. If there was an artificial *rasa*[7], or any opposition to the ultimate truths, Prabhu could not bear it, and became angry. Thus Prabhu did not listen to anything first, and he stipulated this matter of correctness. So the ācārya petitioned Svarūpa: 'A brahman has written an excellent drama on Prabhu. First listen to it, and see if you like it. If you do, then we shall have Mahāprabhu hear is.' And Svarūpa said: 'You are a most noble man, and have a desire to listen to all kinds of *śāstras;* but in the words of indifferent poets there is seeming *rasa*, and it gives me no joy to listen to opposition to the truths.' Those who cannot discriminate between *rasa* and that which seems like *rasa* can never gain the shore of the sea of the perfection of devotion. They do not know grammar, they do not know the art of poetic ornamentation, nor the technicalities of the drama – such worthless people do not know how to describe the Kṛṣṇa-līlā, and especially this Caitanya-part, which is difficult to grasp. That man alone can describe the Kṛṣṇa-līlā and the Caitanya-līlā, whose heart is at the lotus of the feet of Caitanya. It is misery to listen to the poetry of crude poets, as it is delight to listen to true poetry, full of skill... The ācārya persisted for several days, and giving in to his insistence, Svarūpa consented to listen. With all of them, Svarūpa sat to listen, and the poet read the introductory verse:

"Making conscious the endless world, which is naturally inert, he who is as bright as gold [i.e., Caitanya], the soul of Jagannātha,[8] has appeared in this world; may that Kṛṣṇa-Caitanya be gracious to you."

"When they heard the verse, all the people praised it; but Svarūpa said: 'Explain this verse'. And the poet said: 'Jagannātha is the body, which is beautiful, and Caitanya is the most serene essence in it. By his nature he brings consciousness to the inert world, and Mahāprabhu has appeared at Puri.' When they heard this, the minds of all were pleased, but Svarūpa was not happy, and said in an angry voice: 'You are a fool! You have ruined yourself completely. You have no faith that both of these are God. Jagannātha is fully bliss,[9] and his true form is consciousness; yet you have made him inert, transitory, and material in body. Caitanya is himself God, full of the six divine qualities, and you have made him a mere living thing, like a spark to fire. For this offence against them both you will reap misery, for this is the reward of those who describe the truths without knowing them'."

Form follows function, then. If the writer is sincere in his devotion, the form of his writing will be beautiful not only in the truths that it states, but in its metaphor, alliteration, rhyme, and in all the phases of prosody that one more often assocates with careful working and reworking of poetic expression. Further, as Svarūpa bluntly states, those who do not understand and appreciate the ultimate religious and esthetic experience – that of *rasa* – cannot be said to know even grammar, much less the ornaments of poetry. And, as did our unfortunate dramatist, if one thinks that by turning a clever phrase without regard to religious truth he can create poetry, he only brings ridicule upon himself.

For Kṛṣṇadāsa, then, and perhaps for the Metaphysicals as well, the scene of the discourse is literary, to be sure, but more importantly it is religious, it is on the level of metaphysical truth. On that level there can be no hyperbole, for no exaggeration of physical reality can ever do more than suggest the nature of the metaphysical. And on this level there can be no absurdity, for one can here discern the full pattern of the divine purpose, which looks, to limited everyday consciousness, like randomness: physical time and space have no meaning in this sphere. The only expression of truth is beauty; it is a natural relationship. He who has not eyes will not see: the fault is not Kṛṣṇadāsa's.

Finally, by none of the above do I mean to suggest that Kṛṣṇadāsa was unaware that he was treating matters which had actually occurred; rather, he moves in his interpretative way back and forth between the material and spiritual levels of reality with what sometimes seems to the non-devotee disconcerting ease. Yet, Caitanya had been a living, breathing creature, and some of Kṛṣṇadāsa's own teachers had known him well. Thus, even though Puri was really Vṛndāvana, Kṛṣṇadāsa's descriptions of Puri during the Car Festival do reflect some of the colorful ritual and excitement that one gets a hint of even today; Caitanya's being surrounded by Muslim freebooters while he had fallen into a trance during one of his pilgrimages has the ring of truth (though his conversion of these Muslims by rather strange arguments based on the Quran does not); and there are incidents in which Caitanya's personality can be dimly perceived. One could wish, perhaps, that Kṛṣṇadāsa had allowed us more than a glimpse of a figure who changed the course of the religious history of a substantial part of the Indian sub-continent, but he has given us suggestions as to why more than a glimpse is not possible, and that is, perhaps, nearly as important.

Notes

1. This is the so-called *rasa* theory. There are many books on the matter, e.g., Ramaranjan Mukherji, *Literary Criticism in Ancient India* (Calcutta: Sanskrit Pustak Bhandar, 1966), esp. pp. 264–343.
2. Although the name is derived from that of the god Viṣṇu, the Bengali of Gauḍiyā Vaiṣṇavas hold Kṛṣṇa to be himself the high god rather than an *avatāra*.
3. There is a text, the *Karacā* of Govinda-dāsa, which treats of this pilgrimage. However, most scholars consider this text spurious, including as it does loan words from languages with which Bengali, at the time of the pilgrimage, had not come into contact.
4. I.e., a Sahajiyā. See my *The Place of the Hidden Moon* (Chicago: University of Chicago Press, 1966), pp. 52–54.
5. *Ibid*., pp. 72–78.
6. *Caitanya-caitāmṛta* of Kṛṣṇadāsa Kavirāja, 6 volumes (Calcutta: Bhakti-pracāra bhāṇḍar, 1355 B. S.); *bhumikā*.
7. *Rasa* means here an impersonalized state of esthetic experience, enhanced by careful and proper use of the poetic devices.
8. The reference is to the physical image of Jagannātha ('Lord of the World') in the temple at Puri.
9. 'Bliss' is *ānanda*, one of the three characteristics of both the form and the spirit of the godhead; the other two are *sat* ('truth') and *cit* ('consciousness').

PART II

Biographical Traditions and Individual Lives

RENATO ROSALDO

5

The Story of Tukbaw: 'They Listen as He Orates'

As so often happens in anthropological field research I found myself working evening after evening on a project that I did not plan ahead of time.[1] I did not intend to record a life history during our stay in the Philippines; the life story of Tukbaw emerged only gradually, through a series of fortuitous events, and it was not until his narrative was well developed that I decided to ask him to elaborate on it. At the time I came close to assuming that every man has his life story within him; if only Tukbaw had the leisure to speak at length, I thought nature would take its course and an autobiography would emerge. I did not think the task comparable to Socrates' virtuoso questioning of Meno's slave, with the artful, step-by-step revelation that the boy, after all, had known geometry all along. But I did expect Tukbaw's narrative to reveal a person with a deep and intricate inner life; I thought him an extraordinary and introspective person, capable of composing a self-reflective and confessional autobiography. My expectations were disappointed; in retrospect I realize they were inappropriate.

Though Tukbaw never explicitly said so, his narrative seemed to be about a series of critical events through which he came, by incremental steps, to be the sort of public figure he is today. It was as though he emerged at birth as a homunculus-like figure, a pale and miniature sketch of the adult he was to become; a figure to be filled in and fleshed out over the course of a lifetime. His cultural model for manhood was almost exclusively his father: in early childhood he stumbled and tagged after him; in his youth he listened to his advice with great attention and believed in him; in young manhood he took careful note of how his father acted and spoke in public, and was to follow suit. When he told his life story he was a complete and full adult; his youthful trials and errors had led to the realization of his culture's design for the mature social person. In what follows my central concern shall be to interpret Tukbaw's sense of the pattern and shape of his own biography.

How does he view the unfolding of his development as a person? What is his conception of the life cycle? To help in characterizing the design of

Tukbaw's life story I shall allude to Erikson's psychological conception of the life cycle, since his notion of the life stages is as explicit and widely known as any available to English-speaking intellectuals today.[2] By invoking Erikson I wish neither to verify nor to reject his theories; I shall not, as they say, put them to the test. I intend instead to use his theories as a conceptual foil against which to illuminate Tukbaw's conception of his life career: by holding the two conceptions next to one another, and highlighting their similarities and differences, I hope more clearly to perceive the main features of Tukbaw's narrative. For instance, Erikson resembles Tukbaw in that he views each stage in the life cycle as a 'way station' on the path toward adulthood; where he differs, particularly in considering infancy and early childhood, is in that he dwells more than Tukbaw on the characteristic content, or psycho-social crisis, of each stage.

However often I may refer to the work of Erikson, I feel reluctant to 'psychologize' and use Tukbaw's portrayal of his public self to make inferences about his inner mental state. In order to decipher whatever latent meaning may lie beneath Tukbaw's manifest statements, I would require a sense of alternative statements: how else might he have told the story of his life? Had other members of Tukbaw's society written or recited confessional autobiographies I might venture the hypothesis that his self-portrayal as a public figure was but a means of concealing and 'masking' his deeper and perhaps truer self. I do not believe that members of his culture were accustomed to telling their life stories in any form, and certainly not in a way intimate, revealing, and confessional. Narratives, of course, were familiar; Tukbaw often told the tale of a hunt, of a raid, of a fishing trip. What was not familiar was that he himself should be the subject of the narrative. In terms of his own cultural lore and expectations, Tukbaw's narrative was neither appropriate nor inappropriate; it simply was an exploration of little known cultural terrain.

In seeking to characterize the sense Tukbaw had of his own life I begin with an outline of the male life cycle in that society. Such a synoptic view of the generic male biography should convey some sense of the social framework within which Tukbaw lived. Then I tell how I came, almost by accident, to collect Tukbaw's life history as he told it. This is more than a matter of intellectual scrupulousness on my part; my conviction is that anthropological life histories are stories told to a particular person which inevitably reflect this personal relation. To assess and interpret properly the content of a life history one must know something of both the speaker and the listener. Taken together, the generic life cycle and the story of how the life history was collected provide background for lengthy verbatim extracts from Tukbaw's narrative. These extracts are ordered chronologically, from infancy through adulthood, rather than in the order collected; my commentary here is as sparse as possible, providing only sufficient context to make Tukbaw's own words intelligible. Finally, I make certain general remarks about anthropology and biography, and I return to the question of why my expectations of Tukbaw's autobiography were disappointed.

The life cycle in Ilongot society

Tukbaw is an adult male Ilongot of Northern Luzon, Phillippines. The Ilongots comprise a non-Christian group of some 2500, and they inhabit the hills about eighty miles to the north and east of Manila. Like other non-Christian hill peoples of the Philippines, the Ilongots are considered a cultural minority in contrast with the nationally dominant majority of Christian peoples in the valleys. However, they differ from other non-Christian groups in the degree of autonomy that they have maintained. Unlike other dry rice cultivators of Luzon, they have not entered into symbiotic economic relations with their neighbors and they are virtually self-sufficient. That they have thus far retained considerable territorial integrity is doubtless in large part due to their head-hunting forays into the Christian lowlands, at once a distinctive mark of their cultural identity as well as an effective means of keeping insiders 'in' and outsiders 'out'.[3]

Ilongots live in scattered and internally dispersed settlements, with about 40–60 persons in each. The composition of settlements derives in part from the uxorilocal rule of post-marital residence, where the man leaves home and moves into the house of his bride. Subsistence is based on a combination of dry rice cultivation and the hunting of deer and wild boar; the division in subsistence roughly corresponds with the sexual division of labor in which women do most of the continuous agricultural labor while men focus most of their labor on the hunt. Apart from uxorilocal residence and the division of labor, the most striking difference between the sexes over the course of the life cycle is that men, and only men, take heads. However, in general and for both sexes the Ilongot life cycle is divided into the following culturally marked phases: (a) childhood; (b) youth; (c) adulthood; and (d) old age.

Childhood, especially the first few years after birth, is divided into culturally recognized steps in the mastery of motor skills; among these are: feeding at the mother's breast, sitting, walking, venturing outside the house. Ilongots claim that once children have ventured outside the house they are likely to be of an age where they may acquire understanding: that is, they can comprehend and obey the instructions of their elders. In late childhood they are able to grasp more complex kinds of instruction appropriate to their sex; women learn to garden and men learn to hunt. In addition, parents impart moral knowledge concerning what constitutes a good person in that society. For a man to assume the ordeals and privileges of youth he must first learn the traditional lore and become adept at a man's work, ranging from hunting and clearing the forest to more subtle graces of dressing with elegance and tying elaborate rattan knots used in the construction of houses. When a male child becomes a youth, then, he is expected to be a good worker and to have acquired a refined social sense.

Youth as a phase of life is idealized in Ilongot society. At this stage young men are vain, ornamenting themselves with fine jewelry and kerchiefs; they strut, preen, and loll, taking pride in their physical agility and beauty. They often cling together and travel in groups as they move about to visit, court, or raid. Ilongots assert that young men are volatile, often unpredictable, sometimes dangerous, and not to be trusted too far. Youth entails a series of ordeals that must be undergone in order to emerge into full adulthood. Filing one's teeth and taking a head are physical and personal ordeals; courtship and marriage involve a more complex set of social stresses and adjustments. I have known Ilongot men with unfiled teeth, some who did not take a head, a few who never married; nonetheless, the cultural expectation is clear – youth is a time of storm and stress, punctuated by the trying *rites de passage* of teeth filing, taking a head, and marriage. Upon marriage a man leaves his natal household and moves in with his bride; he is entering adulthood.

After marriage a man has moved into a single-room household where his wife's parents also live (and sometimes her married sister as well); in that house the man is made to feel a stranger. He has left a home where he lived with his parents and siblings; he has moved into a house filled with his in-laws. In Ilongot society a person is forbidden to use the personal names of his or her spouse's parents and siblings; hence the man has moved in with people whom he may not name (except by saying 'so-and-so' or 'in-law'), though they employ his personal name in return ('Tukbaw'). Aside from his wife, a man's closest kinship ties are likely to be with the other houses of his settlement, and particularly with other men of his generation who are related as cousins. In old age, the final phase of the life cycle, a man and his wife have become the heads of their household, and the circle rounds itself off as the man's daughters marry, bringing sons-in-law into the house as strangers.

At the time that we knew Tukbaw he was at the peak of his adulthood; he had long since left his youth and he was not yet an old man. He was about forty-five years old, and among his peers he stood out as a gifted and persuasive orator in public meetings (see M. Rosaldo, 1973). He attributed his gift for speech in large part to his capacity to listen and understand what others were saying; I thought that his ability to move and convince others derived from his penetrating human intelligence, his empathy and knack for articulating what others only dimly perceived. He moved people by what I must call sheer force of personality. Apart from his ability to orate and influence, Tukbaw occupied himself like other adult men of his society: he was adept at the hunt and he sometimes labored at clearing the dense forest cover to prepare dry rice gardens for their initial year of cultivation. He had been married once and divorced; he was living with his second wife and because they had no natural children they had adopted two daughters from non-Christian settlers to the region.

My wife, Michelle, and I lived in Tukbaw's house during most of our period of field research. The house was comprised of parents and the families of two married daughters. The tree families were as follows: (1) the parents of Tukbaw's wife (his parents-in-law); (2) the married sister of Tukbaw's wife (his sister-in-law), her husband and their children; and (3) Tukbaw, his wife and their two adopted daughters. At the time of our residence, a number of factors had coincided to make this domestic group prominent in the settlement. In its econonomic productivity, both of rice and meat, the household was outstanding; its plentiful food supply meant that the house became a major locus of social activity, for participants in celebrations and casual visitors alike could count on being well fed there. The men of the household were highly esteemed socially: one was the best hunter of the settlement; Tukbaw's father-in-law enjoyed seniority for he was the elder of two brothers who were pivotal in the composition of the settlement; Tukbaw himself, of course, was a prominent orator.

The prestige of the household members and the dependable supply of food were no doubt the main reasons that we were asked to stay in Tukbaw's house, and it is equally certain that our having stayed there added to the prestige of the house. Nonetheless I should stress that the high status of the household was due to a confluence of reasons, and could easily change as the domestic composition changed. Ilongots themselves insisted that all houses were equal in rank and status; theirs was a long-run view of social life and the domestic cycle. As with the medieval conception of the wheel of fortune, Ilongots saw the larger flow of time and held that the house that is on top today might well be on the bottom tomorrow – in the end, it all evens out.

Collecting his life history, I

In late September of 1967 we arrived in Manila; we were to remain in the Philippines through July of 1969. Our initial stay in Manila was brief; we introduced ourselves to a number of anthropologists and missionaries; we purchased supplies, and we planned our survey of the Ilongot region. Our plan was to take advantage of the airstrips and field stations that had been set up by New Tribes Missionaries active in the area since 1955. We flew to each of four mission stations where we made notes on material culture, recorded census data and collected word lists. In addition, we began to learn the language and we selected a site for our own field station.

Ilongots were familiar with Americans. Older people recalled schoolteachers of the 1930s and soldiers of the Second World War; everyone knew of the missionaries; some had heard stories of William Jones, an anthropologist murdered by the Ilongots in 1909. In recalling how we were initially perceived by the Ilongots I reread our field journals and found that the most indicative anecdote was my solitary hike from a mission station to an interior settlement. The experience was at once exhilarating and unnerving. At first I was guided by an unmarried young man who wore his hair long and was absorbed in playing his flute (he was acting like a 'head-hunter', as missionaries then put it); I imagine it was utter boredom that made him restless enough to pass me on to his cousin. His cousin was wary and vigilant, perhaps suspicious; still, he was willing and otherwise considerate. As we approached the interior settlement we came upon a group of people harvesting rice, and we stopped there to rest.

Much to my suprise one of the harvesters came and spoke to me in evidently rusty English. At the time I recorded the following in my field journal:

"One man about thirty says to me, 'I speak English'. I asked, 'Where did you learn?' He replied, 'All right'. He went on, 'Wash your face. Comb your hair. Brush your teeth. Dirty body, no good." (FJ, 11/1/67)[4]

He went on to explain that he had been to first grade a little after the war; the phrases he recited to me were what he had learned on the first day of school. I felt uneasy. Apart from my dreams of doing field research far from the American classroom, I was forced to confront the aftermath of American colonialism in the Philippines and I felt somehow responsible.

We then walked up a hill to the field shelter where we would eat our evening meal of rice and fresh venison. As we ate I was told that a man who spoke fluent English was to arrive soon; he would translate for me as I explained why I had come to their settlement.[5] After the meal we sat in a low silence; they were tired from the long day's work, and I was not yet capable of carrying on a conversation in the Ilongot language. The silence was shattered by the entrance of a man who announced, in drunken and booming English:

"Good evening, sir. Light. No light? These people, sir, they are no good; they should give you light. I am here to tell these people to follow your orders." (FJ, 11/1/67)

I tried to explain why we had come to Ilongot country, but to no avail:

"He giggles a drunken chuckle now and then, saying he does not understand. Besides he is deaf, so even if I were to shout he would not hear. Then he 'translates' in a kind of chant that I can't follow. People giggle at his speech. I come to the center of the room and very nervously and earnestly explain that I am not a missionary, that I have come to learn their speech, and their customs, so that I can write a book. (FJ, 11/1/67)

Initially, then, the Ilongots were watchful and curious; they knew we were

Americans, but they appeared to wonder: if not missionaries, what are they? We were, after all, strangers and uninvited guests.

COLLECTING HIS LIFE HISTORY, II

After our survey of the four mission stations we decided to live in the interior settlement of Kakidugen. That people spoke in a slow and easy to understand drawl was significant; but the decisive factor was simply that we were charmed by the place. Our enthusiasm was apparent in our dittoed 'survey report' where we wrote:

The five large, square Kakidugen houses are anywhere from 10 minutes to half an hour apart. Between them are rice fields, rice racks – some of a circular kind which we are told is old style – and a slow winding river. Material culture here is rich and largely traditional. Young men wear brass necklaces, bracelets, belts. All men have long hair."

We found the settlement beautiful, nestled as it was in the forest by a slow and winding river. Long hair, red kerchiefs, filed teeth, feather head-dresses, boar-tusk bracelets; all seemed to indicate a rich and traditional culture.

At the time of our first visit the men had gone hunting, so we did not meet Tukbaw. As Michelle wrote in her field journal:

"Our guide called out to the fields for people to come and see the *midikanu* (Americans)." (FJ, 10/27/67)

The people came, and one of the first we met was Tukbaw's wife, Wagi. The journal continues:

"Wagi who wears a sweater shrug as a blouse has a round happy face – five years married and no children; and very anxious for us to stay here, and build an airstrip and bring her clothes." (FJ, 10/27/67)

Our welcome was based more on the commodities we might bring than on friendship pure and simple. But still we found the people engaging, and Wagi was lively, vivacious and energetic; people said over and over, 'See, she pounds rice like an unmarried young woman'. They no doubt were saying that we would be fed well; we had already decided to return to the house of Tukbaw in Kakidugen.

We spent a short while in Manila where we rested, bought supplies, and wrote our preliminary survey report. In early December we returned to Kakidugen for our first extended stay. On our arrival we were taken aback to find that Wagi, a short month before so dynamic and healthy, was ill and seemingly on her death bed. Clearly, the onset of her illness had been abrupt, profoundly painful and beyond explanation for Tukbaw. She was frail and skeletal, and coughed deeply and gasped, as if each breath were her last. Fearing that the blame for her almost certain death would be cast on us, we were reluctant to try our medicine. Fortunately, we had a few days' reprieve; Wagi was then being treated by a non-Christian settler who was known as a curer, and the people dared not mix the two kinds of medicine.

Tukbaw was brooding and pondering over Wagi's perhaps impending death. At the time I wrote the following in my field journal:

"Tukbaw was in a mood – he has been confining himself to his corner of the house for two days. Then he left suddenly. In the evening he returned and whipped the dogs; he told me to write down these words: *bekbek* and *teprat*. He says both of these words mean 'whip' and they may be used either for people or for dogs." (FJ, 12/15/67)

Despite his sorrow and pent-up anger, Tukbaw came and explained that we should try our medicine on Wagi: it would do no harm, and it might work. Sensing our consternation, he added that if our medicine was not effective it was because Wagi no longer had life within her, and no human being could be held to blame for that.[6] As good fortune had it, she did recover. Our penicillin shots helped, but she also still had life within her.

Wagi's turn for the better and her gradual recovery meant that our Ilongot companions became more attentive and tolerant of our presence. It is tempting to report that her recovery led to a dramatic change in our relation with the Ilongots; that we became 'one of the people'; that is was one of those 'magical' moments of acceptance, as Geertz (1971) has reported.[7] Field relations are humanly significant and they do have crucial moments. Yet we did not experience a single and decisive moment. Our relations changed and proceeded toward intimacy over a number of events, with an unsteady and halting gait.

Collecting his life history, III

The first texts of what was to become Tukbaw's life history grew out of our initial efforts to learn the language monolingually. We tried everything we could think of. We read sentences from Tagalog grammars and asked for translations; we pointed to objects and asked what they were called. As we listened to natural conversation we jotted down sounds that seemed like words; later we repeated the 'words' and asked what they meant. We soon started to ask people to tell us stories. We explained that as they spoke we would write down their words, and then we would ask about the words we did not know. For all concerned telling and transcribing stories was an exhausting and trying chore. As I now read them, my transcriptions of these first stories are written in large and uneven script, strangely reminiscent of my writing in the first grade. And Tukbaw ended the second of these stories by saying, 'I am going to the river. I am going to look for snails. I then am going to look for something to wrap and burn them in because I have no lime [snails are burned and turned into lime for use in betel quids]. I am tired of explaining things and telling stories' (LH, 12/12/67).

At this early stage we devoted all our efforts to the language and our teachers' response proved patient and inventive. Ilongots claimed that by following verbal instructions children acquire and demonstrate their capacity for speech. And as with their own children, they spoke to us in imperatives, particularly those of the 'go and get' variety (e.g., 'go and get the cup of water'). Hence, we were asked to fetch water, spoons, betel quids. The people were at once amused to order about their adult guests and pleased to discover our increasing understanding of their language. Early texts from Tukbaw often reflect this imperative mode of instruction. In his first narrative, for instance, Tukbaw says, 'We are making a house, a new house. Put up the house posts. Go and get some people to help. Go and get some rattan to tie it together. Go and get some grass for the roof' (LH, 12/6/67).

In addition to my language learning, the subject of Tukbaw's earliest stories was our relationship itself. On the simplest level, the narrative was about our joint activities, such as drinking sugar cane wine. At about six every morning and evening he and I would drink wine together. In one text he said, 'Liquor makes people fierce. If the liquor is good, then people quarrel. Even if the people are related, they say one thing or another and they begin to fight. Then, when they become sober, they no longer fight with one another' (LH, 2/14/68). Field rats had invaded the sugar cane patches and the wine began to run short, so Tukbaw indulged himself in the whimsical fantasy of organizing a collective hunt against the rats that were depriving us of our daily due. He said, 'If there were many people here now we could hunt them down [the field rats]. We would shoot them with tiny bows and arrows. Does the rat have a bow and arrow to use in its own defence? Anyhow, there are no people to join together with us and hunt for the rats' (LH, 2/3/68).

On a more complex level, the early texts concerned the nature and extent of our commitments to one another. We had arranged to pay five dollars for room and board in alternate months; every other month was 'free'. With this arrangement was coupled the expectation of gifts, according to the 'wishes of our own hearts'. Initially people were uneasy that we might neglect their gifts, or that we might go to Manila, never to return. Tukbaw confronted the dilemma directly; he explicitly told me what to give him, as in the following: 'If only you will think of what I need and help me out. If you remember that I have no blanket, that would be good. But if you do not heed what I am saying, then I will have to say that you are stingy. A relative gives gifts to a relative, and I would do so as well' (LH, 1/4/68). Aside from the request, the text reflects the more subtle problem of the meaning of being 'related'. Tukbaw and I had agreed to call one another 'brother', but whether this was a mere salutation, a bit of etiquette, or entailed other obligations and sentiments was then unclear.

Our sense of 'brotherhood' became more explicit in March of 1968 when Tukbaw and I went together to the lowlands. Our purpose was to treat his back at a hospital in Bambang, Nueva Vizcaya. His back ailment had been chronic; it often kept him awake at night and gave him debilitating shooting pains in his legs.[8] While Tukbaw underwent a brief treatment and was confined to bed, I stayed in a small room in back of the hospital. Perhaps I felt a diffuse sense of loyalty, or of what brothers should do. In any case, my having remained there was a turning point in our growing sense of mutual trust; Tukbaw had been terrified at the thought of being abandoned and left alone in the hospital. As he explained, 'I stayed awake; sleep did not come to me; sleep left me. They frightened me, and that is why I woke up. What if there might be a bad person who would kill me inside the building? But my brother was watching out for me, and that is the reason that I finally went to sleep' (LH, 3/17/68).

After my initial experiences – my lonely hike to the interior and the bombast of my deaf 'translator' – I was deeply moved to hear Tukbaw conclude his tale of the hospital by saying precisely why we had come to Ilongot country. He said, 'Now I am giving my brother words in Ilongot, for that is why he has come to Ilongot country. He wants to learn all the words in our Ilongot language; when he does that he will be very happy. Even I, his brother, will be very happy when he knows our language' (LH, 3/16/68). His narrative was transformed and began to show a complex grasp of our relationship.

The following day Tukbaw told of an uncanny dialogue he had imagined between the two of us. What I said to him (the words he put in my mouth) was as follows: 'I will not leave my brother all alone, for I am fond of him, and he helps me to learn Ilongot. Though there are many Ilongot people, I will not die because my brother will walk with me to any Ilongot place I wish to visit; he is fond of me in the way that I am fond of him. Even if our money is all gone, and finished up, we two brothers will not miss it; we will still have our health. We will find money some other time. Then we will visit whatever place he wishes, even if that place is Manila, the place he says he has never visited. And also, if there is an Ilongot place I wish to visit, my brother will listen and take me to whatever Ilongot place I have never visited' (LH, 3/17/68). What Tukbaw imagined my saying was clear and incisive; it captured the developing configuration of altruistic commitment and egoistic self-interest on both our parts.

Perhaps the confirmation of Tukbaw's brotherly expectations was that in August of that year he and Wagi went with us to Manila, much as he had me say. Our trip was the fulfillment of a promise, one never formally made but always understood to exist. From Manila Tukbaw and Wagi returned to Kakidugen; Michelle and I went to Japan for an anthropological congress. Upon our return from Japan Tukbaw's narratives took on a new shape, that of his biography.

The story of Tukbaw

One evening I asked Tukbaw to tell me the story of his life. He looked puzzled. I was perplexed; I explained it was really quite simple. He should tell me the first thing he could remember, then the second thing, and go on from there in chronological order. Since a life history would take more time than the earlier texts, I suggested that we use a tape recorder. Tukbaw leapt to and eagerly extolled the myriad virtues of the tape recorder; that machine was wiser than any of us, he said, for it spoke any language spoken to it; it made music when played to; indeed it farted if we did likewise – a strange and wonderful machine, the tape recorder. No, Tukbaw wanted me to write his story long hand as we had done before; he wanted to speak deliberately and select his words with care. He told each episode from beginning to end without interruption, in fact with almost no reaction on my part. He spoke as quickly as I was able to transcribe. After he finished I asked him to explain unfamiliar words and to clarify certain events. Usually we worked in the evenings by the light of a Coleman lantern.[9]

Birth

Tukbaw's biography began with the following: 'The place where I was born was called Nanmanukan. I no longer have any memories from the time we were at that place, for I was but a child then' (LH, 11/25/68). His narrative began with his own birth; I might begin my own life story the same way. Or perhaps I might have added that both of Tukbaw's parents had been married and widowed; each had three children by their previous marriages. Tukbaw was their first son and two daughters were to follow. Compare, however, the opening of an Ifugao life history. The Ifugao, residing to the north and west of Ilongot country in Northern Luzon, begins with the following:

"My great-grand-father was a wealthy man and gave my grand-father, his third child, a field from the acquired property. This field my father inherited. My mother ought to have inherited three fields, but really received only two."[10]

Among the Ifugaos, calculation of ancestry is meticulous through four ascending generations and is closely linked to the inheritance of wet rice fields. In contrast, the Ilongot sense of ancestry is not specified beyond the parental generation and is not linked to the transmission of property.

From breast-feeding to standing: Infancy and early childhood

Tukbaw's narrative of his infancy and early childhood is a series of trials and errors. Each stage in the mastery of his motor skills implies another stage as yet unmastered; if he sits he cannot yet stand, and if he stands he cannot yet walk. His first memory is as follows: 'The first thing that I remember was, as they told me later, that I fed at my mother's breast. I do not remember having done that, but that is what they told me' (LH, 11/25/68). His sense of growth and the passage of time is punctuated by developing motor skills; hence: (a) 'I got bigger; I crawled', (b) 'Later than that I learned how to sit up. That time went by', (c) 'I learned to stand up, but I would fall down. That time went by' (LH, 11/25/68). From the viewpoint of Eriksonian psychology Tukbaw has over-differentiated the earliest phases of his life. Where Tukbaw sees his initial development as if in four baby steps (breast) feed; crawl; sit; stand), Erikson would see two major stages: infancy, indicated by 'prone relaxation', and early childhood, indicated by 'being able to sit'.[11]

Placing Tukbaw and Erikson side by side raises the problem of whether their ideas are grounded in comparable kinds of evidence. After all, Erikson's conception is based on actual observation of children. Looking backward, Tukbaw may have placed the design of his adult sense of self on his past life progression. So in retrospect, each early phase appeared more as a prelude than an actual stage. However, Tukbaw lived in a three-family household; he lived in the same room with children at all of Erikson's life stages. Systematic or not, his observations were extensive and his sense of the pattern of Ilongot childhood was deeply informed. Consider, for instance, the following self-portrait at the age he crawled: 'I cried when I was a child; I pissed on my sleeping hide; I shat on my mother's sleeping hide – they took me away and washed me in the river because they did not like the smell of it' (LH, 11/25/68). Unlike breast-feeding, Tukbaw's description is not based on what he was later told; nor does it seem to be an actual memory. Instead, it seems to derive from daily experiences with his adopted daughter (as our field journals from the time amply attest). His narrative of these earliest phases is comparable to that of Erikson, then, in that it is based more on the observation of children around the house than on the vagaries of adult memory."

Walking: Play age

As Tukbaw learns to walk, he models himself on older children and adults. Erikson would consider this the play age, indicated by the ability 'to move independently and vigorously'.[12] Tukbaw did not, however, idealize or even describe this early period as an age of play and freedom. Instead, the closer he comes to being able to imitate his elders the more he tries and fails; he feels an increasing sense of frustration and rage. For instance, his father once made him a toy and the following ensued: "I was contrary and broke what my father had made for me. He said, 'Do you think that I am going to make you another bow and arrow for birds? Do you see? You broke the one I made for you'" (LH, 11/25/68). Or, on another occasion: 'I cried; I howled; I had a tantrum because he did not listen to me, especially when I saw that the other children were getting older' (LH, 11/25/68).

Perhaps the most representative text from this stage of Tukbaw's life is the following:

"I cried to my father; I wanted to walk along with him.
He said to me, 'Why are you crying? Do you think you can do it?'
I lied and I said, 'Yes.'
My father said, 'All right, come along then. But remember, if you cry just see who will carry you.'
I said, 'Yes, I am strong and good at walking.'
He taught me a while longer, then we really went a long ways off. You know, I went and cried.
He became afraid for me and said, 'Stay here; go back to your mother. Was there someone who told you to come along? You said that you were strong and now look at you; you are crying.'
He forced himself to carry me because I was his child." (LH, 11/25/68).

His father's advice: School age

While his earlier attempts to imitate his father were aborted, Tukbaw went on to achieve gradual success in the mastery of male labor. He himself characterizes this stage of his life as follows: 'I grew older and I was nearly a young man; I thought then about learning to work' (LH, 11/25/68). As he remembers it was his father, and only him, whom he listened to at this stage:

"When he saw I was strong enough to work, my father patiently told me how things were done. When I did not know what to do I looked at my father; he told me what I was doing wrong. He said, It is not done like this. Are you doing this the way the others do? Do not do that; I will tell you how it is done'" (LH, 11/25/68). Ilongots saw this kind of instruction as a chain of masculine knowledge linking generations of fathers and sons. Tukbaw's father, for instance, said, 'I have spoken to you with care; I told you only the things that I was told by my father' (LH, 11/25/68). The instruction of the sons by the father is comparable on this level to the acquisition of competence in male labor discussed by Erikson.[13] However, Ilongot instruction, like our own extends beyond labor.

Tukbaw's father gives the following sage and conventionalized advice on how to achieve personal integrity and social esteem: "I will tell you everything. For instance, if you visit somewhere – wherever you choose – nobody should look down on you. You should dress exactly as I do, for you are my son. If you yield to your laziness, you will not be esteemed; however, if you are energetic in your work, you will be highly thought of. People will speak of you by name; people from other places will say, 'There goes so-and-so. He never lacks possessions of any kind; he never wants for rice or anything else; he never lacks anything. Nobody in his house ever goes hungry; he never has to live in a field shelter instead of a house; he is successful in the hunt; his rice is plentiful.' All the people's hearts are boundlessly well disposed, for they speak highly of him; they say he is a good person. Whenever people gather together, they listen as he orates" (LH, 11/25/68). His father, then, speaks to everything from male subsistence labor to his concept of the good man in Ilongot society. As Tukbaw reflects on their relation of father and son he says, 'That is why I love my father; that is why I now weep when I think of my father' (LH, 11/25/68).

Grace and beauty: Adolescence, I

Like Erikson, Ilongots claim that youth is characterized by storm and stress; it is a time of high excitement. Young men are considered volatile. They gossip, sit, and travel together; they visit, court, and raid. They look wistful and dreamy-eyed; they sit with legs intertwined or they stand, embracing one another. In a society that values the studied, taut control of body movement – be it in sitting on the floor or in handing an outsider a betel quid – youths are the most agile, the most graceful, the most beautiful. Physical paragons of beauty, they have not yet acquired social graces; they are shy and easily given to blushing and bursts of giggles.

Tukbaw portrays his youth as a series of physical ordeals followed by public celebrations. These ordeals are the closest Ilongot approximation to rites of passage, yet they are only casual and loose cultural expectations. They may be undergone in any sequence; they should take place before marriage, but they also may take place afterwards. At some point, then, both sexes should have their teeth filed; only men are expected to take a head. Both events dramatize and publicly confirm the painful process of transition from youth to adulthood. What prepares youths to undergo these ordeals seems to be a diffuse sense of competence as manifest in their gradual acquisition of personal belongings. As Tukbaw said, 'What my father told me is really true. What shows that he spoke the truth is that I have possessions. When I think that over I think that I have everything a person may possess' (LH, 11/25/68). His material possessions appear to represent his emerging status as a skilled and virtuous Ilongot male.

Teeth filing: Adolescence, II

The prelude to Tukbaw's teeth filing was a major move by the members of settlement. The move was in accord with the following standard sequence: a few people went to select sites for their gardens; the men cut down the dense underbrush; they returned to cut the living branches from the trees;[14] they burned off the vegetation; they built temporary field shelters to live in during the planting season. To him, his social continuity lay less in the particular place where he resided than in the patterned sequence through which the members of his household and settlement lived their yearly round. His place may have been transient; what endured was the annual cycle of subsistence. After such a long-distance move, then, Tukbaw's father said the following to his mother: 'Kirkir, give some thought to our son. Since we have moved over here to Adiw we should have some kind of celebration; we must do it now when people will help us. If the two of us become old and grey we no longer will be able to have a celebration for our child' (LH, 11/27/68).

The date of the teeth-filing ceremony was set; it was to be for Tukbaw and a few others in their late teens. In Ilongot fashion, the women began to pound rice and the men set off on a hunt; as with any major gathering, they were collecting a store of food. Tukbaw himself anticipated an ordeal and braced himself by saying, 'Since in fact I am an unmarried young man I cannot run away from this, for all the young women are having their teeth filed as well' (LH, 11/27/68). His evident apprehension grew out of his fear of the pain: 'Alas, what if it hurts as much as the others have said when they file my teeth. Probably it will hurt for a long time; I know that immediately after my teeth have been filed off I will feel a thumping pain. Now, when I first feel the pain I will withstand it. Otherwise they would become angry with me for they have gone and made the piece of wood for me to hold between my teeth' (LH, 11/27/68). After his teeth were filed Tukbaw did not dwell on the pain but simply said that he would miss his front teeth as he ate corn and chewed on sugar cane.

Taking a head: Adolescence, III

When Tukbaw was a young boy he learned of a raid that was being planned and he begged to be taken along. As was characteristic of his choldhood, he was premature in asking; but his father capitulated, explaining as follows: 'The reason I wished to leave you behind was because you cannot stand the hunger we undergo in the forest. You deceive yourself in asking; so far in your life you have only lived around the house where you have always had a full stomach' (LH, 4/13/69).

Tukbaw insisted, saying, 'I will be able to stand it; I want to know what raiding and taking a head is all about' (LH, 4/13/69).

Tukbaw's father then began to advise his son on how to act during a raid: 'Be careful! Do not play around! Come here now and sit where I am seated. Do not go outside for I will tell you how things are done on a raid. This is not a game; nor is it like the times when we go hunting. What we call a raid is quite different. We do not talk on and on. If we speak it is in hushed tones; when you talk do not speak in a loud voice' (LH, 4/13/69).

The narrative went on to describe chants and ritual procedures in meticulous detail; it was like a story told by an attentive student bent on memorizing his lessons. It was not until the end of the text that Tukbaw explained that, after all, a victim was not found. The raid had failed, except as a boyhood learning experience.

Some years passed by, then, before Tukbaw said to his father, 'I am able to work; I am a young man. I am able to hunt alone and everything. Father, why have I remain unchanged? Why have I not yet taken a head?'

His father replied, 'Where do we have enemies to raid against?' (LH, 6/14/168).

Again, Tukbaw insisted, 'When you were a young man like myself you would not have felt that way' (LH, 6/14/68).

As it happened World War II was encroaching upon the Ilongots. At first they heard of the Japanese only through distant rumors: 'The news is that we still do not know if those they call the Japanese will reach our place. People say they are in the lowlands; as of now they have not yet marched on and come here to the hills. We hear about them all the time throughout the year: some news comes from Tege, near Kasibur; some news comes from the other side, toward Carranglan' (LH, 12/16/68). By the spring of 1945 the Japanese began to arrive; at first they came as a trickle, in small numbers and as easy prey for raiding parties. It was then that another group of Ilongots came to Tukbaw's father and said, 'Come here and join with us. The Japanese have burst upon us; they drove us from our homes and we have taken flight' (LH, 6/14/68).

A raid was promptly organized against the Japanese. His narrative then shifted in focus and events were told from the point of view of the older people. It was they, and not he in his youth, who organized, discussed, debated, and orated. Tukbaw himself faded into the background; once again he implicitly measured his person against the standard of his father and the adult world. As he said, 'The older people orated together' (LH, 6/14/68). Oratory was the Ilongot vehicle for their protracted process of reaching decisions by consensus. In the elaborate and ornate speech appropriate to the occasion his father said, 'Listen, you our fathers, to what we have to say to you. Now if it should turn out to be the case that you do in fact kill, be sure you think of my son whom it turns out has been left in your care' (LH, 6/14/68).

A member of the other group replied, 'Yes, fine, if that is all you have to ask of us. Should it indeed turn out to be the case that we in fact find a victim, no person other than Tukbaw shall sever the head' (LH, 6/14/68).

They knew full well that the fever pitch of the raid might lead to mindless action; again and again they reminded themselves not to 'try to run ahead of the person who has been entrusted to us, for that would be wrong' (LH, 6/14/68).

They then left and hiked toward the Japanese encampment. Plans for the ambush were not laid in detail until they arrived there. They agreed to lie in wait by a stream where a lone Japanese soldier had been seen to come for water in the first light of dawn; all alone, he made an easy victim.[15] The next morning as the Japanese soldier approached, "Those at the near end of the ambush said, 'Get set; there he is. He has come closer; he has arrived.' He approached those at the near end of the ambush. As I looked at the others I saw that they were tense and fierce. They were moving up and down in anticipation; they were trembling and ready" (LH, 6/14/68). They then shot and ran toward the soldier. As Tukbaw said, 'Then I really went and in an instant I grabbed that head with the short hair' (LH, 6/14/68). The soldier was beheaded: in Ilongot fashion they shouted, tossed the head in the air, and ran into the forest.

A person who had remained behind in the thickets shouted out, 'Who severed the head?'

Another replied, 'It was Tukbaw who severed the head' (LH, 6/14/68).

Someone else called out, 'That is good. What we agreed on in the discussion was carried through then' (LH, 6/14/18).

They then returned home to rest for a few days. In preparation for the collective celebration of the event they did as for any large gathering: the men went to hunt in the forest while the women stayed at home, pounding rice.

Hardship and grief: Young adulthood, I

As the troops retreating before the American infantry were driven into Ilongot country the Japanese trickle became a flood. Ilongots fled before these incursions and sought refuge in the forest; it was a time of severe hardship, of epidemics and starvation. Tukbaw recounted, for instance, the following conversation between himself and his brother-in-law:

"He said to me, 'Alas, the reason that I have come here is that we will no longer see our sisters.'

> I said to him, 'Why?'
>
> He said to me, 'We do not have any way to survive: the Japanese are upon us.'
>
> He wept then and I did likewise. The reason we wept was that we no longer had anything to eat. Many, many Japanese had come and dug up our crops; they took all our rice. They even found what we had hidden away.
>
> My mother said, 'Alas, there is no way we can survive.'
>
> Then all of the women and all of the people, everyone wept. We had nothing to eat." (LH, 12/16/68).

After this period of near starvation and refuge in the forest, they returned within the year to their former way of life. It was about two years later that Tukbaw's father became ill, perhaps as an indirect result of the time of deprivation. As he said, 'My father became ill. He was sick with his cough. He became very thin; he no longer left the house. There were three months during which he was not able to move. The illness endured and hung on. Then he died. When he died he was left in the house for one night before he was buried. The women buried him because at the time there were no men in the house; I had gone to the lowlands, to Pantabangan. I returned. Alas, I did not arrive in time to see him still alive; I arrived only in time to see the freshly turned earth where he had been buried. I then wept. Alas, I was no longer able to see him for he was gone' (LH, 1/20/69).

Courtship and marriage: Young adulthood, II

When Tukbaw felt that he had become a man he began to think about courting and wooing a woman. He said, 'We do not mindlessly go ahead unless we have first looked around. Though there may be many, many women we do not mindlessly decide whom we will court unless we are certain she will look on our attention with favor' (LH, 1/27/69). He conveyed a stiff sense of caution, hesitation, and shyness; relations between a man and a woman appeared delicate, fraught with uncertainty and blushing shame. His first step was to dress up and visit around. He said, 'Give me my kerchief, the one that my older sisters, Riqdeb and Undat, have embroidered and decorated for me. Also, give me all of my belongings: my betel pouch, and my wrapping for piper leaf, my loincloth too, my necklace too, my belt too' (LH, 1/27/69).

He made the following plan: 'What I am going to do, then, is this: I will give her a kerchief. If she does not take it, then she does not like me' (LH, 1/27/69). His confident anticipation, however, was belied by the event itself: "It turned out that I felt ashamed. I said, 'Oh my, what if they do not take it? They will make me feel ashamed.' I forced myself on and I gave it to the mother of the girl" (LH, 1/27/69). His delicate and indirect approach created a further complication: 'Even though, you know, I visit them over and over, they do not know my desires. They seem to think that I am simply visiting and they are not aware of my desires' (LH, 1/27/69).

Eventually Tukbaw married and moved into his wife's house. This marriage lasted only a short time: his wife ran off with another man who was Tukbaw's second cousin. Divorce is a rare and often traumatic event in Ilongot society; under the circumstances, this divorce was destined to prove no exception. Tukbaw was outraged and said, 'I then began to speak my mind. What I said was that I intended to behead the woman because she did a bad thing when she slept with another man. They became frightened at hearing the awful things I was saying. My heart was truly embittered; that is the reason I said that I intended to kill the woman' (LH, 2/11/69). Since the two men were related, in time Tukbaw allowed his anger to be placated by the gift of a large metal pan.

Second marriage: Young adulthood, III

Tukbaw returned to his natal home and lived there for a couple of years. As he remarked, 'I had once again become like an unmarried young man' (LH, 2/11/69). He then began to court Wagi, his present wife. At that time their situation was similar in that they had both been recently divorced. Though they were more experienced than most lovers, they still spoke to one another in private, away from other people who made them blush and feel embarrassed. He recounted one of their conversations as follows:

> "What I said when I spoke to her was, 'Now, what I have to say to you is this: I wish to ask about your true feelings, do you want me? or do you not want me?'
>
> She said, 'Be careful! Do not deceive me in this! If you are not speaking

the truth I will be outraged. Think of the man who came to me before: He has now left me.'

I said to her, 'Friend, do not think I am like him. I too was left by someone'" (LH, 2/11/69)

In time Tukbaw and Wagi were married. As he said, 'Our years together will even last longer than the time my brother, Renato, and I will see one another' (LH, 2/11/69).

Whimsy and responsibility: Adulthood

Tukbaw's narrative was directed toward his assumption of full adult status. His trials and ordeals were steps on the path toward adulthood; whenever he fell short in his youth it was because he was not yet a man. His self-portrayal as an adult ranges from the serious, responsible leader to a comic figure with a sense of self-irony. At the latter extreme was his hunt story. While most hunt stories were told with high drama and maximum suspense, Tukbaw told his with tongue in cheek, amid delighted chuckles of those in the house. Mock heroic, he was evidently amused at a series of mishaps that, nevertheless, ended in his killing a deer. It was the night after he told the tale that he repeated it as I transcribed.

The text began with him at exaggerated ease: "I arrived there. Game had dug for acorns at my hunting site. I made a protective cover so that the game would not see me. When I had finished I sat down; I then pulled off my betel pouch and began to chew betel nut. Once again, I chewed betel nut. So much time finally passed that I ran out of betel nut. After more time had passed, I said to myself, 'Is that game rustling away up there on the hill?' I looked; I stared; I peered. Then I said to myself, 'That really is game. It is coming here'" (LH, 11/25/68).

After it had been shot twice the deer turned and charged at Tukbaw: "That time it turned on me. It came toward me and I climbed a tree. I said to myself, 'It is tearing a hole in the betel pouch on my ass'" (LH, 11/25/68). He escaped from the tree, but still he wondered, "'How will I ever kill it?' Later it came to drink at the stream where I had settled to chew betel. It charged toward me. I said to myself, 'Pheh, it is still alive then. All right, then I will follow after it.' I stopped off to get a small stick of wood to make a handle for my knife. Then I began to stalk the animal; I planned to hurl my knife with a handle. It looked at me again; it then charged me, and I climbed a tree again. I said to myself, 'Pheh, when will it ever die?' It leapt up toward my ass; I moved further up the tree. Finally, it gave up" (LH, 11/25/68). In the end the deer was killed.

At the opposite extreme was Tukbaw as the influential person assuming responsibility for a collective activity. For instance, he told of a fishing trip he had initiated and organized. As people were about to leave the settlement he said, 'Now you, you who have arrived, listen to what I have to say to you; heed my words. What we need, my companions, is for you to hear my oratorical speech; then we may begin to walk. It would seem that I am responsible for this fishing trip' (LH, 5/24/68). He saw to it that each and every person was fed: 'Now you, you who have labored to kill this game, be sure you divide the catch so no person can say he did not receive an equal share; be sure that every single person receives his share' (LH, 5/24/68). He insured their safety: 'Go to those people – borrow my words – and tell them what I have said. Tell them that they should remain alert and watchful' (LH, 5/24/68). Tukbaw had become one of the older people; he was adept in the hunt, accomplished enough to afford self-irony; he was talented in oratory, persuasive enough to lead. He had become a full member of his society.

Anthropology and biography

Tukbaw's portrait of the Ilongot groping toward manhood poses problems of a more general order, concerning the form and validity of anthropological biography. In reviewing these general issues I shall discuss certain similarities and differences between the biographical portrayal I have assembled and more conventional biographical accounts in the anthropological literature. In re-telling Tukbaw's life story I have worked within the traditions of my discipline and at the same time the very nature of his story has impelled me to depart in some respects from canonical form. My biographical sketch has come to be comprised of two interwoven accounts: Tukbaw's autobiography and my own. In assessing his biography I must ask about my expectations of the life history and whether or not it corresponded to my 'brother' as I knew him.

Most studies of lives in anthropology tend toward one of two polar extremes. Some construct a life cycle for a hypothetical typical member of the culture, assuming relative homogeneity in 'primitive' societies such that one person's life is likely to resemble another's. Others record verbatim accounts of the native's autobiography as told to the anthropologist, trusting that what is lost in utility for anthropological analysis is gained in veracity. While I find neither approach wholly satisfactory, I have employed material from both in the construction of my biographical portrait.

It was perhaps Malinowski who first formulated the notion of constructing what is said to be a 'typical' member of a particular society. His intent was to depict the passage of generic persons through the life cycle as a means of understanding the institutional arrangements of a society. Representative of his theoretical stance were ethnographic descriptions such as the following:

"When a boy reaches the age of from twelve to fourteen years, and attains that physical vigor which comes with sexual maturity ... he ceases to be regarded as a child *(gwadi)*, and assumes the position of adolescent *(ulatile* or *to'ulatile)* ... He has already donned the pubic leaf for some time; now he becomes more careful in his wearing of it, and more interested in its appearance."[16]

The above passage is the ethnographer's own amalgam, based on a synthesis of extensive interviews and repeated observations. It shows how the life cycle articulates with more enduring social institutions and thereby increases the time depth and plausibility of accounts of social systems. I myself spoke of the Ilongot life cycle and used a condensed version of the 'biographical approach' to provide social context for Tukbaw's life history, much as one might provide historical background for a modern biography. Yet, however valuable as background and whatever insight it may yield for the study of social processes, Malinowski's approach remains silent about how any particular person has actually lived.

At the opposite extreme from the 'biographical approach' is the life history.[17] Among classic works of this kind are Radin's *Crashing Thunder* (1926), Dyk's *Son of Old Man Hat* (1938), and Simmon's *Sun Chief* (1942). I believe that most anthropologists have assumed that the life history is a natural and universal narrative form. If crudely unmasked it might not be too much of a parody to say that the prevailing anthropological view is as follows: place a tape-recorder in front of Mr. Non-literate Everyman and he will tell the 'real truth' about his life. Or: Oscar Lewis was a man of moderate talents and large budgets for recording instruments. At least I once thought that, if only he were asked, Tukbaw would reveal his authentic life story. I did not anticipate that he would refuse to speak into the microphone; nor did I realize, more significantly, that his autobiography would grow incrementally out of anecdotes told in large part to teach me the language. The narrative was profoundly shaped by the situation: the questions I asked, Tukbaw's intentions, our very relationship. I have attempted to convey a sense of these factors.

In asking about the validity of the life history I begin with the extent to which the narrative corresponded to Tukbaw, the person I knew and admired. His life story concerned his public self as engaged in social action, and indeed, his personal integrity and sheer force of personality led him to be esteemed and respected as a public person. From the first we had recognized these qualities in him; for instance, Michelle wrote the following in her field journal shortly after our arrival:

"*Tukbaw:* Not quick, but so sure and careful – the first time he told us a story he was all in sweat. Never follows a crowd; they follow him. And that sureness, pride, aloneness – he isn't quick or clever – is what we can see of why he's a leader; and others listen and follow. He has a broad mouth that pulls to the side as he chews, and is a handsome kind of ugly (heightened by his wall-like eye); and his smile, lips folding back and wide." (FJ, 12/11/67)

His astute human intelligence enabled him at once to be effective in his local political setting and pensive about what his culture said of the meaning of life.

I remember going on a fishing trip he organized. Initially he moved from person to person, engaging them in private conversation so he could learn their wishes and build an effective concensus on when to leave, the route to take, and where to camp. As he later told me, he became an effective orator by first learning to listen and hear what was in the 'hearts' of others. It turned out that the site had already been fished that season and the trip was a failure; in a foul mood, Tukbaw lay alone for two days beneath the boulders by the river, speaking with no one. Later, when we dove for the few fish to be found, he recited an elegant rendition of a fishing spell and then said to me, 'There may be spirits; then again there may not. How can one be certain if they cannot be seen? In any case, the spell can do no harm.' He doubted and yet was aware of forces outside himself.

He was given to reflect on the tenets given by his culture and at times formulated alternative dogmas and cosmogonies. I once asked Tukbaw, for instance, 'Why does a man take a head?' He began, 'We once were all one people, created by a single maker. Is that not true?' He went on, 'And then your ancestors went to America and mine stayed here.' I agreed. He continued, 'After a while my ancestors started to take heads and we still do today'. When asked the same question others cited youth (coming of age), mourning, and illness, as 'reasons' for taking a head; or they simply said it was an Ilongot custom. Tukbaw's relativistic account was at once original and consistent with his culture's origin myths; he was inventive and had a sense for what I might want to hear. He also speculated of his own accord on the meaning of events in the world around him.

I have already mentioned Tukbaw's insight into the reasons I had come to Ilongot country, as shown in his narrative. His insight grew from an understanding of my desire to learn the language to more complex advice on what I should say about the Ilongots on my return to the United States. He warned me that the story might well take a month to tell and suggested that I begin as follows: 'You will say that their pots hang from hooks above the fire. And when the Ilongots awaken early in the morning they huddle and warm themselves by the fire. Their houses have floors made of split rattan. The men wear little clothing; the women do not decorate themselves with jewelry and fine clothing.' Like other Ilongots, I listened when Tukbaw spoke; I felt that he was a person of fine human insight and depth.

In retrospect I find Tukbaw's narrative sensitive and moving, worthy of my 'brother'. The way in which he took his father as a cultural role, model, imitating him and receiving his instruction, is particularly compelling and revealing of his conception of the formation of character structure. Yet I must confess that at the time I held ethnocentric expectations of the life history and felt disappointed that he did not share my notion of psychological depth (not a minor blunder for an anthropologist nurtured on the doctrine of cultural relativism). Surely there was no reason to expect Tukbaw's life history to be a revelation of the dark and hidden depths of his intimate and private being: why should he construct his autobiography as a spiritual confession, or a psychological journey into his 'inner' or 'deeper' self? In fact Ilongot traditions not only failed to provide models of confessional introspection, but the culture also lacked any conventional form of autobiography. My expectations were ill-founded, at once a-historical and anti-anthropological; I supposed that every human being was endowed with a particular 'modern' conception of autobiography.

The conception of autobiography I had in mind was a rare and historically late development.[18] It seems to have grown out of those fundamental changes that took place in Western Europe during the latter part of the 16th century. Trilling, for instance, gives the following account of the relation between the historical transformations of the late 16th century and the rise of 'modern' autobiography:

"It therefore cannot surprise us that at this point in time autobiography should have taken its rise in England. The genre, as Delany observes, is by no means exclusively Protestant, but it is predominantly so ... Rousseau's *Confessions* exists, of course, in a different dimension of achievement from these first English autobiographies, but it is continuous with them ... The impulse to write autobiography may be taken as virtually definitive of the psychological changes to which the historians point."[19]

My mistake, then, was not to have been sufficiently aware that an autobiography like that of Rousseau was not only extraordinary, but was also the product of a lengthy and cumulative historical development. The kind of autobiography characterized by Trilling was neither 'always there' (as if given by nature) nor did it emerge 'full blown' (as if by divine revelation); it is crucial to bear these facts in mind in order to appreciate and grasp the nature of Tukbaw's sense of his personal development.

Throughout I have attempted to highlight Tukbaw's conception of the configuration of his life by selected juxtapositions with 'modern' notions of self, the life cycle, and autobiography. My own sense of insight and self-knowledge rests on a conception of characer structure as the precipitate of particular life experiences, and it was this psychological orientation that led me to expect introspective analysis in autobiography, with its peculiar underlying sense of self.

I now think that anthropological life histories are intimately bound to culture-specific conceptions of the person. Indeed, recent work on the ways in which notions of the person are peculiar to particular cultures suggests a corresponding variation in the form of life histories from one culture to another.[20] In this respect, the distinctiveness of Tukbaw's narrative consists in his not thinking of crucial episodes, which determine identity, or which lead to either relative 'failure' or 'success'. Rather than anguishing over the road not taken, Tukbaw depicted himself on the pre-ordained path, following in his father's footsteps.

I have attempted to convey a sense of the worth of Tukbaw's conception of his own autobiography. My initial sketch of the Ilongot life cycle, followed by a synopsis of how the life history was collected, was intended to provide a meaningful context for selective, but extensive, citation of his life history. Tukbaw, I think, saw his development in linear terms, as steps along a ladder leading to his adult, public person. His sense was that the lower rungs on the ladder had little intrinsic worth; they were 'way stations' and little more. As he climbed further toward adulthood his narrative became more protracted and his experiences appeared to take on increased worth. Structurally, his story was the opposite of the fall of man; his biography was one of ascent. If he was unworthy in early childhood, it was not because he had fallen, but rather because he had not yet risen to walk and speak in the adult arena of public life. He conceived of his lifetime as a progressive realization of his culture's design for adult manhood.

NOTES

1. Field research among the Ilongots was in part financed by an NSF pre-doctoral fellowship and NSF Research Grant GS-1509. My earliest thoughts on this paper were worked out with the students of Anthropology 57; I am indebted for comments on this paper to Jane Atkinson, Charles Frake, Bridget O'Laughlin, Benjamin Paul, Ellen Rogat, Yosal Rogat, and Michelle Rosaldo.
2. Erik H. Erikson, 'Life Cycle', in *International Encyclopedia of the Social Sciences*, ed. David L. Sills (New York: The Macmillan Company and the Free Press, 1968).
3. For futher information on the Ilongots see Michelle Rosaldo, *Context and Metaphor in Ilongot Oral Tradition* (Ph. D. dissertation, Harvard University, 1972); 'Metaphor and Folk Classification', *Southwestern Journal of Anthropology*, 28, 1 (1972), pp. 83–99; and 'I Have Nothing to Hide: The Language of Ilongot Oratory', *Language in Society*, 2 (1973), pp. 193–223. See also Renato Rosaldo, *Ilongot Society: The Social Organization of a Non-Christian Group in Northern Luzon, Philippines* (Ph. D. dissertation, Harvard University, 1970); and 'Ilongot Kin Terms: A Bilateral System of Northern Luzon, Philippines', in *Proceedings International Congress of Anthropological and Ethnological Sciences*, 1968, Tokyo and Kyoto, Vol. 2 (Tokyo: Science Council of Japan, 1970), pp. 81–84.

4. All citations from field journals are identified as 'FJ' plus the date on which the entries were recorded.
5. This man had married into the central district from a region closer to the lowlands; he later told me that in his youth he had been captured by the authorities and forced to attend school. In the central district few people had attended school at all; the southernmost settlement of the district was a mission station, and our field station was the northernmost settlement of the district. The settlement I had hiked to was south of our field station; neither settlement had any 'believers' and they were relatively uninfluenced by the missionary presence.
6. Tukbaw echoed his statement about Wagi in speaking about the illness of his adopted daughter. He said, 'I will stop off to get the kind of medicine that I know, different kinds of herbs. And I will ask the Americans for medicine. If she does not get better, then that is truly the course her life has to take. But, if she truly has life within her, she will become well in a short time, even with only a little medicine. Really, when I think and think about her, tears well up in my eyes' (LH, 1/4/68). Note that all citations from Tukbaw's narratives are indicated by 'LH' (life history) plus the date on which the narrative was given.
7. Cifford Geertz, 'Deep Play: Notes on the Balinese Cockfight', *Daedalus* (Winter, 1971), pp. 1–37.
8. Unfortunately, the ailment was neither diagnosed nor treated in a way that provided more than temporary relief. References to his infirmity appear throughout the life history. For instance, his father-in-law says, 'We will leave today. We will take Tukbaw with us, and we will leave him in PeNegyaben for his legs hurt' (LH, 1/16/69).
9. The manuscript of Tukbaw's narratives runs to about 160 typewritten pages in the Ilongot transcription, and more than that in the English translation.
10. Roy F. Barton, *Autobiographies of Three Pagans in the Philippines* (New York: University Books, 1963), p. 25.
11. Erik H. Erikson, *Identity and the Life Cycle* (New York: International Universities Press, 1959), pp. 75–76.
12. *Ibid.*, p. 76.
13. *Ibid.*, p. 83.
14. Ilongots cut the living branches from the trees to allow sunlight to reach the rice plants on the ground and at the same time to avoid cluttering their flat gardens with fallen trees.
15. Ilongots try to kill without being killed themselves; they have no notion that death in combat is heroic. As they explain, they cannot conceive of asking their close kin and companions to put their lives in danger. During World War II Ilongots saw American officers ordering their men to move forward into open combat: this was beyond their moral comprehension.
16. Bronisław Malinowski, *The Sexual Life of Savages* (London: George Rutledge & Sons, 1929), pp. 61–62.
17. See Clyde Kluckhohn, 'The Personal Document in Anthropological Science', in *The Use of Personal Documents in History, Anthropology, and Sociology*, ed. Louis Gott-

schalk, Clyde Kluckhohn, and Robert Angell (New York: Social Science Research Council, Bulletin 53, 1945), pp. 78–173, and Lewis L. Langness, *The Life History in Anthropological Science* (New York: Holt, Rinehart and Winston, 1965).

18. The historical origins of Western autobiography and biography seem to date from Greece in the first part of the fifth century B. C. Arnaldo Momigliano characterizes early exploratory writings on the life career in this manner: 'The biographic and autobiographic experiments of the fourth century see a man in relation to his profession, to his political community, to his school; they are portraits of public figures, not of private lives.' The sense of biography held by the early Greeks, it should be noted, resembles that of Tukbaw. See *The Development of Greek Biography* (Cambridge: Harvard University Press, 1971), p. 48.
19. Lionel Trilling, *Sincerity and Authenticity* (Cambridge: Harvard University Press, 1971), pp. 23–24.
20. E.g., Clifford Geertz, *Person, Time, and Conduct in Bali: An Essay in Cultural Analysis*, Cultural Report Series, No. 14 (Southeast Asia Studies: Yale University, 1966).

VICTOR TURNER

6

Religious Paradigms and Political Action:

The Murder in the Cathedral of Thomas Becket

It has been said that almost every schoolchild in England knows the main outlines of the story of Thomas Becket, Archbishop of Canterbury, who was murdered in his cathedral on December 29, 1170, by four knights of King Henry II, the first royal Plantagenet. I beg leave to doubt the literality of this statement after having heard in the Canterbury cloisters last summer a mother tell her ten year-old daughter that Becket was a 'bishop whose 'ead was cut off by old 'Enery the Heigth.' Nevertheless, the tale and the myth of Becket have survived eight centuries and can still arouse fierce partisanship. For there was a clash of wills between monarch and prelate which both masked and milked a fatal affinity of temperament; this was caught up into an accelerating cleavage between Church and State and compounded by the first serious stirrings of nationalist sentiment in England and France. In the complex social field within which both arch-antagonists operated there were many other opposed and developing social trends which reinforced their personal quarrel: the rift between urban and rural social sub-systems, between country aristocracy and town burghers, between feudal relations and market relations; the still unresolved ethnic tension between Norman conquerors and Anglo-Saxon indigenes; the incipient struggle for secular power between the throne and the Barony; the opposition between secular and regular clergy – and other conflicts and struggles which we will encounter in the course of this analysis. These and other social conflicts drew cultural support from divergent theories: one school of thought held that a papal monarchy should direct all the spiritual and temporal affairs of Christendom, another that society ought to be dualistically organized into separate but equal spheres of state and church; then there was the polarization, memorably discussed by Fritz Kern,[1] between the complex of rights summarized under 'the divine right of kings' and the right of resistance to the arbitrary use of royal power, a right which conflated ancient Germanic tribal custom and the Christian tenet that it is one's bounden duty to resist tyrants as expressed in Acts, V: 29, 'We ought to obey God rather than men'. Quite early, too, under the influence of the German monk, Manegold of Lautenback, who wrote in the late eleventh century, the doctrine of popular sovereignty and the vassal's right of resistance in face of the lord's breach of fidelity began to gain ground. In the legal sphere, the burgeoning of studies in canon law, especially at the University of Bologna where the great Gratian and Pope Alexander III (before his elevation to the Papacy) taught and Becket for a while studied, exacerbated the struggle between ecclesiastical and royal courts for jurisdiction over several important categories of offices and for the right to indict and punish clerics who had committed serious crimes. Within the Catholic Church the formal structuring implied by the ferment in canon law was countered to some extent by a renewed stress on the contemplative life by some Cluniac and most Cistercian religious houses. Yet the very success of reformed monasticism increased the operative scope of canon law.

All these conflicts and more besides were caught up into the Becket affair. It is here, I think, that the 'social drama' approach I have advocated in other connections can be shown to be a useful tool for distinguishing between the roles and estimating the significance of such general propensities in specific situations. Indeed, the Becket case lends itself almost too readily to treatment by the 'social dramatistic' technique. Becket's public life was nothing if not dramatic, full of strong situations. This has been gratefully recognized by generations of playwrights, from Will Mountfort and John Bancroft who, in the late seventeenth century wrote a tedious anticlerical play 'Henry the Second' (to which John Dryden contributed a 'hackneyed' prologue) through Lord Tennyson (who in his play *Becket* tut-tutted over Henry's sex life) to such modern celebrities as T. S. Eliot, Christopher Fry, and Jean Anouilh.[2] Novelists have borrowed their plot, lines from Becket's story: for instance, Shelley Mydans' *Thomas* and Alfred Duggan's *My Life for My Sheep*.[3] Historians, too, have seized upon the dramatic aspect of the confrontation between archbishop and king in order to take vehement sides. In the eighteenth century George Lord Lyttleton made a lengthy case for Henry – in three massive volumes – which elicited a slimmer but vigorous ripost in one volume from the Reverend Joseph Berington, who implied that the noble lord falsified his case 'from the prejudications of low bigotry, from dislike of characters, or from a paltry policy'.[4] In the nineteenth century, though respect for the scientific method had grown, nationalist fervor tinctured interpretation and the age of Darwin revived ancient conflicts between Church and State exacerbated by evolutionary theory and in the heat of evolutionist controversy. Thus the Reverend Henry Hart Milman writes of 'the horror of Becket's murder' running 'throughout Christendom' and of 'the Passion of the Martyr St. Thomas', while the Reverend James C. Robertson, the equally clerical but 'anti-Romanist' editor of the major work of historical scholarship, the *Materials for the History of Thomas Becket* (1875) which comprise seven volumes of the Pipe Rolls series, concludes that Becket's program might have made England 'the most priest-ridden and debased of modern countries' rather than 'the freest', manifesting 'a spirit which would aim at the establishment of priestly tyranny and injustice'.[5] The famous legal historians Frederick Pollock and Frederic William Maitland seem to favor Henry who, they say, 'handed down to his successors a larger body of purely temporal justice than was to be found elsewhere'.[6] In fact, Winston Churchill wrote of him that he 'laid the foundations of the English Common Law, upon which succeeding generations would build. Changes in the design would arise, but its main outlines would not be altered.'[7] In the twentieth century controversy has been less acrid and attempts have been made to strike a balance between the conflicting claims of Thomas and Henry, especially in the work of Mme. Raymonde Foreville, author of *Church and State in England under Henry II Plantagenet*, and the Benedictine monk Dom David Knowles, eminent Cambridge University historian of the high Middle Ages, who wrote *The Episcopal Colleagues of Archbishop Thomas Becket* and *Thomas Becket*. Both these modern scholars, however, fully admit the dramatic quality of the main events.[8]

Paul Alonzo Brown *(The Development of the Legend of Thomas Becket)* has asserted that there are 'three Beckets: the Becket of History, the Becket of Legend, and the Becket of Literature', which can be readily isolated though they overlap.[9] I will argue that these three are interrelated in a symbolic field which contains a set of paradigms or models for behavior drawn from the Christian religious tradition. My theoretical concern is not quite that of the historians, though I rely upon their findings, nor is it that of the constitutional historians, though I am indebted to their conclusions. Nor am I operating as a structural anthropologist who might fruitfully analyse the variation of the original Becket legend – as distinct from the abundantly documented Becket history – in terms of mythemic analysis. Since I am a social anthropologist with a long-term bias towards the analysis of micro-events I shall use the social dramatistic framework that I developed first in the study of small-scale Central African village societies and have later begun to apply to the local feuds of medieval Iceland. But I shall use this framework primarily as a device for isolating from the sequence of events dominated by the Becket-Henry confrontation those which unambiguously evince the presence and activity of certain consciously recognized (though not consciously grasped) cultural models in the heads of the main actors which I shall call root-paradigms. These have reference not only to the current state of social relationships existing or developing between actors, but also to the cultural goals, means, ideas, outlooks, currents of thought, patterns of belief, etc., which enter into those relationships, interpret them and incline them to alliance or divisiveness. These root-paradigms are not systems of univocal concepts, logically arrayed; they are not, so to speak, precision tools of thought. Nor are they stereotyped guidelines for ethical, esthetic, or conventional action. Indeed, they go beyond the cognitive and even the moral to the existential domain, and in so doing become clothed with allusiveness, implicitness, and metaphor – for in the stress of vital action, firm definitional outlines became blurred by the encounter of emotionally charged wills. Paradigms of this fundamental sort reach down to irreducible life-stances of individuals, passing beneath conscious prehension to a fiduciary hold on what they sense to be axiomatic values, matters literally of life or death. Root-paradigms emerge in life-crises, whether of groups or individuals, whether institutionalized or compelled by unforeseen events. One cannot then escape their presence or their consequences. I am going to argue that Thomas Becket came more and more fully under the sway of a linked set of such root-paradigms as his relationship with Henry moved from the private to the public sphere, from amity to conflict, and as his attitude shifted from self-interest to self-sacrifice on behalf of a system of religious beliefs and practices, which itself concealed, even from Becket, intuition of the central good of human 'communitas'.

Part of any investigation is the investigator – his motives and circumstances. How and why did I come to select the Becket-Henry drama for detailed attention? I will spare the reader a recital of my personal beliefs and prejudices – these in any case emerge clearly enough in my work as in everyone else's, and are as contradictory as anyone else's who eschews the systematic creation of a *Weltanschauung* as self defence or apologia. The immediate cause of my interest in Becket was an interest in comparative study of pilgrimage systems. This itself was an outgrowth of my investigation of the relations between 'liminality', 'communitas', and 'social structure' in *The Ritual Process*.[10] Pilgrimages, so it seemed to me, were, to put it crudely in social science jargon, 'functional equivalents', in complex cultures dominated by the major historical religions, partly of *rites de passage* and partly of 'rituals of affliction' (rites to cure illness or dispel misfortune) in preliterate, small-scale societies. Since historical religions are ideally 'optative' or 'voluntaristic' in character, as opposed to the 'ascribed' character of 'tribal' religions, and since their ultimate goal is 'salvation', or liberation from the ills of the sensorily perceived social and natural worlds, people *choose* to go on pilgrimages rather than have to undergo initiation, and, furthermore, go for the good of their 'souls' rather than for the health of their bodies. Nevertheless, there remains a strong component of obligatoriness, of the *duty* to go on pilgrimage, in cultures where pilgrimage systems are strongly developed – particularly, of course, in Islam and in Judaism before the destruction of the temple, while many of the faithful of most major religions hope like tribesmen to be cured of the ills or difficulties of body, mind, or soul whether by miraculous power or better morale, by making the penitential journey to some pilgrim shrine. Usually such shrines are 'marginal' or 'liminal' to the major centers of political or ecclesiastical organization, and usually, too, those who have recorded their experiences as pilgrims speak glowingly of what I would summarize as the 'communitas' relationship which develops between travellers to and worshippers at the shrines.

My wife and I decided that we should visit some shrines where pilgrimages were still 'going concerns', to see what their symbolism was and what went on at them. We travelled to Mexico, Ireland, and England, and collected a fair quantity of observational and documentary data at each site studied. Since most pilgrimages are long-established and we wished to study their vicissitudes over time, we were compelled to look at written historical records where these were available and to record oral traditions wherever we could obtain them. Among other fascinating places we came across Canterbury, once one of the four great pilgrim centers of Christendom – along with the Holy Sepulcher at Jerusalem, the apostolic churches in Rome and the great shrine of St. James at Compostella in northwestern Spain. Even today the absence of a shrine to St. Thomas seems to be more potent than the presence of shrines in many other places in drawing hundreds of thousands of visitors – and many of them are *de facto* pilgrims — from all over Europe and, indeed, from America, Asia and Australia as the Canterbury Cathedral Visitors' Book attests. Henry VIII had the medieval shrine destroyed and Thomas' bones scattered – not burnt as one legend has it. Now only a plaque and a circle on the paving stones commemorate the site and fact of the murder, but incessantly throughout the summer months parties of visitors speaking all the tongues of Europe come with their guides to this spot and listen to the grim, heroic story of Thomas' end – with its final question unanswered: did he stage-manage his death through pride or accept it with Christian resignation and humility? Did he seek glory or die for a principle? Did Thomas succumb, as T. S. Eliot makes him fear he might succumb, to the 'last temptation'? 'The last temptation is the greatest treason: To do the right deed for the wrong reason.'

It was not merely the superabundance of available data brought to our attention in the immediate aftermath of the 1970 commemoration of the eighth centenary of the death of St. Thomas Becket' which made me focus especially closely on the career of the Archbishop who had once been Chancellor of the king's domains. By a strange, felicitous fluke the English Thomas story converged with my other main theoretical preoccupation at the time – the study of Icelandic sagas (and Icelandic history generally) as source materials for a comparative study of processual structures. I am interested in the formal aspects of temporality in human social life – how certain events seem to develop along patterned lines so that it is possible to elicit a consecutive series of recognizable phases from the welter of data. It is not only institutionalized processes, such as judicial and ritual processes, that have diachronic form or structure, but also ungoverned events, such as political or religious movements. But where processes are unconditioned, undetermined or unchannelled by explicit customs and rules, my hypothesis would be that the main actors are nevertheless guided by subjective paradigms – which may derive from beyond the mainstream of sociocultural process with its ensocializing devices such as education and imitation of action models in stereotyped situations. Such paradigms affect the form, timing and style of the behavior of those who bear them. Actors who are thus guided produce in their interaction behavior and generate social events which are non-random, but, on the contrary, structured to a degree that may in some cultures provoke the notion of fate or destiny to account for the experienced regulation of human social affairs. Greek tragedy and Icelandic saga are genres that recognize this implicit paradigmatic control of human affairs in public arenas, where behavior which appears to be freely chosen, resolves at length into a total pattern. One has, of course, to account for the almost 'instinctual' manner in which root-paradigms are accepted by the individual and their social consequences are fatalistically regarded – both in the mirror of literature and art and on the stage of history – by the masses. Here I would propose an as yet untested hypothesis: that in man, as in other living species, genotypical goals prevail over phenotypical interests, the general good over the individual welfare – that is, in the relatively rare instances in which there is direct confrontation between the two drives. Almost always there is room for compromise and maneuver. Root-paradigms are the cultural transliterations of genetic codes – they represent that in the human individual as a cultural entity which the DNA and RNA codes represent in him as a biological entity, the species-life raised to the more complex and symbolic organizational level of culture. Furthermore, in so far as the root-paradigms are religious in type they entail some aspect of self-sacrifice as an evident sign of the ultimate predominance of group survival over individual survival. Here, too, I would suspect a connection between root-paradigms and the experience of communitas, an 'essential we' relationship (to quote Buber) which is at the same time a generic human bond underlying or transcending all particular cultural definitions and normative orderings of social ties. The root-paradigm – as distinct from what is probably in each culture a wide range of quotidian or situational 'models for' behavior under the sign of self or factional interest – is probably concerned with fundamental assumptions underlying the human societal bond with preconditions of communitas. Perhaps the best expression of the central Christian root-paradigm is not in the mythic or parabolic forms invoked, as we shall see, explicitly by Becket, but William Blake's passage on the offering up of self as a precondition of 'conversing as Man with Man in Ages of Eternity' in Chapter XLII of his Jerusalem. In it this heretical anti-Churchman compresses the *Via crucis* theme into six lines:

"Jesus said: 'Wouldest thou love one who never died
For thee? Or ever die for one who had not died for thee?
And if God dieth not for Man, and giveth not himself
Eternally for Man, Man could not exist; for Man is Love
As God is Love; every kindness to another is a little Death
In the Divine Image, nor can Man exist but by Brotherhood."

Here the notion of 'Love', as the basal societal bond, is related to the notion of both real and symbolic 'death' – to be in a true social relation to another human being one must die to one's 'selfhood', a term which for Blake is *inter alia* a shorthand for the ambitious, competitive world of social status and role-playing.

I mention all this because I came across an Icelandic saga in the traditional fatalistic vein on the life and death of Thomas Becket which underlined the issues I have just been raising. This was Thomas Saga Erkibyskups, meticulously edited by Eiríkr Magnūsson and published in two volumes of the great 'Rolls Series' in 1875 and 1883 as part of the *Materials for the History of Thomas Becket*, Archbishop of Canterbury, edited as I said earlier, by the Reverend James C. Robertson.[11] Thus pilgrimage, history, myth, and saga met at last, and compelled me to examine the Becket affair. In it one could see a pilgrimage system in its very genesis. The saga style made evident to me the fatalistic quality of Becket's relationship to Henry, its social historical dimension, so to speak, while the other histories dwelt in the main on Becket's freely making the choices which placed him in his final predicament. I will draw on the saga and on the contemporary historical sources, such as William of Canterbury, Edward Grim, Guernes de Pont-Sainte-Maxence, William Fitzstephen, John of Salisbury, and others, to present in social drama form certain crucial episodes in Becket's career. I want particularly to trace in these the development of Becket's commitment to the Christian root-paradigm of martyrdom, of underlining the ultimate value of a cause by laying down one's life for it.

It should be stressed, however, that every sacrifice requires not only a victim – in this case a self-chosen victim – but also a sacrificer. That is, we are always dealing not with solitary individuals but with systems of social relations – we have drama, not merely soliloquy. In the case considered the sacrificer was Henry, who, whether he was directly responsible for the murder or not (and I am inclined to think his grief on first hearing of it was true grief, not just for public effect), at any rate in certain crucial moments almost egged Thomas on to commit himself to the martyr's path. There is constantly a curious complicity between the two, with Henry daring Thomas to make good his asseverations about the honor of the Church. Thomas was at the beginning only reluctantly holy. This comes through clearly in a tale cited by William Fitzstephen, Thomas' friend and one of his best biographers, which, whether myth or truth, rings precisely true to the characters of the great antagonists. It relates of the grand time of their friendship when Thomas was the king's chancellor, and when, as Fitzstephen writes,

"The king and he would play together like boys of the same age: in hall, in church they sat together, or rode out. One day they were riding together in the streets of London; the winter was severe: the king saw an old man coming, poor, in thin and ragged garb, and he said to the chancellor: 'Do you see him?' 'I see', said the chancellor. The king: 'How poor he is, how feeble, how scantily clad. Would it not be great charity to give him a thick, warm cloak?' The chancellor: 'Great indeed; and, my king, you ought to have a mind and an eye to it.' Meanwhile the poor man came up; the king stopped and the chancellor with him. The king pleasantly accosted him and asked if he would have a good cloak. The poor man, who knew them not, thought that this was a jest, not in earnest. The king to the chancellor: '*You* shall do this great charity', and laying hands on his hood he tried to pull off the cape – a new and very good one of scarlet and grey – which the chancellor wore, and which he strove to retain. Then was there great commotion and noise, and the knights and nobles in their train hurried up wondering what might be the cause of so sudden a strife; no one could tell; both were engaged with their hands and more than once seemed likely to fall off their horses. At last the chancellor, long reluctant, allowed the king to win, to pull of his cape and give it to the poor man. Then first the king told the story to his attendants; great was the laughter of all; some offered their capes and cloaks to the chancellor. And the poor old man went off with the chancellor's cape, unexpectedly happy, and rich beyond expectation, and giving thanks to God'."[12]

In this remarkable scene Henry bullies Becket into being good. The style is friendly horseplay, but in it we detect, having historical hindsight, the overbearing, overweening, Angevin temperament that would soon be so menacing for Becket. We can also see in this episode the beginning of Becket's obstinate resistance, and deduce from the quick generosity of the knights and nobles with their offer of cloaks to replace the grudging alms, the strange charm which Becket could exert on members of his own circle. Perhaps, too, we have here a dim foreshadowing, in the poor man's response, of Becket's posthumous miraculous powers.

From this scene of sunlight with a faint shadow I wish to pass to the dark scenario of the Council of Northampton where the wills of Thomas and Henry revealed themselves as implacably opposed, and the causes they stood for seemed just as irreconcilable. I shall discuss this meeting much as I would describe and analyse a major political or jural event in a preliterate society, since the main actors are hardly more in number than those of an African village council, their confrontations are likewise face to face, and their rhetoric and gestures have much in common with those of tribal law men. In brief, I shall study Northampton as a social drama and submit it to 'situational analysis'. But there is one major difference between the two cases. The meeting at Northampton was not concerned with resolving the problems of a handful of villages or even of a whole chiefdom. Within it coiled the tensions of the changing structure of Europe and the form and content of its discourse were drawn from many centuries of literate debate. Although the actors were few, their interactions lend themselves only superficially to small group analysis, for each man there was the representative of many persons, relationships, corporate interests and institutional aims. Each was the incumbent of an office, some of several offices. Such representative figures have carefully to weigh their words, to ponder courses of action, and sometimes to prefer judicious silence to the best chosen words. It is all the more remarkable, therefore, to observe at Northampton how flushed and intemperate great prelates and magnates became, and how overtly dramatic, even melodramatic, grew their deeds. All this clearly betrays the presence of naked confrontation and the absence of adequate means of mediation. It is in this desperate impasse that the root-paradigm we shall discuss came to claim Becket's full attention and to dominate his development from that time forth. When a great man's back is against the wall, he seizes roots, not straws. Yet if we are to sense and weigh what Becket thought and did we must place his actions in their full dynamic context (see *Choronology*, at the end of this article).

The Council of Northampton was at once the climax of a long bout or battle of principles between Becket and Henry and the beginning of a new struggle. Most of us know how Henry, to gain control of church as well as state, had tempted Becket with the double mandate of chancellorship and the see of Canterbury, supreme office of the Catholic Church in England. The king wanted his friend to become the instrument of his will, and through him to make the realm of England obedient to 'government by idea', Henry's idea – one which could not tolerate an 'ungoverned space', such as was represented by the independent sphere of the Church. Becket's insistence on resigning from the post of chancellor, allegedly on the scruple of potential conflict of interests, can now be seen as his first blow for the independence of most ecclesiastical matters from royal control. His resignation flouted the king's wishes and demonstrated his commitment to his new ecclesiastical status which was at the opposite pole to that of monarchy. Becket then threw himself into the practice of religious austerity, further signalizing his separation from the past, when he had been known throughout Europe for the sumptuousness and magnificence of his style of living. To an anthropologist the whole extraordinary business of Becket's life and death after his installation takes on the stylized character of an initiation ceremony – an initiation into the status of martyr. It will become clear that he was propelled along this path or passage by certain images and ideas (which in their patterning made up a paradigm). This pattern, stamped on the real events of history by a primary process at first unpent by royal edict but afterwards governed by its own inner law, took the cultural shape of the martyr's way and brought ever more clearly before Becket's consciousness the glorious goal of the martyr's crown, to be won by a painful death rather than by a meritorious life. It must have been clear to Thomas from the first that he could not make Henry come to Canterbury as Pope Gregory VII, the redoubtable former monk Hildebrand, had compelled the Emperor Henry IV to 'come to Canossa'. William the Conqueror had given the English monarchy too strong a position *vis-à-vis* the English church for that. Force could not conquer the Angevin. Besides, Becket somehow wished to win Henry's soul rather than to destroy him. It is significant that despite his occasional threats to do so Thomas never actually used the ultimate thunders of the church against Henry and England, i.e., excommunication and interdiction. If he would win he must win by antiforce or by demonstrating to the world that if Henry used force against him, such force would be unjust. The paradigm of martyrdom nerved him to dare Henry and the secular power *à l'outrance*.

But some time was left to Thomas yet. Shortly after he became archbishop, Becket identified himself with the church and demanded that certain lands within his diocese be taken from their lay incumbents and restored to their former control by the church. Then he claimed all clerical patronage within his diocese, thus directly challenging a royal prerogative. But what angered Henry most was Becket's insistence that 'criminous clerks' should be tried and punished by ecclesiastical courts under canon law, not civil law. This ran counter to the course being followed by Henry and his competent advisers – including Thomas himself before his installation – of bringing the entire legal system under centralized royal control and devising a system of justice that would be both profitable for Henry and equitable for all. If 'clerks', that is, persons in holy orders of however low a degree, were to be immune from the king's writ, then clearly an absolute limit symbolized by 'the benefit of clergy', had been set to the state's authority. It has, of course, been cogently argued by Lord Acton that one important source of English liberties lay precisely in this legal duality. People could play one set of lawmen against the other. But Henry, though quite disorganized in his personal habits, was always seeking to impose the maximum of discipline and order on others. He could not do this readily if an important area of social control fell outside the scope of his authority. What enraged him was that his friend Thomas, to whom he had entrusted the task of subduing the church to the monarchy, should betray him by declaring that there were many things that might not be rendered unto Caesar. I propose to pass over the complicated tale of the Councils of Westminster (October 2, 1163) and Clarendon (January 14, 1164), in which the openly hostile Henry tried to impose his will on Thomas. Generally, he had his way and it was the archbishop who made the concessions. However, it was Henry's determination to secure the royal prerogative once and for all, and with it, it would seem, Becket's ruin and humiliation as churchman and as man, that drove him on to summon a royal council at Northampton on October 6, 1164.

Something should first be said, however, about the Constitutions of Clarendon which Henry had forced the bench of English bishops to accept at the celebrated meeting there. For it is the Constitutions which set the

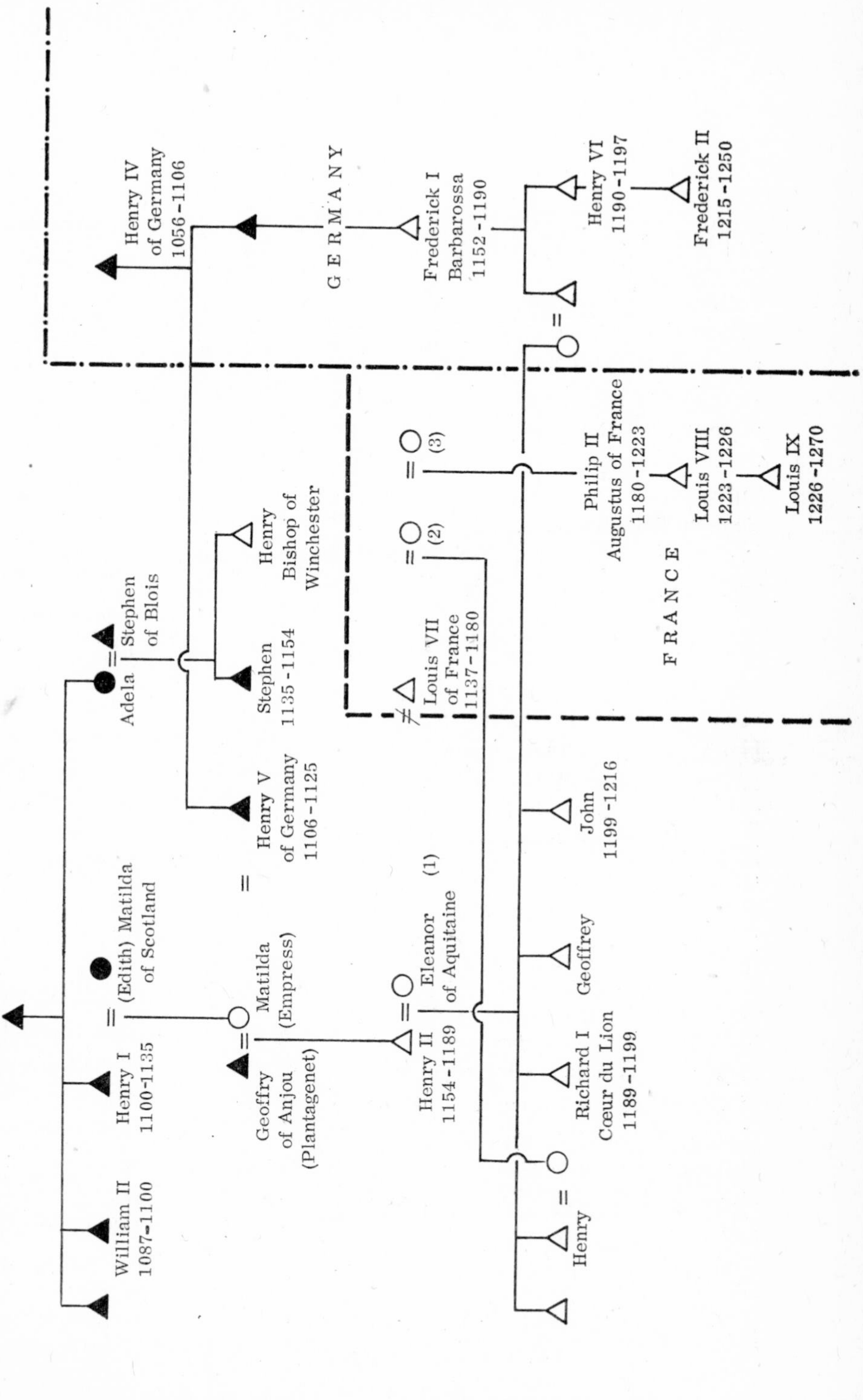

1066 -1087
William II 1087-1100
Henry I 1100-1135
(Edith) Matilda of Scotland
Adela
Stephen of Blois
Henry IV of Germany 1056-1106
Geoffry of Anjou (Plantagenet)
Matilda (Empress)
Henry V of Germany 1106-1125
Stephen 1135-1154
Henry Bishop of Winchester
G E R M A N Y
Henry II 1154-1189
Eleanor of Aquitaine
(1)
Louis VII of France 1137-1180
(2)
(3)
Frederick I Barbarossa 1152-1190
Henry
Richard I Cœur du Lion 1189-1199
Geoffrey
John 1199-1216
Philip II Augustus of France 1180-1223
Henry VI 1190-1197
F R A N C E
Louis VIII 1223-1226
Louis IX 1226-1270
Frederick II 1215-1250

terms of the Northampton confrontation. Becket himself had then quailed and faltered and sought to appease the king. He had not reckoned on Henry's insistence on demanding a solemn assent to a *written* list of propositions; he had thought that a verbal assurance, a gentleman's agreement, would have sufficed, and that subsequent difficulties could have been smoothed away by tact and turning a blind eye, the ancient English 'genius for compromise'. What, then, were these propositions? The Constitutions were given under sixteen headings. David Knowles holds that six of them, at least, 'traversed the rights of the church'.[13] Henry justified the Constitutions by claiming that they were based on the customs of fifty years earlier, in the reign of his maternal grandfather Henry I. Regal custom clashed with canon law. The controversial clauses included the right of the king's justice to summon criminous clerks to come before the king's court 'to answer there concerning matters which shall seem to the king's court to be answerable there' (Clause III). They also declared that 'it is not lawful for archbishops, bishops and beneficed clergy to depart from the kingdom without the lord king's leave' (IV). Again, immunity was conferred against excommunication or interdiction laid by a senior cleric on all who held land primarily from the king and on all officers of his demesne (VII). The king's court was also declared the final court of appeal; indeed 'if the archbishop should fail to do justice, the case must be finally brought to the lord king' (VIII) This article was aimed at preventing appeals to Rome, just as churchmen had been forbidden by Clause IV to visit the Pope without royal permission. Finally, by Clause XII, the king claimed the right to summon the clergy to his own chapel to elect an archbishop or bishop, who would then have to 'do homage and fealty to the lord king as his liege lord for his life and limbs and earthly honour, saving his order, before he is consecrated'. This clause, of course, referred directly to the investiture controversy which divided church and state throughout Europe at the time. Under canon law the church claimed that election should be freely made by 'canonical electors, viz., the clergy of the church with local notabilities, monastic and lay'.[14] Emperors and kings had claimed that the choice be made by the Suzerain himself – as indeed, William the Conqueror had insisted on doing a century earlier – unopposed then by Lanfranc his Archbishop. Clause XVI hit the common people hard – it declared that sons of villeins ought not to be ordained without the consent of the lord on whose lands they were known to have been born. This aimed to strangle one of the few possibilities of upward mobility accessible to the commonality at the time – ascent through ordination and education up the ecclesiastical ladder. Henry aimed to generalize the principles of feudal monarchy throughout all social domains, and decree one law for the lion and the ox.

I have barely touched on the Constitutions and the problems they raise, but the drift is clear. They represent Henry's most determined attempt to mobilize the sanctions of organized and legitimate force behind the protonationalist monarchy and behind the politico-economic structures of feudalism which with all their internal contradictions represent a principle opposed to the internationalism, learning and potential social mobility at that point in history represented by the Catholic Church, in the *fine fleur* of the Cluniac reform, and before the emergent arrogance of Caesaropapalism. Becket, as I said, dismayed the other bishops by giving way, without consulting them, to Henry's demands. As Knowles points out, they had 'stood firm even in the face of the fury of the king – as is the fury roaring of a lion, so is the fury of a king – and the threats of the barons, who at one point broke in upon the bishops threatening violence'.[15] Thus, as Becket's implacable rival, Gilbert Foliot, Bishop of London, was later to point out, Becket's 'sudden tack off course' seemed like defection from the church's cause – an outcome the bishops had always feared from the former King's Chancellor and henchman. For most of the bishops Becket was always an outsider-base-born, never a monk, a wordly sophisticated administrator. It is clear that Becket bitterly repented of his wavering. When he realized that the Constitutions were to be written down, he refused to sign the roll, declaring, 'No seal of mine shall ever be fixed to Constitutions such as these.' Shortly afterwards, in dejection he wrote to Pope Alexander III, begging absolution for his sin of disloyalty. He suspended himself from the service of the altar for the symbolic forty days, until the rescript came to him from the Pope at Sens in France where the Pope himself was then dwelling in exile, a refugee under the protection of the pious French monarch Louis VII from the fury of the Emperor Frederick Barbarossa, who spoke of Rome as his fief and the Pope as his vassal, and who recognized a schismatic anti-pope. Alexander in his usual agony of diplomatic tact reproved Becket for his ostentatious austerities and counselled him not to provoke Henry further. Much of the papacy's financial support came from Henry's treasury, and Alexander could not afford to affront the English monarch too blatantly. But Becket was by now becoming increasingly committed to a policy of steady opposition to Henry's purposes, and this commitment was strengthened by the Pope's condemnation of ten of the Clarendon clauses. Alexander could hardly avoid doing this in view of their assault on ecclesiastical rights. Becket then made two attempts to cross the Channel – both foiled – to confess his fault in person to the Pope: in these he was, of course, contravening the fourth Clarendon clause forbidding clerics to depart from the kingdom without the royal permission. Thomas made one last effort at reconciliation when he waited on Henry at Woodstock. But his former friend merely asked with reference to his abortive flights: 'Do you find my kingdom not big enough for both of us?' The stage was now set for the decisive meeting at Northampton.

In previous studies I have used the notion of 'social drama' as a device for describing and analysing episodes that manifest social conflict. At its simplest, the drama consists of a four-stage model, proceeding from breach of some relationship regarded as crucial in the relevant social group, which provides not only its setting but many of its goals, through a phase of rapidly mounting crisis in the direction of the group's major dichotomous cleavage, to the application of legal or ritual means of redress or reconciliation between the conflicting parties which compose the action-set. The final stage is either the public and symbolic expression of reconciliation or else of irremediable schism. The first stage is often signalized by the overt, public breach of some norm or rule governing the key relationship which has been transformed from amity to opposition. Now there are a number of variations possible with regard to the sequence of the phases and to the weight accorded to them. Again, when there is a rapid sequence of social dramas it is hard to tell whether what one is observing at a given moment in the series is breach, crisis (when sides are being taken, coalitions formed and fissures spread and deepened through a number of coordinated and contiguous relationships between persons and groups) or the application of redressive machinery. In the case of the royal council at Northampton, for example, the action begins when Henry *alleges* that Thomas has broken the law – a breach, incidentally of a constitution issued by the king since Clarendon and bearing the Clarendon stamp. Henry wishes to begin the drama at the redressive stage, and with himself as judge. One cannot decide whether it is Henry who has broken the tacit norm or at least gentleman's agreement between king and archibshop not to meddle in one another's affairs, or whether Thomas' alleged breach of the letter of the new law was the instigating factor. At any rate, the real issue was not the breach of this or that rule, but of who was master. It is obvious that Thomas saw the matter as a test of wills and that Henry was indeed trying to provoke a showdown, converting a power-field into a force-field, potency into act, with the terms materially in his favor. Each contestant was cashing in his resources of power, influence, prestige, wealth, numerical following, organization, internal and external support of every type, in a trial of strength. At any rate breach soon became crisis and crisis grew so severe that available, formal means of redress proved inadequate, throwing back the situation into deeper crisis and preparing the way for the ultimate drama, six years later, of the murder in the cathedral with its symbolic deposits of martyrdom and pilgrimage.

Henry's pretext for Northampton was the affair of John the Marshal. 'This baron, a member of the exchequer staff, claimed land at Mundham that was part of the archiepiscopal manor of Pagham'.[16] The king, as mentioned earlier, had issued a constitution giving a vassal the right of appeal to his overlord 'if the latter failed after two days to do him justice in a plea in his court'. All that he then needed to do was to swear with two oath-helpers that his case had been unjustly delayed. John the Marshal, wishing to ingratiate himself with Henry, followed the procedure, just mentioned, swearing, so his opponents said, upon a troper (a liturgical book) which he had brought with him to elude the charge of perjury, that is, of foreswearing upon the Gospel. [Note here how Becket's mainly clerical biographers impute some sort of blasphemy to many of the actions that support the king's cause.] The king seized his opportunity and summoned the archbishop to answer in the royal court [again in keeping with the Clarendon clause which declared the king's court to be the final court of appeal]. The biographers disagree over what followed. Some say that the archbishop fell sick and sent his excuses, which were not accepted as genuine. Others say that he produced evidence in his favour and refused to answer an unjust summons. In any case, Henry cited him once more to appear in his presence at a royal council at Northampton on 6 October.[17]

There is no lack of documentation on the Council; there are seven lengthy narratives and several briefer accounts; two of the narratives are from eye-witnesses, William Fitzstephen and Herbert of Bosham. It is clear from these that Henry's intention was to run Thomas into the ground, to destroy him. Characteristically he was late for the meeting, for on his way he 'went hawking along every river and stream'. At the start Thomas still had some faint hopes of a reconciliation but the tone was set by Henry's refusal to 'admit Thomas to the favor of a kiss', according to the English custom, after the king had attended his first Mass in the palace chapel. After much wrangling Henry forced his cousin, the elderly Bishop of Winchester, to pronounce the sentence on Thomas in the case of John the Marshal – who never turned up for the proceedings. Thomas had been found guilty of contempt of court for having failed to appear three weeks earlier to answer the suit of John the Marshal, and for having offered no 'essoin', that is, excuse for nonappearance. The main actors at Northampton were the king and Thomas, the king's barons and the bench of bishops. The barons and bishops were by no means solidary groups and Knowles has written a fascinating book detailing the alliances and dissensions within the episcopal ranks as the Becket/Henry drama played itself out.[18] But it is a feature of the present case that the bishops, one by one, some through cowardice, some through knavery, and others out of blank misunderstanding, drew away from Becket as he grew more obdurate. Even the Pope had continually tried to reach compromises with Henry; Becket's opposition to royal demands seemed stupid, arrogant, even uncharitable since it exposed his friends and relatives to royal vengeance. At any rate, in the first round at Northampton, Henry the Bishop of Winchester in an undertone urged Thomas to accept sentence quietly. Thomas retorted ironically: 'This is a new kind of judgment, perhaps according to the new canons promulgated at Clarendon'. The fine proposed was £ 500, and all the bishops, except his ancient enemy Gilbert Foliot of London, 'went bail' for Thomas, i.e., acted as his guarantors.

But Henry was by this time really bloody-minded, and on the following day the monarch demanded that Thomas pay him £ 300 which he had received while the castles of Eye and Berkhamsted were in his charge as Chancellor. Thomas protested that this was a new suit, for which he had not been cited and therefore had had no time to prepare a defence. Besides, he remarked informally, the king knew quite well that he had used the money to repair the Tower of London and the castles themselves.

'Not on my authorization', Henry retorted, 'I demand judgment'.

For the sake of peace Thomas agreed to pay this; remarkably, a nobleman,

William of Eynsford – whom Becket had recently excommunicated and absolved – came forward to offer security for the debt (the sum Thomas owed the king has been computed at about $32,000 in modern American cash terms). He was joined in this by the Earl of Gloucester–which indicated that Thomas had some support at this time from the baronry. But next day the financial demands went on. Henry probed Thomas to the root. What happened, he asked to the thousand marks (two-thirds of a pound) that Thomas had borrowed during the Toulouse War? Notice how Henry seems to be reminding Thomas of his moral debt – rather than his financial one – to the king when Thomas had as client been the King's Chancellor. Thomas replied that the money had been a gift expended, in fact, in the king's service. Henry demanded more security. Five laymen came forward and offered to go bail for Thomas. But the king was implacable. He asked Thomas to account for all the proceeds of the archbishopric during its vacancy, and for the revenues of all the other bishoprics and abbacies he had held during his chancellorship. The sum demanded was at least 30,000 marks (c. $800,000 today). Thomas said that he needed time to do the proper accountancy work; he would do it if time were granted. Henry said, 'You must then give security'. Herbert of Bosham writes that at this 'all (Thomas') wisdom was devoured'. He could hardly speak but he yet asked to consult his clergy. This was quite a tactical move for it made clear to Henry that the bishops were not to be classified as barons – though in terms of the royal writ inviting them to the council they had been summoned in their role as English feudal magnates – but as representatives of the universal Church. Thomas thus hoped to divide the bishops from the barons and precipitate a manfest state-church confrontation. But all Thomas succeeded in doing was in estranging his friends in the baronry and dividing the churchmen. Thomas spent the whole of Saturday in consultation with his bishops and abbots. Gilbert Foliot reminded Thomas of his commoner origin – he was a burgher of London, of the Norman merchant class, not of the landed gentry to which Foliot and several other bishops belonged – and urged him to resign 'to avoid ruining the Church and all of us'. Henry of Winchester, the royal bishop once a playboy but now an elder statesman, defended Thomas' position, arguing that if the primate of all England resigned how could any future prelate oppose the king's will? Others urged various forms of compromise. Several said that it would be better for Thomas to suffer than the whole

English Church. But the true tenor of Henry's desires became clear when Winchester went to the king with an offer of two thousand marks to get Thomas off the hook. Henry turned it down flat. Now the good men of God really had the fear of God in them, for they saw that Henry wanted to doom Thomas, no less. No compromise seemed possible. All the king's demands had been trumped up; what he lusted for was the downfall of Thomas, possibly his imprisonment and the lingering death this often entailed. The king demanded that the bishops themselves should pass sentence on Thomas, since the Barons had declared themselves, as laymen, incompetent to do this. The next day Thomas found that only Winchester and Worcester of the bishops seemed to realize that the principle of ecclesiastical freedom – and perhaps beyond that, freedom in the realm of England – was at stake; it was not just a matter of the king's protecting himself from the past financial dealings of a supposedly dishonest official.

On Monday, Thomas fell ill; the tension of the debates, his long ride from Canterbury to Northampton, the king's delay in coming, all these stirred up his old complaint, kidney stone, and he writhed with renal colic. Henry believed that as before he was merely feigning illness and sent the Earl of Leicester and the Earl of Cornwall – the highest ranking officials of the kingdom – to find out the true facts. They realized he was really sick but asked him whether he was prepared to submit his accounts. Thomas replied that he would appear in court next day, if he had to be carried there, and would then 'answer as God wills'. They then 'encouraged' him by telling him that some nobles were conspiring to kill him, and that the king, following certain Angevin and Norman precedents, was planning to have him imprisoned for life or mutilated – his eyes put out and his tongue cut off.

This was Thomas' low-point, the rock-bottom of his life, Black Monday. Picture the gloom and desperation of the scene. There was Thomas, sick on his pallet in St. Andrew's monastery outside Northampton town, having been debarred by royal pressure from taking up the more comfortable quarters to which his rank entitled him – but in a strange way foreshadowing his exile among Cistercial monks in Pontigny and his attempt to emulate the humility of the ideal monk. The king was all cold cruelty, masked in moral law and accusation. The weather was dank and dull, as I have often known it myself in the Northampton area in autumn. The savage, illiterate barons had uttered their appalling menaces. Becket was auined man, foredoomed.

How could this tall man, always intent on glory, snatch victory from this disaster, this unnerving mood? Almost all the bishops, his recent Job's comforters, had abandoned him, quailing from the physical threat in the castle where the king and his barons revelled and raved. The great lords had rejected him. It was in these circumstances that courage came back to Becket from the paradigm glowing redly in his mind, the *via crucis* pattern of martyrdom. Years ago, Becket had gone to school at Merton in Surrey. His teacher had been a Prior Robert. This Robert's successor at Merton was another Prior Robert, and out of some quirk of nostalgia Thomas had appointed the second Robert his confessor. In his darkest hour Thomas confessed his despair and Prior Robert in the Abbey confessional encouraged him to say a votive mass next morning, Tuesday, the 13th of October, – not the regular mass of the day according to the ceremonial of the Roman Church – but the Mass of the Protomartyr of the Christian Church, St. Stephen, whose day as all know, follows Christmas, the celebration of the birth of Jesus Christ.

All the historical evidence points to Thomas' decision to say this challenging Mass as the turning-point towards his martyrdom. Henry had browbeaten him once more, as in the friendly affair of the cloak, just a further step towards the martyr's crown. Tuesday was thick with symbols. It has not passed unnoticed by the makers of the Thomas legend that Tuesdays were crucial days for the Archbishop. As Tennyson puts it in his *Becket*, following Robert of Gloucester's late thirteenth century metrical history of the Life and Martyrdom of Thomas Becket:

> On a Tuesday was I born and on a Tuesday
> Baptised; and on a Tuesday did I fly
> Forth from Northampton; on a Tuesday passed
> From England into bitter banishment;
> On a Tuesday at Pontigny came to me
> The ghostly warning of my martyrdom;
> On a Tuesday from mine exile I returned,
> And on a Tuesday – [he was murdered].

Not only did Becket say St. Stephen's Mass out of season but he said it in St. Stephen's Chapel at the Cluniac monastery of St. Andrews. Before he set forth, on this day scheduled to be the last of the great council, most of the bishops, led by Foliot of London, called on Thomas. They tried to persuade him to resign and throw himself on Henry's mercy. But he was already resolved to fight matters out with the spiritual sword for he replied vigorously: 'The sons of my own mother (i.e., the Church) have fought against me' – a citation from the Canticle of Canticles I: 5 (Vulgate): 'Filii matris meae pugnaverunt contra me'. He then ordered the bishops to excommunicate any of the laity who might raise their hands against him. Foliot, leader of the king's party among the bishops, refused to accept this injunction. Thomas then dismissed them and they hurried off to court. Nevertheless, the bishops of Winchester and Salisbury lingered after the rest to give him a few words of encouragement before he went to celebrate Mass.

St. Stephen's Mass has for its opening words or Introit: 'Princes sat and spoke against me: and the wicked persecuted me ... but thy servant is occupied in thy statutes' (Ps. 118). I have given the impression that apart from his immediate entourage and a few sympathetic bishops Thomas was without support. This was decidedly not the case, for the common people of Northampton thronged around him whenever he moved from St. Andrew's Abbey to the Castle and back again. Anouilh was literally incorrect – he followed Thierry, the nineteenth century French historian translated by Hazlitt in this – when he declared Becket to have been an Anglo-Saxon, for Becket's parents both came from near Caen in Normandy to settle in London, but he was right in stressing the support given him by the masses, most of whom were of indigenous origin, Anglo-Saxons or Celts. The London burghers, merchants, and guild-craftsmen, also gave him considerable support – and for years St. Thomas Becket was the patron saint of the Brewers' Company, of which he was allegedly the founder. On the morning of the 13th of October, despite the persecution of princes the commonality gathered round Thomas like a shield as with his procession of priests and choristers, wearing his most sacred garments, including the pallium, a circular band of white wool symbolizing the fullness of the episcopal power enjoyed by the Pope and shared in by archbishops, Thomas entered the Chapel of St. Stephen to say Mass. Even the pallium has martyrological associations, for the pallia are made of the wool of two lambs blessed in the church of St. Agnes in Rome on her feast day. St. Agnes was a 4th Century Virgin-Martyr, beheaded, at the age of thirteen, at the order of the Prefect of Rome under the Emperor Maximian Herculeus. Becket, always a highly conscious man with a flair for the symbolism of public life, was probably not unaware of the multivocal meaning of the pallium – which symbolized not only his archiepiscopal authority devolving from the Papacy but also the image of martyrdom in the cause of Church against Empire.

In the presence of his own 'sheep and lambs', as Becket often called the people of England committed to his pastoral care, Becket celebrated the Mass of the Protomartyr, with its Gospel reference (Matthew, 23: 34–39) to Zachary slain between the altar and the temple – a curious prophecy of his own fate in his own cathedral of Canterbury just over six years later. Thomas is recorded as having become so caught up in the emotions stirred by the words of the Epistle recording Stephen's stoning for defending the early Christian church, and of the Gospel with its reference to the persecution of 'prophets and wise men and scribes' that 'he wept and sighed frequently'.[19] To my mind the confession on October 12th and the martyr's Mass on October 13th, in the desperate circumstances of Northampton represented Thomas' decisive conversion to the role of champion of the Church, who would prevail as 'a lamb led to the slaughter' over the 'lion king', Henry the raging Angevin. Becket knew that if he was to be a winner he would have to be a loser, since he had no force at his command, other than the spiritual weapons of the Church, excommunication and the interdict. Such weapons clearly did not terrify all, since the de Broc family who gave Becket's four slayers hospitality and guidance before the martyrdom lay under excommunication by Becket at the time. It was the root-paradigm of martyrdom – with its rich symbolism of blood and paradise – which gave him a frame and fortification for the final trial of will with Henry whom he had loved and whom he could never really hate. And there is about all this still the curious suggestion of an initiation scenario: just as in many initiation rituals Becket the neophyte went through ordeal, in this case at the king's hands, the king being an unconscious initiator. Becket was enclosed from secular society in his abbey – a liminal place if ever there was – while the king and his baronry were lodged in the Castle where the jural-political meetings also were held. What we will now describe is Becket's 'ritual of reaggregation', as Van Gennep might have called it, in which he returned to society as an initiated defender of the Church – though his vision of the Church does not seem to have coincided with that of his fellow bishops, nor even with that of Pope Alexander – who saw the field of Church-State relationships as a cockpit of perrenial intrigue, *raisons d'état et d'église* (hardly severable), balance of power, administrative strategies, etc. For

Becket the Church seems to have been connected in some way with the virtues of *caritas* and *humilitas*, as the many traditions relating to his alms-giving, personal penances, and ceremonial feet-washings of the poor before dawn at Canterbury seem to indicate. Yet he was no St. Francis – he was a combative, masterful man, skilled in arms, as his exploits before Toulouse in Henry's service demonstrated, a brilliant administrator as Chancellor and Archbishop, skilled in canon law and civil law. He put these propensities and gifts at the service of the Church, yet could not do so wholeheartedly until he had identified himself with the root-paradigm of martyrdom. In many superficial respects he remained worldly, but his rich robes literally covered a verminous hair-shirt, discovered on his body after his death. Once he knew that he would have to die to get his own way and the way of the Church, with which he seems to have identified his own, he achieves a peace and certitude of mind and consistency of action which never fails him until the bloody climax. Writers have argued over the centuries; was Becket 'humble' or 'proud'? Was his end, like a Japanese *harakiri* suicide, an attempt to shame King Henry in an unanswerable fashion, a final pride? Or was he truly a sacrificial lamb, unresistingly slain at the altar? – many icons have sentimentally portrayed him as dying thus meekly despite the eye-witness accounts which tell of an almost arrogant provocation of the king's knights on that last dark afternoon. After all, he hurled Reginald Fitz-Urse to the ground in his full armor, before, almost ironically, offering himself to the sword that sheared off his skull-cap. My own view – developed in my books on African ritual symbolism – is that Becket became himself a powerful, 'numinous' symbol precisely because, like all dominant or focal symbols, he represented a coincidence of opposites, a semantic structure in tension between opposite poles of meaning. Becket was at once lion and lamb, proud and meek. The energy of his pride gives drama and pathos to his self-chosen role of lamb, just as, I have argued, the orectic or sensory pole of dominant symbols gives life and color to the virtues and values at the other pole. Martyrs were, after all, the warriors of the Church; like Icelandic heroes they died indomitable, proclaiming their faith in the face of torture and a variety of sticky ends. The intriguing feature of Becket's end was that while formally it was a lamb's fate, psychologically it was a lion's. The Icelandic saga genius saw this, and portrayed Thomas like some Gunnar, Skarphedinn, or King Olaf who half-deliberately places himself in an untenable position, refusing aid or chance of escape, and dies in full heroic integrity, knowing that his death will be 'worth at least a song'.

But let me conclude this presentation by following David Knowle's account of Becket's last day at Northampton. Northampton was the real break in Becket's life; the murder ratified it. Knowles' synoptic and scholarly narrative shows clearly Becket's contradictory yet oddly consistent character, shrewd yet bold, humble and angry. I shall supply exegetical notes and cross-refer to other writers on appropriate occasions.

Knowles writes that after saying St. Stephen's Mass, 'still wearing some of the priestly vestments under a cloak, preceded by his cross, and carrying secretly the sacred Host to serve as Viaticum [i.e., holy communion given to those in danger of death] should the worse befall [Becket] took horse for the castle'.[20] His cross, incidentally, 'was a solid piece of work, for the four knights, six years later, had thoughts of braining him with the haft'.[21] The Icelandic saga of Archbishop Thomas bluntly states that 'Thomas took for his protection the body of Our Lord [i.e., the Host, the consecrated communion bread], both for the sake of natural fear and strong faith in the mercy of God'.[22] Becket, knowing that Henry still hesitated to attack directly any aspect of the sacramental system, tried to guarantee his physical immunity from violence by letting it be known he carried the Host under his cassock. In this way, too, he would be protected while he said his say in the uncongenial and menacing company of Henry's drunken baronry. Knowles continues:

"Dismounting in the courtyard, as the gate shut behind him [thus shutting out his popular support], Becket took from his [cross-]bearer the archiepiscopal cross. [This same cross-bearer – and the Archbishop of Canterbury was entitled to have one wherever he travelled – was a young Welshman who had formerly rebuked him at Clarendon when he had bowed to the king's will.] Some bishops were at the door of the castle, among them Gilbert of London. One of the archbishop's clerks, Hugh of Nunant, later bishop of Coventry, approached him: 'My Lord of London, can you stand by while the archbishop carries his own cross?' 'My dear fellow', replied Foliot, 'the man always was a fool and he'll be one till he dies'. Robert of Hereford, Becket's old master, tried to take the cross from him in vain; Foliot approaching from the other side, told the archbishop sharply that he was a fool and endeavored to wrest the cross from him. (Bishop) Roger of Worcester (a cousin of Henry II, but a supporter of Becket's) rebuked Foliot: 'Would you prevent your Lord from carrying his cross?' only to be told sharply that he would live to be sorry for those words. The bishops then fell aside and Thomas entered alone, bearing his cross, and passed through the hall himself; the others followed, and Foliot again remonstrated: 'Let one of your clerks carry it.' Thomas refused. 'Then let me have it; I am your dean [this was true, the Bishop of London acted as Canterbury's dean, or senior prelate on great state occasions]; do you not realize that you are threatening the king? If you take your cross and the king draws his sword how can we ever make peace between you?' 'The cross *is* the sign of peace', answered Thomas. 'I carry it to protect myself and the English Church'."[23]

Full analysis of the social structure and symbolism of this phase and its contextualization in the on-going process of State/Church and intra-ecclesiastical relations would be matter for another paper, but it is worth pointing out that Becket was beyond all compromise by this time while Foliot wanted at any cost to avoid direct confrontation of the clerical cross by the royal sword. He wanted to avoid the scandal of the cross, but most of all he did not want to provoke the royal wrath which had led to the mutilation of bishops before at the hands of some of Henry's ancestors. Today one can hardly avoid the phallic connotations of cross and sword – perhaps at the unconscious level Becket wished to avoid what is still common in Africa where the priests of the earth – the ecclesia of West African societies – are collectively and symbolically known as 'the wife' of the Paramount Chief, who represents quintessential politico-legal authority. Both Becket and Henry wished to be 'husbands' here; Becket's heavy wooden cross would confront Henry's sword and sceptre, holy machismo would challenge kingly machismo. But, as Knowles writes, after the bishops drew away from Becket, whom they thought doomed, leaving him alone with his two clerks and later biographers, Herbert and Fitzstephen, in the inner chamber, anticipating the worst, 'a touch of bitter comedy ... was provided by the entrance of Roger of York [the Archbishop who contended with Canterbury for the primacy over all the metropolitans and bishops of England]. He had arrived late to the council, partly to ensure attention, like a queen at the theatre, partly, so the chronicler suggests, to have secure alibi should he be charged with having worked the archbishop's downfall [it is said that he had been secretly intriguing with the king]. He now entered with his unpermitted cross borne before him [unpermitted because only Canterbury of all the bishops was allowed to have a cross carried before him outside his own diocese], and there were thus two crosses in the castle, as it were two hostile lances at rest (*quasi* '*pila minantai pilis*', as Fitzstephen writes, citing Lucan's *Pharsalia*). [History was never more speedily repeated as farce, though Thomas carried his own while Roger usurped the privilege of Canterbury by having his carried.] The bishops were then summoned to council with the king, who had retreated to the upper floor (of the castle) at the news of Thomas' advent.'[24]

This retreat was a curious matter – and I do not think I have seen it noted in any history of Northampton – for it reverses the Henry/Thomas situation at Clarendon. There Henry was dominant and sure and Thomas hesitant and on the retreat. Perhaps it began when Henry's spies reported to him from St. Stephen's Chapel in the early morning that Becket had celebrated the Protomartyr's Mass, for our sources report that 'certain king's folk and clerks' rushed out to tell him that Thomas was comparing Henry and his nobles to the persecutors of the first martyr. William Fitzstephen calls this interpretation 'malicious', but it was true enough. My own hunch is that Henry then grasped very clearly what Thomas was intent upon, and he knew that in his own time and society he had no defence against the strategy of martyrdom. Thomas had told Henry rather earlier at a private meeting, also in Northampton, that he 'was ready to die for his Lord', and Henry could now see that he meant business. Henry could intimidate the bench of bishops, even if they were, as Knowles says, perhaps the most able group of bishops in medieval England. But he knew Thomas' mettle from the days of their friendship. When he heard that Thomas was coming with cross and Host he may well have gone into a blue funk. Winston writes that 'Henry would have no part in dramatizing a confrontation of *regnum* and *sacerdotium*' and that 'he feared his own temper',[25] but I think that he knew now subliminally that the root-paradigm of the martyr's *via crucis* was archetypally in control of Thomas and that he could only use direct force against him at the expense of giving him what he wanted and what would strengthen the Church's position at home and abroad – the martyr's crown. I honestly believe that Henry felt panic at that moment. But he soon rallied sufficiently to bully the bishops whom he had summoned to attend upon him upstairs. They told him that Thomas had reprimanded them and forbidden them to judge him henceforth on any secular charge. Angrily, Henry replied that this was a clear violation of Article XI of the Constitutions of Clarendon, which bound the bishops to participate in all of the king's trials and judgments unless these involved the shedding of blood. Still unwilling to go to the lower hall, where the Cross awaited him, Henry sent several of his barons to ask whether Thomas intended to present the accounts of his chancellorship, as had been requested on the previous Friday, and to provide sureties for his debts. More importantly, Henry learned that Thomas had appealed from his judgment that the bishops should pronounce sentence on Thomas – his scheme for dividing them from their official head – the Pope. This was an open rebuff to the Clarendon rules. He sent a deputation down below to Thomas to ask whether he stood by his appeal. 'Thomas answered at some length; as for moneys spent as chancellor, he had received formal quittance; as for guarantors, his colleagues and friends were already too deeply engaged to undertake more; as for the appeal it had been lodged against suffragans [i.e., diocesan bishops subject to the Archbishop as their metropolitan bishop] who had condemned him against justice and ecclesiastical precedent; he therefore held to his prohibition and appeal, and commended himself and the Church of Canterbury to the Pope.'[26] This was rank defiance of the monarchy. Thomas had burnt his boats behind him.

It is not possible to dwell here on the ebb and flow of the subsequent events, each rich in symbolism and drama. The upshot was that the bishops did not want to cut the cord which bound them at one and the same time to Canterbury and Rome, and they knew that if they pronounced a criminal sentence on Thomas they would greatly weaken their position *vis-à-vis* Rome, which had condemned most of the Clarendon clauses. Meanwhile, the passions of the barons had been rising – several suggested the castration of Thomas. Among the bishops, Thomas' arch-enemies, London, York, and Chichester, tried to find a way of getting rid of Thomas while keeping their own hands clean. Smart old Foliot finally thought up a way: they would lodge an appeal to the Pope which would accuse Thomas of having perjured himself and forced them to disobey against their oath – they might thus obtain Thomas' deposition. Henry promptly accepted this tactic. But he had no intention of waiting for a papal decision; he wanted action now, if others would do the dirty work for him. One can imagine what Thomas' feelings must have been, sitting in apparent calm in the lower room with his two clerks – rather like a student waiting in the coffee lounge to hear the result of an important oral exam perhaps. In the end, Henry sent all the bishops to torment Thomas, having committed them through Foliot to a united attack on him before the Pope. Robert of Lincoln, we are told, was in tears, others near weeping. But Hilary of Chichester, who never liked Thomas, had the words. He said that Thomas' obstinancy had put them between the hammer and the anvil, for he had ordered them to make a promise at Clarendon, and then at Northampton he had prohibited them from making that promise. What could they do, then, but appeal to higher Church authority – to the Holy Father himself? Thomas replied that two wrongs did not make a right. He now saw that the Clarendon constitutions were uncanonical – and canon law was the law of God at work in history. Thus no one was bound to keep an oath which he should never have taken. If all fell at Clarendon, all could rise now. The bishops went up to the king, who was shrewd enough to then excuse them from taking part in the trial of Becket, which was still unconcluded. At that, they returned to sit with their Archbishop.

The long day was ending. The barons, unfettered from episcopal restraints, and roaring out the word 'traitor', condemned and sentenced Becket – to what, never appeared, but probably to that perpetual imprisonment which he is known most to have dreaded. The whole baronial mob, augmented by sheriffs and lesser men, surged down the stone stairs to pronounce sentence, leaving Henry and a few others above. Thomas did not rise to meet them, but remained sitting holding his cross. No one wanted to be spokesman, but the Earl of Leicester, a not unsympathetic figure, eventually took on the unpopular role – for Becket, like Henry, was not an easy man to outface. Leicester had hardly come to any point when Becket interrupted him, and brusquely forbade all present to pass judgment on him. Leicester stammered and stopped, the Earl of Cornwall refused to take over from him, and it was left to the smooth Bishop of Chichester to interpolate that the treason was clear, and that the archbishop must hear the judgment. Thomas then, with one of those surprising strokes of which he was master, suddenly rose, exclaiming that it was none of their business to judge their archbishop, and strode through the hall towards the door. All hell broke loose. Some barons, roaring 'traitor' again, picked up rushes and less reputable debris from the floor to throw at Thomas. In the melée he tripped over a cord of firewood and there was another howl of imprecation. Hamelin, the king's illegitimate half-brother and Randolph de Broc (who would later give Becket's killers hospitality in the castle of Saltwood, taken from the Canterbury holdings and given to the de Brocs by King Henry after Becket's flight) joined in the cry of 'Traitor!' Now Thomas showed himself as less the meek Christian and more the Norman descended from the Danish vikings of Count Rollo who wrested land from the Carolingian kings. He rounded on Hamelin and spat: 'Bastard lout! If I were not a priest, my right hand would give you the lie. As for you (to de Broc) one of your family has been hanged already.' Here speaks the London burgess' son, on the defensive among men who counted as aristocrats, violent, illiterate, and savage though most of them were. Then with his group of attendants he broke out of the room. The gate of the bailey was locked, and the porter was engaged in a private scuffle – everyone that day was overwrought – but a bunch of keys hung by the wall, and the first that was tried opened the door – this was later to form one of the legends of Holy Saint Thomas. The archbishop's horses were standing ready bridled, and he and his entourage rode off across the town, to the cheers of the ordinary people – many of whom he invited to share his supper at St. Andrew's monastery that night, after the model of Christ's parable of the wedding feast, to make up for the many clerics and nobles who had defected from his household out of fear. I have to conclude the narrative here almost; after Thomas, in disguise and with only three companions, left the church at midnight and rode off into darkness and a violent thunderstorm, we have a new social drama, that of Thomas' 'Odyssey' of escape from England, and his 'Exile' first at the Cistercian monastery of Pontigny and later in various French refuges, as prelude to the final darkness of the martyrdom. One must note, again, that Henry did not try to prevent Thomas' escape. It's hard to separate love from hate in the relationship between these two men, and harder to define the nature of either.

My intent here has been to show how symbols are dynamic entities, not static cognitive signs, how they are patterned by events and informed by the passions of human intercourse, in friendship, sexuality, and politics, and how paradigms, bodied forth as clusters and sequences of symbols, mediate for men between ideals and action in social fields full of cross purposes and competing interests. I have used a few decisive incidents, composing a social drama, from the history of friendship that turned sour, to show how personal and state of affairs may both achieve a memorable form and generate legend as well as archives due to the action of root-paradigms in people's heads that become objectivated models for future behavior in the history of collectivities such as churches and nations.

Chronology

B.C. 516? Zachary, prophet, slain
A.D. 33 Crucifixion
A.D. 35 Stephen martyred

Europe	*England*	*Thomas*
	597 St. Augustine in England	
910 Start of Cluniac reform		
962 Otto 1st Holy Roman Empire		
	1012 Archbp. Alphege martyred by Danes	
	1066 Archbp. Lanfranc pushed Cluniac reforms	
1072–85 Pope Gregory VII		
1077 Emp. Henry IV 'went to Canossa', penitent to Gregory		
1095 Reforms of Council of Clermont		
	1097 Archbp. Anselm exiled by Henry I	
		1118 Birth of Thomas
		1148 Entered Archbp. Theobald's household
	1154–89 Reign of Henry II	1154 Became archdeacon
	1155–72 Struggle between Church and royal court system	1155 Became chancellor
1162 Pope Alexander III exiled by Barbarossa to Sens		1162 Became Archbp. of Canterbury
	1163 Council of Westminster	

CHRONOLOGY *continued*

Europe	*England*	*Thomas*
1164 Antipope Paschal III appointed by Barbarossa	1164 Jan. 14 Constitutions of Clarendon Oct. 6 Council of Northampton	1164 Jan. 14 Constitutions of Clarendon Oct. 6 Council of Northampton Oct. 12 Thomas sick Oct. 13 Tues. Mass of St. Stephen; Thomas fled
1166 Vézelay excommunications		1166 Vézelay excommunications
1170 July 22 Fréteval reconciliation		1170 July 22 Thomas reconciled with Henry Dec. 1 Returned to England
	Dec. 24 Henry: 'Who will rid me of this low born priest?' Conspiracy of knights	
		Dec. 25 Preached sermon prophesying his death Dec. 29 Tues. Murder of Thomas in cathedral
		1173 Canonized
	1174 Henry's penitence at Canterbury	
1177 Defeat of Barbarossa by Pope's forces		
		1220 Translation of body to new shrine. 200,000 present

NOTES

This essay is also printed in Victor Turner, *Dramas, Fields and Metaphors*. Cornell University Press, 1974.

1. Fritz Kern, *Kingship and Law in the Middle Ages* (New York: Harper Torchbooks, 1970).
2. T. S. Eliot, *Murder in the Cathedral* (New York: Harcourt, Brace, 1935); Christopher Fry, *Curtmantle* (London: Oxford University Press, 1961); Jean Anouilh, *Becket of the Honor of God* (London: Coward-McCann, 1960).
3. Shelley Mydans, *Thomas: A Novel of the Life, Passion, and Miracles of Becket*, 1st ed. (Garden City, New York: Doubleday, 1965); Alfred Duggan, *My Life for My Sheep* (London: Coward-McCann, 1955).
4. Rev. Joseph Berington, *The History of the Reign of Henry the Second* (Basil: Tourneisen, 1793).
5. Rev. James C. Robertson, ed., *Materials for the History of Thomas Becket*, 7 vols. (London: Her Majesty's Stationery Office, Kraus Reprint, 1965). Vol. I. See also Rev. W. H. Hutton, *St. Thomas of Canterbury: An Account of his Life and Fame from the Contemporary Biographers and Other Chroniclers* (London: Nutt, 1899).
6. Frederick Pollock and Frederic William Maitland, *The History of English Law before the Time of Edward I*, 2nd ed, reissued (Cambridge: Cambridge University Press, 1968).
7. Winston Churchill, *The History of the English-Speaking Peoples*, 1st. ed., 4 vols. (London: Cassell, 1956–1958), Vol. I.
8. Raymonde Foreville, *L'Eglise et la Royauté en Angleterre sous Henri II Plantagenet, 1154–1189* (Paris: Bloud and Gay, 1943); Dom David Knowles, *The Episcopal Colleagues of Archbishop Thomas Becket* (Cambridge: Cambridge University Press, 1951) and *Thomas Becket* (London: A. & C. Black, 1970).
9. Paul Alonzo Brown, *The Development of the Legend of Thomas Becket* (Philadelphia: University of Pennsylvania Press, 1930).
10. Victor Turner, *The Ritual Process* (Chicago: Aldine, 1969).
11. Eiríkr Magnússon, ed., *Thomás Saga Erkibyskups* (London: Longman, 1875).
12. W. Fitzstephen, in Robertson, ed., *Materials*, Vol. III, p. 22.
13. Knowles, *Thomas Becket*, pp. 89–92.
14. *Ibid.*, p. 92.
15. *Ibid.*, pp. 87–88.
16. *Ibid.*, p. 94.
17. *Ibid.*, p. 94.
18. *The Episcopal Colleagues of Archbishop Thomas Becket*, *supra*.
19. Richard Winston, *Thomas Becket* (New York: Knopf, 1967), p. 183 (From *Materials*, Vol. III).
20. Knowles, *The Episcopal Colleagues*, pp. 77–79.

21. *Ibid.*, p. 71.
22. Robertson, ed., *Materials*, Vol. I, p. 209.
23. Knowles, *The Episcopal Colleagues*, p. 77.
24. *Ibid.*, p. 79.
25. Winston, *Thomas Becket*, p. 185.
26. Knowles, *The Episcopal Colleagues*, pp. 79–80.

RICHARD A. HUTCH

7

Ralph Waldo Emerson: The Birth of a Seer

THE NATIVE SEER

Late in 1832 Ralph Waldo Emerson, recently bereaved of his wife, embarked on an extended trip to England. On his return in the fall of 1833 he immediately accepted the opportunity to lecture in the Lyceum series sponsored by the Masonic Temple of Boston. While he remained available for preaching responsibilities until 1838, he had to all intents and purposes abandoned the ministry in 1832 in favor of public lecturing. His new career required him to spend the rest of his life travelling throughout the continental United States.

His lecture circuit took him at first as far west as St. Louis, Missouri and Chicago, Illinois (1850, 1853, 1867) and later in life he spent time in California (1871), in addition to making several trips to England (1847, 1873) as the distinguished American scholar. These lecture tours were significant because of the seeds he sowed and the harvest he reaped. By means of his travels, a diverse and fragmented 'second generation' of United States citizens was able to savor the spirit of the Revolution of 1776 which severed its fathers from 'Mother England'. Emerson literally 'gathered in' the populace with the arc of his sweeps westward, then eastward, then back again. Audiences were literally 'taken in' by what this keeper of tradition from the Puritan past had to say. Not only did his message of 'self-reliance' fit the exigencies of the farmer, pioneer, or entrepreneur; it served the larger purpose of calling a populace to nationhood at a time when the flow of immigration from abroad began to mount. One could say that the harvest of Emerson's travels after 1833 rested finally in the fact that he facilitated the formation of an American culture distinct from that of England and distinct from that of a colonial past.

On the face of it, it would appear that Emerson, on his return to America, abandoned a religious career. Various Emerson scholars have suggested this.[1] However, I would like to develop the view in this paper that Emerson abandoned the Unitarian ministry and its theological doctrines only to embark on a religious mission of greater import and based in personal experience – the mission of the seer. To be sure, Emerson has been referred to as a seer in a casual manner by several commentators.[2] But Emerson himself did not take the appellation of seer lightly. He points, for example, to such a self-understanding in a poem which he wrote on October 9, 1832, two months before departing for Europe. It is called, appropriately, 'Self-Reliance':

> *Henceforth, please God, forever I forego*
> *The Yoke of men's opinions. I will be*
> *Light-hearted as a bird, and live with God.*
> *I find him in the bottom of my heart,*
> *I hear continually his voice therein*
>
> *The little needle always knows the North,*
> *The little bird remembereth his note,*
> *And this wise Seer within me never errs.*
> *I never taught it what it teaches me;*
> *I only follow when I act aright.*[3]

It is reasonable to assume that the form of a sonnet lurks in the background of this poem – suggesting the grave seriousness of the heroic mode. In any case, the poem suggests that the vocation of the seer was beginning to impress itself on him as he embarked for England, and that he took this vocation very seriously.

What does it mean to be a religious seer? What are the dominant features of the seer? One of the few, though brief treatments of the seer-type of charismatic authority is that of the historian of religion, Joachim Wach. Wach, like Max Weber, believed that consideration of the 'ideal types' of religious authority would prove fruitful in bringing conceptual order to bear upon social phenomena.[4]

As a type of charismatic authority, the seer model has roots not in the world of the ancient Near or Far East but in the ancient Greco-Roman world. Wach suggests that 'hero worship' was unknown in Israel, for example, but that it was quite characteristic of the Hellenic world. The worship of heroes developed into the 'veneration of the *theios*', or the process by which affinities were recognized between prophets and a king, philosophers and a seer. The 'types', Wach submits, largely influenced Christian hagiography. Therefore, Emerson fits quite nicely within this tradition, especially when one realizes his own penchant for 'hero worship' (he wrote a long series of lectures and essays on 'Representative Men') and, in the specific case of the seer-type of authority, his own inclination to identify himself with Plato and the neo-Platonist, Plotinus.[5]

According to Wach, the major features of the Hellenic seer are quite specific and they can be enumerated here: Usually a seer is aristocratic, enjoying 'prestige' mostly during the second half of his life; he passively interprets his times by means of 'intuition' rather than according to processes of methodical divination; he relies on 'inner experience' more than on external signs; his attitude suggests a tendency toward passivity as evidenced by his lack of concern 'with developing norms of judgment and rules of action'; he deals with 'individual situations', not with generalities; hence, he relates to others 'personally', especially in that he has learned that a successful incubation comes about only to the degree that one succeeds in being a master's disciple; he is a lonely figure, subject to dreams and grand visions; he is credited with a 'particularly close connection with the past ... (he is) the keeper and guardian of tradition'; he does more to guarantee 'in his person and message' the 'spirit of his heritage' than he does to hand down the literal content of the oral and written lore; and his 'insight' tends to be 'an overpowering burden' which contributes greatly to the 'tragic undertone' in his existence. These, then, are the marks of the Greco-Roman seer.

Wach also suggests that in addition to the Hellenic thrust, the seer expresses charismatic authority which is a precursor of the authority of the Hebrew prophet-type. The Hebrew religion assists one in defining the seer-type even though the seer's connection with 'hero worship' is more Greco-Roman than Hebraic. One is aided particularly on philological grounds which lend the patently 'visual' quality to the pattern of this kind of charisma. The terms *ro'eh* and *chozeh*, the former applied to Samuel and the latter to Gad, have the meaning 'to see', 'to look', or 'to gaze'. But because the seer was not a prophet, perhaps by tradition less engaged in historical processes than the Hebrew prophet, the seer's charisma remains fundamentally Hellenic. One needs only to note, as Wach himself does, that the seer, *mantis*, was well-known in ancient Greece; and that the Greek *hypophetes* was definitely a seer and not a prophet-type. Thus, it might be said that Emerson 'the seer' was not so much aloof from his times as he was concerned to draw upon a very different charismatic tradition from that of the 'prophetic' revivalists of his day in shaping a national identity.

In the discussion to follow, I should like to trace the events in Emerson's life which led to his adoption of the role of the seer. With such a retrospective glance we can gain considerable insight into the personal and religious significance of his becoming the nation's seer during the nineteenth century, perhaps even to this day. My discussion will center on two events which, quite literally, enabled Emerson to focus on the personal and religious possibilities inherent in the act of seeing.

SEEING, NOT SEEING, SEEING AGAIN

For some time now the Victorian period of American cultural life has been the focus of renewed scholarly interest. If what the historian Paul Carter calls the 'Gilded Age' was inextricably linked, as he put it, to the 'visible decline' of New England and the Puritan ethos of the seventeenth and eighteenth centuries during the nineteenth century, then Ralph Waldo Emerson found the spiritual crisis of America at that time particularly troublesome.[6] Anxiety about establishing and preserving a new cultural autonomy as a nation was characteristic of the spirit of his age. Certain psychological inclinations, however, predisposed Emerson to negotiate the nation's spiritual crisis in a particular way. Furthermore, his inclinations can be said to bear a striking similarity to the style of cultural reflection of another person who also is interested in America's ongoing 'identity crisis', the psychologist Erik H. Erikson.

When he talked about the value of observing children in the process of playing with toys, that is, observing so-called 'play constructions', Erikson suggested he could see connections between the behavior of the children and their wider cultural milieux. Indian children, for example, hid what they would point to as the 'most exciting scene' within a seeming confusion of many toys scattered about the 'stage'. American children, on the other hand, created their 'most exciting scene' usually with a minimum of toys, and each staging was quite clearly delineated so all could tell easily which it was. For our purposes what the children actually did with their scenes is not important, but what Erikson did while watching is, in effect, our 'most exciting scene'. He observed the children in a particular way, noting that he thought of himself as a 'seeing type' and sought 'over-all configurational impressions' of the children's behavior and their cultural backgrounds.[7] Erikson's eyes played with the children as much if not more than the children played with the toys. Thus, vision and the process of seeing configurations with one's eyes (or mind's eye) are the activities going on beneath Erikson's style of reflecting along psychohistorical lines. The same style is no less characteristic of Emerson's inclinations, at least those promptings which were less deliberate than he may have wished.

Emerson was preoccupied with seeing in a manner not unlike Erikson's watchful style. Seeing was the source of Emerson's art. It has been suggested recently that along with Jonathan Edwards and William James, Emerson drew on a so-called 'aesthetic sensibility' in the American experience.[8] Whether he helped shape the American religious consciousness as a result of his visual rendering of the aesthetics of the land is debatable. Nonetheless, Emerson displayed his particular visual preoccupation on two separate occasions which deserve our special attention in a moment. Besides being interesting psychologically, each occasion serves to suggest the ritual dimension of Emerson's life. That is, seeing his way clear of the past and into a future of recognized autonomy would be not only vocationally innovative, but also culturally significant. The ritual he effected in his person would shift the spiritual crisis of the Gilded Age into the larger and similar crisis of the transition from a colonial to an independent people. The American national identity was at stake and Emerson supplied a kind of authority – the seer's authority – at a time when it bore considerable significance in supplying a thread of meaning to the hard work of nation-building.

Erikson's work is helpful in getting a hold on the ritual process involved in Emerson's visual preoccupation. Taking a cue from words Erikson himself has used in passing comments (especially the word 'configuration'), one may turn to that body of research generated from studies of seeing, namely, classical Gestalt theory. If one is to understand Emerson's life as it was lived on two occasions in particular, especially as it was lived with cultural significance attached to it, then further cues can be taken from the notion of configuration, the central notion of Gestalt theory. Simply, one would want to know, given the record of Emerson's life, that is to say, the 'parts', how those parts configurate into a distinctive 'whole-quality' which is greater than the sum of them all. It is possible to say from the start that what allows Emerson's life to 'hold together', as it were, is the whole-quality of seeing. More to the point, the pattern of 'expansion within diminishment' characterizes best not only the nature of Emerson's two occasions of visual ritualizing, but also points to a particular ritual process which he carries on, in effect, on several different but interrelated levels – personal, social, vocational, historical, cultural. It is a ritual which every child learns to use with his mother. More about this in a moment.

Emerson's father died in 1811 when young Ralph was eight years old. His wife, Ruth Haskins Emerson, raised her five sons with an eye toward pressing them into a ministerial career like that of her prestigious Boston Brahmin husband. Certainly the intermittent help Ruth received from her sister-in-law, Mary Moody Emerson, energized the household intellectually. This was so if only for the tradition embodied in the presence of Emerson's paternal aunt. Seven generations of Emersons had been clergymen; and that a new harvest was at hand after 1811 seemed clear to the women in Emerson's life. Young Ralph was the only son to take a parish later on, and this alone suggests that he, out of all the Emerson sons, was faithful to the composite maternal wish. From the time he was eight until he turned seventeen there were few if any significant masculine influences in his life, aside from his brothers.

Needless to say, Emerson found separating himself from his mother and his aunt difficult throughout the first thirty-five years of his life, years fraught with vocational conflict. It was no coincidence that toward the end of that time, when he was resigning from his brief ministerial charge at Boston's Second Church (1829–32), he described himself as 'severing the cord' that bound him to that church and a career in the Unitarian ministry according to the maternal wish.[9] This simple picture, which suggests a concern for separating from his mother, implies a particular psychological style Emerson adopted. It can be understood as an extension of a ritual process, in particular, the ritual process of '*peek-a-boo*'. What does this ritual imply?

Of central importance in this game that is played between a mother and her child is the matter of 'seeing' and 'being seen', or 'recognizing' and 'being recognized'. The game demands that the child perform a certain task, namely, the task of establishing clear lines of psychological autonomy on the backdrop of maternal trust. As the child plays 'peek-a-boo' with his or her mother, an already established instinctive trust of the mother can be relied on at any time, to be sure. This determines, of course, how the child responds to the risk involved in the game, that is, the hazard faced by going too far in asserting autonomy or separation from the mother's protective care. The thrill of 'peeking' is derived from being peeked at. However, an equally thrilling moment comes when withdrawing, or 'booing', is coaxed toward new peeking. Thus, the game might be said to have three stages – peeking, booing, peeking. As the game is played over and over again the child establishes a sense of personal autonomy or a sense of being separated from his or her mother. The point here is that the child is enabled ritually to explore the 'heights' and 'depths' of autonomy and, most importantly, to do so visually. Or, as Erikson has shown, to do so in terms of an infant's delighted trusting in the sight of its mother's face.[10] Emerson, this self-made man, was, on a more basic psychological level, a man made by his mother.

Emerson's ritual of 'peek-a-boo' takes the form of the pattern, 'expansion within diminishment'. Here, expansion is like the exhilarating heights of 'peeking'. Diminishment resembles the risk of cutting oneself off from his mother's face, or hiding in the depths of 'booing'. As we turn to look at the two occasions when seeing was critically important for Emerson the three stage sequence of the ritual process of 'peek-a-boo' will be noted. For example, on the first occasion peeking is embodied historically in terms of a particular college relationship Emerson described in his journals, hoping no one else would read about it. Next, several years later, booing takes shape in terms of another relationship into which Emerson stumbled necessarily during the first weeks of his studies for the ministry at the Harvard Divinity School. Finally, seven years later, the booing of ministerial preparations comes to issue forth in a new, invigorated sense of peeking. Then he resigns from his ministerial post and asserts his new-found sense of autonomy as a national lecturer and writer. He then literally 'sees beyond' his vocational crisis of the past toward the spiritual crisis of American national identity. As the two occasions are examined we will want to keep in mind how, on the basis of each of these events (the college relationship and the divinity school relationship), wider cultural vistas related to establishing autonomy radiated outward from Emerson's ritualized vision.

The Gay and Norton episodes

The first episode, the accentuation of peeking, occurred in 1820–22 when Emerson was involved in a relationship with a college school-mate, one Martin Gay. The relationship not only coincided with the commencing of his voluminous journals, but it was described in those journals in a strikingly visual way as well. For example, when he was a junior at Harvard College in 1820 Emerson first noticed, as he put it, 'a strange face in the Freshman class'.[11] He went on to say later that he had begun to believe in the 'Indian doctrine of eye-fascination', because the 'cold blue eye' of Martin Gay had intimately connected itself with his 'thoughts and visions'.[12] Later, because he and Gay had had 'two or three long profound stares at each other', Emerson saw intensely Gay's 'pale but expressive face and large eye' and instantly invested him with 'complete character'.[13] In 1822, after having graduated from college a year before, Emerson was inclined to summarize his peculiar relationship with Gay. In his summary statement more than anywhere else Emerson lets us know just how exclusively visual his relationship with Martin Gay was. He says that never once during their two years of acquaintance did either he or Gay exchange any conversation with the other![14] 'From the first', Emerson said, he sought to preserve the terms which 'kept alive so much sentiment' in regard to Gay, rather than to engage in a 'more familiar intercourse' which, he speculated, would have ended in 'indifference'.[15] Peeking, as it were, served as the pretext for undertaking vocational preparation for the ministry during 1825, though nothing is heard ever again about Martin Gay in the pages of Emerson's letters and journals after 1822. Therefore, having thrilled at peeking at Martin Gay, booing, as the next stage of Emerson's ritualized vision, pertained to hiding from a ministerial commitment of a permanent sort.

The second episode when seeing (or not seeing) was critical occurred when Emerson entered the Harvard Divinity School, in accord with the maternal wish, and began to study Biblical theology at the feet of Andrews Norton, Boston's so-called 'Unitarian Pope'. Less than a month after beginning school Emerson went partially blind, and he requested to be excused from Norton's required recitations, since blindness was making reading and preparing for lessons impossible. Though Norton granted Emerson's wish (what else could he do?), the student withdrew, going so far as to drop out of school altogether and not return for a year (and then he returned under the noncommital guise of 'graduate resident'). Toward the end of 1825 Emerson's eyesight gradually returned and by January of 1826 he could return to his journals, his 'ancient friend and consoler', with 'mended eyes'.[16] No reason was given as to why his eyesight failed him, especially why his vision worsened in the face of coming to grips with Andrews Norton and classes in Unitarian Biblical theology. Nevertheless, we can say that when this episode of blindness is understood in terms of the experience of 'peek-a-boo', it can be set alongside the episode of Emerson's relationship with Martin Gay. This is to say, 'peeking' had its counterpart in 'booing' and vice versa. Now 'seeing' Gay was having counterpart in literally 'shutting his eyes', as it were, in the face of Andrews Norton.

Closing his eyes in Norton's classes was also booing the viability of a career in the Unitarian ministry. During the seven years from 1825 to 1832 Emerson made various attempts to fit himself into the mold of the Unitarian ministry. However, each time he did he became ill and withdrew. This psychological tactic followed the pattern of his lost eyesight. For example, in 1826, after being licensed to preach by the Middlesex Association he soon found himself with all the symptoms of tuberculosis. It was evidently a mild case of the disease, but he believed it to be catstrophic nonetheless. He withdrew from his very good chances in the local market and sailed to the South for about six months. When he returned to Boston, he resisted taking on lengthy, though temporary, ministerial assignments on account of his health, or as he put it, his need to maintain a 'lounging capricious unfettered mode of life' so as to be able to pen sermons.[17]

Other examples abound and follow the same pattern of becoming ill and withdrawing from imminent ministerial commitments, right on up to the weeks preceding his resignation when he was inexplicably drained by acute and prolonged diarrhea. His dread of the ministry became most articulate during 1828–29 when he actually became a parish minister. Offered the position as the minister of Boston's Second Church toward the end of 1828, Emerson not only delayed giving the Society of the church his answer for over a month, but he also believed his accepting the offer was to 'enter into captivity'.[18] Things escalated. When he thought of his approaching ordination day several months later he felt he was nearing his 'execution day'.[19] When Emerson resigned from the church late in 1832 his seven year booing of the Unitarians ended. Vocational reticence in becoming a minister served as the pretext for becoming a nation's seer. It might very well be said that going blind in the face of Andrews Norton was the beginning of the ritual arc which would bring Emerson around to the thrill of staking out a national vision – an indigenous cultural life with the seer at its center. Transcendentalism, we know, had the notion of 'self-reliance', or autonomy, as its major axis.

Generally, if Emerson was 'booing' the Unitarians in 1825, his ritual action was sustained through his resignation from Second Church in 1832. Thus, its energy and sway derived from the pay-off of 'peeking' once again. That is, he soon would see his way clear from the church and toward a place on the lecture platform of the American lyceum movement. Then he would be 'recognized' in the limelight of audiences' eyes. Usually Emerson is not remembered as a Unitarian minister, but as an author, poet, philosopher – a seer. This reputation of the transcendentalist issues out of his work after his 1832 resignation from the church. However, at second sight, the years from his birth in 1803 up to 1832, because they are, as it were, 'obscure' or 'hidden' vis-à-vis popular opinion, have been subject to contemporary 'booing', at least by those scholars who prefer to dwell on Emerson's literary achievements alone. However, this brief study is an attempt to set the record straight; that is, to suggest that our own 'peeking' into those earlier years facilitates a psychological and religious understanding of Emerson's cultural contributions to American life. Generally, this thrust is contained in what has been called the ritual of 'peek-a-boo', or the style of the seer's charisma.

The vision of self-reliance

The style of the seer, at least Emerson's reflection of it, can be translated easily into what can now be called the visual pattern of 'expansion within diminishment'. This is done by way of noting more thoroughly the cultural impact of this American seer's life. Booing is not unlike 'diminishment', and peeking is not too different from a sense of 'expansion'. Vocationally speaking, for Emerson the 'diminished' prospect of the Unitarian ministry (a 'denominational' focus) gave rise to the 'expanded' vista of lecturing (a 'national' focus). Autonomy was implicit for both Emerson and his countrymen. The pattern of Emerson's vocational conflict sustained itself in the broader cultural domain as well. We can allude to this by way of drawing this study to a close.

As an American, Emerson could play 'peek-a-boo' with English culture. In fact, he would visit the famous English man of letters, Thomas Carlyle, several times and those visits would bear ritual significance for the American author. Carlyle was one of the first Englishmen to applaud the new American literary achievement of the nineteenth century, and Emerson was thought to be the brightest star rising over that literary horizon to the west. The task faced by Americans during the first decades of that century was precisely to establish collective solidarity and unanimity of a deliberately independent sort. Besides, it was necessary for Americans to "see beyond" the consciousness of the colonial past; but to do so while preserving a fundamental line of continuity with national origins. Vestiges of the Puritan past were readily at hand.

It was the seventeenth century Puritan governor, John Winthrop, who first described the new world venture as an 'experiment'. Emerson himself referred to the experimental nature of the American republic many times, and employed the Puritan imagery to do so. Winthrop described the Puritan establishment in Massachusetts as, in his words, 'A Citty upon a Hill', upon which the 'eies of all people' were watchfully fixed in the 1600s.[20] Emerson beseeched, 'Let the young American withdraw his eyes from all but his own country' so that 'the eyes of the world' will be drawn by the brilliance of tried and true 'free institutions'.[21] As far as Winthrop could see, the future of the spiritual life of the world its last best *hope* in the new world venture. For Emerson, the United States was the hope of all nations for free institutions. Therefore, 'hoping', which according to Erikson, issues out of basic trust, and 'seeing', or the form trust takes in the mother-infant relationship, already were fused in Emerson's cultural heritage. As the Puritans did during the seventeenth century, Emerson himself used a voyage away from home as a means of cutting the cord which bound him and his forefathers to 'Mother England'. He did so during 1832–33, after resigning from the ministry. For a nation to be dependent on 'another man's consciousness', he said in 1838, was for America to 'suck at (its) mother's teat' like a dependent son.[22] By leaving the ministry Emerson was weaned from

English culture as well as from the shame and self-doubt endemic to colonial subjugation.

All in all, Emerson's ritual of seeing, as it reached its height in his relation with Martin Gay, and as it dove into the obscurity of withdrawal in the face of Andrews Norton and for seven years thereafter, helped establish autonomy for Emerson and, later, propelled him into the national limelight as a seer. Emerson's personal autonomy became the legacy of self-reliance which, one may note, most commentators agree is central to the shape and the tenor of the American consciousness. Emerson saw his way to the pattern of his vision, 'expansion within diminishment', or the Gestalt which the seer-type of charismatic authority may reflect. The process of his particular style of visual patterning, thus, is characterized by the ritual behavior of separation, or the ritual of 'peek-a-boo'. And, finally, the charisma he bore was that of the religious seer who, as he says in his manifesto of 1836, *Nature*, like a 'transparent eyeball' is able to 'take in' the universe.[23]

The model of the seer-type of religious authority is an 'ideal type'. Therefore, it is not necessarily inherent in any one particular culture. Nonetheless, the model of the seer is hardly 'unreal'. As Zevedei Barbu, the historian, puts it, the ideal type contains the 'general vectors in the psycho-social field'.[24] The point here is that, Emerson notwithstanding, the early nineteenth century bore vectors characterized best by the model of the seer, the model being a trans-cultural type. Emerson's times did, in fact, lend themselves to an accentuation specifically of the 'visual' sensibility. This is suggested by the fact that early in the century outdoor landscape painting blossomed in America, making the age an 'ocular' one.[25] Moreover, the notion and fact of the 'frontier' itself, which was to reach to the Pacific during the nineteenth century, implied an ever-widening visual 'horizon'. Generally, therefore, we have seen how Emerson was psychologically inclined to draw upon the general vectors of the seer-type of religious authority. We have seen how his visual preoccupation, once coupled with the task of establishing a personal sense of autonomy to counter shame and self-doubt, was able to reflect the national struggle to make the new, independent American experiment work.

Emerson was a holy man because he showed Americans how to trust themselves. Indeed, he secured for his countrymen a firmament that stretched from coast to coast, from sea to shining sea. Such was the hard-won vision of self-reliance.

NOTES

1. See Ralph Waldo Emerson, *The Early Lectures of Ralph Waldo Emerson*, ed. Stephen Whicher and Robert Spiller (Cambridge: Harvard University Press, 1959), Introduction; and Henry Nash Smith, 'Emerson's Problem of Vocation', in *Emerson: A Collection of Critical Essays*, ed. Milton Konvitz and Stephen Whicher (Englewood Cliffs: Prentice-Hall, 1962).
2. Several examples are the following: O. B. Frothingham, *Transcendentalism in New England: A History* (Gloucester, Mass.: P. Smith, 1965), Chapter Heading, 'The Seer'; Robert Gay, *Emerson: A Study of the Poet as Seer* (New York: Doubleday, Doran, 1928.)
3. Ralph Waldo Emerson, 'Self-Reliance', in *Poems*, ed. Edward Emerson (Boston: Houghton Mifflin, Household Edition, 1904), p. 394.
4. Joachim Wach, *Sociology of Religion* (Chicago: University of Chicago Press, 1962), pp. 331–374; 351–353.
5. John S. Harrison, *The Teachers of Emerson* (New York: Haskell House, 1966). The point is that out of all the intellectual influences bearing on Emerson, Platonism can be shown to have made the greatest impression in the long run. It is this idealistic tradition which most readily can be couched in terms of vision.
6. Paul A. Carter, *The Spiritual Crisis of the Gilded Age* (DeKalb: Northern Illinois University Press, 1971), p. x.
7. Erik H. Erikson, *Gandhi's Truth* (New York: W. W. Norton, 1969), p. 40.
8. William Clebsch, *American Religious Thought: A History*, Chicago History of American Religion Series, ed. Martin E. Marty (Chicago: University of Chicago Press, 1973).
9. Ralph Waldo Emerson, *Letters*, 6 Vols., ed. Ralph L. Rusk (New York: Columbia University Press, 1939), Vol. I, pp. 357–358.
10. Though he has alluded to the centrality of the face of the mother as the first firmament of the infant in several places in his writings, Professor Erikson shared this thought with me in person during conversations on October 26, 1973, in San Francisco while attending the meeting of the Society for the Scientific Study of Religion.
11. Ralph Waldo Emerson, *The Journals and Miscellaneous Notebooks*, ed. Gilman, Clark, Ferguson, Davis, et. al. (Cambridge: The Belknap Press of the Harvard University Press, 1960+), I, p. 22.
12. *Ibid.*, I. p. 39.
13. *Ibid.*, I, p. 39; pp. 52–53.
14. *Ibid.*, I, pp. 39–40.
15. *Ibid.*, II, p. 59.
16. *Ibid.*, II, p. 340.
17. Ralph Waldo Emerson, *Letters*, I, pp. 229–230.
18. *Ibid.*, p. 242.
19. *Ibid.*, p. 264.
20. John Winthrop, 'A Modell of Christian Charity', *Winthrop Papers, 1623–1630*, II (Boston: Massachusetts Historical Society, 1931), pp. 282–284; 292–295.

21. Ralph Waldo Emerson, *Journals and Miscellaneous Notebooks*, III, pp. 31–32.
22. *Ibid.*, V, pp. 465–466.
23. Ralph Waldo Emerson, *Nature*, in Brooks Atkinson, ed., *The Selected Writings of Ralph Waldo Emerson* (New York: Modern Library, 1964), p. 6.
24. Zevedei Barbu, *Problems of Historical Psychology* (New York: Grove Press, 1960), p. 218.
25. Neil Harris, *The Artist in American Society* (New York: George Braziller, 1966). The chapter on transcendentalism and its relation to open-half painting is most to the point.

DONALD CAPPS

8

Newman's Illness in Sicily: The Reformer as Biographer

Biographers are universally agreed that even important events in an individual's life are not of equal significance. Certain events stand out as being of extreme importance. Biographers of John Henry Newman (1801–1890) have taken the view that there were three very significant events in his life. The first was his conversion experience at age fifteen which marked his initial commitment to a religious vocation. The second was his illness in Sicily (1833) immediately preceding his venture into Oxford Movement activities. The third was his conversion to the Catholic Church (1845). Newman himself singled out these three major events in his *Apologia Pro Vita Sua:* his conversion experience at age fifteen directed him quite irrevocably toward a religious life; his illness in Sicily firmed his resolve to throw himself into ecclesiastical controversy; and his conversion to Catholicism marked his disengagement from public life and completed the 'growth of mind'. Thus, his autobiography presents a spiritual odyssey which begins at age fifteen and culminates at age forty-five. Neither the years prior to age fifteen nor the years after age forty-five receive any significant attention. This limitation of his life history to these thirty years was quite deliberate, for, on the one hand, he noted that in his conversion experience at age fifteen he assumed a new 'identity' and, on the other hand, he suggested that his life underwent no further 'movement' after his conversion to the Catholic Church. Thus, his life consisted of three critical events, each roughly fifteen years apart, and the fact that two involved 'conversion' and the third had prominent conversion elements underscores their character as turning points.

For the purposes of this essay, I shall limit discussion to Newman's illness in Sicily. I am restricting the discussion to this event because it was immediately followed by his publication of a collection of biographical studies of saints, studies which reflected his preoccupation with this significant turning point in his life. Thus, the biographies are not only generally autobiographical, as various commentators have pointed out, but they are also autobiographical reflections on a specific event.[1] In focussing on his illness in Sicily, therefore, I am not interested simply in the biographical reconstruction of the event, nor am I only concerned to demonstrate the view that Newman's biographies of saints are, in a general sense, autobiographical. Rather, my concern is to augment our understanding of what must strike the Newman scholar as a rather remarkable 'coincidence', that immediately after this critical event Newman turned to biography. I shall therefore view this event in light of its influence on his biographical study of saints and, conversely, consider the biographies for what they reveal concerning his own self-reflections as prompted by this event. In the course of my discussion, I will be viewing specific aspects of this reciprocity of life and biographical art, in particular the influence of the traditional heroic model of the reformer.[2]

THE ILLNESS IN SICILY

Newman's nearly fatal illness in Sicily at the age of thirty-two was the climax of a series of episodes which began six years earlier. In 1826, at the age of twenty-five, he was appointed a public tutor at Oriel College, Oxford. In the months following his appointment as tutor, he became increasingly popular with Oriel College students. This popularity began to disturb him because it evoked thoughts of further advancement in the University, thoughts which he had resolved to put out of his mind when he accepted the position: 'I am becoming somewhat worldly; thoughts about livings, the Provostship, promotion, etc., come before my mind ... I *do* struggle against this, but *how* difficult it is.'[3] This problem reached a critical juncture when, in November 1827, he received news that Edward Copleston, the Provost of Oriel College, had been appointed to a bishopric. Newman had been examining students for their degrees at the time and the news of Copleston's promotion precipitated a temporary nervous breakdown. Clearly, Copleston's promotion had direct implications for his own career. As one biographer points out, Newman 'saw a field of promise suddenly opening before him and he dreamed about it for two nights in a row'.[4]

But why was it significant enough to precipitate a nervous collapse so severe that he was compelled to withdraw from the examinations? One major reason was that it placed him in an extremely awkward moral position, for his decision as to which of his colleagues to support for successor to Copleston would have direct bearing on his own professional future. The leading contenders for the position of Provost were Edward Hawkins and John Keble. In spite of vigorous opposition from his closest friend and fellow tutor, Hurrell Froude, Newman campaigned vigorously for Hawkins and he was elected over Keble. More than fifty years later, Newman acknowledged that Hawkins' election was largely due to his own influence: 'Let me add what I have never yet brought out, that it was a longing on my part for some stricter discipline *which was the direct cause of Hawkins' election.*'[5] If we take the italicized words seriously, we should conclude that Newman is here acknowledging his responsibility for the election of Hawkins. However, in spite of his explanation that his support of Hawkins was prompted by a longing for stricter discipline in the college, most of his biographers have found his choice of Hawkins over Keble mystifying, if not downright inexcusable. For it was Hawkins who subsequently dismissed Newman from his tutorship and Keble who became an important ally in the Oxford Movement. As Meriol Trevor points out, 'In helping to put Hawkins rather than Keble at the head of his college, Newman was unknowingly cutting his own throat, for the Provost was to prove one of the stiffest of his opponents. For Keble, it meant a lifetime of obscurity in country parishes.'[6] How could Newman have been such a poor judge of character in this instance as to prefer Hawkins over Keble?

If we view Newman's support of Hawkins in the context of his concern for his own professional advancement, this preference of Hawkins over Keble is not so mystifying. Since Hawkins was Vicar of St. Mary's Chapel at the time Copleston stepped down from his Provostship, his election as Provost would leave that post vacant. Because Newman was then his curate, it would be natural enough for him to succeed Hawkins as Vicar. On the other hand, if Keble had been elected Provost, Newman's professional situation would have remained unchanged. Thus, through his vigorous campaigning for Hawkins, he gained the 'living' and 'promotion' which he had dreamed of, quite guiltily, for some months. This is not to say, of course, that he thought solely of his own advancement in achieving the election of Hawkins. But it is to say that his motives for supporting Hawkins need to be considered in light of the consequences of this support. It is doubtful that Newman, already thinking about promotion, would have neglected to consider these consequences. And the fact that even fifty years after the event he was still attempting to explain his support of Hawkins would seem to indicate that it continued to evoke guilty feelings.

Newman's dreams of promotion were therefore fulfilled. But, having helped Hawkins become Provost, he immediately found himself in conflict with his superior. Less than eight months following Hawkins' election, Newman and two other tutors who had been students of Keble, Robert Wilberforce and Hurrell Froude, were contemplating changes in the curricular organization of the college. Again, the fact that Newman fell immediately into conflict with Hawkins has caused his biographers some consternation. They attribute this sudden reversal in the relationship to Hawkins' alleged change in demeanor after taking office. While Hawkins, now safely ensconced in office, may have made life difficult for his younger supporter, Newman's conflicts with him are not so mysterious if we consider that his support of Hawkins had been prompted more by personal ambition than by respect for him. In any case, the conflict between Hawkins and his young tutors was quick to develop, and it centered on proposed curricular changes. In a letter written to Newman in September, 1828, Wilberforce summarized a number of changes which they agreed would be beneficial to the better students and then concluded by suggesting that they seek Provost Hawkins' approval of the changes.[7] But this suggestion was apparently overruled or neglected by Newman and Froude. For, in a letter to another friend in February, 1829, Newman pointed to all the changes they had effected in curricular design and then cautioned that 'we do not want this to be talked about'. He went on to explain that Hawkins, though he had not taken the initiative in these innovations, nonetheless always approved. However, when Hawkins learned that numerous changes in the tutorial system had been made without his knowledge, he immediately demanded an explanation. In seeking to justify their decision not to notify him, Newman and the other tutors contended that the University statutes allowed them to structure tutor-pupil relations as they saw fit. According to the statutes, they were answerable only to the senior tutor and not to the Provost.[8]

The curriculum dispute was not settled amicably. By May, 1829, the conflict had reached such an impasse that Newman sent the Provost an 'ultimatum' demanding his approval of the changes or dismissal of the tutors. In June, Hawkins reluctantly followed his predecessor Copleston's advice, and informed the three tutors that he would not submit to their ultimatum and was therefore not assigning them any new students. Obviously unprepared for this response to their ultimatum, Newman and the other tutors cast about for a countermove. Believing the University statutes supported his position, Newman considered taking his case to the University Chancellor but then decided against it. One year later he completed work with the students in his charge and thus his tutorship was ended. As a lifetime Fellow of the college, he remained in residence at Oxford and participated in a limited number of college activities.

Newman remained in limbo for more than a year following his completion of his tutorial work. Then, in 1832, he accepted, but with considerable misgivings, Hurrel Froude's invitation to accompany his father and himself on a tour of sourthern Europe. The tour was intended to be rehabilitative for the younger Froude, who was then in the initial stages of the illness which was to claim his life in 1836. Newman himself went out of some vague sense that it was his duty to go.[9] As he travelled, however, it became increasingly clear that he was wrestling with some very crucial vocational conflicts. Given the unfortunate results of his altercation with Hawkins, what was he to do now? He could, of course, continue his research and writing as he had during the year between his dismissal and his embarking on the tour. (He was working at this time on his history of the Arian controversy.) But was this enough? Was a private life of studying and writing what God had destined him for? He expressed his misgivings regarding the private life in a letter written to a friend during his travels. As he expressed it, 'If God willed me a private life, the happier for me; and I think I do feel this. O my God; so that if Thou wilt give me retirement, Thou wilt give me what I shall rejoice and prefer to receive except that I should be vexed to see *no one* doing what I could do in a measure myself.'[10] Here, Newman expresses attraction to the continued private existence which his dismissal as tutor had secured for him. But he also felt responsible for engaging in activities which would otherwise go undone. As we shall see, his illness in Sicily enabled him to resolve this vocational dilemma.

Newman set sail with the Froudes in December, 1832. They toured the Mediterranean countries, finally arriving in Rome in February, 1833. Rome was to be their last stop before returning to England. However, when they arrived in Rome, Newman surprised the Froude's by announcing that he would not be returning home with them, that he had decided to postpone his return and tour Sicily again, this time unaccompanied. The Froudes accepted this decision and they parted company. A few weeks after striking off on his own, however, Newman fell deathly ill of typhoid fever. The fever struck in early May and forced him to stop travelling; a month elapsed before he was able to resume his travels. As he lay on his strange bed in a strange country, with no friends to keep him company, he considered that the illness had some 'meaning' for him if he could only discern it. On the first day of his illness, he recalled asking why God was permitting this suffering: "Many thoughts came over me. I felt God was fighting against me, and felt – at last I know why – it was for self-will. I felt I had been very self-willed that the Froudes had been against my coming [to Sicily] ... I said to myself, 'why did no one speak out, say half a word? Why was I left now to interpret their meaning?'"[11] Thus, his first thought was that he had been struck with the fever because he had been headstrong, determined to return to Sicily against his perception that the Froudes were opposed to it.

On the second day of his illness 'the self-reproaching feelings increased'. On that day he reflected on his dismissal as tutor and felt that in this case he had also been obstinate in his dealings with Hawkins: 'I thought I had been very self-willed about the tutorship affair, and now I viewed my whole course as one of presumption. It struck me that the 5th of May was just at hand, which was a memorable day as being that on which (what we called) my Ultimatum was sent into the Provost; and that on the third anniversary I should be lying on a sick bed in a strange country. Then I bitterly blamed myself, as disrespectful and insulting to the Provost, my superior.'[12] He confessed to feeling this self-blame so keenly that he vowed 'not to preach at St. Mary's or anywhere for a length of time as a penitent unworthy to show himself'. Later, in the *Apologia*, he reiterated this belief that he was at fault in the curriculum dispute and observed that although they had each provoked the other, his own fault was much greater because 'in me such provocation was unbecoming ... because he was the Head of my College'.[13] And, in a private memo written in 1860, he described their relations from 1829 as 'a state of constant bickerings, of coldness, dryness, and donnishness on his part, and of provoking insubordination and petulance on mine'.[14] Thus, his efforts to understand his illness had now penetrated beyond considerations of his decision to return to Sicily, especially what this decision meant with regard to his relationship to Mr. Froude, to reflection on his disrespectful actions toward Provost Hawkins. As penance, he vowed that he would not engage in public activities immediately on his return to England. Evidently, he was coming to some resolution that he would engage in public affairs on his return and that his penance would serve as a temporary restraining from such engagement.

However, Newman's self-reproach did not end with these reflections on his earlier altercation with Hawkins. As he expressed the matter himself, 'I felt God was fighting against me'. His initial efforts to understand why God was fighting him by visiting this illness on him centered on his self-assertiveness with the Froudes and, somewhat further back into his guilty past, with Provost Hawkins. However, it appears that he felt especially guilty for having postponed his return to England, for having allowed himself to be drawn back to Sicily. For, in commenting on his return to Sicily, he observed that it is 'Satan [who] lures us by the authentic traces of a lost Paradise'. Hence, in postponing his scheduled return to England with the Froudes, he had allowed Satan to assume control of his life. But God fought against him in this flight to Sicily and, by visiting him with a near-fatal illness, cut him down in such a manner as to suggest both his displeasure with Newman and his determination to insure his obedience in the future. If this interpretation is accurate, we may then say the flight to Sicily not only involved going against the better judgment of the Froudes but that it also, and in a much more fundamental sense, involved placing considerations of his own feelings in the matter above the larger considerations of the work which God had destined him to carry out in England. Viewed in this light, Newman's complaint during his illness that he possessed 'little love' and 'little self-denial' captures this newly-won insight that he had placed personal considerations above the will of God. His whole course had been one of presumption – toward the Froudes, toward Hawkins and even toward God himself. The illness, then, was God's way of 'fighting against' him, signifying to him that there was no escaping the destiny to which he had been ordained.

How strong was Newman's psychological resistance to a 'public life' in England? While it is rather apparent that he was using the trip to prepare himself for future service, his reluctance to reinvolve himself in University controversy was genuine. Consider, for example, a dream which he related in a letter to his mother in April, 1833, about two weeks after setting out by himself in Sicily. As he confessed in the letter, which included an account of the dream, he had been thinking a great deal about events back at Oxford and was especially concerned about the approaching competitions for fellowships offered by Oriel College. He was hoping that one or two of his own students would be selected, thus vindicating his efforts to reform the curricular structure in the college, and was regretting that he would not be there to cast his vote. Thus, the dream was evidently prompted by the same remorse suggested above, that he was avoiding University controversy by remaining in Sicily.

The dream centered on the Provost and Fellows of Oriel College. The scene was the tower at Oriel and the Fellows were discussing the college budget. In the course of working over the budget, Provost Hawkins and Jenkyns, another Fellow, fell into a serious dispute: 'Jenkyns and the Provost had been quarreling (what a shame! I suppose they never did in their lives) and the latter had left the room, and Jenkyns to expedite matters had skipped on in the accounts and entered more items without the Provost's sanction.'[15] After this was done and the budget was completed, Newman stood to shake hands with the other Fellows, recognizing that his closest friends were not among them: 'I shook hands first with one Fellow then with another. At last I got a moment to shake hands with the gallant Dornford, then Copleston (these were the new tutors in our place).' Then he shook hands with the new Fellows elected that year, observing that they were not his own students and were a clumsy, unpromising lot to boot. With this, he recalled feeling a great "longing to get away, and with a sickness of heart. When I got away at length, I could find no means of relief. . . . I wished to retire to the shrubberies, which were those of Ham [his boyhood home] . . . 'There', I thought to myself, 'on this seat or that arbour, which I recollect from a boy, I shall recover myself'; but it was not allowed me. I was in my rooms or some rooms, and had continual interruptions. A father and son, the latter coming into residence, and intending to stand for some Sicilian scholarship. Then came in a brace of gentlemen commoners with hideous faces, though I was not a tutor. . . ."

Now, it requires no unusual psychological expertise to recognize that this dream captures the substance of Newman's vocational conflicts, especially with regard to his genuine reluctance to reengage in University controversy.

The first part of the dream centers on his earlier difficulties in the curriculum dispute. Here, he has substituted Jenkyns, 'who had never quarreled with Hawkins', for himself. Significantly, the dream portrays Jenkyns going over the budget with Hawkins but, in point of fact, Newman was the treasurer of Oriel College at the time of the curriculum dispute.[16] Thus, Newman not only substituted Jenkyns for himself in the dream but also changed the conflict situation by couching the quarrel in terms of budgetary matters instead of curriculum changes. Given these alterations of person and situation, Jenkyns' auditing of the accounts following Hawkins' departure from the room is most intriguing. As we have seen, the changes which Newman initiated in the curriculum – the cause of his dismissal – were also made in secret, behind Hawkins back. And, like Jenkyns' tampering with the accounts, his rationale for taking matters into his own hands had been that of 'expediting matters', of making necessary changes which Hawkins would not have thought to initiate himself. In both situations, however, Hawkins' subordinates had taken actions which evidently only he had authority to carry out. As Newman describes Jenkyns' actions following Hawkins' departure, he 'entered more items *without the Provost's sanction*'. Thus, Newman was recreating and only thinly disguising in this part of the dream his own insubordination in the curriculum dispute.

The focus shifts to the present situation in the second part of the dream. Here Newman has obviously lost the struggle in Oxford affairs. His own students have not been awarded the college fellowships (here Newman's premonition was unfounded since one of his students did in fact win the competition). The fact of this loss, together with his generous but humiliating act of shaking hands with the new tutors in his place, causes him to seek relief from college affairs. He escapes to his boyhood home. And, in a later footnote to this reference to his boyhood home at Ham, he added, 'When I dreamed of heaven as a boy, it was always Ham'. It would be fair to view this impulse to hide away in his boyhood home as expressing the wish for a private life apart from public affairs at Oxford. Significantly, then, his comparisons of Sicily as well as his boyhood home to heaven (Sicily 'retains the authentic traces of a lost paradise') indicated that extending his tour to include the trip to Sicily was psychologically similar to the return to his boyhood home, away from the controversy and humiliating experiences of Oxford. By invoking the image of his boyhood home, the return to pleasurable scenes of childhood, Newman was revealing the profound emotional depths of his desire to remain away from public life. On the other hand, the dream continues and, in the third part of the dream, he is back in his rooms at Oriel College and subject to continual interruption, 'though I was not a tutor'. His depiction of the gentlemen commoners with hideous faces suggests that he anticipated his return with great trepidation, and yet the dream does affirm the necessity of his return in spite of strong inclinations to remain away. In short, the dream captures his genuine ambivalence regarding a return to controversy at Oxford. Yet, like his illness, the dream tells him that his return is expected of him. He might postpone his return, but God will not allow an indefinite postponement of his spiritual destiny.

Newman returned to Oxford on his recovery, and while en route home, wrote a poem which begins to anticipate the biographical studies written in the months after his return. The poem was based on the Old Testament prophet Jonah, and his theme is the prophet's moral weakness: 'Sloth had sapp'd the prophet's strength,) he fear'd, and fled from God'. Like Jonah, Newman had also attempted to avoid the humiliation which was the consequence of his earlier skirmish with the authorities. But, through his illness – his shipwreck on the Mediterranean as it were – he began to consider his return to England in a new light. He would be returning not in a mood of assertiveness toward the likes of Edward Hawkins, but in a mood of obedience and submission to a *higher* authority. Thus, again like Jonah, he was given a second chance to make amends through his physical recovery. His determination not to disobey God a second time is expressed in the following recollection of his thoughts while recovering from the fever: 'I had a strange feeling on my mind that God meets those who go on in His way, who remember in His way, in the paths of the Lord; that I must put myself in His path, His way, that I must do my part, and that He met those who rejoice and worked righteousness, and remembered Him in His ways.'[17] Here, in almost hypnotic repetition, he proposes the resolution of his conflict regarding private and public life through implicit trust in the God who controls all things. Thus, while the unfortunate conclusion of the curriculum dispute had apparently caused him to doubt the trustworthiness of God (in a manner similar to Jonah's first venture in Ninevah), his illness and especially his providential recovery convinced him of God's concern to favor his work in England. He arrived in Oxford on July 9 and the following

Sunday John Keble preached the Assize Sermon in the University Pulpit on the topic of 'national apostasy'. As Newman observes in his *Apologia:* 'I have ever considered and kept the day, as the start of the religious movement of 1833'.[18]

THE BIOGRAPHER'S ART

Let us turn from Newman's illness in Sicily to the biographical studies written after his return to Oxford. Newman's early biographical studies were published in 1833 under the title *The Church of the Fathers.*[19] Written immediately following his illness in Sicily and during the early months of the Oxford Movement, these studies include sketches of Basil, Gregory, Anthony and Augustine. Newman's study of Basil draws an immediate parallel between his own life and that of the early saint. There is strong evidence that Newman was brought up by his grandmother in the country home belonging to his father. Similarly, Newman points out in the beginning of his account of Basil that the saint located his monastic retreat 'close by the village where lay his father's property, where he had been brought up in childhood by his grandmother'.[20] In noticing this 'coincidental' similarity in their upbringings, Newman puts his reader on notice that his life has been prefigured in certain essential aspects by that of Basil. However, the segment of the Basil study which bears directly on his illness in Sicily is the discussion of Basil's own confining illness. The circumstances of this event were as follows: Basil had been living in retirement for three years (exactly the length of time between Newman's dismissal from his tutorship and his falling ill in Sicily). But when the attack of the Arians on the Church of Caesarea had 'made his loss felt', his friend Gregory of Nazianzus began to initiate a reconciliation between Basil and the Bishop Eusebius in order to effect Basil's return to action. Finally, a letter from Eusebius to Basil had its effect, but precisely at a time when Basil was lying ill of a deadly fever. This fever, Newman points out, seems to have been the result of an epidemic and was for this reason unusual. Thus, the circumstances of Basil's illness were sufficiently out of the ordinary to suggest divine intervention. Basil conveyed to Eusebius his eagerness 'to fly straight to Syria' but this, of course, was impossible. As he lay ill, however, he reflected on the positive aspects of his illness, especially the fact that the illness increased his trust in divine mercy: 'But it is the scourge of the Lord which goes on increasing my pain according to my deserts; therefore I have received illness upon illness, so that now even a child may see that this shell of mine must for certain fail, unless perchance God's mercy, vouchsafing to me in His long-suffering time for repentence, now, as often before, extricate me from the evils beyond human cure. This shall be as it is pleasing to Him and good for myself.'

Now, to be sure, the fact that Basil suffered an illness similar to Newman's is not striking in itself. Nor is the fact that both men interpreted the illness as a scourge from God. But what is striking is the fact that, in both cases, the illnesses were intimately bound up with their return to ecclesiastical activity after periods of absence. Too, Basil is being encouraged to return to service by a friend who hopes to overcome his resistance to reengagement by effecting a reconciliation between the bishop and Basil. As we have seen, Newman's reluctance to reinvolve himself in ecclesiastical controversy was prompted in part by his previous altercation with Hawkins. In Newman's case, Hurrell Froude served as such an intervening friend, not however by effecting a reconciliation between Newman and Hawkins but by encouraging a movement at Oxford intended to restore episcopal power to its former prominence. In short, the Basil study focuses precisely on the saint's reluctance to involve himself in ecclesiastical controversy, but recognizes illness as the key to overcoming this reluctance.

As we turn to Newman's study of Gregory, we find our biographer plumbing further the reasons for a saint's reluctance to engage in public affairs. As Newman says of Gregory, 'He professes that he could not bring himself to make a great risk, and to venture ambitiously, but preferred to be safe and sure.' This reluctance to engage in public controversy was prompted, according to Newman, by Gregory's dislike for controversy: 'He disliked ecclesiastical business, he disliked publicity, he disliked strife, he felt his own manifold imperfections, he feared to disgrace his profession and to lose his hope; he loved the independence of solitude, the tranquility of private life; leisure for meditation, reflection, self-government, study and literature'. Newman points out, however, that all this changed with the death of his friend Basil. Gregory 'admired, yet he playfully satirized, Basil's lofty thoughts and heroic efforts. Yet, upon Basil's death, Basil's spirit, as it were, came unto him'. Gregory proceeded to form a congregation for orthodox worship in a heretical metropolis and was stoned by the populace. Newman asks: 'Was it Gregory, or was it Basil, that blew the trumpet in Constantinople, and waged a successful war in the very seat of the enemy, in despite of all his fluctuations of mind, misgivings, fastidiousness, disgust with self, and love of quiet?' Here Newman describes Gregory's resistances to a public and controversial ministry in terms similar to his own inner wrestlings concerning a private or public life. At the same time, he describes how Gregory succeeded in overcoming his desire for retirement from ecclesiastical strife, suggesting that the influence of Basil's death was a most critical factor in this resolve. There was, as it were, a transfer of power from Basil to Gregory.

Now, as we have seen, Newman's tour of the Mediterranean was prompted by the serious illness of his friend, Hurrell Froude. It became clear as the tour continued that the trip could not save Froude and on his return to England he was confined to his father's house. As the Oxford Movement gained momentum his condition steadily worsened and yet, as Newman described him in the *Apologia*, Froude remained 'a bold and daring rider' in ecclesiastical matters. As Froude's physical powers were washing away, Newman was assuming an increasingly dominant role in the movement. If such were against his natural inclinations for peace and solitude and if it belied his own unsettledness regarding ecclesiastical points of view, it was nonetheless in keeping with the 'lofty thoughts and heroic efforts' which he admired in Froude. As Newman put it, 'Such was the power of the great Basil, triumphing in his death'. In short, Newman's study of Gregory probes the psychological reasons both for his reluctance to engage in ecclesiastical controversy and for his eventual reinvestment in such controversy. With the impending death of his friend Basil, he would make Basil's power his own. It is interesting to note, therefore, that the Gregory study exactly reverses the identities assigned Gregory (Froude) and Basil (Newman) in the Basil study. But the fundamental issue of involvement in ecclesiastical conflict remains the same. And here, in the Gregory study, Newman makes quite explicit his understanding that he, like Gregory, was committed to waging a successful war in the very seat of the enemy. Thus, in the Gregory study, Newman further plumbs the saint's reluctance to engage in ecclesiastical controversy, but at the same time he isolates those factors that effected the overcoming of this reluctance.

Newman's study of Augustine strikes the very same note, but this study is unique in that it focuses on a single event, the 'memorable event' of Augustine's conversion. Newman's account of the conversion begins with Augustine's decision to leave Africa, 'his native country, first for Rome, then for Milan'. He makes a point of noting that Augustine came under the influence of St. Ambrose in Milan at the age of thirty-two, precisely Newman's age during his trip to Rome (which also included a stop in Milan). He views Augustine as a troubled young man at the time, especially burdened with vocational conflicts. The issue, for Augustine, was whether to continue in a secular calling which was ostensibly serene and secure, or whether to follow his higher aspirations into a religious calling and an unpredictable future. Like Newman had been in Sicily, Augustine was torn between 'self-will' on the one hand and 'the beauty of religious obedience' on the other. But, as with Gregory, the death of Augustine's young friend Alypius was a stimulus toward religious obedience.

Thus, Augustine was 'converted'. Newman's account of the actual conversion follows Augustine's own account in the *Confessions* almost verbatim and need not detain us here. However, his description of Augustine's life in the period which immediately followed the conversion is important because it develops the view that Augustine now became head of a group of young converts. Thus, like Newman, Augustine was no longer engaged in the formal tasks of teaching. However, again like Newman, he had gathered a group of young men around him on his return to his native country and this group 'naturally looked up to him as the head of their religious community'. Then, however, Newman betrays some of his own ambivalence about being, as his opponents alleged, 'the head of a party'. For, as a consequence of the success of the community, Augustine's fame spread and he became involved in activities uncongenial to the religious life to which he had hoped to dedicate himself. Indeed, Newman exclaims, Augustine's 'talents were of too active and influential a character to allow of his secluding himself from the world, however he might wish it'. In short, Augustine's resistances to public engagement were overcome in his conversion, but the leadership of a group of young converts placed new obstacles in the path of his carrying out his vows of religious obedience.

From this brief survey of Newman's early biographical studies, then, it is evident that Newman views his biographical subjects as reformers. These are men who, after much soul searching, enter into ecclesiastical controversy with a mind toward institutional change. Basil has conflicts with the Bishop, Gregory forms a congregation for orthodox worship in a hostile setting, and Augustine creates a community of young converts to serve as a catalyst for reform. Thus, the event of his illness in Sicily establishes similarities between his life and theirs, i.e., their common, if belated, commitment to ecclesiastical reform.

Conclusion

In the foregoing discussion of Newman's biographical response to his illness in Sicily, we have seen how he interpreted the lives of saints in light of his own recent experience, and we have also noted his tendency to understand this experience in terms of insights gained from lives of saints. Now, in recent decades, there has been a movement in Newman studies to combat what one scholar has called the 'sentimental myth' which characterized earlier biographies of Newman. As an instance of this recent movement, Maurice Nedoncelle cautions that 'Newman's glory, even his sanctity, do not stand to gain from extravagant wavings of censers by poor hagiographers'.[21] Inasmuch as Newman himself rejected such hagiographical forms of biography, this more recent movement in Newman scholarship merits our enthusiastic support. However, our present study also indicates that, in one important sense, hagiography and biography may be inextricably mixed, i.e., when the biographer's identification with the saints exerts a decisive influence on his own self-understanding. While Newman vigorously rejected the suggestions of friends that he was himself a saint, there is little doubt that he saw his life mirrored in the lives of various Christian saints. Thus, efforts to expunge hagiographical concerns from Newman biography are necessary to establish it on a firm historical-critical foundation. At the same time, we need to appreciate and even honor the basic intuition behind the 'sentimental myth' of Newman, that in a certain sense Newman does indeed 'belong' to the hagiographers. As a biographer profoundly affected by the lives of his saintly subjects, he allowed the heroic models evident in their lives to shape and refine his own self-understandings. Thus, his own biographical writings, based on the conception of life as a developmental, chronologically ordered process, were written in the best historical-ciritical mode.[22] However, in selecting for these studies aspects of the lives of individual saints which especially illumined his own experiences, *his* life thereby assumed the mythical cast which identification with the saints inevitably accorded it.

This is not to say that Newman viewed his life as the replica of that of any individual saint. Rather, the very range of his biographical studies indicates that he was more concerned with the biographical pattern of Christian sainthood than with personal identification with any individual saint. And, too, if Newman gave his life a mythical cast through identification with the saints, this should not be understood as an act of self-glorification. Rather, I would understand it as the expression of what he described, in his subsequent account of his illness in Sicily, as his 'rhetorical or histrionic power to represent' certain religious truths. As our account of his illness indicates, Newman had come to recognize the potential value of his own life as a dramatic instrument of truth.[23] His identification with the reformer saints confirmed this self-appraisal. As he said of Augustine, "He had 'counted the cost', and he acted like a man whose slowness to begin a course was a pledge of zeal when he had once begun it".

Notes

1. In his introduction to a collection of Newman's biographical studies, Charles Frederick Harrold points out that there are "enough autobiographical intimations in it to preserve its value for any student of Newman's life and thought". John Henry Cardinal Newman, *Essays and Sketches*, Vol. 3, ed. Charles Frederick Harrold (New York: Longmans, Green and Company, 1948), p. x.
2. In his typology of religious authorities, Joachim Wach places Newman in a subgroup of reformers whose principle method was theological criticism. Wach includes in this subgroup Castellio, Erasmus, Newman and Kierkegaard. The linkage of Newman and Kierkegaard is especially felicitous. For a comparative analysis of these two nineteenth century reformers, see my unpublished doctoral dissertation, "John Henry Newman: A Study of Religious Leadership" (University of Chicago, 1970). See also Wach, *Sociology of Religion* (Chicago: University of Chicago Press, 1944), pp. 331–374.
3. John Henry Newman, *Autobiographical Writings*, ed. Henry Tristram (New York: Sheed and Ward, 1957), p. 210.
4. A. Dwight Culler, *The Imperial Intellect* (New Haven: Yale University Press, 1965), p. 59.

5. *Ibid.*, p. 63. My italics.
6. Meriol Trevor, *Newman: Light in Winter* (New York: Doubleday and Company, 1963), p. 71.
7. John Henry Newman, *Letters and Correspondence of John Henry Newman*, ed. Anne Mozley (New York: Longmans, Green and Company, 1890), Vol. 1, p. 168.
8. One of Newman's students at the time pointed out, 'His politics occupy an earlier place in the memory of his pupils than his theology, for he had analyzed the Constitution and history of every state in the world, ancient or still existing'. In appealing to the statutes, Newman was claiming to have the University 'constitution' on his side. Rev. Thomas Mozley, *Reminiscences Chiefly of Oriel College and the Oxford Movement* (Boston: Houghton, Mifflin and Company, 1882), Vol. 1, pp. 34–35.
9. His friend Thomas Mozley pointed out: 'The tour he was about to make was in those days more of an epoch in a man's life than it is now, and it might be a turning point in his career, as many have since felt that it really came to be in Newman's. But he was now just over thirty. A man has made up his mind at thirty, if he ever made it up, he used to say.' Mozley also pointed out that Newman at this time circulated among his friends a collection of poems titled *Memorials of the Past*, and included 'a motto which showed that a change was passing over him, and he was entering upon a future'. *Ibid.*, p. 293.
10. *Letters and Correspondence*, Vol. 1, p. 363.
11. *Letters and Correspondence*, Vol. 2, p. 365.
12. *Autobiographical Writings*, pp. 125–126.
13. John Henry Cardinal Newman, *Apologia Pro Vita Sua*, ed. Charles F. Harrold (New York: Longmans, Green and Company, 1947), p. 7.
14. Cf. Walter E. Houghton, *The Art of Newman's Apologia* (New Haven: Yale University Press, 1945), pp. 80–81.
15. *Letters and Correspondence*, Vol. 1, pp. 345–346.
16. Some people believed that he would use this position as college treasurer to effect reform in the college. The Bishop of Llandaff wrote Newman in October, 1828: 'It is well that Oriel has so good a treasurer as yourself. Without meaning any reflection on former treasurers, I think you will improve the system; at least you will not be content with copying precedent blindly, but will accomodate your methods to the changes which time is forever bringing on and study continual improvement, which is the way in all things to prevent both degeneracy and revolution.' *Letters and Correspondence*, Vol. 1, pp. 171–172.
17. *Letters and Correspondence*, Vol. 1, p. 368.
18. *Apologia Pro Vita Sua*, p. 32.
19. *Essays and Sketches*, Vol. 3
20. *Essays and Sketches*, Vol. 3, pp. 58–59. Cf. Donald Capps, 'A Biographical Footnote to Newman's 'Lead, Kindly Light',' *Church History*, Vol. 42, No. 4 (December, 1973), pp. 480–486.
21. See Francis V. Reade, 'The Sentimental Myth', *John Henry Newman: Centenary Essays* ed. Henry Tristram (London: Burns, Oates and Washbourne, 1945), pp. 139–154.

23. Erik H. Erikson makes a similar point concerning Gandhi: See *Gandhi's Truth: On the Origins of Militant Nonviolence* (New York: W. W. Norton, 1969), pp. 410–440. Nedoncelle's remarks appear in his essay 'The Revival of Newman Studies – Some Reflections', *The Downside Review*, Vol. 86 (October, 1968), p. 391.
22. In his introductory remarks to his later biographical study of St. John Chrysostom, Newman chides earlier hagiographiers for their tendency to structure their biographies according to the 'virtues' of the saints. In contrast, he argues for a biographical approach to the lives of saints which attends to the matter of biographical form in a developmental way, basing the study on 'events' as opposed to 'virtues'. He writes: 'I prefer (speaking for myself) to have any one action or event of [a saint's] life drawn out minutely, with his own comments upon it, than a score of virtues, or of acts of one virtue, strung together in as many sentences'. Hagiography written according to virtues, he continues, 'is not history, it is moral science; nay, hardly that: for chronological considerations will be neglected; youth, manhood, and age, will be intermingled. I shall not be able to trace out, for my own edification, the solemn conflict which is waging in the soul between what is divine and what is human, or the eras of the successive victories won by the powers and principles which are divine. I shall not be able to determine whether there was heriosm in the young, whether there was not infirmity and temptation in the old. I shall not be able to explain actions which need explanation, for the age of the actors is the true key for entering into them.' However, Newman's analysis goes further than simply an insistence on chronology as the key to developmental biography. In addition, he insists on a 'connectedness' of events which captures the essential unity of the life. He continues: 'Perhaps I shall be asked what I mean by 'Life'. I mean a narrative which impresses the reader with the idea of moral unity, identity, growth, continuity, personality. When a Saint converses with me, I am conscious of the presence of one active principle of thought, one individual character, flowing on and into the various matters which he discusses, and the different transactions in which he mixes.' *Essays and Sketches*, Vol. 3, pp, 166–169. Newman here has adopted a fundamentally Aristotelian understanding of biography. See Georg Misch, *A History of Autobiography in Antiquity*, Vol. 1 (Cambridge: Harvard University Press, 1951), pp. 292–293.

PART III

Individual Lives and Cultural Innovation

GANANATH OBEYESEKERE

9

Personal Identity and Cultural Crisis

The Case of Anagārika Dharmapala of Sri Lanka

Introduction

Sri Lanka (Ceylon) is probably the oldest Theravāda Buddhist country, and its major ethnic group, the Sinhala, has always been conscious of this heritage. They have called their country Dhammadvipa, 'the Island of the (Buddhist) Doctrine'. Buddhism is on the one hand a universal religion; on the other hand, like all universal religions, it had to be institutionalized in the local culture into which it diffused. This transformation of Buddhism, as Weber called it, occurred on several levels, one of them being its conversion into the state and national religion of each South Asian society which accepted it. In Sri Lanka as elsewhere in South Asia, Buddhism was the state religion and the kings were defenders of the faith. On the level of the community of believers Buddhism and ethnic identity were one: to be Sinhala was to be Buddhist, and vice versa. So it was in Burma, Thailand, Cambodia and Laos. The identity 'Buddhist' is inseparable from ethnic, in this case, Sinhala, identity.

This notion of a Sinhala-Buddhist identity was expressed in the myths and chronicles of the Sinhala people. I have dealt with these myths at length elsewhere,[1] but let me briefly mention a few. According to the great chronicle of the Sinhala, the Mahavamsa, the Buddha himself visited the Island three times, banished the demons and evil spirits that inhabited it, set his footprint on the peak Samanala (Adam's Peak), and visited other places in the country which today are popular places of Buddhist pilgrimage. The significance of the myth is that the Island has been consecrated by the Buddha. Evil forces have been banished or subjugated preparatory to the arrival of the founder of the race, Vijaya. Vijaya arrived in Sri Lanka on the day the Buddha died; on his arrival he was blessed by the god Vishnu, on the instructions of Sakra, the guardian god of Buddhism. The Buddha himself prophesied before his death that Sri Lanka would be a place where Buddhism would flourish.

These myths, which are repeated in various contexts – literary, ritual and historical – crystallized Sinhala identity until about the 16th century. This identity is simply Sinhala-Buddhist. The myths also express the self-perceived historical role, decreed by the Buddha, of the Sinhala nation as the guardian and protector of the sāsana. In a sense, myths are more powerful than actual historical events, for Sinhala 'history' in the modern sense of that term is a series of events which have little bearing on or meaning in the lives of the people. Myths, by contrast, are always present in the minds of the people at any given point in history, and sum up for them the 'meaning' of their country's history. Historical events, which we know from verifiable sources to have occurred, may also be mythicized, to become part of the larger corpus of myth that gives meaning to the self-perceived historical role of any nation. Historical events become mythicized when they have been repatterned in according with the pre-existent dominant myths of a nation.

The historical events as depicted in Sri Lanka's chronicles until the 16th century had an unvarying pattern. With a few exceptions, Sri Lanka was consistently invaded by South Indian peoples who were generally Tamil speakers. Thus there were historically two major opposed ethnic identities, Sinhala versus Tamil (Shaivite unbelievers). The historical conflicts between Sinhala and South Indian invaders reinforced and stabilized Sinhala-Buddhist identity.

The wars between the Sinhala and the Tamils continued until the 16th century. In the 10th century the old capital of Anuradhapura had to be abandoned owing to the Tamil invasions, and the capital was moved east to Pollonnaruva. The low point in Sinhala fortunes commenced in the late 10th century with more systematic invasions from South India, unlike the sporadic incursions of the earlier periods. Sri Lanka was a principality of the Tamil Cola kings till 1070 when the Sinhala Chieftain Kirti raised the standard of revolt and assumed the crown as Vijayabuhu I (1059–1114 A.D.). Under Prakramabahu Sinhala civilization reached new heights, and Pollonnaruva, the new capital, became a great city. But the respite was temporary. In 1214 Magha of Kalinga landed in Sri Lanka with a large army of South Indian mercenaries and devastated the old kingdom. As a result of these invasions the centers of the old civilization in the Northern Dry Zone of Sri Lanka were abandoned, and the Sinhala kings gradually moved to the South-west. The new capital was Dambadeniya to the south of the Old Kingdom; then Gampola near Kandy (central Sri Lanka) in the middle of the 14th century. In the beginning of the 16th century there were three virtually independent kingdoms in the country – Kandy, Kotte near Colombo, and the independent Tamil kingdom in the northern Jaffna peninsula. The existence of a Tamil kingdom in the North implied the existence of an ethnically homogenous Tamil community which persists to this day. By the beginning of the 16th century there were also groups of Tamil-speaking Moslems scattered in various parts of the Island having an identity distinct from, and opposed to, both Sinhala and Tamil.

The period of the decline of the old Sinhala civilization may have resulted in the demoralization of the Sinhalese, but did not otherwise affect their identity. Sinhala still implied Buddhist, and was opposed to Tamil (and Moslem). The division of the country into separate autonomous Sinhala kingdoms no doubt produced conflicts between Sinhala people, but similar divisions had existed in previous periods. The Sinhala ethnic identity transcended political boundaries, and is perhaps one reason for the instability of these boundaries and the massive crossing over of people from one kingdom to another. The radical change in ethnic identity came with the advent of European powers, beginning with the arrival of the Portuguese in 1505.

By the end of the 16th century the Portuguese were in virtual control of the coastal region known today as the 'low-country'. The kingdom of Kandy alone remained independent. In 1655 the Dutch defeated the Portuguese, and retained control of the seaboard until they were defeated by another Protestant power, the British, in 1795. In 1815 the British marched into Kandy, defeated the last king, and brought the whole country under their rule.

The advent of European powers had serious implications for Sinhala identity, for the historic equation of Sinhala-Buddhist ceased to have the universal validity it once had. As a result of European proselytization, Sinhala people were converted to Catholicism and later to Protestantism. In the areas that came under Portuguese rule, Catholicism was the dominant religion. Later with the Dutch and the British, Protestantism became politically dominant, and Sinhala Protestants became economically dominant also. Thus the old Sinhala ethnic identity split into several contrastive sets:

Sinhala Buddhist × Sinhala Catholic
Sinhala Buddhist × Sinhala Protestant
Sinhala Catholic × Sinhala Protestant

There developed then three separate Sinhala identities, distinguished by religion – Buddhist, Catholic, Protestant. Furthermore, these identities were characterized by regional, occupational and class differentiation. The bulk of Sinhala peasants living in villages were Buddhists while Catholics were largely confined to the fishing communities on the coast. Protestants became a bureaucratic elite in the Dutch and British areas. To compound matters the Tamil ethnic identity was also split in the same fashion, and there were the Moslems who could also be characterized as an ethnic group. From the point of view of most Sinhala Buddhists the Chirstians were one group, *āgama* ('religion' lit., 'tradition'). Perhaps this term developed because the missions claimed their religion was the only religion, or *āgama*. In opposition to *āgama*, the term *Buddhāgama* was used to refer to Buddhists, which is now also a self-reference term. This is a new term, but one which has persisted as a result of the split in Sinhala identity into Christian and Buddhist.

Let us briefly sum up the effects of colonial rule on the Sinhala identity. First, there was the split in Sinhala identity, as mentioned earlier. Secondly, Buddhism ceased to be the official and dominant religion. It lost prestige, and Sinhala-Buddhists simultaneously lost political and economic power. Under British rule Protestantism was dominant and Protestant churches were built near old Buddhist temples, symbolizing the supercession of the old religion by the new. The demoralization of the Sinhala people is manifest in the millenial myth which became popular in British times among Sinhala peasants, the Diyasena myth. According to this myth a new Sinhala culture hero, Diyasena, will arise, kill all the Christians and non-believers, and reestablish the glory of the Buddha *sāsana*. This millenial fantasy is the product of the plight of Sinhala-Buddhists, demoralized and unable to take positive rational action to reestablish lost prestige. Though demoralized, the bulk of the Sinhala were still Buddhist, living in peasant villages. Yet power was in the hands of colonial rulers, and a minority of educated and westernized Sinhala Protestant elite in the cities.

The middle 19th century saw a revival of Buddhism in Ceylon. This revival has been documented by Malalgoda.[2] It was initially spearheaded by educated monks, who in general ignored their internal differences and conducted a vigorous campaign against the Christian missions. The climax of this campaign was a debate in Panadura in 1873 between the Buddhist monks led by a fiery orator, Miguttuwatte Gunananda, and several Protestant clergymen, in which the former trounced the latter. In the 1890s the campaign against the missions, as part of the wider nationalistic revival, was initiated by Anagārika Dharmapala, whose biography we record here.[3] This man, in resolving his personal identity problems, helped forge a new and unified Sinhala Buddhist identity, healing the split which had resulted from the effects of colonial rule.

Early life and social background

Anagārika Dharmapala's father was a carpenter of the *goyigama* (farmer) caste who left his native home in Hittatiya, a village near Matara in the Southern province, in order to seek his fortune in Colombo. He was eminently successful, and established the firm of H. Don Carolis, which exists to this day as Sri Lanka's foremost furniture establishment. Hevāvitāranalāge Don Carolis married the daughter of Don Andiris Perera (later Muhandiram Dharmagunawardene), a wealthy Colombo businessman who was also of village background. Don Carolis and his father-in-law were often referred to as 'appuhāmi', a term used for respectable villagers of the *goyigama* caste. Many *appuhāmis* from the villages in the Southern and Western provinces were in small businesses in the city of Colombo. Some of them, like Don Carolis and Don Andiris Dharmagunawardene, became extremely wealthy and supported the Buddhist revival movement.

These Colombo *appuhāmis* were neither of the village (which they had left for good) nor of the English speaking Protestant elite that dominated the urban political and social life. From the point of view of the elite they were *parvenus*, attempting to emulate elite life styles. This generation of *appuhāmis*, barred from marrying into elite ranks, was complelled to inter-marry. Wealthy but socially and politically inconsequential, they nevertheless aspired to elite ranks. Techniques for approaching elite status were (a) emulating elite life style, made possible by their wealth, and (b) converting their children into elites via the educational system, through an exclusive

English education in Colombo and sometimes in England. In addition, *appuhāmis* sought status through honours from the Colonial government, in particular titles of office like Muhandiram and Mudaliyar.[4]

Into this stratum of society Anagārika Dharmapala was born on 17 September, 1864. He was the oldest son of H. Don Carolis. He was named Don David, and was registered as Hevāvitāranalāge Don David. The personal name Don David (like Don Carolis), followed the surname in Sinhala fashion, but when the family became more 'respectable' they reversed the names to the English order. Later in his life Anagārika Dharmapala explained his Western personal name:

"...children of Buddhist parents had to be taken to a church where the minister would record the name of the parents and the date and birth of the child, the Christian minister would give a biblical name for the infant."[5]

It is true that births could only be registered at a church until this law was abrogated in 1884, but this was not the only reason for his name. During this period many Sinhalese were voluntarily adopting English names, such as Dharmapala's father's name, Don Carolis (from the Portuguese, Don Carlos).

Dharmapala's early education was inconsistent and contradictory. His family resided in the Pettah, the 'native' business quarter. Dharmapala reminisced: 'As an infant I was sent to a girls' school in the Pettah where Dutch Burgher girls were taught English'.[6] It is not likely that a 'native' child was happy there. At six he was moved to the Pettah Catholic School, 'now known as St. Mary's School'. At age eight he was moved to a Sinhala school in the Pettah. Here

"...I had to go through Sinhalese textbooks as were taught in the Buddhist temples in Ceylon. My Sinhalese teacher was a strict disciplinarian who impressed in my mind the necessity for keeping everything clean and using plenty of water to keep the body in physical purity."[7]

While Dharmapala gained a good Sinhala education here, this school was not Buddhist, but Baptist.

In 1874 Dharmapala's family moved to the predominantly Catholic suburb of Kotahena where, he said, 'my father had a beautiful garden house'. With the move, the ten-year-old Dharmapala changed schools again. He went to St. Benedict's College in Kotahena, a famous Catholic School with an English curriculum. Since the child came from a 'native school' he was put in the lowest form at St. Benedict's, but after some months was 'promoted to a higher class'. Between 1876–1878 he was in a Methodist English Boarding School, and in 1878 he was sent to the highly prestigious Church of England school, St. Thomas College, Mt. Lavinia, where he remained till 1883.

Thus his education shifted from Catholic to Protestant and from Sinhala to English. It was, one might say, a rootless education – ironically, and unintentionally from the parents' viewpoint – reflective of the social rootlessness of the family, which was neither of the village nor of the city. Dharmapala explains his mission school education:

"The reason is that the Buddhist temple school in Ceylon had been forcibly closed because, in view of a commission appointed by the government to investigate them, the children attending them were too loyal to the traditions of old Ceylon."[8]

It is true that a reasonably good education was available only in mission schools, but Dharmapala's early education also reflected status changes in his own family. The schools he attended show an increasing order of prestige.

Dharmapala's early life and education had serious implications for the identity problems of an intelligent and sensitive child. First, we noted that his father who belonged to the *goyigama* (farmer) caste had given up his primary group identities (his kinship and caste obligations) and emigrated to Colombo where he was not entirely accepted into Colombo's Protestant elite society. Dharmapala's family had not established place in the community. It is likely that Dharmapala was conscious of this fact and later attempted to find roots, not in any specific locality or grouping, but in the whole historical tradition of Sinhala Buddhism.

Secondly, the religious education he received in the schools was in stark contrast to the religious education in his home, posing a moral dilemma as well as an identity dilemma of the first magnitude to the child. In school he was nurtured in Catholicism, and later Protestantism:

"...in the years six to ten I was associated daily with Catholic teachers. I was a favorite with my padre teachers because I brought flowers from my father's garden to decorate their altars on feast days..."

In all likelihood he was a 'good', obedient pupil, as he was a 'good' son, at least on the surface, and he probably reflects on his own attitudes when he says: 'As boys, the Sinhalese are good and obedient and love their teachers'. At twelve he was reading the Bible 'four times a day' in the Protestant boarding school. 'During the two and a half years I stayed there I was taught very little history or arithmetic, but pored over Bible lessons from morning till evening.'[9] Though later he developed a great hatred of the missions, he respected the Bible, particularly the New Testament, and the personality of Jesus himself. Wherever he went he carried copies of Buddhist texts as well as the Bible 'heavily underlined with references and cross references and falling apart from constant use'.[10]

At the same time, Dharmapala was being taught Buddhism at home. The village Buddhism of his father's ancestral home in the South, with its heavy orientation towards magic and exorcism, had little relevance in the urban milieu in which Dharmapala was raised. The Buddhism practiced by his parents had a more fundamentalist character, partly because they and his maternal grandparents were closely associated with the monkish intellectuals who spearheaded the Buddhist revival. The scholar Hikkaduve Sri Sumangala and the great orator Miguttuvate Gunananda were closely associated with the Hevāvitārāne family. In this environment the kind of Buddhism that Dharmapala learned was the intellectual doctrinal tradition imparted by the monks.

'My family, which is Sinhalese, has been Buddhist without a break for twenty-two hundred years.'[11] This sentence shows that Dharmapala identified his family primarily with an idealized Buddhist identity.

"All the members of my family were devout. I had to recite passages from the *sutras* and holy poems to my mother: and always she had ready, as a reward for good work, special sweets which she knew I liked..."[12]

His mother's charity toward the poor, and his mother's sister's qualities of a 'ministering angel' created in him, he says, a sensitivity to 'human suffering from bodily privation, and I always want to help those who are poor'.[13] The whole family observed the precepts, meditated and fasted 'once a month on full-moon day'.[14] The contrast between Buddhism at home and Christianity at school comes out dramatically in the following reference to his early childhood: 'Every half an hour the class had to repeat a short prayer in praise of Virgin Mary, and I got accustomed to Catholic ways, *though I was daily worshipping my Lord Buddha*'.[15]

The conflict between the home and the school environment was manifest in the child's sensitive conscience at a very early age. He speak of the humiliation that Buddhists and Buddhism bore through the taunts of the missionaries. He says of the Catholic mission school:

"The *padres* gave us bonbons and stroked our hair to show us that they loved us. But they also would say to us constantly: 'Look at your mud image. You are worshipping clay.' Then the small Buddhist boy would turn in shame from his native religion."[16]

"I remember on a certain Sunday, I was reading a Buddhist pamphlet on the Four Noble Truths, when he (the boarding master at Christian College) came to see me and demanded the pamphlet from me, and had it thrown out of the room."[17]

For a sensitive child, the loss of self-esteem suffered as a result of these onslaughts must have been great. The young boy, not yet ten, reacted to these insults by abusing the *padres* in fantasy.

"But my teachers could not win me away from the Buddhist training I had received at home. The *padres* were great pork eaters. I thought: 'The dirt pigs eat is disgusting. These fellows must be very dirty.' That thought was enough to breed any early contempt for my missionary teachers."[18]

At twelve, while studying in the Protestant mission school, an incident occurred which profoundly affected him, for he repeated it several times in his writings.

"One day when I was at this school [...] I saw one of my teachers go out into the field with his gun and shoot down a bird. I was horrified. I said to myself – and at that time I was reading the Bible four times a day – 'This is no religion for me. He is a preacher of Christianity and he goes out cold-bloodedly and kills innocent birds.' The teachers in that school also drank liqour, a practice that was against my earliest teachings. Not long after this time one of my classmates died. As we looked at him, lying so still on his bed, our teacher told us to pray. Suddenly I realized that we were praying because of fear. From that moment freedom of thought was born in me. I ceased to pray. And I soon became very critical of the Bible."[19]

Later he became openly rebellious: 'I became a Biblical critic in the boarding school, and I was threatened with expulsion if I continued to attack Jesus Christ.'[20]

Thus it seemed that the home environment prevailed, due largely no doubt to the influence of his devout mother and the monks with whom he came into contact. At ten Dharmapala listened to Gunananda's famous debate with the Christians. On his way to St. Thomas' College, at age fourteen, he passed Gunananda's temple daily, and from Gunananda he came to hear of the Theosophical Society and of Colonel Olcott and Madame Blavatsky. From the age of fourteen he took a great deal of interest in theosophy and was a voracious reader of the occult sciences.

We have mentioned two types of conflicts – the social and the religious – that posed problems of identity to the growing child, and now we must mention the third – the familial. Dharmapala's father was a hardworking, wealthy and upwardly mobile man who probably had little time for his son. It was his mother, however, whom Dharmapala adored.

"Often, in the midst of my play, I would say to myself, 'May my mother enter *nirvana* when the next Buddha comes'."[21]

Later he wrote about other 'mother figures': 'I owe everything to my parents, to the late Madame Blavatsky and to the late Mrs. Foster of Honolulu.' The latter was his patroness who helped him financially and morally, and he referred to her as 'my foster-mother'.[22] His biographer refers to her as his 'other mother'; and to Blavatsky as 'another mother'.[23]

Dharmapala's identification with his mother is suggested in a reference to the loss of his baby sister at the age of two, when he was seventeen: 'When I saw her quietly weeping over the loss of *our* precious baby...'[24] One can speculate that his identification with his mother was fostered by certain social circumstances. The relation between father and son in Sinhalese society is often one of reserve, and Dharmapala's father was probably hard-working, with little time for his family. Dharmapala, in his reminiscenses, reflected on his respect for his father, but never spoke of him in the loving and endearing terms he reserved for his mother and for other mother figures. This situation was compounded by the extremely poor relations he had with nearly all his teachers. The harshness of the child's external world may have pushed him closer to his mother for love, nurturance and support, contributing thereby to his identification with her.

An event in his later school life at Christian College, Kotte, is revealing. In 1876, at age twelve, he was sent to this boarding school, and as a result saw his family only during school holidays. The loss of familial support and mother's love took a severe toll on the boy. 'The food that we had to eat was horrible, and my father had to remove me when he saw how lean

I had become.'[25] We can interpret this statement differently. The rejection of food is a standard cultural expression of the feelings of being rejected, of loss of love. In children food rejection is also an attempt to gain parental attention and solicitude. Dharmapala succeeded, for in 1878 his father removed him from school. After recuperating at home for two months Dharmapala resumed his schooling at St. Thomas' College.

The school background of the growing child, the reserve he probably had towards his father, and the oedipal resentment towards him (to be discussed below) probably contributed to the boy's adoration of and identification with his mother. In this regard an incident that occurred at age nine is interesting.

"In my ninth year I was initiated into the Brahmachariya vow by my father at the Temple, and on that day he advised me that a Brahmachari should be contented with what he is given to eat, and that he is expected sleep little. The vow was taken only for 24 hours; *but in my case it had made a permanent impression in my mind.*"[26]

The reference is to the custom of observing meditation on holy *(pōya)* days. One of the ascetic vows which one observes on such days is *brahmachariya*, total sexual abstinence. Perhaps we are not reading too much into this incident if we infer that the strong impression of the *brahmachariya* vow on the child was due to his identification with his mother, and the association of sex with incest. Much later the British noted in their confidential files that Dharmapala was a homosexual. While there is no independent evidence for this, it is likely that he was at least latently homosexual. He was fond of keeping young boys around him as disciples or acolytes. In his adolescence he was closely associated with the English theosophist Leadbeater who, it was later discovered, was homosexual. In any case, homosexuality, latent or otherwise, has often been associated with a child's early and close identification with his mother.

THE RESOLUTION OF AN INDENTITY CRISIS

The life of Anagārika Dharmapala clearly reveals the situation which arises when the identity crisis of an individual has significance for the group. Let us sketch the manner in which his crisis came about and was resolved through his adoption of an historic role.

At age sixty-nine Anagārika Dharmapala asked himself why, in spite of all the pressures brought to bear on him as a child, he had not become a Catholic. His answer was the correct one: that the strong Buddhist environment at home prevailed.[27] However, there were other influences on the child. One was that of the intellectual monks of the Buddhist revival, particularly Miguttuwatte Gunananda and the gentle scholar Hikkaduve Sumangala, the only older males with whom Dharmapala had positive relationships. He always spoke of them with affection and respect. Though these monks were males they were in a sense outside the kinship and secular status system; as monks they were 'sexless'. Furthermore, their vows of chastity, asceticism and sexual abstinence had a strong appeal to a child who at age nine had felt the indelible effect of the Brahmachariya vow. If we are correct about our inference of Dharmapala's homosexuality, then the monk role with its ideal of celibacy would have great appeal to him. He idealized the good monks (holy bhikkus, he called them) as he castigated the bad, and held up monkish behavior as a model and as a contrast to that of the Christian padres.

"In contrast to my wine-drinking, meat-eating and pleasure-loving missionary teachers, the bhikkus were meek and abstemious. I loved their company and would sit quietly in a corner and listen to their wise discourse. [...] I was fortunate in knowing well the Venerable H. Sri Sumangala, the most learned and beloved of bhikkus. [...] Another Buddhist monk whom, as a friend of my family, I saw nearly every day was Mohottiwatte (Miguttuwatte) Gunananda [...] a golden tongued orator."[28]

It is the golden orator with his whiplash tongue and fiery dialectic that became his 'role model', rather than the meek scholar, Sumangala. He tried, we shall show later, to be meek and full of *maitreye* (compassion), but could hardly sustain it.

Through these two monks Dharmapala was introduced to the theosophists, Blavatsky and Olcott, another powerful influence on his life. It came about in the following manner.

An account of the Panadura controversy was published in English, and Dr. J. M. Peebles, an American spiritualist visiting Sri Lanka, showed it to Madame Blavatsky and Colonel H. S. Olcott, the founders of the Theosophical Society of New York. Olcott, who was president of the Theosophical Society, opened correspondence with Sumangala and Miguttuwatte Gunananda and Blavatsky presented a copy of her book *Isis Unveiled* to the latter.

Olcott expressed his wish to help the Sinhala Buddhists and his letters were translated and widely publicized among Buddhist intellectuals. In 1879 the Theosophists transferred their headquarters to Adyar near Madras and in May, 1880, Olcott and Blavatsky, accompanied by five Indian delegates and an Englishman, arrived in Sri Lanka. They were given a hero's welcome as Western champions of Buddhism during their two month tour of Sri Lanka. During this visit Olcott founded the Lanka Theosophical Society (the 'scientific' branch which soon became moribund) and the Buddhist Theosophical Society (B.T.S.), which, as Malalgoda shows, was Buddhist rather than Theosophist.

Even before they arrived in Sri Lanka Dharmapala was impressed by the Theosophists: 'My heart warmed towards these two strangers so far away and yet so sympathetic, and I made up my mind that, when they came to Ceylon I would join them'. He was sixteen when they arrived.

"I remember going up to greet them. The moment I touched their hands I felt overjoyed. The desire for universal brotherhood, for all the things they wanted for humanity struck a responsive chord in me [. . .] as I walked in the gardens overgrown with fragrant plants or along the shore shaded by teak and coco-palms, I pondered on the conversation I had with the two theosophists."[29]

Elsewhere he writes that he was 'drawn to Mme Blavatsky intuitionally never expecting that four years later who *(sic)* would forcibly take me with her to Adyar in spite of the protests of my father, grandfather, the High Priest Sumangala and of Colonel Olcott'.[30]

In 1883 an incident occurred that profoundly affected Dharmapala as it did many Buddhists. A Buddhist procession was attacked by Catholics as it went past St. Lucia's Church in Kotahena towards its destination, the Temple of Miguttuwatte Gunananda. The government condoned the event, but the Buddhists were outraged. To Dharmapala it was not only an attack on his religion, but on the monks whom he idolized. He was nineteen at this time and a student at St. Thomas College. He wrote,

"I had to leave school without even passing the Matric examination because my father being a rigid Buddhist objected to my going to a Christian school after the Catholic riots of March 1883."[31]

More likely the son had already made up his mind to work with the Theosophists, and persuaded his father to remove him from the school.

On leaving school he read voraciously in Theosophy and the occult, and when Olcott and Blavatsky arrived in Sri Lanka again in 1884, he persuaded Olcott to initiate him as a member of the Theosophical Society. He also wanted to go with Blavatsky and Olcott to the Adyar Headquarters.

"I went to my father and told him I wanted to go to Madras and work with them. At first he consented. But, on the day set for my departure, he announced solemnly that he had a bad dream and could not allow me to go."[32]

Clearly this was not the type of career planned by the father for his son. Everyone – the monks, grandparents, and Olcott himself – supported his father, but two women, Blavatsky and his mother, did not.

"Though I did not know what to do, my heart was determined on this journey, which I felt could lead to a new life for me. Madame Blavatsky faced the priests and my united family. She was a wonderful woman, with energy and will power that pushed aside all obstacles. She said: 'That boy will die if you do not let him go. I will take him with me anyway'. So the family were won over. My mother blessed me and sent me off with the parting words, Go and work for humanity'. My father said, 'Go, then, and aspire to be a *Bodhisatva*, and he gave me money to help me in my work.[33]

The passage to Madras was also a rite of passage for the young man from confused adolescence to mature adulthood. He cut his connections with his family and sought a new identity under the guidance of another mother figure. Dharmapala was so enamoured of Blavatsky that he wanted to study occultism, but, to Blavatsky's credit, she encouraged him to devote his life to the 'service of humanity' and to Buddhism. Back in Sri Lanka the same year he took over the management of the Buddhist section of the Theosophical Society. His father, with his high aspirations for his son, was in a dilemma. On the one had he was a fervent Buddhist and supported the B.T.S. (Dharmapala's maternal grandfather was its president). On the other he wanted his son to move into an elite career through a job in the bureaucracy. He persuaded his son to accept a job as a clerk in the education department, urging him to 'see if you can't be practical'.

In 1886 Olcott and Leadbeater visited Sri Lanka and Dharmapala obtained three months leave from his governent job to go with them on a tour of Sri Lanka in Olcott's 'travelling cart'. Olcott left for Madras in two months and Leadbeater and Dharmapala continued the trip. The impact of this tour was profound, for Dharmapala was convinced of the decay of Buddhism, the necessity to regenerate it, and his own role in its regeneration. He wrote a letter in Sinhalese to his father and mother indicating his resolve to devote his life to the Buddhist cause. Though addressed to both parents, the letter is in fact directed to an obdurate father.

Let me summarize its contents.[34] First, Dharmapala says that he joined the B.T.S. with the firm intention of devoting his life to the Buddhist cause. For the two years of his involvement with the B.T.S. he has observed the five Buddhist precepts uninterruptedly. 'It is difficult to convey to another the happy sense of peace that fills a man who leads a pure life.' Such a man sees the impermanence of all mundane life. 'Hence as long as life lasts I will work, in accordance with the Buddhist precepts, for the progress of the world.' He has followed a path similar to that trod by the Buddhas; he too has forsaken his home for the Society's (i.e., the B.T.S.'s) Halls. Secondly,

"I have realized that to be a head of a household, protecting home and property, bringing up children, is one of suffering. Hence I have decided to live as a brahmacharin. Though I would like to become a monk I have decided not to do so, but instead become a lay brahmacharin for life. *A life of a monk is suitable for a person who is concerned with his own selfwelfare. But for those concerned with the welfare of others the brahmacharin life is suitable, useful for meaningful wordly work (lokārthadāyaka väda)*" (my italics and translation). He asks his father's permission, with his hands placed on his head in obeisance, to become a brahmacharin. This is a clear statement of the personal ideals he sets for himself: celibacy (brahmachariya) and this-wordly asceticism. He realizes that monastic life is a selfish one; the Sinhala word *ātmārtakāma* could mean 'self-welfare' or simply 'selfishness'. Asceticism must be practised in the world; he must do 'meaningful wordly work'.

That his rejection of sex is rooted in deep personality problems is seen in the following excerpts from his letter. He writes, 'I am not suitable to lead a life in a household as its head', which may mean 'I don't want to be like my father'. He continues:

"A physically weak person that I am it would be a grave injustice of I were to enter into the bondage of household life. Nothing good will come out of the offspring of a physically weak person. They will be poor in physical beauty and intelligence."

He says that he wants to extinguish the sexual passions that hinder man's other wordly aims. He need not belabor this point, for surely his parents as good Buddhists understand it. The letter ends by saying that he can live cheaply and requests an allowance of five rupees per month for his sustenance.

I have demonstrated elsewhere that sexual anxiety and guilt are expressed in Sri Lanka in terms of bodily weakness, generally the loss of semen either due to legitimate or illegitimate sex, night emissions, and often passing with the urine.[35] Here too the notion of damaged or deteriorated semen is implied in his reference to his physical weakness and the possibility of poor offspring. It is likely that the sexual guilt which prompted the decision of celibacy is due to unconscious incestuous feelings towards his mother, and to 'impotence anxiety'.[36]

Among other things, the latter was a request for the parents' warrant or permission to adopt the new role, such permission being culturally obligatory. For the father this meant the end of the secular ambitions he had for his son. The son had already made up his mind and had resigned from his government job in spite of a promotion he had received. The father took him 'to the colonial secretary who asked me to withdraw my letter of resignation'. But he refused and for the first time explicitly went against his father's wishes. 'With delight I left', he wrote later.

From this point on Dharmapala devoted his full and energy to Buddhism. He renounced sex, took the Brahmachariya vow, and became Anagārika, 'the homeless one'. He shed his Western name, Don David, and his family name, Hevāvitārāne, and adopted a new name, Dharmapala, 'guardian of the doctrine'. His new role could fully mobilize and express in a creative and sublimated form the psychological tension in the individual's life. It must be noted that the *family problem* of attachment to and identification with the mother, is resolved in the new role of *Anagārika*. He initially breaks away from the mother and home largely with the help of a mother-figure, Madame Blavatsky, and takes to the homeless life dedicated to a cause. Guilt feelings regarding sex are also resolved through the *Anagārika* role with its ideal of chastity. The ascetic denial of sex, originally a personal psychological problem, becomes a higher, impersonal way of life.

His lack of roots in the traditional social structure – the absence of village, caste or regional identities – impelled him to seek his identity in Buddhism. Moreover, insofar as he lacked local identities like caste, he could appeal to all sectors of the educated Sinhalese. His religious conflicts led him to be an inveterate and implacable foe of the Christian missions, and he brought to Buddhism the zeal, enthusiasm and bigotry that characterized the missionary dialectic. The style in the following is typical:

"The sweet gentle Aryan children of an ancient historic race are sacrificed at the altar of whiskey-drinking, beef-eating belly god of heathenism. How long, oh! How long will unrighteousness last in Lanka,"[47]

and

'Arise, awake, unite and join the army of Holiness and Peace and defeat the host of evil."[38]

He became a Protestant-Buddhist, a reformer of the Buddhist church, infusing that institution with the Puritan values of Protestantism. These had tremendous influence on a group of people who were in a sense like Dharmapala himself, alienated from the traditional culture of the village, and from the politico-economic system controlled by the British and the English educated elite of Colombo. Later, he had an impact on Sinhala Buddhists as a whole.

Apprenticeship and maturation: 1886–1906

Malalgoda, in his comprehensive and scholarly study of the 19th century revival of Buddhism in Sri Lanka, notes that before 1880 (when Colonel Olcott arrived) lay participation in the movement was minimal.[39] The monks who led the movement attempted to counter the Christian missions on three fronts: education, preaching, and the press, beginning around 1860. On the latter two fronts 'the Buddhists, within two decades, were able to thrust themselves forward decisively in opposition to the missionaries. But on the third front – that of education – the missionaries, during the same period, held their ground with no difficulty whatsoever.'[40]

The reasons are not difficult to find. The monks had two types of schools: temple *(pansala)* schools scattered over the country where village children were educated, and monastic colleges for monks. In none of these was a 'modern' education imparted, which meant that Buddhist children had to attend mission schools for a 'good' education. By 1880 only four Buddhist schools received government grants, indicating government approval of the quality of education imparted. The monks lacked competence and interest in subjects like math and geography, and they also lacked organizational skills to compete with the missions in the field of lay education.[41]

This need of competence and organizational skills was filled by Colonel Olcott and the B.T.S. Olcott, a colonel in the United States Army, a lawyer and an ex-Protestant married to a daughter of a Protestant minister, was a highly intelligent man with great organizational ability. The Buddhist Theosophical Society he formed had a lay as well as a clerical section. The lay section began to take an active interest in Buddhist education under Olcott's leadership. "The result of all this was that, in Ceylon, theosophy began and developed not so much as a new exogenous movement as a stage of an older indigenous movement. 'Buddhist Theosophy' had very little Theosophy in it; what it did have was a great deal of Buddhism."[42] While Buddhist, the theosophy movement was not a traditional Buddhist organization, rather it was what I have elsewhere called 'Protestant Buddhism'. Many of the norms and organizational forms of the new movement are historical derivatives from Protestant Christianity; but it is also a protest *against* Christianity. Thus Protestant organizational models were used explicitly by the B.T.S. in its fights against the missions.

It is this organization that Dharmapala joined in 1884; in November 1885 he took up residence at the B.T.S. headquarters, and in 1886 in his new role as Anagārika he devoted all his time to the activites of the B.T.S. Dharmapala learned much of his managerial and organizational skill from Olcott. Let me recount some of his activities during the period of 1884–1890, when he worked for the B.T.S.

He was general secretary of the B.T.S., assistant secretary of the Buddhist Defense Committee, and manager of the new system of Buddhist schools founded by the B.T.S. Within ten years of its establishment the B.T.S. had sixty-three schools registered under its aegis.[43] Dharmapala was also manager of the Buddhist Press and the Sinhala newspaper, *Sandaräsa*, published by the B.T.S. in 1880. As editor, columnist and unpaid labourer he worked night and day on this journal. During this period he travelled extensively in India with Olcott. He was deeply impressed by the decline of Lumbini, the birthplace of the Buddha, and Gaya, where the Buddha attained enlightenment. The neglect of the sacred pilgrimage places, which showed him the decline of Buddhism in India, set him on his later career of champion of 'ecumenical' Buddhism. Leadbeater had developed a Buddhist catechism which, during this period, Dharmapla helped translate into Sinhala! (Later, in 1925, he was to encourage Payne to produce a Buddhist Bible.) In 1889, when he was in Japan with Olcott, the new five-coloured Buddhist flag was hoisted for the first time by Olcott, who had devised it with Sumangala's advice. Later, Dharmapala popularized the flag.

Thus the period 1884–1890 was a time of training and apprenticeship, following the adoption of the anagārika role which had helped resolve his identity crisis. But it is not likely that the Anagārika would have taken second place for long in any movement or organization. Given his oedipal conflicts and his early school experience with mission teachers, it is unlikely that he would have tolerated a male who stood in a position of authority over him. Furthermore he was gradually formulating his own ideas regarding his role vis-ā-vis Buddhism and Sri Lanka. He saw his goals clearly by 1890: he was interested in rejuvenating Buddhism in Asia and he wanted to resuscitate the Sinhala race and Buddhism in Sri Lanka. These major goals came into sharp conflict with the 19th century liberalism of Olcott who seemed to despise some of Dharmapala's religiosity, particularly his veneration for sacred places and adoration of Buddha relics. To Dharmapala the sacred pilgrimage places represented a Buddhist, rather than national heritage. The relics were also associated with the Sinhala Buddhism of Sri Lanka, i.e., the tooth relic in Kandy was traditionally associated with the soverignty of Sinhala kings. He enjoined people to go on pilgrimages both in Sri Lanka and in India; he exhorted them to attend and encourage Buddhist festivals. Such ideas were anathema to Olcott and by 1890 the two of them had drifted apart. Their final and violent altercation was over the tooth-relic, which Olcott said was an animal bone. This was too much for Dharmapala, and they severed their relationship completely in the early 1900s. Perhaps their antagonism was facilitated by the exteremely bad relations which had developed between Olcott and Miguttuwatte Gunananda, Dharmapala's old hero. The extraordinary success of the B.T.S. meant that the monks took second place in the movement. Gunananda probably resented this and in 1887 there was a confrontation between him and Olcott. Gunananda started his own paper, *Rivirăsa* (sun-rays) in opposition to the B.T.S. *Sandarăsa* (moon-rays).

It is likely that Dharmapala felt drawn towards the strong nationalist interests of his old hero. Moreover, Olcott was an alien; probably he could not lead for long a national Sinhala-Buddhist movement. He had a critical role to play at a certain juncture in history in involving lay Buddhits in education and forging an organization to meet the missionary challenge. But this role, if not redundant, was no longer as relevant in 1890. The B.T.S. never became, indeed *could not* become, a movement involving a mass of people; it continued after 1890 as essentially an organization for developing Buddhist schools, many of them modelled on the mission schools and equal to the best of them. Dharmapala had a key role in the development of these schools, but his place in the B.T.S. was a narrow, constricting one. He had to play his role in a broader arena of history.

The period 1890–1906 saw Dharmapala fully emancipated from the B.T.S. and acting on his own. He travelled widely in India, the United States, Japan, Burma, and Thailand. Dharmapala's Asian travels were for the purpose of getting the support of Asian Buddhists in restoring the Buddhist pilgrimage centers in India, and he became a successful fund-raiser. His work also extended beyond Asia. In 1892, he visited Chicago as a delegate to the World Congress of Religions where he, along with Vivekananda, the Hindu delegate, made a strong impact on his audience. On his way home he met his life-long benefactress, Mrs. Foster, in Hawaii. These travels abroad made him strongly conscious of his wider historical role – not only among Asian Buddhists, but as a missionary to the West. During his travels to Japan, the United States and Europe, he was profoundly impressed by the economic advance in those countries. In 1904, he established an industrial school in Benares on the Western model, using money he had raised on his travels, much of which was from Mrs. Foster. The 'meaningful worldly work' to which he had dedicated himself in his early manhood received objective validation in the economic advance he saw in Japan and the West.

Violence and the oedipal rage

In a previous section I emphasized Anagārika Dharmapala's relationship with his mother, and mentioned his reserved relationship with his father. There is no explicit indication in his own writings of open hostility toward his father. However, there is much indirect evidence of a strong oedipal rage which he had to hold in precarious control. Let me show how these oedipal conflicts were expressed indirectly, and channelled into his social role of religious reformer and nationalist Buddhist.

During the period 1890–1906, after he had gradually broken away from the B.T.S., Dharmapala was for the most part abroad and had little time for work at home. On the one hand this preoccupation with the outside world was due to the explicit goals he set for himself as an Asian (ecumenical) Buddhist, a propagandist, and a missionary of Buddhism to the West. On the other hand his avoidance of home reflected his avoidance of his father. There were reasons beyond the oedipal one which led Dharmapala to avoid his father and these reasons probably prevented him from more fully assuming a nationalist role at home.

Dharmapala's father, Don Carolis, like the other Colombo *appuhamis*, wanted to move into elite ranks. His other sons were given fine educations and one became Sri Lanka's first M.D. trained in Edinburgh. For himself Don Carolis aspired towards honours from the Imperial government and he was made a Muhandiram and towards the end of his life, a Mudaliyar. Dharmapala detested this, and even during this period he warned people not to be cheated by the medals, honours and inducements the British gave them. It is obvious that his role as Sinhala nationalist would involve an attack upon his father, who represented what he despised. As a loyal son he did not wish this to occur; hence his avoidance of his home country and his travel abroad for the Buddhist cause.

The year 1906, though, was crucial for Anagārika Dharmapala, for he started devoting most of his time to his work in Sri Lanka, until 1915 when he was intered as an exile in Calcutta. 'The noble Dharmapala's nationalistic light became more bright and intense during this period.'[44] In 1906 he carried on an open conflict with the B.T.S.; he objected to the word 'theosophist' in the title of the society and wanted it eliminated. He started his own Sinhala newspaper, the *Sinhala Bauddhaya* (Sinhala Buddhist; note the title). If the English journal he founded had ecumenical Buddhism as the primary interest, the Sinhala newspaper was strongly nationalistic, and was influential among the Sinhala intelligentsia. His style of writing was innovative. He did away with the stilted literese then in fashion and the heavily Sanskritized diction of the literati, and substituted instead a folksy, racy, polemical, forthright idiom. From public platforms he thundered and railed against the British and those Sinhala people who aped foreign ways. The psychological backdrop of this wrath was the oedipal rage against his father, which some further incidents document.

Colonel Olcott met with an accident in 1906, and died the following year. Dharmapala's own father died in 1906. With the death of his father, the necessity for avoiding Sri Lanka no longer obtained, and Olcott's death made him the undisputed Buddhist leader of Sri Lanka. After these two deaths it was as if a dam had burst, and the rage which had been contained within rushed forth in a torrent. It is likely that Dharmapala was himself aware of this rage and troubled by its contradiction with the Buddhist ideal of *maitreye* (compassion). His biographer notes this contradiction: "Often he tried to control his anger by repeating to himself 'I am good, I am good'. But often this was unsuccessful."[45]

Dharmapala's invective was often directed toward those who, like his father, succumbed to honorifics, medals and titles offered by the British. One form of dress he particularly detested was the curved comb worn on the head by village officials, or those who have been given a title. He called the comb a horn and frequently and mercilessly castigated its wearers as *gon tädi* (stupid bulls). Dharmapala's father wore such a comb, at least as part of his ceremonial dress. Similarly, at a ceremony at Vidyodaya College he noticed a Muhandiram wearing a tie, a sarong, trousers under the sarong, hat and a stick. 'Who is the wild-elephant with a walking stick', he raged, and grabbed the man from his waist, pushing him against a wall.[46] Surely such excessive and gratuitous violence against an old man must have referred in part to his father who was also a Muhandiram.[47]

His invective was also against the English. The only man of high status whom Dharmapala admired was John Kotalawala, the father of Sir John Kotalawala, one of Sri Lanka's former Prime Ministers. John Kotalawala was a thug who assaulted Englishmen. Physical attack against the English is what Dharmapala surely would have liked to do himself, but he couldn't by virtue of his role. Instead he taught:

"You should assault the lawless British wherever you see them. In front of every house make a scarecrow of the white-man with banana trunks, deck the scarecrow with a pair of trousers, and beat it in front of your children. Then when your children grow up they will assault the alien British."[48]

If the source of his rage was primarily oedipal, this rage was directed to father-figures like those wearing officialdom's insignia. Yet on another level this rage was transformed into the legitimate and patriotic hatred of the authority of the British, the foreign missionaries, and Sinhala who represented a senile tradition. In Dharmapala the rage was harnessed to a leadership role, providing that role with psychological direction – not towards the ideal of *maitreye*, which he could not sustain, but towards resentment of established authority. Culturally, this type of behavior became a model for others, thereby creating a political community influenced by his ideas and by the phenomenal charisma he had for people of all ages and both sexes, wherever he went.

The impact of Anagarika Dharmapala

No charismatic leader affects all strata of society equally. First, Dharmapala influenced the Buddhists who, like his own family, were moving into elite positions via wealth, education and the professions. In Dharmapala's lifetime the Colombo elite expanded to include many affluent Buddhists. For example, the descendants of Dharmapala's brothers are now fully accepted members of the elitist establishment. These are the people whom Dharmapala addressed in much of his English writing, for he feared that their loss of identity and their denationalization would result in the denationalization of Sri Lanka. 'Aryan Sinhalese have lost his (sic) true identity and become a hybrid', he lamented.[49]

Many persons in his own stratum of up-and-coming Buddhist elites sympathized with his Buddhism, but not with the extreme nationalism which they felt threatened their elite aspirations. Politicians felt that his nationalism endangered the negotiations they were conducting for constitutional reform. Respectable Buddhists of Colombo, whose children were receiving an elite education, were perturbed by his attack on Western ways, particularly on English language usage, dress and styles of life. His brothers supported him in many of his activities, but did not change their Western personal names, nor their life styles. Dharmapala resented this: 'We also have an elephant-doctor (referring to his brother) but he (ū, extremely contemptuous pronoun form) wears the trousers of the foreign whites.'[50] In sum, the Buddhist elites were ambivalent towards Dharmapala. They felt more comfortable with the ethos of the B.T.S. than the Mahabodi Society and the *Sinhala Bauddhaya*. Nevertheless he did give all Buddhists a sense of self-respect, so that his generation could take pride in its Buddhist identity. While his brothers did not change their own names, they did give Sinhala names to their children.

A second and more profound effect of Dharmapala was on the Sinhala educated village intelligentsia. Part of this intelligentsia was the monks, and it was Dharmapala who more than anyone in Sri Lanka helped to politicize them. Even more important was a village elite, generally school-teachers, ayurvedic physicians, and minor government officials in villages like headmen, registrars of marriages, and village notaries. Many were products of the British bureaucracy, and all were educated in the rapidly expanding village schools. They lived in the village and had close relationships with peasants, but they were not of the peasant class. Yet they were also far removed from the city elites, and cut off from sources of political and economic power. This was a new stratum, quite different from a traditional feudal bureaucratic class. Dharmapala provided a way of life and a new identity to these people. This village intelligentsia constituted the leadership in Sinhala villages. They mobilized the village vote for the first time in 1956 and brought the popular Prime Minister Bandaranayake into power.[51] Bandaranayake, though himself unaware of it, reaped the heritage of Dharmapala. This was also the stratum that led the 1971 insurrection in Ceylon. The ascetic dedication, rigid Puritanism, and organizational skills of the 1971 rebels, and their nationalist adaptation of Marxism, reflect at least partly the heritage of Anagārika Dharmapala.

Affirmation of the Sinhala-Buddhist identity

Anagārika Dharmapala provided a new identity for this stratum in the villages, and for other Buddhists as well. An identity in the making requires continuing affirmation and symbolic validation. Dharmapala initiated the process of identity affirmation which has continued into our day. He had to affirm his own Buddhist (Sinhala) identity. On the personal level identity affirmation helps enhance individual self-esteem, which has been lowered as a result of shame of humiliation. Dharmapala's message was also directed to others: he insisted that they too affirm their identity. Here the needs of the individual matched the needs of the group, so that today Sinhala Buddhists are still affirming their collective identity as an ethnic group. As a collective phenomenon identity affirmation is a process whereby an ethnic group displays its unity through visible symbols and self-conscious overt symbolic actions, or through the reiteration of grandiose ethnic myths. Sociologically viewed, the process is complicated and probably always occurs as part of ethnic identity-consciousness. It is accelerated in times (a) when there is an actual or perceived threat to the unity of the group, so that the ethnic group must affirm its collective solidarity and self-image; (b) when the ethnic identity is disintegrating and attempts are made to reconstruct or resurrect the ethnic identity, as happened to the Sinhala under European rule; or (c) when an ethnic group attempts to define or redefine itself for political, economic or other purposes where the self-image is not.

The immediate effect of Dharmapala's teaching was quite dramatic. There was massive name changing. Names are identity badges, and name changing implies self-consciousness about one's identity. European names were changed to Sinhala or Buddhist names. At first this name changing was confined largely to the alienated intelligentsia, but it soon became the general pattern so that by the 1930s practically all parents – Sinhala Christians included – gave Sinhala or Buddhist personal names to their children, even if they did not change their own names. A similar dramatic effect was almost immediately felt in female fashions. Well-to-do Sinhala women in the low country – that area which was subject to three centuries of Western contact – wore Dutch or British types of dresses. Dharmapala mercilessly ridiculed these clothes in his speeches and in cartoons in his newspaper. Again, the technique was the same – shaming, lowering of self-esteem and the provision of an alternative. He exhorted women to wear the Indian *saree*. Anagārika's own mother was the first to wear this new dress in 1894 on a pilgrimage to India; soon it became the standard 'national' dress for women in the low-country. Another important innovation was the Buddhist flag, mentioned above. Hitherto Buddhists had no flag. Since the Sinhala identity has implied Buddhist, the Sinhala national flag was all that had been necessary. With identity affirmation initiated by Dharmapala, the Buddhist flag soon became popular, so that on all ceremonial and ritual occasions this flag was hoisted also. The Buddhist flag has been effectively assimilated into the national life to the extent that few are aware of its comparatively recent origin.

As Erikson says, identity makes no sense except in relation to the 'core of the communal culture'. Traditionally the core of the Buddhist culture was adapted to a peasant way of life. In the twentieth century, social changes had produced urbanization and massive economic change. Dharmapala provided a new orientation in Buddhism, consonant with the new identity. This orientation was active involvement in the world. The modal for active involvement was Protestant: the *anagārika* is the modern Sinhala Buddhist analogue of an early Calvinist type of reformism with its increasing this-wordly asceticism. Though Anagārika Dharmapala is more a symbol than a person for most contemporary Buddhists, the *anagārika* role is a function of a specific socio-political context. In the Buddhist Pāli texts, the term *anagārika* (homeless) was exclusively applied to monks. The resurrection of the term *anagārika* by Dharmapala to designate a specific status intermediate between monk and layman was an innovation. Its popular acceptance was due to the need for a model of the 'homeless life' *(anagārika)* in the world.

The life and work of Anagārika Dharmapala anticipated much of contemporary Buddhism. In his Sinhala writings his audience was never the peasantry; it was the educated Sinhala speaking or bilingual intelligentia. He not only enhanced its sense of self-worth, but also provided a 'charter' for modern Buddhism. Let us consider this charter.

Dharmapalas 'this-worldly asceticism': The modern Buddhist charter

Anagārika Dharmapala taught modern Buddhists how to live and behave and how not to live and behave. He himself served as an exemplary model for his negative and positive teachings.

In contrast to Europe's and America's reliance on modern science, Dharmapala sometimes saw Asia as full of opium eaters, ganja smokers, degenerating sensualists, and superstitious and religious fanatics. 'Gods and priests keep the people in ignorance', he said.[54] He scoffed at the typical village monk leading what he thought was an idle life: 'Monks who without working for the race and the nation and ruining the Buddhist order, exist only to fill their spittoons...' Only one with Dharmapala's charisma could have gotten by with such critical statements. His scorn of the gods was no less devastating. He rejected the major deities of Hindu and local origin, who were immediately below the Buddha in traditional worship. Belief in these gods was, for him, superstition antithetical to orthodox Buddhism. Only 'idiots' worshipped gods and demons like Vibisana, Gale Bandara, Mahason, Moratu Yaka, and Pattini.[55] His rejection of the authority figures in the pantheon probably had psychological roots in his relationship with his father and other father-figures.

While castigating Sinhala laziness and superstition, he exhorted his people to positive worldly action orthodox worship. He emphasized thrift, saving and hard work, and urged parents to interest their children in meditation which was an innovation at that time, when it was traditionally confined to old persons. Again and again he condemned consumption of meat and alcohol, the negative Western habits, while urging adoption of the positive Western worldly work.

The thrust of his positive teachings becomes clear in the code of lay ethics for Buddhists which Dharmapala lay down in 1898. Buddhist doctrine has no such systematic code for the laity, although rules of conduct for the order *(Sangha)* are minutely regulated, with great emphasis placed on personal decorum. Only broad generalizations were available for laymen in texts like the *Sigālōvada Sutta.* The lack of specificity of lay ethics facilitated the spread of Buddhism among peasant societies with diverse and even contradictory moral codes. But the publication of Dharmapala's pamphlet of daily ethics, 'The Daily Code for the Laity', codified daily behavior for Sinhala Buddhism.[56] The nineteenth edition appeared in 1958 and 49,500 copies were sold. Behavior in the following areas was minutely regulated, among the 200 rules under twenty-two heads which the Anagārika set down:

The manner of eating food (25 rules)
Chewing betel (6)
Wearing clean clothes (5)
How to use the lavatory (4)
How to behave while walking on the road (10)
How to behave in public gatherings (19)
How females should conduct themselves (30)
How children should conduct themselves (18)
How the laity should conduct itself before the *Sangha* (5)

How to behave in buses and trains (8)
What village protection societies should do (8)
On going to see sick persons (2)
Funerals (3)
The carter's code (6)
Sinhalese clothes (6)
Sinhalese names (2)
What teachers should do (11)
How servants should behave (9)
How festivities should be conducted (5)
How lay devotees (male and female) should conduct themselves in the temple
How children should treat their parents (14)
Domestic ceremonies (1)

The Anagārika's rules suggest some general conclusions about the character of his teachings. First, the pamphlet is addressed to a literate Sinhala intelligentsia; it is a code of conduct for an 'emerging Sinhala elite'. Proscriptive rules refer to habits which peasants are generally given to, such 'bad' eating, dress, and lavatory habits, indiscriminate betel chewing, and use of impolite forms of address. (Yet the Anagārika used some of these same terms on occasion, as in a letter to one of his servants.) Secondly, many Western norms for conduct are found alongside traditional norms. Even the condemnation of peasant manners is based on a Western yardstick. The Anagārika's code is based on traditional norms as well as those prevalent in the wealthy, Protestant influenced society in which he was reared. Thus Protestant and Western norms have been assimilated as pure or ideal Sinhala norms. This is particularly interesting in the case of the Anagārika, whose avowed intention was to reject Western ways. Yet regulations about the correct use of the fork and spoon are included in his code. Elsewhere, his admiration for the West breaks through the polemic and comes into the open. 'Europe is progressive', he once said. 'Her religion is kept in the background for one day in the week and for six days her people are following the dictates of modern science. Sanitation, aesthetic arts, electricity, etc., are what made European and American people great.'[57]

Anagārika Dharmapala himself provided a role model for Buddhist this-worldly asceticism. In his own day his influence was with the 'not yet emerged' Sinhala elite. For it he provided a model which included a national consciousness, a nativistic sense of past glory and present degeneration and an ascetic involvement in this-wordly activity. Few people since his day have actually adopted the anagārika *status* with its associated vestment. But the anagārika *role* has come to stay. A this-wordly asceticism composed of the Puritan type of morality is part of the higher code of urban elite Buddhism. This contemporary Buddhist code emphasizes a greater commitment to the doctrine, living by a 'rigid' moral code, meditational activity for the young and old, an intolerance towards other faiths, an identification of Ceylon with Buddhism and the Sinhala language, and an involvement in social and political (though not economic) activity. However, there is an important difference between the anagārika role symbolized by Anagārika Dharmapala and the contemporary adoption of that role. The anagārika status is a 'bachelor' status; the contemporary 'Puritanism' is for all, including married persons. The Anagārika Dharmapala emphasized the doctrinal aspects of Buddhism and scorned the intercessionary powers of *dēvas* (gods) and demons. But for contemporary elite Buddhists involved in the family and the larger society this emphasis is not easy, for the Buddha is not a conventional deity who grants favours. Today's elite Buddhists therefore still depend on *dēvas* in contradiction to the doctrinal position.

Conclusion

In this paper I have attempted to show the articulation of the personality and the social role of a charismatic leader, and the consequences of his role for the specific stratum he influenced directly and for the larger society. Personality problems constitute a sublimated driving force for the role, so that the one cannot be fully understood without reference to the other. The role, and the individual playing it, could only have been effective at a certain juncture in history, in a specific constellation of social and political events characteristic of a historic period. Had he been born in our day Dharmapala would not have made an impact on Sri Lanka. For example, his mode of addressing social inferiors would have been resented by most modern Sinhala people. Dharmapala also did not believe in social equality (though he probably did not approve of traditional caste inequalities). He himself maintained distance from social inferiors and generally travelled first class by train (in contrast to Gandhi). He was a firm believer in hierarchy, consistent with the views of the stratum he influenced. Yet in his day he was a powerful figure who set an indelible stamp on his society. However, it should be noted that a charismatic leader's influence on the group makes sense only if, for historic and sociological reasons, the group *wants* to be influenced. This was the case in Sri Lanka of Dharmapala's time: Dharmapala's own problems of identity represented in exaggerated form the identity problems of a larger society.

NOTES

1. Gananath Obeyesekere, 'Ethnic Identity and Buddhism: Ceylon' (Paper presented at Burg Wartenstern Symposium No. 51, September 5–13, 1970).
2. Kitsiri Malalgoda, *Sociological Aspects of Revival and Change in Buddhism in Nineteenth Century Ceylon* (Unpublished Ph. D. thesis: Oxford University, 1970).
3. This paper draws heavily on my earlier article on the Buddhist identity, *op. cit.* I have deliberately refrained from discussing Dharmapala's missionary role and his contribution to ecumenical Buddhism. These topics require further research, and they are also not directly related to the theme of this paper.
   I have used three sources for the present work – the two collections of English and Sinhala writings collected and edited by Guruge (1963, 1965) and a biography written in Sinhala by one of Dharmapala's disciples, David Karunaratne (1965). All three works are highly uncritical. The biography in particular is extremely bad, written in a stilted and pedantic style. I have not been able to look at his unpublished writings. One of these is a diary which contains his temptations and sinful thoughts but I have not been able to locate it.
   It should be obvious to my readers that the interpretation and frame of analysis are influenced strongly by Erik Erikson and Max Weber. I have in a sense attempted to relate Erikson's psychological orientation to Weber's sociological one.
4. See Patrick Pebbles, *The Transformation of a Colonial Elite: The Mudaliyars of Nineteenth Century Ceylon* (Ph. D. thesis: University of Chicago, 1973).
5. Anada Guruge, ed., *Return to Righteousness. A collection of speeches, essays and letters of the Anagarika Dharmapala* (Colombo: The Governement Press, 1965), p. 697
6. *Ibid.*, p. 697.
7. *Ibid.*, p. 698.
8. *Ibid.*, p. 653.
9. *Ibid.*, pp. 683–684.

10. *Ibid.*, p. 682.
11. *Ibid.*
12. *Ibid.*
13. *Ibid.*
14. *Ibid.*
15. *Ibid.*, p. 698. My italics
16. *Ibid.*, p. 683. My italics.
17. *Ibid.*, p. 699.
18. *Ibid.*, p. 683.
19. *Ibid.*, p. 684.
20. *Ibid.*, p. 699.
21. *Ibid.*, p. 682.
22. *Ibid.*, p. 769.
23. David Karunaratne, *Anagarika Dharmapala* (Sinhala) (Colombo: M. D. Gunasena and Co., 1965), p. 47.
24. Guruge, *op. cit.*, p. 686. My italics.
25. *Ibid.*, p. 699.
26. *Ibid.*, p. 698. My italics.
27. *Ibid.*, p. 698.
28. *Ibid.*, pp. 684–685.
29. *Ibid.*, p. 685.
30. *Ibid.*, p. 701.
31. *Ibid.*
32. *Ibid.*, p. 687.
33. *Ibid.*
34. This letter is quoted in full by his biographer, David Karunaratne, *op. cit*, pp. 46–48.
35. 'The Impact of Ayurvedic Ideas on the Culture and Individual in Ceylon', in Charles Leslie, ed., *Towards a Comparative Study of Asian Medical Systems*, fo rthcoming.
36. *Ibid.*
37. Guruge, *op. cit.*, p. 484.
38. *Ibid.*, p. 660.
39. Kitsiri Malalgoda, *Sociological Aspects of Revival and Change in Buddhism in Nineteenth Century Ceylon* (Ph. D. thesis, Oxford University, 1970), pp. 370 ff.
40. *Ibid.*, p. 361.
41. *Ibid.*, p. 369.
42. *Ibid.*, p. 381.
43. *Ibid.*, p. 387.
44. Karunaratne, *op. cit.*, p. 95.
45. *Ibid.*, p. 203.
46. *Ibid.*, pp. 116–117.
47. It should be noted that while his father sought the despised Mudaliyar dress, his mother voluntarily rejected the Western dress she wore for that recommended by her son.

48. Karunaratne, *op. cit.*, p. 103.
49. Guruge, *op. cit.*, p. LXXIII.
50. Karunaratne, *op. cit.*, p. 108.
51. W. Howard Wriggins, *Ceylon: Dilemmas of a New Nation* (New Jersey: Princeton University Press, 1960).
52. Guruge, *op. cit.*, p. 510. My italics
53. *Ibid.*, p. VLII.
54. *Ibid.*, p. 717.
55. Karunaratne, *op. cit.*, p. 166.
56. Anada Guruge, ed., *Dharmāpala Lipi* (Letters of Dharmapala) (Colombo: Government Press, 1963), pp. 31–46.
57. Guruge, *op. cit.*, p. 717.

ROBERT MICHAELSEN

10

The Beecher Family

Microcosm of a Chapter in the Evolution of Religious Sensibility in America

> How did man's need for individual identity evolve? Before Darwin, the answer was clear: Because God created Adam in His own image, as a counter-player of His identity, and thus bequeathed to all man the glory and despair of individuation and faith.

It was God who called the true self forth, who created man in His own image and, after man's fall from grace, restored that image. But how was that miracle of restoration or transformation effected in one's own life? Through a sacramental system, said the Catholic tradition. Through saving faith, said Puritan Protestantism and, by virtue of this, consigned sensitive men and women to lifelong soul searching. One sought to know and to obey the truth. But above all one wanted to feel it, to experience it, to be sensibly assured of God's saving power in one's own life.[1] Given the magnitude of man's sin and of the consequent gulf between him and God, this was no easy matter. Just any experience would not do; even 'peak' experiences could be the result of false exuberances or enthusiasms. A miracle was required, a miracle as great as the incarnation: indeed, saving faith was the miracle of the incarnation reenacted in the individual soul. Hence the experience of saving faith was a special experience, a discreet experience, which had its own unique quality. Jonathan Edwards compared it with the taste of honey: it was that real – and that ineffable.

This Puritan stress on a distinctive inward experience made a deep impact on American spirituality. A controlled inward spiritual intensity was sought. Treatises were written and sermons preached to help men to discern the signs within themselves. A whole religious system was built to elicit the coveted experience. And spiritual autobiography became nearly as common as the farmer's almanac.

I turn to the Lyman Beecher family to illustrate the personal results of this kind of Puritan spirituality at a critical and relatively late stage in its development. This family graphically illustrates the dialectical dance that went on between thought or belief and expe ience. What one believed colored his experience, and one's experience affect d his belief. The experience of Lyman's children could not support or endure his thought system. That experience forced a closing of the gap between God and man and a blurring of the focus on the distinctiveness of the experience of saving faith.

Lyman Beecher, who was born on the eve of the American Revlution and died during the Civil War, called his revised Calvinism 'clinical theology'. Under the tutelage of his Yale mentor, Timothy Dwight, followed by more than thirty years in the pastoral ministry, Lyman became an accomplished minister to sick souls. His home was his primary clinic. He sired thirteen children by two wives, and he labored mightily for the salvation of every one of the eleven who survived infancy.

Henry Ward, Lyman's most famous son, labelled Lyman's system '*alleviated* Calvinism'. The 'alleviation' was such, however, as to put even greater pressure on the individual than had unrelieved Calvinism. Lyman lifted the will out of the endless chain of cause and effect into which Edwards had bound it By doing so he gave greater weight to individual effort in the salvation process. At the same time, however, he did not abandon original sin total depravity, eternal punishment, and the mysterious ways of a righteous but inscrutable deity. The conversion experience was crucial. That determined whether one was bound for heaven or for hell. It was an experience in which one repented for his sin and gave up his own will for God's will. But the experience could not be achieved by will alone. It also required divine action. At the same time, the individual was under indictment if the experience was not achieved.[2] Professor Henry F. May correctly points out that Harriet Beecher Stowe and her generation 'had to confront not neo-orthodoxy, but orthodoxy. Hell was not a metaphysical necessity or an absence from God, but a real place full of real fire [. . .] In this place oneself and most of the people one loved were probably destined to spend an eternity of torture.'[3]

By 1819 Lyman was the father of eight children by Roxanna Foote, who had died three years earlier. The five oldest ranged in age from eight to nineteen. These were the critical years, as Lyman himself recognized in a letter to his oldest son, William, who was then seventeen: 'You occupy that period of life in which there is more hope than in any other'.[4] There began about that time a series of written exchanges between father and children, letters which are filled with urgency, poignancy, longing, and turmoil; letters which illustrate the trials of this intelligent, articulate and relatively strong-minded quintet of young people in their efforts to fit with integrity into their father's scheme. This correspondence, together with Lyman's letters to younger children, exchanges among the children themselves, and other types of personal and semi-personal Beecher documents, constitute a rich source from which to document a marked change in American spirituality. (Thomas, one of the younger sons, reports that when he was eleven his father said to him: "This is the most important year of your life, my son; you have come to the turning point of your history"; and thereafter "by many letters and words I was certified four times a year or oftener that I was at an 'important', critical', 'decisive' turning point..."[5] When James, the youngest child, went to Dartmouth at the age of sixteen the father remonstrated with him over his 'eternal destiny'.[6])

The Beecher home was not all morbidity or dullness. As a conscientious evangelical Christian and ministerial father, Lyman did agonize over the state of his children's souls. But he was also an indulgent father who loved to take his children hunting and fishing, who could turn routine household work into a game, and who, on occasion, even danced an old routine for his children's delight. From 1810 to 1826 the family was located in Litchfield, Connecticut, a community of extraordinary cultural depth considering its location. There the Beechers were very active participants in community life. The romantic poets and the novels of Scott were read in their home. Outside the home the old order was changing. The Congregational Church was disestablished in Connecticut in 1817, a move which Lyman fought but later came even to value. Unitarianism was on the rise in the state to the north. Lyman was a sworn enemy of that development and moved into the heart of Unitarian territory in 1826 to do battle. Good strategist that he was, he set out to learn all he could about his adversaries. In the process, his children also learned. Lyman was also a vigorous and vocal moral reformer. The Beecher home was very much alive to the moving issues and ideas of the day.

The very vitality of the Beecher home no doubt increased the burden of concern with the soul experienced by the children. Exposure to the ideological storms and stresses of the time increased psychological pressures within them. It is perhaps remarkable, then, that so many of the Beechers not only survived but went on to achieve some distinction in their own right. (Seven of the eleven who reached maturity were considered important enough to be included in the *Dictionary of American Biography*.[7])

'I have no child prepared to die', wrote Lyman to William in 1819. 'My son, do not delay the work of preparation. Awake to the care of your soul. Time flies; sin hardens; procrastination deceives. [...] Do not put off the subject.' Then he summarized the state of the other accountables in his family:

"I talked and prayed with Edward before he left home [for Yale], and shall attend to Catharine, and Mary, and George, and Harriet, with the hope that God will bless them with salvation. A family so numerous as ours is a broad mark for the arrows of Death. I feel afraid that one or more of you may die suddenly, and I be called to mourn over you without hope. [...] But, oh my son, save me from such an hour on your account. Let me not, if you should be prematurely cut down, be called to stand in despair by your dying bed, to weep without hope over your untimely grave. Awake, I beseech you, my dear son, and fly to Christ. So your affectionate father prays with weeping."[8]

Poor William never quite made it. 'I am completely down in the dumps', he wrote his oldest sister Catharine five years later. 'I was an imaginative boy, somewhat romantic with a sprinkling of minor notes – a sort of sad longing – a feeling I never should be anything – a sort of black sheep feeling.' He complained that he did not know how to study and hence could not keep up with his younger brother, Edward, who went on to success at Yale and Andover. William was in and out of a dozen or more jobs. When not regularly employed, he often returned home where, he reported, 'the great question was: What shall we do with William?' Finally he was converted while working in a hardware store in Boston. Then, surprisingly dissuaded by his father, he decided to become a minister. And there followed a life of itinerancy from one poor and dissatisfied congregation to another.[9]

The experience of Edward, the second son, contrasted sharply with that of William. He too had his soul troubles, especially after he went to Yale in 1818. But during his senior year he attained the coveted experience, the first of the Beecher children to do so. While that experience, as we shall see, did not quite fit the Lyman Beecher system, Edward's description of it was sufficiently persuasive that Lyman triumphantly welcomed him to the firm.[10]

And with that there began a correspondence between Edward and his brothers and sisters in which the second son occupied a surrogate fatherly role.

The one who looms largest in this early correspondence is Catharine, the oldest of the brood. Hers is an especially poignant story, and yet she emerges in the end as perhaps the strongest of the lot. When Lyman's first wife, Roxanna, died, much of the care of the seven younger children fell to the sixteen year old Catharine. She was a strong and capable young woman who managed superbly to rise to the occasion.

Catharine put the crucial religious question in an early letter to Edward: 'How can I make myself feel?'[11] How can I have the right feeling, the requisite sense experience? Shortly after she put this question her situation was immeasurably complicated by the accidental drowning of her 'affianced lover', Alexander M. Fisher of Yale. Fisher apparently also had not received the desired religious experience. Hence, his ultimate destiny was much in doubt. The anguished Catharine asked her brother: 'Oh, Edward, where is he now? Are the noble faculties of such a mind doomed to everlasting woe?' [...] 'Could I but be assured that he was now forever safe, I would not repine. I ought not to repine now', she continues in self-condemnation, 'for the Judge of the whole earth cannot but do right'. But there was the difficulty. 'Right', according to the received Calvinist view, would be condemnation to eternal hellfire if the young man had not had that experience which certified his chosen status.

Catharine was plunged into a period of deep religious questioning and despair: She is greatly afficted. She knows not where to turn for comfort. She longs for God to 'take possession of the heart that He has made desolate', but most of the requisite signs are not to be found within her. 'I feel no realizing sense of my sinfulness, no love to the Redeemer, nothing but that I am unhappy and need religion; but where or how to find it I know not.' Her case, she concludes, 'is almost a desperate one'.

For more than a year Catharine opened her troubled heart to both her father and her brother, but to no avail. 'When I began to write to you on the subject which now occupies my thoughts', she complains to Edward, 'it was with a secret feeling that you could do something to remove my difficulties. But this feeling is all gone now.' To her father she confesses that she is "like a helpless being placed in a frail bark, with only a slender reed to guide its way on the surface of a swift current that no mortal power could ever stem, which is ever bearing to a tremendous precipice, where is inevitable destruction and despair."

"If I attempt to turn the swift course of my skiff, it is only to feel how powerful is the stream that bears it along. If I dip my frail oar in the wave, it is only to see it bend to its resistless force."

"There is One standing upon the shore who can relieve my distress, who is all powerful to save; but He regards me not. I struggle only to learn my own weakness, and supplicate only to perceive how unavailing are my cries, and to complain that He is unmindful of my distress."

Lyman assures his daughter that help is available. At the same time, like a good consulting clinician, he observes to Edward that Catharine's case is 'awfully interesting', that 'there is more *movement* than [...] ever before [...] and she is now [...] handling edge-tools with powerful grasp.' The prognosis is positive.

For nearly two years following Fisher's death, Catharine lived with his parents in Franklin, Massachusetts where she taught his two sisters, studied mathematics with his brother, and listened to the 'fearless and pitiless preaching' of Nathaniel Emmons, one of the most unyielding of the proponents of 'consistent Calvinism'. (Emmons' preaching was significantly influential in driving Horace Mann from orthodoxy to Unitarianism.) During that time Emmons preached a memorial sermon on Professor Fischer in which he lauded Fisher's worldly accomplishments but left Fisher's ultimate status very much in doubt. 'I felt', she wrote to her father after hearing this sermon, 'that I *could not* bend the knee, not open my lips to pray to a Being whose character, to my blinded eyes, was so veiled in darkness and gloom. And for a time, with mournful desperation, I thought I would seek religion no more.'[12]

Catharine did not have the coveted conversion experience during this desperate period, and apparently never in her lifetime. She climbed slowly out of the pit of despair through a resolve 'to do good', to pursue a course that would lead 'to a more extended usefulness'.[13] With the help of Edward and her sister Mary she opened, in Hartford, 'a school intended exclusively for those who wish to pursue the higher branches of female education.' She quickly developed a theory of education which was based on the assumptions that 'all intelligent beings are formed with a supreme desire for happiness, and are continually regulated by this principle...' and that God has so made men and women that they can promote their own happiness by '*doing right*'. Pupils should be taught, by appeal to their reason and their affections, that rectitude will lead to their happiness. 'No other motives can operate so powerfully [...]' in producing a good life. It is clear that this is a theory which is a far cry from even 'alleviated Calvanism'.[14]

In the meantime, Edward was having his difficulties. Seemingly a successful minister-scholar, he too continued to be deeply troubled by a view which seemed to make God a wrathful tyrant who punishes man for not doing the good which man is incapable of doing. This seemed to be the father's view, but it was not congenial to Edward's mind or to his heart. All through his childhood, according to Catharine's account of what Edward related to her, 'as far back as memory could reach he never had a feeling of conscious alienation from God, or of hostility or revolt'. At the time of his conversion he sought to know God 'face to face, as a man talked with his friend.' Seeking such a friend, he turned to the New Testament and found there a God who suffers with man and thus reveals human qualities. Edward was still troubled, however, by the Calvinist notions of original sin, total depravity, and eternal punishment. How could these be squared with the suffering God – the face to face friend – that he had found in the New Testament? Finally Edward hit upon the truth of the *pre-existence of souls* – hardly a Calvinist notion! Man in this life suffers and atones for sins committed in his own *previous* lives, not for the sin of Adam. This truth came to him, Edward reported to his younger brother Charles, as 'a virtual revelation'. There was something akin in Edward's experience 'to that of the apostle when he was caught up to the third heaven and heard things which it was not lawful to utter'. Like 'Moses descending from the mount – his face transfigured – must he needs draw a veil over his countenance'. In other words, his new view was so unorthodox that he could not publish it abroad and did not do so until twenty-five years after the initial 'revelation' in 1827. Lyman 'had no place in his system for this new revelation' to his son, nor did any of the other 'great champions of evangelical faith.' But in the intimate circle of his siblings Edward could privately communicate his views. Charles reports that at the age of fourteen he 'instantly as by a kind of intuition' accepted Edward's new doctrine. Sixty years later he wrote that he had 'never doubted it since'.

Charles, who was the most articulate theologian in the family, carried the doctrine further in developing a kind of Christian spiritualism.[15]

Edward's 'revelation' was also of keen importance to the spiritual development of his younger sister Harriet. As child number six, Harriet stood near the middle of the Beecher brood of thirteen. The relative anonymity of this location was aggravated by the death of her mother when Harriet was four and the remarriage of her father a year and a half later. (She clearly felt a 'generation gap' between herself on the one side and her father and his second wife on the other. This is evident in the autobiographical treatment of the character of Dolly in *Poganuc People*.) Harriet was a bright youngster with a great range of imagination. She developed early in life habits of careful observation of her fellows and of herself. She understood her introspection, quite naturally, in the language of religious search. At the age of twelve she wrote a surprisingly adult composition on the subject 'Can Immortality of the Soul be Proved by the Light of Nature?' Two years later, while hearing her father preach a communion sermon on the Johannine text, 'Behold, I call you no longer servants, but friends', she experienced what she took to be a genuine conversion. The preacher's theme, Harriet wrote later, 'was Jesus as soul friend offered to every human being', as a person 'patient with our errors, compassionate with our weaknesses, and sympathetic for our sorrows [...] Oh! how much I need just such a friend.' But before she could freely receive Jesus as a friend, according to the clinical formula, she had to come to terms with her own 'conviction of sin' or rather her lack thereof. She concluded quite logically, however, that if Jesus was the right kind of friend he could even take care of that apparent lack. She could 'trust Him for the whole', and she said, 'my whole soul was illumined with joy, and as I left the church to walk home, it seemed to me as if Nature herself were hushing her breath to hear the music of heaven'. As soon as she could get Lyman's attention she rushed into his arms and eagerly announced that she had given herself to Jesus, 'and He has taken me'. 'I never shall forget the expression on [my father's] face [...] it was so sweet, so gentle, and like sunlight breaking out upon a landscape. 'Is it so?' he said, holding me silently to his heart, as I felt the hot tears fall on my head. 'Then has a new flower blossomed in the kingdom this day!'[16]

But was the conversion genuine? That question came back to haunt Harriet. The business about the 'conviction of sin' seemed, on reflection, to be a suspicious short-cut, a subterfuge. The scarred older sister, Catharine, had her doubts. She 'was afraid that there might be something wrong in the case of a lamb that had come into the fold without being first chased all over the lot by the shepherd.'[17] These doubts were reinforced by the earnest probings of the pastor of the First Church in Hartford which Harriet sought to join soon after her conversion.

In her late teens and early twenties Harriet experienced much doubt and melancholia. This is evident in her correspondence, much of it with Edward who became her chief spiritual counselor; once having confessed herself to her father she apparently felt uneasy about turning to him again. 'My whole life is one continued struggle', she wrote to Edward when she was sixteen.

"I do nothing right. [...] My deepest feelings are very evanescent. [...] I don't know as I am fit for anything, and I have thought that I could wish to die young [...] You don't know how perfectly wretched I often feel: so useless, so weak, so destitute of all energy [...] I wrote rules; made out a regular system for dividing my time; but my feelings vary so much that it is almost impossible for me to be regular."

It costs her great effort 'to express feelings of any kind' to her fellows. Yet 'the desire to be loved forms [...] the great motive' for all her actions. She wishes that 'the Saviour were visibly present in this world, that I might go to Him for a solution of my difficulties'. But she wonders if God 'really loves sinners before they come to Him?' Edward assures her that God is her friend, that in Christ he grieves and suffers with her. But she responds that the book of Job, which she has just been reading, does not contain the views which Edward presents to her. Her case, like Job's, seems hopeless. It is "exactly as if I had been brought into the world with such a thirst for ardent spirits that there was just a possibility, though no hope, that I should resist, and then my eternal happiness made dependent on my being temperate."[18]

In the summer when she became eighteen, Harriet thought she had reached a distinct turning point. While she began that summer 'in more suffering' than she had felt 'ever before', she later reached the high point where she could say that she had 'never been so happy'. She now had reason to hope that her 'long, long course of wandering and darkness and unhappiness' was over. She confided in Edward that now she could speak of Christ as a friend, just as Edward could:

"Oh, Edward, you can feel as I do; you can speak of Him! There are few, very few, who can. Christians in general do not seem to look to Him as their best friend, or anything of his unutterable love."[19]

But her 'long course of wandering' had not ceased. Two remarkable passages emerge from letters written in 1832, the year she reached the age of twenty-one. In these passages she appears as a kind of burned-out case, and she very perceptively understands her soul struggles in their American religious context. First, she announces a firm resolve to think positively:

"[T]his inner world of mine has become worn out and untenable, I have at last concluded to come out of it and live in the external one [...] to give up the pernicious habit of meditation to the first Methodist minister that would take it, and try to mix in society somewhat as another person would [...] I have come to a firm resolution to count no hours but unclouded ones, and to let all others slip out of my memory and reckoning as quickly as possible."[20]

Some months later, after having moved with the family from Boston to Cincinnati where Lyman took up the job of establishing Lane Theological Seminary, Harriet observed that in America vehement and absorbing feelings become

"deep, morbid, and impassioned by the constant habits of self-government which the rigid forms of our society demand. They are repressed, and they burn inward till they burn the very soul, leaving only dust and ashes. It seems to me the intensity with which my mind has thought and felt [...] has had this effect. It has withered and exhausted it, and though young I have no sympathy with the feelings of youth. All that is enthusiastic, all that is impassioned in admiration of nature, of writing, of character, in devotional thought and emotion, or in the emotions of affection, I have felt with vehement and absorbing intensity, – felt till my mind is exhausted, and seems to be sinking into deadness. Half of my time I am glad to remain in a listless vacancy, to busy myself with trifles, since thought is pain, and emotion is pain."[21]

How could a daughter of Lyman Beecher live only externally and 'count only the sunny hours' (Harriet's rendering of *Horas non numero nisi serenas*, an inscription on a sun-dial in Venice)? And, most significantly, how could she do so without assurance of salvation? Surely the 'pernicious habit of meditation' must continue until that assurance was achieved. And just as surely there were still live coals in the ashes of that soul, coals which would be fanned into flame again and again as Harriet endeavored to express the intensity of her emotions in a thousand different ways. And repeatedly she would experience what she later called 'the burning *inward* of a deep, unsaid dissatisfaction'.[22]

Harriet spent the next eighteen years in Cincinnati. During that time she married Calvin Stowe and gave birth to six children. In that bustling border city she was exposed at first hand to some of the harsher realities of slavery. Like most of the Beecher family, she agonized over what the Christian could say to that evil. For twenty years after writing the above, her soul was pitched back and forth between despair and hope. Then, out of the depths of these inner struggles, she spoke her word against the evil of slavery.

In 1843 Harriet's brother, George, regarded by some as the most promising of Lyman's sons, killed himself. A verdict of suicide seems to be a reasonable reading of the evidence despite the finding of the coroner's jury that George met his untimely death by accident.[23] This event, Harriet wrote, 'shook my whole soul like an earthquake.' She saw in it a threat to all – 'father, brothers, husband', and – not least herself. Now at the age of thirty-two, she experienced deeper anguish than she had ever known before. She was not prepared for this threat to her world. She felt 'haunted', 'pursued', 'harassed', 'anxious', and 'alone'. She had not fully submitted herself to God. She must endeavor to do so with even greater resolve. She is rewarded within a year by another high: '*All* changed', she wrote to her half brother Thomas in June of 1845.

'Whereas once my heart ran with a strong current to the world, now it runs with a current the other way. [. . .] The will of Christ seems to me the steady pulse of my being. [. . .] I seem to see the full blaze of the Shekinah everywhere.'

But again the relief is temporary. The effort is great and the circumstances difficult. Calvin is away much of the time. The children are young. Cincinnati weather and atmosphere depress her. 'I am sick of the smell of sour milk, and sour meat, and sour everything', she writes her husband with some complaint. The 'clothes *will* not dry, and no wet thing does, and everything smells mouldy; and altogether I feel as if I never wanted to eat again'. While she finds Calvin's letter to be 'a very agreeable contrast to all these things', she must confess that her own health is 'bad enough and daily growing worse'. 'Upon reflection', she concludes, 'I perceive that it pleases my Father to keep me in the fire, for my whole situation is excessively harassing and painful'.[25] Things grow worse until she reaches a state of near collapse. Then the family rallies to her aid and enables her to spend nearly a year seeking rest and 'a cure' in Brattleboro, Vermont. Temporary relief is found again. But six months after her return to Cincinnati, her eyesight begins to fail and she finds herself in a 'strange state'. Then cholera ravishes Cincinnati and, while Calvin is in Europe, the dread disease takes her youngest son, Charley. That experience was the final burst of flame which tempered the steel of her soul to its point of remarkable productivity. It was at Charley's 'dying bed and his grave', she wrote later,

"that I learned what a poor slave mother may feel when her child is torn away from her. In those depths of sorrow which seemed to me immeasurable, it was my only prayer to God that such anguish might not be suffered in vain. There were circumstances about his death of such peculiar bitterness, of what seemed almost cruel suffering, that I felt I could never be consoled for it, unless this crushing of my own heart might enable me to work out some great good to others."[26]

Within two years of Charley's death the family moved to Maine, Harriet gave birth to her seventh child, and she began to write *Uncle Tom's Cabin*. She often said later of that work, which made her famous, that it was not she but God who wrote it. Whatever the case, it is clear that the book represented a kind of culmination of her own inner struggles. It was Harriet's theodicy. As a daughter of Lyman she was appalled at human slavery. As a sister and a mother who had experienced the death of her loved ones, she identified with the sufferings of slaves. As a tormented soul who must know God as a friend, she declared him as such even to those who knew the depths of human misery. 'This story', she wrote of *Uncle Tom's Cabin* or *Life Among the Lowly*, 'is to show how Jesus Christ [...] has [...] a mother's love for the poor and lowly, and that no man can sink so low but that Jesus Christ will stoop to take his hand.'[27]

Harriet was forty when she began writing *Uncle Tom*. For the next thirty years she turned out an average of nearly a book a year. Many of these, as Charles H. Foster has shown in *The Rungless Ladder*, were started under the impact of her own inner experience. Religiously, that experience led her in various directions. When her oldest son Henry was accidentally drowned at the age of nineteen, Harriet was plunged into a state of spiritual and emotional turmoil similar to that which Catharine had experienced many years earlier at the drowning of Professor Fisher. "Our dear boy was but a beginner in the right way", she wrote. "Had he lived, we had hoped to see all wrong gradually fall from his soul as the worn-out calyx drops from the perfected flower." But he was taken while the state of his soul was still uncertain. And his mother experienced "utter darkness and separation, not only from him but from all spiritual communion with God."[28] Shortly after Henry's death, two similar and unusual "phenomena" occurred, one to Calvin in the family home and the other to Harriet travelling in Italy: "phenomena" which led both to speculate that Henry's spirit might be endeavoring to communicate with them. But Harriet could not be sure. Her good friend Oliver Wendell Holmes wrote to her that it was understandable that she might find comfort in spiritualism, which modified "the sharp angles of Calvinistic belief, as a fog does those of a landscape".[29] Her Italian experience led Harriet to identify briefly in her imagination with Roman Catholicism *(Agnes of Sorrento)*. Finally, she joined the Episcopal Church where she hoped, in Foster's words, to find "a stay against religious and moral confusion".[30] Toward the end of her life her contact with reality steadily diminished and for the last decade she needed to be almost constantly attended by another person.

Calvinist orthodoxy precipitated psychological and ideological crises which it was unable to resolve. The Beecher family illustrates this in microcosm. While the father, in his efforts to preserve and advance what he regarded as the essential elements in the Calvinistic understanding of the supernatural self, stressed sharp discontinuity between God and man and between the old self and the new self, the children came to assert continuity. The father belonged to an elite corps of Calvinist evangelicals which sought to bring the populace up to the stern demands of a distant and rigorous ruler God. The children tended to ally themselves increasingly with popular sentiment for a humanized God and a divinized man. Catharine settled early on moral resolve and assumed moral responsibility. She and Harriet both later found some solace in the dignified formalism of the Protestant Episcopal liturgy. Edward, Harriet, and Henry stressed the love, even the mother love, of Christ as contrasted with the stern justice of the Father-God. Nearly all the Beecher offspring found comfort and inspiration in a benevolent deity's presence in the seemingly friendly world of nature. Several flirted with spiritualism and one, Isabella, the youngest daughter, actually became a Spiritualist. She also declared that she was to be the new messiah, an equal partner with Jesus Christ. George, the third son, developed a fatal romance with perfectionism. He completely exhausted himself in his efforts to live at that high level of spiritual and emotional transport which had been exhibited on occasion by Sarah Edwards (Jonathan's wife), and at the age of thirty-five, while serving as minister of a New School Presbyterian Church in Chillicothe, Ohio, he took his own life.[31] There is a considerable range of spirituality and its effects in this microcosm. But all exhibited the same tendency to narrow the gap between God and man and to blur the Edwardsian focus on discreet religious affections.

None exhibited the above tendency more clearly than the most popular and most influential of the Beecher sons, Henry Ward. Henry was the seventh child and the fourth son. His mother died when he was three and, as noted, Lyman remarried a year and a half later. Henry seems to have suffered considerably under these circumstances. He, more than any of his brothers and sisters, complained of a lack of mother love, on the one hand, and the seeming distance of the father, on the other. Henry was slow of speech and, although he was not the youngest of the first wife's children, he was often treated as the baby. Even so, his older sisters were not entirely adequate mother surrogates and his stepmother seemed cold and distant. All of his life he was to contrast the warmth of his real mother with the coolness of his stepmother. Of the latter he wrote:

"Although I was longing to love somebody she did not call forth my affection and my father was too busy to be loved. I think it would have been easier to lay my hand on a block, and have it struck off, than to open my thought to her. [. . .] I was afraid of her. I revered her, but I was not attracted to her. I felt that she was ready to die, and that I was not."[32]

She impressed him as saintly but distant. He needed someone close and loving. That is the image he had of his real mother. From his early life he later recalled a particularly revealing experience. Suddenly, in the darkness and while separated from the family by a closed door, he shrieked in fright. Hearing only the echo of his own voice, he shrieked again, louder. Then, he says,

"I remember seeing the light stream in from the dining room, and being taken up in loving hands. The face I do not recall, the form I do not recall; but I remember the warm pressure. It was my mother. [. . .] She took me to her bosom. [. . .] Now I could not paint my mother's face; but I know how her bosom felt [. . .]. I know how her arms felt."[33]

Henry's sense of being low man on the sibling ladder is perhaps implied in his first known letter, written at the age of five in reference to his stepmother: 'Dear Sister, We are al wel. Ma haz a baby. The old sow has six pigs.' Of his soul troubles as a youngster he wrote later:

"[A]t intervals for days and weeks I cried and prayed. There was scarcely a retired place in the garden, in the woodhouse, in the carriage house, or in the barn that was not the scene of my crying and praying. It was piteous that I should be in such a state of mind and that there should be nobody to help me and lead me out into the light [. . .]. I wanted to be a Christian. I went about longing for God as a lamb bleating longs for its mother's udder."[34]

From such longing developed an idealization and idolization of his real mother which was to shape his own understanding of religion. At the age of fourteen or fifteen, he reports, he 'began to be distinctly conscious that there was a silent, secret, and, if you please to call it so, romantic influence which was affecting me'. This was his mother with whom he came to 'have more communion [. . .] than with any living being'. No 'devout Catholic ever saw so much in the Virgin Mary as I have seen in my mother'.[35] In Henry's religious novel, *Norwood*, the young hero, Barton Cathcart, 'desires the (religious) truth as an unweaned child yearns for its mother's breast.'[36]

At the age of sixteen Henry experienced a conversion when 'there arose over the horizon a vision of the Lord Jesus Christ as a living Friend'. Young Beecher had "an intoxicating sense of God as one who loves 'from the fulness of His great heart' [. . .]." After describing a similar experience, Barton Cathcart was asked if that experience had left any lasting effect. 'In truth it did', he replied: 'It awakened all my mother in me'.[37]

Henry never split openly with his father. As a lad he attempted to escape the intolerable psychological pressures of the Beecher home by running away to sea. But old Lyman – who wanted every Beecher boy in the ministry – outsmarted him. Harriet later described the incident in *Men of Our Times*:

Now the wood pile was the principal debating ground and Henry felt complimented by the invitation, as implying manly companionship.

'Let us see', says the Doctor, 'Henry, how old are you?'

'Almost fourteen!'

'Bless me how boys do grow! – Why it's almost time to be thinking what you are going to do. Have you ever thought?'

'Yes – I want to go to sea!'

'To sea! Of all things! Well, well! After all, why not? – Of course you don't want to be a common sailor. You want to get into the Navy?'

'Yes, sir, that's what I want.'

'But not merely as a common sailor, I suppose?'

'No sir, I want to be a midshipman and after that a commodore.'

'I see', said the Doctor cheerfully. 'Well, Henry, in order for that, you know, you must begin a course of mathematics and study navigation and all that.'

'Yes, sir, I am ready.'

'Well then I'll send you up to Amherst next week to Mount Pleasant and then you'll begin your preparatory studies and if you are well prepared I presume I can make interest to get you an appointment.'

And so Henry went to Mount Pleasant Collegiate Institute at Amherst and Lyman remarked shrewdly, 'I shall have that boy in the ministry yet.'[38] It was while he was studying in this preparatory school that Henry found Jesus as a friend. This he hinted to his father and that seasoned shepherd quickly took measures to drive this would-be rebel into the fold. Under Lyman's ministrations, Henry joined his father's Boston church and entered Amherst College to prepare for the ministry.

While at Amherst, Henry found other friends outside the family circle. There began a series of close relationships – relationships of dependency, one might say – which was to continue throughout his lifetime. Henry required warmth, affection, and even adulation in those close to him. Under such circumstances he became remarkably adept at playing upon the more tender notes of human emotion.

Over a long ministry, which spanned the middle years of the nineteenth century, Henry moved farther and farther out of Lyman's orbit. In the process he came as close as any nineteenth century minister to being the national chaplain of his time. His sermons were often front page news. His writings were widely read. He was the object of much adulation. Henry did not speak as clear and distinct a word as Lyman had. In fact, his published work often seems bland and confused in comparison with Lyman's. But in that, too, he spoke to his age. It was a time to make the rough edges smooth, to take the harshness out of religion, and to put a smile on the deity's countenance. It was a time to exalt even the humblest sentiment and to give play to even the commonest emotion.

No son or daughter of Lyman Beecher openly rebelled against him, but, in one way or another, they all appropriated views which clearly differed from his. Still, most of them shared their father's zest for life, his moral zeal, and his Protestant patriotism. There was an enormously human quality about the man and despite all of his advertisements of eternity he thoroughly relished this life. At his last public appearance, when he was well past his alloted three score and ten, he said that if God gave him an option either to enter heaven immediately or to begin his life over again and work once more he '*would enlist again in a minute*'.[39] Any true Beecher would have chosen to enlist. That much of the energizing force of consistent Calvinism came through loud and clear. Without that the second generation modifications of Lyman's views might simply have thinned out into sheer sentimentalism.

Notes

1. Owen C. Watkins, *The Puritan Experience* (London; 1972).
2. For Lyman Beecher's difficulties, see *Autobiography, Correspondence, etc., of Lyman Beecher, D. D.*, ed. Charles Beecher, two volumes (New York: 1864). This source was published again, under the editorship of Barbara M. Cross, by Harvard University Press (Cambridge: 1961). See also Vincent Harding, *Lyman Beecher and the Transformation of American Protestantism*, Ph. D. dissertation, University of Chicago, 1965. For Henry Ward Beecher, see William C. McLoughlin, *The Meaning of Henry Ward Beecher* (New York: 1970).
3. Henry F. May, Introduction to *Oldtown Folks*, by Harriet Beecher Stowe (Cambridge: 1966), pp. 8 f.
4. Lyman Beecher, *Autobiography, Correspondence* ..., Vol. I, p. 390.
5. *Ibid.*, Vol. II, p. 504.
6. Letter, July 13, 1844. In Thomas K. Beecher papers, Cornell University Library, 12 letters from Lyman Beecher to his son James, while the latter was a student at Dartmouth College.

7. The *Dictionary of American Biography* contains articles on Lyman, Catharine, Edward, Harriet, Henry, Charles, Isabella, and Thomas.
8. Lyman Beecher, *Autobiography, Correspondence* . . ., Vol. I, pp. 390 ff.
9. Lyman Beecher Stowe, *Saints, Sinners and Beechers* (Indianapolis: 1934), pp. 138 ff. Also Catharine Esther Beecher to Edward Beecher, March 26, 1825, Beecher family documents, Mount Holyoke College Library, chiefly letters from Catharine Esther Beecher to Edward Beecher, Edward Beecher to Lyman Beecher, and Lyman Beecher to Edward Beecher.
10. Robert Merideth, *The Politics of the Universe: Edward Beecher, Abolition, and Orthodoxy* (Nashville: 1968). See also letters from Edward Beecher to Catharine Esther Beecher, August, 1822, and Edward Beecher to Lyman Beecher, March 27, 1822, in Papers of the Beecher and Stowe families, chiefly letters from Esther Beecher to Charles Edward Beecher and Lyman Beecher. See also Lyman Beecher, *Autobiography, Correspondence* . . ., Vol. I, pp. 428, 460 and 476.
11. Edward Beecher in response to Catharine Esther Beecher, March 29, 1822, Radcliff Mss
12. Lyman Beecher, *Autobiography, Correspondence* . . ., Vol. I, pp. 479–497.
13. Charles E. Stowe, *The Life of Harriet Beecher Stowe Compiled From Her Letters and Journals* (Boston: 1890). See also Lyman Beecher, *Autobiography, Correspondence* . . ., Vol. I, p. 508; and Edward Beecher to Catharine Esther Beecher, August 23 and August 30, 1822, Radcliffe Mss.
14. Catharine Esther Beecher, *Suggestions Respecting Improvements in Education* (Hartford 1829), pp. 44 ff. See also Catharine Esther Beecher, *Letters on the Difficulties of Religion* (Hartford: 1836): 'God does not require anything of us but what we have *full ability* to perform'. See also L. B. Stowe, *op. cit.*, pp. 96 ff; also Catharine Esther Beecher to Edward Beecher, August 23, 1828, Radcliffe Mss. Catharine did join her father's church, but apparently without the requisite conversion. Some sort of filial and perhaps personal compromise must have been effected. Harveson mentions the church affiliation but does not document it: Mae Elizabeth Harveson, *Catharine Esther Beecher: Pioneer Educator* (Philadelphia: 1932), p. 32.
15. Robert Merideth, *op. cit.*, pp. 47–49. Also Catharine Esther Beecher to Edward Beecher, August 23, 1828, Radcliffe Mss.
16. Cf. Charles E. Stowe, *op. cit.*, pp. 33 ff.
17. *Ibid.*, p. 35.
18. *Ibid.*, pp. 36–47.
19. *Ibid.*, p. 48.
20. *Ibid.*, p. 50.
21. *Ibid.*, p. 67.
22. Lyman Beecher, *Autobiography, Correspondence* . . ., Vol. II, p. 488.
23. See Catharine Esther Beecher, *The Biographical Remains of Rev. George Beecher, 1809–1843* (New York: 1844), p. 341. Also Barbara M. Cross, Introduction to the *Autobiography, Correspondence, etc., of Lyman Beecher* (Cambridge: 1961), p. xII.
24. Lyman Beecher, *Autobiography, Correspondence* . . ., Vol. II, pp. 493 ff.

25. Charles E. Stowe, *op. cit.*, pp. 111 f.
26. Charles H. Foster, *The Rungless Ladder: Harriet Beecher Stowe and New England Puritanism* (Durham: 1954), p. 27.
27. Charles E. Stowe, *op. cit.*, p. 154.
28. Charles H. Foster, *op. cit.*, p. 130. Also Harriet Beecher Stowe letter in Annie Fields, *Life and Letters of Harriet Beecher Stowe* (Boston: 1898), pp. 280 ff.
29. Charles H. Foster, *op. cit.*, p. 130.
30. *Ibid.*, p. x.
31. On nature, see McLoughlin, *op. cit.*, pp. 19 ff. Also Catharine Esther Beecher, *Letters on the Difficulties of Religion*, p. 189, and *The Biographical Remains of Rev. George Beecher*, pp. 19, 66 and 84. On Isabella, see May, introduction to *Oldtown Folks*, p. 16, and *The Dictionary of American Biography*. On George, see Catharine Esther Beecher, *The Biographical Remains of Rev. George Beecher*, pp. 71, 78, 180 and 83 ff.
32. See McLoughlin, *op. cit.*, p. 66. Also Paxton Hibben, *Henry Ward Beecher* (New York: 1927, 1942), p. 19, and William C. Beecher and Samuel Scoville, *A Biography of Henry Ward Beecher* (New York: 1888), p. 66.
33. Beecher and Scoville, *op. cit.*, p. 47.
34. McLoughlin, *op. cit.*, pp. 14 ff.
35. Lyman Beecher Stowe, *op. cit.*, p. 24.
36. McLoughlin, *op. cit.*, p. 14.
37. *Ibid.*, pp. 17, 76.
38. Lyman Beecher Stowe, *op. cit.*, p. 243.
39. Lyman Beecher, *Autobiography, Correspondence* . . ., Vol. II, p. 552.

DENNIS KLASS

11

Psychohistory and Communal Patterns

John Humphrey Noyes and the Oneida Community

William James spoke of one variety of religious experience as that of religious geniuses who 'do not remain mere critics and understanders of their intellect. Their ideas possess them, they inflict them, for better or worse, upon their companions or their age.'[1] In so doing, they change the structures by which we lesser men find our bearings, define our reality, and channel our energies. Most of us are born into or find a world, defined by an ideological system, which gives us the institutions and meaning systems by which we live, work, play, have babies, fight, are reconciled, learn, show ignorance, are out of sorts, get in touch, get sick, get well, bury our dead, and die ourselves. But some men create the structures for others. Erik Erikson has called these few people ideological innovators, a term somewhat broader than James' religious genius, but directed toward the same relationship between biography and social systems.

This essay is a study of that relationship between one religious genius, John Humphrey Noyes, and one small world, the Oneida Community. Beyond that, it is a study of Noyes' failure at trying to use the rituals of the world into which he was born, and thus it is a study of his motivation to create a new world. The process by which Noyes moved from this failure to generating the new community is far too complex to compress into this brief paper, but the dynamics of the innovations themselves, by way of his early biography, can be set out. The outline of this study is first, to explore some psychological concepts which are useful to our task; secondly, to examine Noyes' unsuccessful attempt to fit into the ideological system to which he was born; thirdly, to look at his earlier life for some understanding of his failure; and finally to analyze his innovations for some understanding of their success.

I

A distinction drawn from Erik Erikson's epigenetic stages will be useful in our study: the difference between shame and guilt. While in common parlance the two are often used interchangeably, Erikson has shown that they are in fact rooted in different epigenetic stages and thus function differently in the psychic organization.[2]

Shame is rooted in the anal or autonomy stage. It is a violation of the ego ideal which develops with the internalization of ideal social models. Those models are too externally formed to be called identity at this point, but should be understood as identification referents which serve as guidelines and standards of behavior. Usually, of course, the models are the same sex parents, but the child's world is large enough to include heroes, astronauts, cowboys, and the like. In effect the models are ideal types of the social world into which the child is being introduced. The stage is devoted to establishing a mobile, independent personhood in a fixed world and thus is focused on a good deal of control: control of the bodily functions like the large muscles, but also the bowels and bladder; control of the emotions, 'big boys don't cry'; and to a limited extent, control of the interpersonal environment, the two year old's 'No!'. The converse of autonomy is self-doubt and shame, the feeling of failure to live up to the standards contained in the models. It is a feeling of being exposed as inadequate in a situation where one has no control, embarrassment which is literally 'being caught with your pants down'. When we fail in our eyes, we are conscious of the eyes, we are conscious of the eyes of others and thus blush and cannot return their gaze. While guilt may be shared and even punishment is a form of communication, shame isolates us and makes us lonely. Conscious of ourselves, our weakness, and our failure, we cannot risk the exposure of intimacy. To be a healthy functioning person, at least part of the ego ideal must be realized some of the time. That is, it is good for a person to feel relatively satisfied with himself sometimes. For this to happen, both the ego ideal and the self-perception or self-image must be based in an achievable reality. When this is the case, there is a healthy measure of narcissism. When a person does not feel relatively satisfied with himself often enough, he will have to do something to alleviate the constant shame.

Guilt, on the other hand, is based in the third or genital stage. Erikson holds to the Oedipal theory in which the object of love and hate is introjected to form the superego. The love and hate are thus redirected toward the ego. Therefore an offense against the superego has an objective character in that it is a violation of an other. Guilt is guilt for something, an act or nature of being, and against something, another person, or a divinity, or society, We do not judge ourselves, guilty, but feel ourselves judged in the court of law, religion, or psyche.

It is difficult to differentiate shame and guilt when we confront the actual symptoms in present or historical persons. Both can manifest themselves as depression, resistance to introspection, overconfidence, etc. Indeed they are commonly found in tandem. But when we try to respond to the symptoms we discover which predominates. Judgment and therefore mediated forgiveness is possible for guilt; however, shame only grows in judgment, and since it is against a self-chosen standard, forgiveness is impossible. Thus confession and acceptance by another can help guilt. With shame an examination of the concretes of the ego ideal for 'reasonableness', and building the patient's regard for his own ego potentialities, are in order.

The traditional forms of the Christian doctrine of atonement are primarily designed for the problem of guilt, for they are premised on man's disobedience against a righteous God. Revivalist preaching in the early nineteenth century was formed to a guilt pattern: hearing the Word, conviction of sin, learning of salvation, repentance and conversion. Indeed, we might characterize the Calvinist preaching as being centered around two points: the righteousness of the sovereign God and the depth of man's innate and total depravity. At the time such preaching and subsequent conversion experiences constituted the most prominent available form of 'therapy'. The point of the preaching was to make the listener aware of the offense he presented to the divine order and then to open the means by which he might be reconciled to that order.

But what if the problem were shame and not the guilt the revival conversion was designed to resolve? It would seem that some further development would be necessary for the person to find a resting place in which to feel comfortable in his world. If a person were one of those Erikson has called ideological innovators, we should be able to understand the ideological structure he generated as designed to alleviate the shame which the conversion could not. That is, a disequilibrium between the prevailing social system and his psychological organization could force him to innovate ideas, institutions, and patterns of interpersonal interaction which would channel the same and either resolve it or take away its power. John Humprey Noyes and the community he generated seem to be such a case.

II

The disequilibrium between Noyes and the prevailing ideological system is portrayed most clearly in one event and the year that followed: his conversion to Calvinist revivalism and the year of cycles of depression at Andover Seminary.

In mid-September, 1831, Noyes, just turned twenty, attended a four day revival in his home town of Putney, Vermont. He wrote:

"I was at Glens Falls on a visit when I first began to ascertain the determination of my own mind as to the impropriety of the four days meeting. I knew that such a meeting was to commence at Putney on the thirteenth, and I felt a dread of being present at it. I looked upon religion, at least I endeavored to do so, as a sort of phrenzy to which all were liable, and feared lest I should be caught in the snare. However, my aversion to it was such, and my love of the pleasures of the world so strong, that I concluded to yield to the force of circumstances which seemed to summon me to the spot; and trusting in my own strength to resist the assaults of the Lord I attended the meeting on the fourteenth. I knew mother was exceedingly anxious that I should receive the word, but I told her plainly that she would be disappointed. She asked why I went, and I replied to please her. However, I think that curiosity and perhaps a twinge of my own conscience were among the motives which led me thither."[3]

His attitude, then, was highly ambivalent, perhaps best characterized as a dreading anticipation. He feared getting caught in the phrenzy, but was drawn to it.

His ambivalence continued during the meetings, yet focused on specific conflicts. During the second meeting he wanted to put his name in when those wanting the congregation to pray for them called out, but he did not because he was afraid that after the excitement died he would revert to his former state and 'should thus expose myself to ridicule'.[4] By the last meeting he still had made no outward indication, but the conflict had emerged starkly as symbolized in the professions of law versus divinity.

"It seemed I must make up my mind whom I would serve, and I determined to brace myself for the conflict. The consideration which weighed most within me was that religion would make it necessary for me to quit the law and take to divinity."[5]

But after the meetings were over, Noyes appears to have actively sought in private the conversion he had feared having in public. The sabbath service signaled the end of the revival preaching. That afternoon Noyes was 'almost sick with a cold' and took to his bed. He suddenly thought this was the perfect time to submit to God in that 'the severity of my cold suggested to me the idea of the uncertainty of life'.[6] Although his account was written several years after the event, we still might note that he first said he was almost sick and then that the cold was severe enough to suggest death. In light of what immediately followed, we might wonder to what extent the illness was usefully psychosomatic. He then decided to seek the religion he had so recently avoided.

"I felt as if the crisis had come, and my destiny was to be decided. I then, after some hard thinking determined to obtain religion and set about conquering my pride."[7]

That pride was first understood as a fear of exposing his thoughts to others.

"The first duty which presented itself was that of overcoming my fear of man, and though it was like cutting off the right hand God enabled me to resolve and to execute the resolution of communicating to mother my determination."[8]

He had gone to the revival, he said, to please his mother, though he had cautioned her not to raise her hopes. Now we find his mother's desires internalized to a striking degree. Before he told her of his resolve

"I pondered in my mind as to what would probably be her advice, and from former experience I knew that she would bid me resort to prayer. I then determined to anticipate her, and actually bent my knees and offered up an incoherent heartless petition."[9]

Determined as he now was to seek a conversion experience, he faced a major stumbling block: the absence of a conviction of sin. The theology said that sinners guilty before God were forgiven by grace, atoned to Him, and thence walked in a new light. Noyes did not feel guilty before God, so he had a hard time working into a saving experience. It is here that we see most clearly the disequilibrium between Noyes' discomfort and the ritual provided to ease that discomfort.

"I read the Bible, prayed and meditated, until I actually sweat; and still I was calm and dispassionate. I shed no tears; I still felt no disposition to mourn on account of sin; and this lack of the usual sensibility troubled me exceedingly."[10]

But his desire to have the experience could, in the short run, overcome this obvious discrepancy between Noyes' psyche and the theology. In the intimacy of the sickroom, alone with his mother, he seems to have regressed to a level of trusting acceptance which the inner conflict was resolved for at least a short time. He wrote, 'In the course of the afternoon Monday, I read the Bible to mother. . . . From that time my anxiety diminished.'[11] But still he could not trust his feelings, for he still had not conformed to the expected guilt pattern.

"Before night I had become so far tranquil that I began seriously to fear the return of my former stupidity. Accordingly the next day I set about my old work of forcing myself into convictions with renewed vigor."[12]

Still conviction never came. Yet,

"when I surveyed, and compared my spiritual views, I found to my surprise an entire reversal of my tastes and affections. The Bible seemed a new treasure of precious thought; Christians seemed kindred spirits, and the matters of God and of eternity alone seemed worthy of attention."[13]

When an experienced believer (probably his mother who had been his spiritual counselor so far) told him that these were evidences of conversion, he slowly went into an ecstatic state which lasted several days. Thus he had a change in theological perspective; his world view was changed; but he never did undergo the conviction of sin and thus forgiveness.

But the ecstasy soon turned into what seems to have been a deep depression. Almost a year later when he thought he had recovered from the 'spiritual desolation' he wrote in his diary:

"July 1, 1832. – On the eighteenth of September 1831 I hope I gave my heart to God. There was much of delight, and as I view the case now, much of sin in my first spiritual exercises. I became so much absorbed in meditation on the goodness of God and on the novelty of my situation, that my mind seemed to lose its faculty of self-control, and I was for several days at the mercy of my imagination. My physical system sank under the intensity and protraction of the discipline, and I was forced to divert my mind by every means in my power from reflection on religious subjects. In this fact I can see a reason for the spiritual declension which succeeded, and which maintained its domination over me during the following winter."

"I determined from the first to become by the permission of Providence a minister of the gospel, and commenced soon the study of Hebrew. My health was such as forbade much application or much effort of any kind, and accordingly I came to Andover on the first of November unprepared to enter the seminary, and in a state of spiritual desolation."[14]

It seems, then, that while he had found a new theological world view, he had by no means found peace or even emotional stability.

It was not that Noyes failed to go through an emotional catharsis during the conversion experience, but that it was the wrong kind. While he badly wanted to believe, shame elements bothered him when he wanted guilt. He did not publicly call for prayer for fear of 'exposing myself to ridicule'. The most difficult task of the episode was not confronting a judging God, but telling another person of his quest. So it would appear that in the conversion experience shame was quieted briefly, but the conversion was not an appropriate ritual by which the shame could be channeled and resolved.

III

An overwhelming experience of shame probably made Noyes first dreadingly anticipate and then actively seek the saving experience. But even before that, Noyes' life was marked by constant shame. We will now turn to an examination of his life before the conversion.

A reporter once asked Noyes how he had the 'moral courage to radically defy the usage of society as he did thirty years ago and still does'. Noyes replied, 'I don't think it was courage. I was always bashful and timid, and lacked confidence in myself'.[15] The bashfulness was especially pronounced when young women were involved. Two years before the conversion while at Dartmouth he wrote a sonnet which, while not good poetry, had summed up his feelings about himself.

I hate garrulity and self-conceit,
And vain display of learning or of wit,
Where'er I meet it. But a greater curse
(In man 'its bad enough, in woman worse)

Is that affected modesty called cold reserve,
Which holds in stiff subjection every nerve,
Ties down the tongue to merely 'Yes' or 'No'
And chokes the fountains whence kind feelings flow.

And this vile canker-worm, this deadly pest
To every joy that kindled in the breast,
Is called by some 'good breeding', and by some

Is named 'politeness'. By my halidom!
What good it breeds, or where its merits lay,
'Twould match the far-famed Oedipus to say.

But identifying a problem did not make it go away. The bashfulness itself became an occasion for shame, a personal failure like a bad habit.

"I am a fool! And why? Because I cannot conquer a habit which will be my ruin! To relieve the reader's anxiety I will premise that this habit is not tobacco or dram-drinking. It is that infernal diffidence, natural or acquired which makes me when in company appear to myself and to everybody else a stupid dunce. Oh! For a brazen front and nerves of steel! I swear by Jove, I will be impudent! So unreasonable and excessive is my bashfulness that I fully believe I could face a battery of cannon with less trepidation than I could a room full of ladies with whom I was unacquainted."

Noyes himself identified the bashfulness with shame. 'I can feel my cheek burn with shame frequently when I ruminate upon occurrences occasioned by this plague of my life.'[16]

When Noyes called his diffidence 'natural or acquired' he was probably referring to the fact that the problem ran in the family. His father's four brothers, who were from Atkinson, Massachusetts, all married cousins because, it was said, they suffered from the 'Atkinson difficulty' – they were too bashful to propose to anybody but kin. It would seem that we should read this trait as an overriding sense of shame in intimate situations. Noyes' father did not marry until middle life, and only then when his bride forced the issue. Noyes once said the reason his father left the ministry and teaching was that 'he was too bashful for the pulpit, and I cannot think he was at ease as a teacher'.[17] His granddaughter described him at age seventy as 'of a reticent nature and studious habits, never alluding in any familiar way to the thoughts and feelings connected with his affections'.[18]

Noyes' world was a divided one. His father had been a minister for a year. After a faith crisis he had left the church and gone into business just before he married. He made a success of business and retired early, entering politics for a short time. He was elected to the state legislature and served a term in the House of Representatives in Washington. For as long as Noyes could remember he had been a well-educated, emotionally reserved agnostic. Noyes' mother was a devoted Calvinist Congregationalist. She dedicated him to the ministry at his birth, saw that he had a sound religious education, and took him to revivals when he was eight and sixteen years old. We can see, then, that Noyes was born into a world of contrary ideologies, identification models, and ego ideals.

During his college years and the year he spent reading law, Noyes was trying hard to live in his father identification. The 'Atkinson difficulty' was a negative part of that model, but using the control of that identification, he tried to force himself out of his bashfulness.

In the early part of his year at law he thought he had realized the ideal of a young sophisticated bachelor on his way to being a successful part of his father's secular world. In October, 1830, he reviewed the changes of the last year in his journal. Although he admitted that 'It may be that I have less stability of character than most men; but I must confess that my views of man and things change so often and so essentially even in the course of a single year, that I almost lose all acquaintance with myself', all the changes can be seen as attempts to fit the father identification model without the millstone of the 'Atkinson difficulty'.

"I will endeavor for experiment's sake to trace these changes for the last year."

"First, I was simple and credulous; averse to all society, especially that of the opposite sex; consequently unpopular. I studied because it was my duty, and not from any fondness for the employment. . . ."

"Suddenly the stamp of my character was completely changed. I became ambitious of popularity. I studied human nature and learned to live with men."

"Now science began to have attractions in herself. I looked deeply and eagerly into the secrets of philosophy. My views embraced a wider scope than hitherto; and I panted after *eminence in learning* as the height of human felicity."

"Another change came over my spirit. Its details would be tedious. It is sufficient to say that I sought happiness and distinction in *philosophic stoicism.* The fit lasted but a brief space, and next I found myself seeking the bright phantom in the mazes of dissipation. Another revolution placed me on far higher ground. Virtue, honor, and the dictates of conscience stood preeminent in my estimation as the guarantee of happiness."[19]

But the next month he admitted to himself that things were not going as well as he wanted to believe.

"November 19, 1830. – Three months of mingled mirth and misery are gone, and with them are gone – various things – no matter what. I came here expecting to enjoy everything that society could furnish, and thanks to the depravity of human nature society has been a constant source of misery to me [...] In short my fancy was wrought up to such a pitch that I imagined I had at length found that perfection for which I had hitherto sought in vain. [...] Any one considering the subjects of my meditations by day and my dreams by night might reasonable conclude that I was happy; but the true state of the case was far different."[20]

The father identification was beginning to crack. Shortly thereafter, two failures showed him conclusively that he would find no peace in his father's world. First he did very badly in his first law case.

"Yesterday I made my debut as an advocate, and a most shabby performance it was. I was frightened beyond all reasonable bounds. I stammered and trembled, and for a few minutes was utterly unable to fabricate a decent concatenation of words. It is true, before I had finished I had disfurnished myself of a portion of my trepidation; but still the conclusion of the whole matter is that (in the taunting words of Squire Spaulding) I 'did not plea worth a damn!' However, when I consider the disadvantage under which I labored, my speech being wholly unpremeditated, although I must bear the curse of other people's contempt, still my opinion of myself has suffered no incurable deterioration.'[21]

While the deterioration might not have been incurable, it was still deterioration and the squire's word focused the shame he felt.

We have little information on the second failure, perhaps because the shame was too great to write about. In the tow of his fellow clerk, Putnam, Noyes had led an active party life in the early part of his year at law. In the spring he fell in love with a girl named Caroline. She was due to leave town; Noyes wanted to propose. The 'Atkinson difficulty' showed itself. Rather than face her, the others in town, or his own inability, he fled home to Putney. His law days were over; Noyes would never again attempt to live in his father's world.

His discontent, then, as the revival started the following fall, was based in shame, both the pervading shame of the father identification and the special shame of the failures to live up to the ego ideal of the sophisticated lawyer. The same had made his world unlivable.

But what alternatives did he have? At that point he knew only one mechanism to reconcile the differences between him and his world – that of the religious conversion experience. He also had only one alternative identification model to try: his mother's faith. Within this context the internalization of his mother's desire during the conversion becomes understandable. Noyes' decision to seek the saving experience would thus seem to be a decision to stop the discontent he was feeling and to be positively reconciled to his world. But as we have seen, that mechanism was not appropriate to his problem, so that try as he might he could not fit himself into the expected guilt pattern. His mother had dedicated him to the ministry at his birth and had reminded him of her vow throughout his life. His change from law to divinity thus starkly symbolized his changed identification model. But while he did fully leave his attempt to live in his father's model, his mother's model did not have the social structures of ritual and dogma into which he could channel and therefore reconcile his psychic structure.

Hence the year he spent at Andover Seminary was one of severe cycles of depression, alleviated only by the discipline of a compulsive study program and the group discipline within the Brothern, a small band whose members had all dedicated themselves to overseas missions. We get an idea of the severity of his condition and the psychological controls he had to muster to overcome it in the contrast he drew between his year at Andover and his subsequent term at Yale, when his ideological innovation was just beginning.

"By systematic temperance, fasting, exercise and prayer I had overcome the bodily infirmities which troubled me at Andover. I was no longer tormented with inordinate alimentiveness and other temptations to sensuality. I had conquered my nervous system, which for a long time after my conversion had been morbidly excitable. I could now study intensely twelve or even sixteen hours a day without injury. Preaching which once would shake and disorder my nerves, had become a delight and refreshment to me. I was constantly cheerful and often happy."[22]

IV

Noyes had a long way to travel between the unsuccessful conversion of 1831 and the generating of the community in which he finally found peace. He went through, among other things, two psychotic-like episodes, several groups of associates, and a largely imaginary love affair. But it is beyond the scope of this paper to deal with the process by which he developed the ideology which structured the community's patterns. An analysis of the practices of the Oneida Community, however, will show how they were designed to resolve the shame problem and thus will show Noyes 'inflicted' on the community his solution to the disequilibrium between himself and Calvinist revivalism.

Noyes began gathering the group that was to form the core of the Oneida Community in 1838 at Putney. His first converts were three of his siblings. By 1846 the structures which were to characterize the community for the rest of its existence had emerged. In 1849, driven from Putney by the ill feelings and legal action of their fellow townsmen, the fewer than thirty people from the Noyes community joined a group which had just begun a community on the Putney model at Oneida, New York. Although the community expanded to over three hundred people in sometimes as many as six locations, no major changes were made until its breakup in 1880. Noyes did live a few years after the breakup, but he was into his dotage by the late 1870's, as were most of the founding members. We can say then, that for thirty-five years one group of people found a productive and creative life in the community patterns which Noyes generated.

We can discern four distinctive marks of the community: Perfectionist Theology, Mutual Criticism, Complex Marriage, and Male Continence.[23]

Perfectionist theology

The community members believed that they were no longer sinners, but were perfect. Noyes explained:

"I do not pretend to perfection in externals. I only claim purity of heart and the answer of good conscience toward God. A book may be true and perfect in sentiment and yet be deficient in the graces of style and typographical accuracy."[24]

Noyes began with a theory that the second coming of Christ was not a future event, but had already happened – in 70 A.D. at the time of the destruction of the temple in Jerusalem. But this 'realized eschatology' did not mean that history had thereby come to an end. Rather than the usual 'end of the world', Noyes said the Greek meant 'the end of the age'. He then developed a theory of three ages or dispensations in history: the Jewish dispensation, the Gentile dispensation, the new dispensation. The first two ages were alike in that they had a beginning with a new revelation of God, criteria for living under that revelation, and judgment at their end. The Jewish dispensation began with Moses and was characterized by the law. Holiness was right action defined as obedience to the law; sin was wrong action or disobedience to the law. Judgment for that age was at the second coming. The Gentile dispensation was inaugurated on the day of Pentecost and carried forward by Paul. Instead of right action, the criterion for living in this age was right intent, or love. Because right intent would result in right action, sin as action was merely external, but was not essential to the nature of man. The work of Christ had been not only to free man from the consequences of sin, but from sin itself. 'You that were sometimes alienated, and enemies in your mind by wicked works, yet now hath he reconciled... to present you holy and unblamable and unreprovable in his sight.'[25] As there had been a long time between the sowing and the harvesting in the Jewish dispensation, so the history between Pentecost and the present was a history in which the Gentiles were prepared for the harvest.

A major stubling block to Noyes' theory proved to be Paul's statement that he was the 'chief of sinners', for if Paul sinned, then man was still under the law and the flesh. Here Noyes found a strange ally. His teacher at Andover, Moses Strart, had argued that the verse was meant as a description of Paul's life before his conversion. Noyes accepted his old teacher's interpretation, but took it further to mean that all men could now be free from the law's demands. But this did not mean that all were therefore perfect, or even that the Gentile dispensation was devoted to perfectionism. He found in the writings of Paul two classes of believers: those who believed, but were still in a carnal state, and those who were perfect. Noyes went through several different ways of thinking about the end of the Gentile age, finally believing that it would pass aways slowly and that the new age of full spirituality would come gradually.

In the new age no one would be under the demands of the law, and love could be the standard of all men. Thus in the new age it would be on earth as it is in heaven. Until 1845 Noyes believed the new dispensation to be in the near future, but as the community formed and especially after he had what he believed to be a miraculous healing, he felt that resurrection power was immediately available. On June 1, 1847, after Noyes had presented the idea and the proofs, the community voted unanimously that 'the kingdom of God has come'.[26] Thus the community was the first fruit of the new age and could leave the law behind.

These ideas are interesting in terms of shame. If shame is caused by the disparity between ego ideal and self-perception, one must modify either the ideal or the self-perception to alleviate the shame. Noyes did the latter, changing the self-perception and externalizing the shameful attributes. If one was a believer with his whole heart attuned to God, he was perfect in God's eyes, and therefore in his own eyes. Those faults which formerly had been signs of depravity were now simply external and correctable matters – deficiencies 'in graces of style and typographical accuracy'. Why strive to obey laws which are no longer in force when the real goal is rightly to intend and when this has been made possible by the resurrection power now available? Noyes could now have the ego ideal of the man of the new age, and have the self-perception of a creature fit for the new times. As St. Cyril said centuries earlier,

"O how wonderful it is! You were naked before the eyes of all, without feeling ashamed of it. Verily, that is because you bear within you the image of the first Adam who was naked in paradise without feeling ashamed."[27]

Mutual criticism

We can see this resolution of the shame problem more clearly on a practical level by examining the ritual which formed the basis of governance in the community. Since the community was living in the new age in which the law had been superseded, it would have been contradictory to have a set of communal rules and a judicial system for enforcing those rules. So order in the community was enforced through the system of Mutual Criticism.

The interpersonal relations of over three hundred people living and working in close quarters over a long time could have been troublesome. When one reads the records of other communist societies which failed, one gets the impression that petty quarreling was a large factor in their demise. So one must be impressed that Oneida ran over a quarter of a century with a minimum of friction. Members always attributed this to Mutual Criticism. While there were variations over the years in the way the groups were formed, the method remained the same over the life of the association. Each member would offer himself periodically for criticism, though in problem cases or when a member had been exposed to the 'world' for some time, others might strongly recommend criticism. A group of other members would spend a few days considering and watching the subject, and then would sit down with him and criticize his character while he listened in silence. The areas of criticism ranged from what were considered to be inherited characteristics like possessiveness, to manners of dealing with relationships, such as withdrawal, to small irritants like rushing by in the hall without exchanging greetings. In 1863, for example, the following summary of a criticism session was published:

"Criticism of M. this evening. He was commended for kindness of disposition, readiness to serve and oblige others, affection and warm-heartedness, versatility of talent, and force of character; and was censured for lack of purpose, selfishness in his dealings, for a strong love of dress, or foppishness, and pleasure-seeking in social matters [a community way of saying he had failed at Male Continence – a serious breach we will examine later], for the lack of the spirit of *improvement*, and indisposition to qualify himself intellectually to do business properly. Was advised to withdraw himself from the Peddling Business, and take hold of some steady employment here at home – to put himself to school intellectually and spiritually, etc."[28]

Criticism was praticed regularly in the governance of the community, but was also used on special occasions such as to cure illness or to raise a sagging morale in either the whole community or in a small group. A community pamphlet explained:

"Criticism bathed in love wounds but to heal; bathed in personal feelings it leaves poison in the wound."

"There must not only be love but respect. Whatever a person's faults, Christ is still in him if he is a believer, and there is a sense in which it may be said: 'Who shall say anything to the charge of God's elect. It is God that justifieth, and who is he that condemneth?' Criticism should carry no savor of condemnation. There should be discrimination between a person's superficial character and his heart where Christ is. The object of criticism is only to destroy the husk which conceals his inward goodness."[29]

Yet we should not assume that a feeling of essential perfection made the criticism easy to take while it was being administered. One member describing his first criticism said:

"Every trait of my character that I took any pride or comfort in seemed to be cruelly discounted. And after, as it were, being turned inside out and thoroughly inspected, I was metaphorically stood upon my head and allowed to drain until all the self-righteousness had dripped out of me. [...] There was not a word or thought of retort left in me. I felt like pouring out my soul in tears, but there was too much pride left in me yet to make an exhibition of myself."[30]

The idea of criticism was not original; it was taken from the Brothern group at Andover. Welded to Noyes' theology, however, it was expanded to become the central religious practice of the community, doing what the revival had failed to do. The psychological dynamic was as powerful as the metaphors used to describe it: surgery and threshing. The person was shown the disparity between his externals and his internal goodness, which is to say the shame-producing disparity between reality and ideal. The whole ritual of criticism was to work shame to a high pitch until the subject was so ashamed he felt nothing good about himself. But the ideology kept the shame impersonal, that is, it controlled the isolating aspects of shame, while at the same time channeling the shame into constructive self-improvement. The cycle was broken. No longer did the individual feel shame, then do something to alleviate it, only to have the shame return as before. "One brother says that while he was undergoing the process he felt as though he were being dissected with a knife, but when it was all over he said to himself: 'These things are true, but they are gone, they are washed away'."[31]

The power of the shame was mollifed by the fact that it was external; and the process of shaming had a goal – the creation, by the surgery or threshing, of a more externally perfect man who would be a better member of the community which was the first fruit of the new age.

Complex marriage

Noyes characterized the main idea of all the nineteenth century socialist communities as 'the enlargement of the home – the extension of family union beyond the little man-and-wife circle to large corporations'.[32] At Oneida the extension of the family was an oft-stated principle. Members sang:

Where the pure currents flow
From all gushing hearts together,
And the wedding of the Lamb
Is the feast of joy forever.
Let us go, brothers, go!
We will build us a dome
On our beautiful plantation,
And we'll all have one home,
And one family relation.[33]

The community insisted that, as members of the household of God, it was one family in fact as well as in theory.

"Our communities are *families*, as distinctly bounded and separated from promiscuous society as ordinary households. The tie that binds us together is permanent and sacred, to say the least, as that of marriage, for it is our religion. We receive no members (except by deception or mistake), who do not give heart and hand to the family interest for life and forever."[34]

In practice this meant the abolition of conventional marriage in favor of a system called Complex Marriage, in which every man was considered the husband of every woman, every woman the wife of every man, and the children progeny of all. As there was a sharing of material goods, there was complete interpersonal communality. The aspect of this which most enraged outsiders was that sexual relations were part of that communality.

"In the kingdom of heaven, the intimate union of life and interests, which in the world is limited to pairs; extends through the whole body of believers; i.e., complex marriage takes the place of simple. The abolishment of sexual exclusiveness is involved in the love-relation required between all believers by the express injunction of Christ and the apostles and by the whole tenor of the New Testament. 'The new commandment is that we love one another.' And that not by pairs, as in the world, but *en masse*."[35]

The other side to this more inclusive love was that there should be no exclusive love. The members were to love all equally and none more than others. Married couples entering the community were expected thereafter to show no 'partiality' to their mates after the 'worldly fashion'. Young couples who showed too much interest in each other were separated by sending one to another branch of the community. Pierrepont Noyes, who spent his first ten years in the community, remembered:

"It was not alone that the Community religion rated 'special love' between the sexes as a sin, but any friendship that excluded others came in for censure, and those Perfectionists believed in uprooting pairs as soon as they showed themselves."[36]

As a child he was separated for periods of time from another boy when they became too close. In the same way children who were too 'sticky' with their mothers were deprived of visits until they got over it, as were mothers who showed 'partiality' to their own children.

The community thus had extended intimate relationships, but with a good measure of isolation built in. There is, of course, a complicated history to this radical innovation, but we can see the relationship to shame with the data already given. Sexual relationships among a large family were fully in keeping with the 'cousin clause' of the 'Atkinson difficulty'. Noyes' problem with bashfulness had been in face to face situations, not in genital relationships. At Oneida adolescent romances were labeled 'special love' and were frowned upon. It was precisely that kind of relationship with Caroline that had driven him back to Putney the spring before his conversion. Thus the feeling of personal isolation that shame brings was institutionalized at Oneida. The emphasis on individuals as members of a whole group could, with the help of Mutual Criticism, cultivate the aloneness of shame while avoiding the feeling of loneliness. Instead of feeling shame at their inability to handle intimate situations, members could concentrate the power of shame on avoiding these intimate inclinations. We might think of this stress on the independence of each individual within the community as a forced autonomy. While all were responsible for the life of the group, within the group each was responsible only for himself. Living for others meant constant awareness and development of one's own perfection. A member did not need to concern himself with providing for his mate or caring for his children. Rather, energy was directed toward individual 'improvement', so each person could be a better citizen of the new age. The communal framework thus fostered not mutual dependence, but mutual autonomy. Such autonomy is the converse of shame. At the same time the radical sexual practice was a denial of any shame worldly standards might bring to bear. After all they were new creatures in a new age.

"To be ashamed of the sexual organs, is to be ashamed of God's workmanship [...] of the most perfect instruments of love and unity [...] of the agencies which gave us existence [...] is to be ashamed of the image of the glory of God – the physical symbol of life dwelling in life, which is the mystery of the gospel."[37]

Noyes had once been afraid to ask for public prayer for fear that he would 'expose myself to ridicule'. Any intimate situation was an occasion for shame. Now he could expose himself shamelessly in a complex web of relationships which were intimate, but intimate at arm's length.

Male continence

While Complex Marriage was intimacy with tightly controlled isolation, this denial which looks like bold exhibitionism to cover embarrassment was balanced with a rigidly proscribed use of the sex organs: Male Continence. Simply stated, Male Continence was withholding semen after prolonged and motionless insertion of the penis in the vagina. Both the man and the woman felt sexual satisfaction, though the man had no orgasm (the woman might have multiple orgasms). Such a practice was, of course, a method of birth control. Though it may seem inconceivable (so to speak) in our pill-crazed age, Carden points out that at most thirty-one children were accidentally conceived between 1848 and 1869 in a sexually active community of about two hundred and fifty adults. She also points out that Masters and Johnson have shown that spermatozoa are found in preorgasmic fluid, so not all those thirty-one cases necessarily meant a failure at Male Continence.[38] Sexual life was open to Mutual Criticism, the women reporting the men's lapses, so it would appear that the practice was nearly universal in the community.

The theoretical breakthrough which allowed Male Continence to develop was the division of sex into two functions: the social or amative, and the propagative. Noyes analyzed this division in two ways, by an analysis of the sex organs and by analysis of the sex act. He noted that while the genitals are normally called the organs of reproduction, they actually have three functions, each with its own parts: urinary, propagative, and amative. The reproductive organs, the testicles and the uterus, are not really part of the actual instruments of union. The amative function is an interpersonal exchange.

"Sexual intercourse pure and simple, is the conjunction of the organs of union, and the interchange of magnetic influence, or conversation of spirits, through the medium of that conjunction."[39]

The second, an analysis of the sex act, divided sexual intercourse into three phases: presence, motion, and crisis. The first two are voluntary, the third is not. Noyes said that the greatest pleasure is in the first.

"I appeal to the memory of every man who has had the good sexual experience to say whether, on the whole, the sweetest and noblest period of intercourse with a woman is not that *first* moment of simple presence and spiritual affusion, before the muscular exercise begins."[40]

For Noyes, then, 'amative' was defined as interpersonal magnetism or spiritual affusion. Magnetism was a term he took from popular theories of the day, not dissimilar from modern E.S.P. or 'psychic' beliefs. Noyes thought the scientific explanaton of Biblical miracles, the Holy Spirit, and the doctrine of the soul could be found in magnetism.[41] It referred to a spiritual energy which transferred from one person to another. Spiritual affusion meant the joining of two persons spiritually so they became one. This Noyes said was the most enjoyable part of sex.

While it is cast in a genital mode, this kind of language sounds strikingly like the adolescent romantic language the 'Atkinson difficulty' precluded. The Caroline affair was in fact only the first of several flights from romantic interpersonal situations.[42] Yet now we find him using the language of spiritualized interpersonal relations. He seems to have been able to do this because of the extreme control of Male Continence. Shame is, as has been noted, rooted in the autonomy stage which is the time when control, emotional, physical, and interpersonal, develops. The feeling of shame is the feeling of being exposed in a situation over which one has no control. Thus in Male Continence the body was mastered to the extent that the affinity could be enjoyed with no fear of uncontrolled passion to follow. Noyes himself made the connection between Male Continence, shame, and adolescent romance:

"Ordinarily sexual intercourse (in which the amative and propagative functions are confounded) is a momentary affair, terminating in exhaustion and disgust. If it begins in the spirit, it soon ends in the flesh; i.e., the amative, which is spiritual, is drowned in the propagative, which is sensual. The exhaustion which follows naturally breeds self-reproach and shame, and this leads to dislike and concealment of the sexual organs, which contract disagreeable associations from the fact that they are the instruments of pernicious excess. Thus undoubtedly is the philosophy of the origin of shame after the fall. Adam and Eve first sunk the spiritual in the sensual, in eating the forbidden fruit; and then, having lost the true balance of their natures, they sunk the spiritual in the sensual in their intercourse with each other, by pushing prematurely beyond the amative to the propagative, and so became ashamed, and began to look with an evil eye on the instruments of their folly. On the same principle we may account for the process of 'cooling off' which takes place between lovers after marriage and often ends in indifference and disgust. Exhaustion and self-reproach make the evil eye not only toward the instruments of excess, but toward the person who tempts to it. In contrast to all this, lovers who use their sexual organs simply as servants of their spiritual natures, abstaining from the propagative act, except when procreation is intended, may enjoy the highest bliss of sexual fellowship for any length of time, without satiety or exhaustion; and thus marriage life may become permanently sweeter than courtship or even the honeymoon."[43]

Psychologically, then, we see the control of shame freeing the interpersonal relationship. This control provided the balance for the exposure in Complex Marriage. But this control was from within; it was not external as was the old control of the law. It was autonomous control, though to be sure it was reinforced by the community in criticism. Such autonomy is the converse of shame. In setting out this doctrine, Noyes answered the objection that such control was unnatural by saying such autonomous control was, in fact, the glory of man in the Kingdom.

"But every instance of self-denial is an interruption of some natural act. The man who virtuously contents himself with a look at a beautiful woman is conscious of such an interruption. The lover who stops at a kiss denies himself a natural progression. It is an easy descending grade through all the approaches of sexual love, from the first touch of respectful friendship, to the final complete amalgamation. Must there be no interruption of this, natural slide? Brutes, animal or human, tolerate none. Shall their ideal of self-denial prevail? Nay, it is the glory of man to control himself, and the Kingdom of Heaven summons him to self-control in ALL THINGS."[44]

In the patterns of the Oneida Community – Perfectionist Theology, Mutual Criticism, Complex Marriage, and Male Continence – we see structures which are designed to channel and resolve the shame Noyes could not channel and resolve in his attempted conversion to Calvinist revivalism. It would appear, then, that the disequilibrium between Noyes' psychological organization and the world into which he was born forced him to generate a new world, one with structures appropriate to his personality. And, for the personalities of one small group, the patterns which Noyes generated were apparently suited as well.

Notes

1. William James, *The Varieties of Religious Experience* (New York, 1958), p. 36.
2. Erik Erikson, *Childhood and Society* (New York, 1950), pp. 251–258. In addition to Erikson's work, the following present more detailed treatments of the subject: Gerhart Piers and Milton Singer, *Shame and Guilt, A Psychoanalytic and a Cultural Study* (Chicago, 1953); and Helen Merrell Lynd, *On Shame and the Search for Identity* (New York, 1958).
3. George Wallingford Noyes, ed., *The Religious Experience of John Humphrey Noyes* (New York, 1923), p. 36.
4. Noyes, *Religious Experience*, p. 36.
5. *Ibid.*
6. *Ibid.*, p. 37.

7. *Ibid.*
8. *Ibid.*
9. *Ibid.*, pp. 37–38.
10. *Ibid.*, p. 38.
11. *Ibid.*
12. *Ibid.*, pp. 38–39.
13. *Ibid.*, p. 39.
14. *Ibid.*, p. 42.
15. Quoted in Robert Allerton Parker, *A Yankee Saint* (New York, 1935), p. 272.
16. Noyes, *Religious Experience*, pp. 20–21.
17. *Ibid.*, p. 6.
18. *Ibid.*, p. 211.
19. *Ibid.*, pp. 24–25.
20. *Ibid.*, p. 28.
21. *Ibid.*, p. 29.
22. *Ibid.*, pp. 67–68.
23. There are several good sources available on the community which will not be footnoted except for quotations. Readers who wish further information on community life can read the following. The first is a primary document written by Noyes himself. The second and third are collections of primary source material, and the fourth is a modern study: John Humphrey Noyes, *History of American Socialisms* (republished, New York, 1966); George Wallingford Noyes, ed., *John Humphrey Noyes, The Putney Community* (Oneida, 1931); Constance Noyes Robertson, ed. *Oneida Community, An Autobiography, 1851–1876* (Syracuse, 1970); Maren Carden, *Oneida: Utopian Community to Modern Corporation* (Baltimore, 1969). Those interested in the theories behind the community will find the following recently republished: John Humphrey Noyes, *The Berean, Male Continence, Essay on Scientific Propagation* (New York, 1969); (Oneida Community), *Bible Communism* (New York, 1973).
24. Noyes, *Religious Experience*, p. 120.
25. Colossians 1 : 21–22.
26. George Wallingford Noyes, *John Humphrey Noyes, The Putney Community*, p. 238.
27. Quoted in Mircea Eliade, *Images and Symbols*, tr. Philip Mairet (New York, 1969), pp. 155–156.
28. Robertson, *Oneida Community, An Autobiography*, p. 141.
29. Noyes, *Putney Community*, pp. 101–102.
30. *Ibid.*, p. 111.
31. *Ibid.*, p. 101.
32. Noyes, *History of American Socialisms*, p. 23.
33. 'Community Song' quoted in Robertson, *Oneida Community, An Autobiography*, p. xviii.
34. *Ibid.*, p. 282.
35. *Ibid.*, p. 267.
36. Pierrepont Noyes, *My Father's House, An Oneida Boyhood* (New York, 1937), p. 49.

37. *Bible Communism*, p. 54.
38. Carden, *Oneida: Utopian Community to Modern Corporation*, pp. 51–52.
39. Noyes, *Male Continence*, p. 12.
40. *Ibid.*, p. 8.
41. Noyes, *The Berean*, pp. 65–78.
42. Those familiar with the years of Noyes' life we have passed over will especially want to examine the language of the New York Perfectionists which Noyes specifically rejected.
43. Noyes, *Male Continence*, p. 14.
44. *Ibid.*, pp. 9–10.

PETER HOMANS

12

The Uses and Limits of Psychobiography as an Approach to Popular Culture: The Case of 'The Western'

1. The context for a psychobiographical approach to popular culture

The serious study of popular culture is relatively new, but its novelty has been more than matched by the attention and energy devoted to it. Since the 1950s popular culture has become increasingly important as a phenomenon of study for university-related intellectuals, who have approached it from the point of view of many, very different disciplines. These two features – recency of appearance and variety of fundamental approaches – are the most prominent, general characteristics of popular culture studies today. From the latter comes a richness of approach, but also a lack of methodological integration. And the latter characteristic forms the context for any discussion of popular culture and biography.

The approaches available for the study of popular culture are best characterized as *multi*-disciplinary, rather than *inter*-disciplinary. We possess a pluralism of disciplines, each at times willing to share insights derived from another, but there is little engagement at the level of methodological assumptions. Sociologists have created two kinds of studies – broad, functional analyses which assign to popular culture a specific function, and large-scale empirical studies focussing on attitudes, opinions, influence and the like. Literary critics have treated popular culture as a series of texts, and have brought to their work of interpretation one of their most fundamental and favorite distinctions, the separation of high from low culture. Anthropologists have viewed popular culture as folk culture, analyzing it as an element in a cultural system. Historians and philosophers of culture have viewed popular culture as mass culture, interpreting it in terms of massification and depersonalization resulting from the fragmentation of those ontological structures which have come to constitute the essence of Western culture. Psychological studies, for the most part psychoanalytic in character, have dwelt upon fantasy processes in popular cultures, and have emphasized its escapist character.

Popular culture has in effect been a gathering place for a variety of disciplines, a gathering as lacking in communication as it is rich in resources.

In point of fact, however, some development between disciplines has occurred, enough for us to focus here a problem central to all approaches to popular culture, a problem lying at the heart of the study of popular culture itself. The most systematic discussions of popular culture have come from literary criticism and sociology. These discussions have created a tension between an analysis of the inner nature of the art form and the circumstances – historical, sociological and psychological – of its creation, and production, and consumption. This tension between inner structure and outer circumstance is the most identifiable particular feature in the development of popular culture studies. Robert Warshow captured well its essence when he observed that the literary critic in effect says, 'It is not to the movies I go, but to art'; and the sociologist in effect says, 'It is not I who go to the movies, but the audience'.[1] I will call this tension or conflict between symbol and social context 'Warshow's dilemma'. Despite the fact that it was uttered more than twenty years ago, it still points up the fundamental problem, no more resolved now than then, in popular culture studies.

Warshow's work constituted a plea for a more direct focussing upon what he called 'the immediate experience' of popular culture. He wanted more direct involvement between critic and text, and his own writings displayed that involvement, without at the same time losing the equally necessary element of critical distance. But Warshow's focus on immediate experience is even broader than he himself realized. While he used the notion of immediacy to emphasize the relation between critic and text, immediacy also occurs in relation between author and text. It follows that the critic responsible to his own immediate experience is also the critic who will be equally concerned to learn about the immediate experience of the author.

In the case of both critic and author we may view 'Warshow's dilemma' as a call for a more explicit psychology of popular culture. Psychology is the discipline, more than any other, which takes as its subject matter immediate experience, and it is therefore in an advantageous position to contribute to the study of popular culture, either by focussing on the inner experience of the critic in his role as a member of the audience, or on the inner experience of the author as producer of popular art forms. Psychology,

I believe, especially the particular form of psychology known as psychobiography, contains considerable potential for resolving Warshow's dilemma.

Such a psychology has until very recently been lacking. Most psychological criticism of popular culture (and the only kind available to Warshow) has taken the form of applied psychoanalysis, and in this it repeats both the literary and sociological errors which together comprise Warshow's dilemma. The psychologist in effect says, 'It is not to the movies I go, but to the dreams of society'; or he says, 'It is not I who go to themovies, but my patients'. In doing so, he loses the very dimension of immediacy his discipline is intended to capture.

However, if we were to think of psychology as the study of immediate experience, and if we were to focus on the relation of author to text as well as that of critic to text, then we would be in a position to understand connections between the internality of the text and its outer, social and psychological contexts. For immediate experience is both psychological and sociological – i.e., it includes not only the history of the author's personal relations, but also his relation to everyday social reality. Such a psychological approach, were it to be as effective as it promises, could resolve much of the tension between symbolic analysis and social context.

This attempt to develop correlations between a text and its author's personal and also social circumstances is no longer foreign to dynamically-oriented psychology, but in fact constitutes a recent development within psychology itself. The so-called psychobiographical or psychohistorical approach, grounded in the writings of Erik Erikson, can with little modification be adapted to the study of popular culture. Through the interpretive perspective of this psychology we can view the text as a synthesis of trends in personal life with prevailing social trends, especially as these take the form of shifting role-models for work offered by society to the author. Unlike psychoanalytic approaches, psychobiography does not view popular culture as either a distortion of a social unconscious, nor as the result of psychological trauma undergone by the author. Yet it shares many of the fundamental assumption of psychoanalytic psychology.

In this paper I test the validity of such a psychobiographical approach in relation to one form of popular culture, 'the Western'. The Western is an ideal form for testing such a new hypothesis. It is the most studied of the various narrative types of popular culture. Unlike some forms of popular culture, there is considerable knowledge of its social and historical conditions. The genre is familiar to those who do not study popular culture, as well as to the specialist. And further, excellent psychobiographical material on the Western already exists.

The first part of this paper defines the psychobiographical method. The second part illustrates the approach by noting the inescapable parallels between texts, social circumstances and personal trends in the case of Owen Wister and of Frederick Remington, two men who together established the Western as the major genre of American popular culture.

However, the psychobiographical method also has limits. In fact, it breaks down completely when we study the generation of Western writers following Wister and Remington. To this 'second generation' belong such writers as Max Brand and Zane Grey. In the case of Brand and Grey the biographical and sociological elements of personal experience no longer bear the same kind of meaningful relationship to their stories, their texts. In short, we conclude that the psychobiographical method works with high culture, or with popular culture in a 'high culture phase', but not with mass-produced texts for mass consumption by a mass audience. In the latter case the lines of relation between an author's life, his social circumstances, and his work, must be understood in quite a different manner. The third part of this paper therefore attempts to formulate the limits of the psychobiographical approach, and it makes some fresh methodological proposals which result from recognizing these limits. The paper in effect calls for a structural re-formulation of the psychobiographical approach.

2. Three Elements Comprising a Psychobiographical Approach to the Western

Erikson's full-length studies of Luther and Gandhi and his shorter reflections on G. B. Shaw, William James, Kierkegaard, Freud and others form the basic sources for the psychobiographical approach.[2] Erikson developed his theory by exploring 'high culture' figures, and the studies influenced by his work follow this. However, Erikson selected these types of figures not simply because they were high-culture figures, but also because of his interests in leadership, ideology, and the psychology of adolescence. In each of these cases patterns of adaptation to everyday social reality are paramount.

Erikson's psychology is especially relevant to the psychology of social change and mass movements. It is, in short, deeply relevant to the psychology of popular culture, to what Warshow called 'the immediate experience'.

The core of what we are calling the psychobiographical approach lies not in Erikson's lengthy discussions of Luther and Gandhi, but in his far briefer but more methodologically substantial discussion of Freud and the origins of psychoanalysis.[3] Erikson refers here to three crises which, cumulatively, form three dimensions of psychological discovery. Freud, so Erikson's argument goes, underwent a three-fold crisis which eventuated in new psychological knowledge, and Erikson's intepretation of this crisis becomes the paradigm for his own work. Erikson's three dimensions of psychological discovery will form the nucleus of our own psychobiographical approach to the Western.

First, and most obviously, Freud underwent a crisis in theoretical formulation. He found it necessary to reject the explanatory paradigms of 19th century science and medicine, and to develop his own notion of dynamic, unconscious mental functioning. This crisis in theory-making was accompanied by a crisis in vocational self-understanding. Freud was forced to abandon the conventional work-role of the 19th century physician, along with its related techniques, in order to allow for a new work-role, that of the psychotherapist, and for a new work-technique, the recognition and analysis of the transference. This technique, requiring imaginative participation by the doctor, replaced the fact-giving role of the Victorian physician. Erikson notes that, concurrent with these two changes, Freud underwent a purely personal crisis as well. He had developed an excessively intense relation to a friend, Wilhelm Fliess, a Berlin physician, a relation Erikson has called a transference relation. Psychological discovery, Erikson argues, consisted in the interlocking of a personal crisis, new theoretical formulations, and a new sense of one's work-role, one different from those offered by the social conventions of the day.

Erikson's categories can be adapted to the analysis of popular culture by broadening them somewhat and by applying them to figures who have either created new genres or have innovated new styles within genres. The dimensions of psychological discovery found in Luther, in Gandhi, and in Freud are also present in Wister and Remington, who together established the Western as a definite form of popular culture. The problem of leadership remains central in all three cases, and its psychology remains constant.

Erikson's notion of work-techniques is highly specific. It refers to the specific work-roles a society offers a person and their relation to his psychological development. Work-roles are in effect the way society makes felt its demand for certain types of performances. As such they are indices of basic patterns of social stability and change, as these shape everyday life and make their impact upon the immediate experience of the subject. Because of this broader reference we will use the term 'ethos' instead of 'crisis in work-techniques', and mean by it the marks of everyday life, as these are shaped by social structure and as they are experienced by individual subjects.

For Erikson's elaborate and often intricate discussions of personal crisis in the lives of the men he studied, we substitute a broader but no less dynamically sophisticated notion, that of 'person'. Person refers to: (1) basic attitudes in a subjects' emotional relationship to his parents during childhood; (2) specific interests and talents as these emerged in childhood and adolescence and the response of parents to them; and (3) the degree to which an individual integrates his own interests with his parents' attitudes towards him and his interests.

Third, in lieu of Erikson's dimension of 'theoretical or conceptual discovery', we substitute the broader notion of 'text'. It should be noted that from this more generalized perspective Freud's theoretical discoveries are themselves texts. Evidence for this assertion lies in the fact that some scholars have insisted that his writings require interpretation[4] – just as it can be said that Luther's theology, Shaw's art, and James' psychology require interpretation. The notion of text refers to what the author creates, constructs and projects – it is what he produces. While it possesses an autonomy of its own, it is also to be viewed as a synthesis of the effects of personal trends and social conditions – i.e., of person and ethos. The text is a product or objectification of the articulations between person and ethos, while at the same time transcending these.

So, the psychobiographical approach centers upon a mutual interplay between person, ethos and text: the text is a synthesis of person and ethos, but the person is also deeply affected by his ethos and by the works he produces; and changes in ethos are created by the person of the author and by the works he produces.

We now need to explore this interplay in the case of 'the Western'.

3. Psychobiography and 'the Western': Owen Wister and Frederick Remington

Wister and Remington are of especial interest and value for a psychobiographical approach to the Western. The artistic works (i.e., the texts) of each were instrumental in establishing the Western amongst Eastern producers and audiences. Since Wister wrote and Remington painted, we have in the two men evidence of the flexibility of the Western, its adaptability to both narrative and visual media. The vocational energies of both men were largely devoted to Western art, and their personal lives were deeply enmeshed in both Western art and the experience of the West. In a recent work by G. E. White this cogwheeling of text, ethos and person is amply supported.[5]

The psychobiographical approach generates the following series of questions: what was the general tenor of the emotional relations which Wister and Remington had with their parents? What talents, vocational interests, and abilities emerged during childhood and adolescence, in each case, and what parental responses were produced? Did prevailing work-roles and vocational identities support emerging vocational trends, or force their suppression? To what extent did the creation of Western art allow each man to resolve conflicts within and between the dimensions of person and ethos?

And to these questions the psychobiographical approach gives the following answers: as children both Wister and Remington experienced ambivalent relations to their parents; this ambivalence centered around tension between their own vocational interests, the demands of parents, and the emerging, new work-roles of their society. Both men withdrew from parental and social demands and lived in the American West for a period of time. Both men returned East to take places in the social order of the East as sought-after artists, thereby resolving their vocational conflicts, both in their personal and social dimensions. The psychobiographical approach shows the interconnection between person, ethos and text – i.e., it shows the personal and social dimensions behind the text, and it argues that these dimensions are necessary for an understanding of the text. We must, therefore, proceed by examining each dimension in the case of each author.

Text

We cannot in this discussion develop an analysis of the text of the Western, nor is this necessary for the accomplishment of our task. Rather, we need only recognize the fact of its existence, and its most central features. First, then, let us note that a particular type of popular art exists which is identified by writers, critics and audiences as a Western. Even though each of these groups may disagree as to what a Western is, all agree that the genre exists. Put in another way, there are definite rules for the formation of a Western, and these rules are recognized both by the self-conscious critic and the unreflective observer. Children, who know nothing of such things as hermeneutics, structural analysis, or theme can write Western stories and could describe, if asked, their basic conventions. We are more concerned with the correlation between person, author and the fact that Westerns exist than we are with correlations with the specific features of Western texts.

However, we cannot establish 'the fact of a Western' without noting at least its most salient characteristics. In an earlier discussion I developed an analysis of the basic elements for all Westerns, focussing on narrative structure, on typical persons and their patterns of social inter-relationship, and on primary scenes or images.[6] For the present psychobiographical discussion, we need only note that all Westerns conceive of a hero in a special relation to a frontier society. This society is progressive – i.e., it is expansionist, pursuing goals of economic development and especially land development. The hero always has a double relation to this society. On the one hand he protects it, while on the other hand he steadfastly refuses to join it wholeheartedly. Speaking purely descriptively, the hero participates in the world of Western everyday life, but he also stands outside this world. As such he possesses a quality of personal uniqueness and depth of character which is not accorded to the other types of persons who regularly frequent the Western story.

This tension between hero and frontier society is seen in the figure of the cowboy, which attracted both Wister and Remington. It is this central feature of the text, this double relation between hero and social order, which we need to relate to the person and ethos of each Western artist. They too stood in a double relation to their social order.

Ethos and life

White cogently argues that the ethos or social conditions surrounding Wister and Remington were extremely important factors in their development as artists of the West.[7] Both men were caught in a major sociological change, the decline of the post-bellum, landed gentry and the rise of a new entrepreneurial, professional class. The forces behind this change were rapid industrialization and urbanization, which created a need for professional specialization, especially in banking, business and law. The personal prerequisites for success in the new work-roles were ambition, persistence, competitiveness, and self-confidence, accompanied by a willingness for self-discipline and by good health. These work-roles were anti-intellectual, and therefore incompatible with vocational interests in art.

The clash between old and new ethos structured the personal development of Wister and Remington. The parents of both had strong connections with landed aristocracy and both sons felt its influence, for both developed artistic inclinations. On the other hand there was parental pressure to adapt to the work-roles, creating an intolerable conflict for each. The solution to this conflict lay in a withdrawal from it, occasioned in each case by the convenient onset of a mysterious illness. Both men decided to live in the West, and both returned from this experience to the East as successful Western artists. Through their art they were able to integrate the pressures of family and tradition with the socially defined demands of the new work-roles.

Owen Wister

Wister's mother was generally cold, and represented for him the intellectual aspects of life. She had correspondence with Thackeray, Browning, Henry James and Mendelssohn. Wister studied music at Harvard. His father was emotionally warm to him, and also encouraged a business career, to the point of helping his son acquire employment first in a bank and then in a law firm. Wister did his best to please his father, and attempted law school. However, he despised this vocation, and his health broke down. He decided to travel in the West. During this sojourn he was able to discover his vocation as a writer. This discovery, however, was inseparable from the West as a subject matter for art, suggesting a very intimate connection between the nature of Western life and Wister's own conflicts with parents and the social order in the East.

When Wister returned East he did so as the author of *The Virginian*, and also, we should add, no longer burdened by the mysterious illness. The Western experience had functioned to provide him the opportunity to synthesize the parental conflict between his mother's encouragement of the artistic and his father's support of the practical. As an artist he combined an appeal to both aristocratic and entrepreneurial social forces. In becoming a successful writer he synthesized those personal and social conditions which had the most influence upon him.

But person and ethos cannot be separated from text. *The Virginian* depicts a hero whose relation to his society is both one of readiness to involve himself in it, as well as a special kind of aloofness from it. This double attitude, as we have noted, is the central characteristic of all Western heroes, and of all Westerns.

Frederick Remington

Frederick Remington spent his childhood in a small, upper New York village. As in the case of Wister, Remington's mother was emotionally cold. She was, however, of a practical nature, and was continually concerned about her son's capacity to make his way in the world. Remington's father, a Civil War officer, was committed to military life. He displayed an attitude of emotional warmth and acceptance towards his son. As in the case of Wister, Remington's parents together displayed sharply contrasting, generalized emotional attitudes towards him, and towards his vocational interests.

Before adolescence, Remington had developed a strong interest in painting, and especially in the portrayal of scenes of adventurous military life, drawn no doubt in large part from his father's experience. As he entered adolescence this interest and talent grew. Remington's father encouraged both his painting and the types of scenes he was found of depicting. His mother, however, strongly disapproved, viewing such interests as a threat to his capacity to maintain himself economically in the world. As she was wont to remark, 'He will never make a living painting pictures'. Despite this disapproval Remington studied art at Yale College. Like Wister, he experienced contrasting parental responses to those talents and interests which were very much associated with his developing sense of personal uniqueness.

Shortly after his studies at Yale, Remington entered a phase of life characterized by personal disorganization and subsequent life-integration. His father died, and his mother pressed him to take on employment, even to the point of finding situations for him. His life was further complicated when a marriage proposal was rejected. He was unable to maintain interest in the work situation his mother obtained for him. His health broke down, and his solution to all this consisted in a trip to Montana of eighteen months duration. While living in the West, Remington continued to paint, and his original interest in adventurous military life turned to those typical scenes of life in the West with which his name is so closely associated.

When Remington returned East, he began to sell his paintings to *Harpers Weekly* and *Harpers Monthly*. His work was soon in considerable demand, and he began to develop a reputation as a major artistic interpreter to the Eastern reading public of Western American life. In doing so Remington re-entered the new, entrepreneurially-oriented world of the East as a successful member of it, but on his own terms. He had created a work-role for himself approved by the new entrepreneurial criteria – he was 'successful' according to the emerging urban industrial milieu; yet he was able to achieve this success without abandoning his personally unique talents and interests, as these grew out of the more traditionalist elements in his boyhood experiences. Through this commitment he was able to synthesize the tension between his mother's practical goals for him and his father's approval of his interest in painting.

And, as in the case of Wister, these elements of person and ethos are related to his texts. In the case of Remington the correlation is more difficult to locate, because his art was visual rather than narrative, but it is very much in evidence. To find it we must consider visual portrayals of the Western hero, rather than his characteristic patterns of relationship as they developed along a narrative line. The Western hero embodies a special and peculiar kind of fusion of intense energy and equally intense motionlessness. When not engaged in acts typical of his role, as hero, his manner is one of contrived indolence. On the other hand, in climactic moments he displays extraordinarily intense and focussed energy. At the right time he is all movement, all motion, all energy. This fusion of contrived indolence and readiness for the discharge of energy is the most characteristic *visual* feature of the Western hero. It is the *visual* counterpart to the central narrative feature of the Western, namely the hero's double relation to society, his commitment to it as well as his detachment from it. For, in his most focussed, energetic moments the hero is also participating in the social order, and in his indolent moments he is least involved.

If we focus our perceptual capacities on Remington's works, we find his cowboys, horses and other animals, together display a fusion of apparent energy with a more subtle motionlessness. The elements of energy indicate involvement and participation in the work-roles of everyday life, whereas the quality of motionlessness – more subtle and requiring more perceptual effort to discern – betray reluctance, a 'holding back', a detachment from everyday life. To this observation we should add, too, the more obvious fact that Remington's scenes display little interest in the types of people associated with the expansionist ethos of Western, frontier life, suggesting that the element of detachment outweighs that of involvement in his work.

In sum, it is possible, at least in the case of Wister and Remington, to sketch in important lines of relation between trends in the popular artist's personal life, the social circumstances surrounding his personal vocational development, and certain major features of his artistic productions. There are linkages between the Western as a popular culture genre and the person and ethos of its authors. The Western 'text' is a construction and synthesis of childhood conflicts, vocational crisis created by social change, and idiosyncratic talent. And the West itself assumed a central function in the resolution of the life situations of these two men. Psychobiography does help us understand this form of popular culture. Presumably, it could be applied to other genres as well.

4. The limits of psychobiography: The writings of Max Brand and Zane Grey

White's study and its characteristic method, which we have followed rather closely, would seem to be a viable and promising model for further study of the Western, and by implication of other genres of popular culture. To test this proposition we should explore it in relation to other types of Westerns created in different circumstances. The evolution of the Western genre not only permits this inquiry, it actually encourages it. Wister and Remington were instrumental in establishing the Western as a genre. They siginified its arrival as a form of popular culture. In the next phase of the Western's evolution its presence as a genre of popular culture is established and unquestioned. In this phase Max Brand and Zane Grey were extremely prominent figures. They signified the presence of the Western as a self-evident part of popular culture. Brand and Grey were as effective working within the form as Wister and Remington were in establishing it. Brand and Grey therefore provide the most appropriate focus for any further testing of the psychobiographical hypothesis. For we want to know whether the same method works for a genre, once established, as it did for its inception. Do person, ethos and text correlate in the same fashion, or are these categories of analysis limited to one particular phase in the evolution of a genre?

The answer to this question is most disappointing, although it also opens the way for more advanced methodological experimentation. The progression of our discussion has led us to believe that psychobiography is a new psychological method for the study of popular culture. We find instead in the case of Brand and Grey a very different situation.[8] First, we find no similar correlations between person, ethos and text – at least we find none of the cogwheeling of clearly discernible patterns between the life, work and thought of these authors. Secondly, we find that the tensions comprising each of these dimensions, which endowed them with considerable analytic power, are largely absent. More precisely, it is not that the three dimensions are absent, but rather that their contents and interrelations have changed considerably. From this we conclude that a different method is necessary for the psychological analysis of the established forms of popular culture. We can only briefly suggest the nature of this different method, but in doing so we note the intimate parallels between a major shift in the evolution of the Western and the type of method useful for the analysis of this popular culture.

Ethos and life

By the time Brand and Grey had begun to write, the ethos of the Western artist or author had changed considerably from that at the time of Wister and Remington. First, we note that the old order, with its landed gentry, intellectualism, inherited money, and sensitivity to family and traditional ways, was not a source of conflict for these writers. Both were born into the new entrepreneurial ethos and, moreover, accepted it without question – without any sense of there being an alternative work-role such as the role of artist for the writer.

This lack of tension at the level of ethos was due to the fact that urbanization and industrialization were considerably further advanced. Brand and Grey were men of the city (New York) and they worked for publishing houses located there, whose products were mass-produced by the techniques of industrial technology. They modelled their writing of Westerns on the basis of this situation. They expected of themselves what the publishing houses expected of them. If their stories were rejected, they re-wrote them in an instrumentally efficient way, or sought other publishers.

Behind this readiness to accept the new ethos was a very new and different sense of vocational craft. Wister and Remington worked as artists, drawing on dimensions of inwardness nourished by tradition. In and through their work they attempted to synthesize the tension between traditional and emerging forms of experience. Brand and Grey worked as technocrats, deriving their sense vocation and craft, not from a sense of artistic calling, but from what readers and publishers wanted. Associated with this was an indifference to intellectuality. Grey never aspired to an association with letters, and while Brand struggled all his life to produce great literature, most of his energies went into his popular stories. Frank Gruber, a figure who could be easily included with Brand and Grey, scornfully announced his superiority over the novelist Thomas Wolfe entirely on the basis of volume of sales.

It is not surprising, then, to notice as well that the lives of Brand and Grey displayed the kinds of energy, ambition, health, confidence and persistence which the new professionalism required. Gone was the mysterious illness which drove Wister and Remington westward – intense doubt, preoccupation with self, and personal isolation. In fact, the very notion of 'a breakdown in health' is incongruous with these 'new Westerners'.

Personal life circumstances were equally different. This is not to say that there was an absence of personal conflict of the sort which characterized Wister and Remington – far from it. Grey exhibited delinquent behavior as an adolescent and Brand had many personal difficulties throughout his life. Nor are we suggesting that parent-child conflicts were absent. But two important differences between the two groups of men must be noted. First, personal conflict with parents in the latter case was experienced and worked out as a matter of course, through the more customary and largely unconscious processes of ordinary development. Neither saw personal conflict with parents as the occasion for the kind of self-reflection which would lead to major decisions regarding self-image and the choice of a vocation. As children Brand and Grey took their cues more from their own inclinations and from the social order than from their parents.

Secondly, their own vocational conflicts and decisions were not subject to intense parental concern. The family was not a locus of vocational conflict. In brief, Brand and Grey were extroverted, and fundamentally unalienated from their parents and society. Wister and Remington were introverted and profoundly alienated both from their parents and from the ethos of their times. No longer is there active tension, in the case of Brand and Grey, between person and ethos, and, as we will next show, between these and their writings or texts. There is a relation, but it is one of adaptation and not of conflict.

In this regard we should also note that neither Brand nor Grey endowed the West, taken as a geographical location, with any special significance for their personal situations. Wister's and Remington's travels West were important for their personal development and their work. The West contained considerable symbolic character for ordering their lives and their experiences of society. Not so for Brand and Grey; for them the West was a place to visit and to write about. In the light of this it is not surprising that from time to time both Brand and Grey wrote stories having nothing to do with the West – Brand created the Dr. Kildare series, and Grey wrote about fishing and baseball. The Western experience was not 'psychobiographical' for these writers.

Text

These shifts in person and ethos are reflected in the texts. Brand and Grey created enormous amounts of work. Nevertheless, it is still possible to detect in their work the disappearance – or rather, transformation – of the major characteristic of Wister's work, a focussed tension between the inwardness of the hero and the frontier society from which he is alienated. An explicit contrast between the hero's personal inwardness and the rational, expansionistic character of the frontier ethos is blurred. In fact, inwardness of this sort is lacking in the heroes of Grey and Brand. This textual feature coordinates, I think, with the shifts in ethos and person just summarized. Grey and Brand do not depict this alienation in their art because they did not experience it in their social ethos, nor was it reflected in any personal, generational conflict. The text is not a self-conscious resolution of the tensions of person and ethos.

On the one hand, then, we can indeed see an interlocking of text with personal and social factors, although it is of a very different sort from that found in Wister and Remington. Entrepreneurial work-roles are positively linked to absence of vocational conflict with parents, and both are reflected in the text. On the other hand, this interlocking is of little analytic, explanatory, or hermeneutical value. For it is precisely that double tension, so characteristic of Wister and Remington, within the author's person and between that person and its ethos which created the Western, and which also gives us a significant and important perspective on the Western. But in the case of Brand and Grey the life of the author no longer exercises positive effects upon the formation of the text. The text can hardly be a synthesis of a set of conflicts which have disappeared. The dimensions of person, ethos and text remain, but their inner structure and inter-relation are different. They neutralize each other, or complement each other, rather than reciprocally effecting one another.

To make the same point in a different way: the Western is a genre which has travelled the route from high to low culture, and in this process it has lost its psychobiographical character. The limitation of the psychobiographical method lies in its dependence on certain characteristics in the author's life which, as we have seen, do not exist when a popular culture genre truly becomes established. We have in sum, moved from a world of persons to a world of types.

What can we say of this limitation of the psychobiographical method? Are there new roads of analysis which it can point to? There are, I think, but based heavily upon an analysis of the distinction between person and type, between author and genre.

5. Conclusion: The inconsequentiality of the author in the Western

The nature and limits of psychobiography can be well seen in the shift from the work of Wister and Remington to that of Brand and Grey. I can summarize my conclusions regarding this shift by speaking of the use of 'the inconsequentiality of the author' in the Western. By this I mean that the personal uniqueness of the life-experiences of the author, what we have called the dimension of 'person', does not produce significant effects upon his texts. The author's personal situation, his peculiar personal and social circumstances and the tensions these create, and his peculiar struggle with them and final command over them, has disappeared. In fact, there seems to be an inverse relation between authorial effects and the genre character of the text: the more stereotyped the Western becomes, the less important is the personal situation of the author. But in fact in popular culture the author has not disappeared. Facts about his personal life are available. However, these facts are of no interest or value for retracing the process by which a text was created. As we have said, there is a shift in the relation between the three dimensions, as well as in the character of those dimensions.

In the case of the personal dimension there is, as noted already, a decline in importance of earlier, childhood experiences as determinants of the text. Further, whatever personal trends remain no longer bear the stamp of an intense vocational preoccupation. The question of craft and vocation is closely linked with the dimension of ethos, through the social-psychological factor of work-roles. As the significance of the author's personal experience diminishes, the work-role of the author becomes more organizational. Large and powerful organizations for the production of Westerns rendered the role of the author more entrepreneurial. He was less concerned with the integrity of his work than he was with its acceptability for production and consumption.

This reduction of tension between person and ethos is reflected in changes in text. The firm distinction between frontier society and the life of the hero is blurred. The text becomes more and more stereotyped. To this we add the speculation that the audience itself becomes more and more invisible, more massive, and more passive. A sophisticated electronic technology has been developed to manage these characteristics of the audience.

By way of summarizing these observations we could argue that we have discovered that popular culture is really a reflection of social change, not personal change, as the psychobiographical method insists. Popular art reflects ethos, not person; or, popular art is the 'mirror of society', as the saying goes. It is the ethos which shapes the author's person, and his text as well. However, as we just noted one of the characteristics of established popular culture is not only the inconsequentiality of the author, but also the invisibility of the audience. In the latter we are in effect speaking of the 'inconsequentiality of the ethos'. Through survey techniques we could make the audience more visible, as has already been done, but this would not necessarily illumine the text. Knowledge of how many people watch Westerns, their socio-economic status, etc., will not lead us to the meaning of Westerns.

The inconsequentiality of both author and ethos therefore calls for a new approach, one which allows us to re-think the significance of each dimension without, however, necessarily abandoning them. The inconsequentiality of author and the invisibility of the audience likens popular culture more to folk tale and myth. In each case we are confronted with narratives, presented at a popular level, in which authorship and social circumstances are irrelevant for appreciation. Therefore, I wish to suggest that the most fruitful line of investigation is broadly structural in character. By structural I mean: (1) abandoning the search for the author's intention as the privileged key to the meaning of the text; (2) granting an autonomy to the text at least equal to other factors; and (3) searching within the text for recurrent elements – i.e., searching for and correlating recurrent types of narrative pattern, and recurrent types of central images.

In making such a suggestion I am not proposing a simple transfer of methods from the structural study of folk tale and myth to that of popular culture, for popular culture is created by self-conscious persons for a self-conscious society. But structuralist methods might be adapted to the conditions of mass society – of mass production, mass media, and mass consumption. The problems of person and ethos could then be re-thought along structuralist lines, for these two dimensions are, in their original forms of statement by Freud and Marx, the essence of modernity. What is important is to begin by focussing on the text and then, under the guidance of principles established in that analysis, search out correlations between texts, ethos and person.

On the one hand, one could view such a proposal as a revised program in psychobiography. On the other hand, it seems that psychobiography, regardless of how extensive a revision it may receive, seems destined to be the handmaiden of high culture, not of popular culture, and possibly for the analysis of the way high culture products lead to the creation of popular genre. Psychobiography seems to work best with the great texts, at least with those texts, usually great, wherein authorship is a central, identifying and problematic feature of the text.

In conclusion we must also note that the personal, authorial element, so dear to the criticism of high culture, and so central to psychobiography, has not entirely disappeared from the popular culture scene. It has, I think reappeared in the 'auteur theory' of film direction, wherein the director has replaced the author in providing the personal element. This is a fruitful point where psychobiography can continue to focus without essential methodological modification on popular culture. At the very least, it is an avenue of inquiry which needs to be explored.

But the 'auteur theory' will not help us understand Westerns. For Westerns are stories which people submit to, without care for the intention of the author, or director, and without self-conscious desire to penetrate the meaning of the text. But it is precisely the reason people go to Westerns and the nature of the satisfactions they derive from them, which we, as students of psychology of culture, wish to understand.

NOTES

1. Robert Warshow, *The Immediate Experience* (New York: Doubleday, 1962), p. 27.
2. Erik Erikson, *Young Man Luther* (New York: W. W. Norton & Co., 1958);
   —, *Gandhi's Truth* (New York: W. W. Norton & Co., 1969);
   —, *Identity and the Life Cycle* (New York: International Universities Press, 1959);
   —, *Insight and Responsibility* (New York: W. W. Norton & Co., 1964);
   —, *Identity: Youth and Crisis* (New York: W. W. Norton & Co., 1968).

3. Erikson, 'The First Pyschoanalyst', in *Insight and Responsibility.*
4. See for example, Paul Ricœur, *Freud and Philosophy*, tr. Denis Savage (New Haven: Yale University Press, 1970); and Philip Rieff, *Freud: The Mind of the Moralist* (New York: Viking Press, 1959).
5. G. Edward White, *The Eastern Establishment and the Western Experience* (New Haven: Yale University Press, 1968).
6. Peter Homans, 'Puritanism Revisited: An Analysis of the Screen Image Western', *Studies in Public Communication*, No. 3 (Summer, 1961).
7. G. Edward White, *Op. cit.*
8. Robert Easton, *Max Brand: The Big 'Westerner'* (Norman: University of Oklahoma Press, 1970); and Frank Gruber, *Zane Grey* (New York: World Publishing Company, 1970).

PART IV

From Individual Life to Hagiography

JOSEPH M. KITAGAWA

13

Kūkai as Master and Savior

Students of Buddhism are already acquainted with the figure of Kūkai (774–835), the founder of the Shingon or Esoteric sect in Japan. That he transmitted the Esoteric tradition of Buddhism from China and made great contributions to the religious and cultural life of Japan is well known. During his lifetime Kūkai undoubtedly was a towering figure in scholarship, spiritual perception, and religious leadership.

More significant perhaps, from the standpoint of *Religionswissenschaft* (History of Religions), is the fact that after his death Kūkai, under his posthumous title Kōbō Daishi, has continued to hold a special place in the hearts of Japanese Buddhists. Even today, 'his memory lives all over the country, his name is a household word in the remotest places, not only as a saint, but as a preacher, a scholar, a poet, a sculptor, a painter, an inventor, an explorer, and ... a great calligrapher'.[1] It is interesting to note that historically Kūkai was neither the first nor the only patriarch who was given the title of Daishi (or Taishi, 'Great Master'), but in the course of time he became the Daishi *par excellence*. Moreover, in the eyes of the faithful Kūkai was more than a Great Master who had acquired the secret teaching *of the Buddha; he himself* became a semi-divine saviour, a worthy object of adoration and worship. Thus, it is widely believed that Kūkai did not die, and that he is still walking around in various parts of Japan under the disguise of a pilgrim helping those who need his help.

Even such a brief characterization of the life and influence of Kūkai raises a number of important and difficult questions to a historian of religions. Essentially, the figure of Kūkai as we now know him is a composite of many factors – what he actually was, how he was remembered, and the ideal virtues and qualities that were attributed to him by pious tradition. There is little doubt that he was a remarkable individual who reflected the religious and cultural ethos of his time and yet transcended his environment. He was also a learned Master and patriarch, having acquired understanding and proficiency in the profound doctrines and intricate practices of Esoteric

Buddhism. Moreover, he might be regarded as what Joachim Wach calls the 'classical figure' of Japanese religion, not only in the sense that he was an outstanding representative but also because his personality, activities and influence illuminate the nature and character of the religious heritage of the Japanese. In dealing with such a multi-dimensional figure as Kūkai, a historian of religions is naturally intrigued by the cultural situation which nurtured him and the manner in which various kinds of attributes and legends came to be homologized in his person. In so doing, he has to know something about Kūkai's understanding of Buddhism, even though it is not his task to determine whether or not Esoteric (Shingon) Buddhism, transmitted and propagated by Kūkai, actually revealed the sacred truth of the Buddha. He would also like to inquire about the characteristics of the soteriological yearning of Japanese Buddhists who have found in Kūkai an image of a saviour.

Our first task is to reconstruct, as concisely and accurately as we can, the life and career of 'Kūkai, the Master' and the cultural and religious milieu which nurtured him, and then to discuss the main features of 'Kūkai, the Saviour', realizing of course that these two dimensions are inseparably interrelated. Throughout all this, our aim is to depict and understand the significance of such a paradigmatic figure as an important phenomenon in the history of religions.

Kūkai, the Master

Any effort to reconstruct the life of Kūkai is frustrated by the difficulties in sorting out facts from legends. Although he was a prolific writer throughout his life, he seems to have been more interested in explicating the doctrines of Esoteric Buddhism than recording his autobiography. Even when he made references to himself, Kūkai was more concerned with the development of his thought than with the details of his life. For instance, his first work, the *Sangō-shiiki* (Indications of the teaching of three religions),[3] which compared the doctrinal characteristics of Confucianism, Taoism, and Buddhism, was written to affirm the superiority of Buddhism. The *Sangō-shiiki*, however, may be regarded as the record of Kūkai's conversion to Buddhism, which marked an important turning-point in his life. In the *Shōrai-mokuroku*

(The list of newly-imported scriptures),[4] which he presented to the court upon his return from China, Kūkai included an account of his encounter with Hui-kuo at the Chinese capital, describing how he received the secret transmission of the Esoteric Vehicle from this celebrated master. Important though this experience was, and it might be regarded as Kūkai's second conversion, his reference to it was again motivated by his desire to advocate the efficacy of Esoteric Buddhism.

A number of so-called biographies of Kūkai throw very little light on the actual life of Kūkai. There are, however, a few notable exceptions. One is the *Kūkai-sōzu-den* (The biography of Abbott Kūkai), which was probably written shortly after his death by Shinzei (800–860).[5] Another is the *Zo-daisōjō-Kūkai-wajo-denki* (The biography of Archbishop Kūkai). Its authorship is ascribed to Kūkai's younger brother and disciple, Shinga (801–879), who however was dead before the year 895 when this work was reputedly completed. Many scholars today are inclined to believe that this biography was actually written by Shobo (832–909).[6] A more controversial, and yet indispensable, source for the life of Kūkai is the *Goyuigō* or *Yuigō* (The last instructions), consisting of twenty-five injunctions supposedly given by Kūkai to his immediate disciples on his deathbed in 835. Officially the Shingon ecclesiastical authorities have always affirmed Kūkai's authorship of *Yuigō*, but many scholars, including some of the leading Shingon scholars, have come to the conclusion that while it was no doubt based on Kūkai's teachings and instructions, the compilation of them in the form of the *Yuigō* was done later by one of his disciples. To make the matter more complex, there are at least four different texts of the *Yuigo* with considerable discrepancies and contradictions among them.[7] Nevertheless the *Yuigō* provides important data that are not available anywhere else regarding the early life of Kūkai. For this reason practically all the biographies of Kūkai written in later centuries depend on the *Yuigō* as their basic source.

It is to be noted in this connection that in the cases where the *Yuigō* and other accounts do not agree, the Shingon authorities and biographers invariably accepted the former as authoritative. Thus, for example, it is widely held that Kūkai was born in the year 774. This assumption is based on the account given in the *Yuigó*, and depends on the rejection of the chronology of the *Zō-daisōjō-Kūkai-wajō-denki.* Since pious legends later regarded Kūkai as the reincarnation of Amoghavajra or Pu-k'ung, the celebrated master of Esoteric Buddhism, who died in China on the fifteenth day of the sixth month of 774, many biographies of Kūkai take it for granted that he was actually born on that very day.[8] Similarly, the dates usually given for Kūkai's conversion and ordination are based on what might be called a 'pneumatic exegesis' of the references given in the *Yuigō*. Notwithstanding these and other difficulties and ambiguities involved, we must try to piece together available data and reconstruct the portrayal of the human figure of Kūkai.

As far as we can ascertain, Kūkai was born in or around 774 in the Sanuki province (present Kagawa prefecture) of Shikoku island. His father was Saegi Ataegimi (Masauji), and is mother was Ato Tamayori.[9] Evidently the Saegi family and the Ato family were related.[10] Although we are not certain exactly how many brothers and sisters Kūkai had, we know that one of his brothers, Shinga, became a disciple of Kūkai, and that two famous Shingon prelates, Shinga and Shinzen, were Kūkai's own nephews.[11]

When Kūkai was born, he had of course no way of knowing that he was destined to spend his childhood and youth in a very critical period of Japanese history. The impact of the Chinese civilization which began to penetrate Japan in the sixth century transformed many aspects of Japanese society and culture. The introduction of a written language and of Chinese art and classical literature inevitably created a sharp division between the Sinified upper strata and the uneducated masses. Politically, the Yamato kingdom which earlier had been a *de facto* confederation of autonomous clans became a centralized empire governed by a series of rescripts and legal codes patterned after the Chinese system. Confucianism provided a coherent system of personal and political ethics hitherto unknown in Japan, while Taoism and the Yin-yang system contributed lofty cosmological theories as well as magical practices. By far the most far reaching new influence was Buddhism, which quickly overshadowed the indigenous Shintō religion. Prince Regent Shōtoku (573–621) adopted a multi-religious policy which attempted to preserve a division of labor, so to speak, among Buddhism, Confucianism, and Shintō.[12] However, Shōtoku's pious hope of maintaining a harmonious relationship among the three religions was not to be easily attained. During the second half of the seventh century the imperial court under the influence of Confucian-trained bureaucrats attempted sweeping reforms.[13] One of the important measures of the reform was the establishment of an educational system based on the teaching of the Confucian classics.[14] Partly as a reaction to the excessive Confucian emphasis of the previous century, eighth-century Japan witnessed an "ecclesiastification" of culture under the influence of Buddhism.

It is worth noting in this connection that the glorious culture of the eighth century (the Nara period) was more than the imitation of Chinese culture to which it has often been reduced by superficial critics. Rather, it would be more correct so say, following the metaphor used by Langdon Warner, that 'the T'ang dynasty of China was hanging like a brilliant brocaded background, against which we might look at Japan and its capital city of Nara to watch the eighth century, while *the Japanese were at work weaving their own brocade on patterns similar but not the same*'.[15] What was involved in this process of 'weaving' was the integration of diverse threads, great and small, foreign and indigenous, old and new. The establishment of the first permanent capital at Nara, for instance, resulted in dividing sharply the mode of living of the capital, which was greatly influenced by continental customs, from the traditional way of life of the uneducated peasants in the countryside. The exposure to Chinese civilization made the Japanese elite in turn conscious of their own heritage, as evidenced by the compilation of the *Kojiki* (Records of Ancient Matters) and the *Nihongi* (Chronicles of Japan) at the same time as the first collection of Chinese verse by Japanese poets, the *Kaifūsō* (Fond Recollections of Poetry). Officially, the government was still committed to the reform measures of the seventh century promoted by the Confucian-trained bureaucrats, but those measures virtually collapsed because of repeated revisions made for the benefit of the former clan chieftains and local magnates now emerging as court nobles.

By far the greatest issue of the Nara period was religion. Little need be said about the six schools of Buddhism established during this period, e.g., the Kusha (*Abhidharmakośa*), the Jōjitsu (Satyasiddhi), the Hossō (Yogācāra), the Sanron (Mādhyamika), the Kegon (Avatamsaka), and the Ritsu (Vinaya). The extravagant support given to Buddhism by the court, plus the religious vitality inherent in Buddhism, gradually transmuted Shintō to the extent that it easily became subservient to Buddhism. It was more difficult for the Buddhist hierarchy to deal with the unorthodox Buddhist holy men called *ubasoku* (*upāsaka* ascetic, magician, healer, or medium) who were greatly influenced by the shamanistic folk piety of the pre-Buddhist period. Their influence was such that the court felt compelled to solicit their support for the construction of the great Buddha statue and appointed Gyōgi (670–749), their leader, to the rank of archbishop.[16] Buddhist leaders were also confronted by rivalry on the part of learned Confucianists who controlled educational policies and institutions.[17] Some of the orthodox Buddhist priests, dissatisfied with the scholastic emphasis of the established schools in the capital city, sought enlightenment by undergoing austere physical discipline in the mountains and forests in the vicinity of the Hiso Temple at Yoshino.[18] Moreover, certain sutras and practices of Esoteric Buddhism, which enjoyed royal favor in China at that time, infiltrated Japan, and the Hiso Temple came under their influence.

When Kūkai was born in 774, the once glorious culture of Nara had already begun to disintegrate. Shortly before, an audacious attempt by a Buddhist priest named Dōkyō to usurp the throne then occupied by a superstitious empress had failed, and in 770 a minor prince was suddenly enticed to ascend the throne as the Emperor Kōnin. The new emperor, inheriting a nation suffering from overtaxation, political intrigue and general apathy, attempted to rectify the situation by appointing a number of competent bureaucrats well versed in Confucian learning. Among them were Saegi Imaemishi and Saegi Mamori, both cousins of Kūkai's father, and Ato Ōtari, Kūkai's uncle. It was the Emperor Kōnin's son, the Emperor Kammu (reigned, 781–806), who moved the capital from Nara, first to Nagaoka and again in 794 to the present Kyōto. Understandably, the young Kūkai's outlook was greatly influenced by the political and cultural changes that were taking place during this period.[19]

From all accounts, it appears that Kūkai was initially given a Confucian education at the university in the capital. He was thereby following in the footsteps of his uncle, Ato Ōtari, a Confucian scholar and tutor to the Emperor Kammu's son, Prince Iyo. Kūkai's brilliant academic career, however, was suddenly terminated by his conversion to Buddhism. He thereupon left the university and became a hermit.[20] There is no doubt that he had a genuine religious experience, even though his conversion was in no small measure the result of intellectual inquiries into the teachings of Confucianism, Taoism, and Buddhism. Probably Kūkai was also disillusioned by the unpredictable nature of government careers, so easily ruined by intrigues at court.[21] Kūkai's activities following his conversion seem to imply that he followed for some time a path of seeking enlightenment by undergoing austere physical disciplines in the mountains near Hiso Temple mentioned earlier. Sometime around 798 Kūkai received the traditional priestly ordination at Tōdai-ji, the national cathedral during the Nara period and the main sanctuary of the Kegon (Avantansaka) school. Meanwhile, by chance he came across the Dainichi-kyō (Mahāvairocana Sūtra), and became a seeker after the truth transmitted in the Esoteric tradition of Buddhism.

Shortly after the turn of the ninth century Kūkai aspired to study in China, and sent a petition to the court to this effect. In 804 he was permitted to accompany the Japanese envoy, and after an eventful trip reached Ch'ang-an, the capital of T'ang China. There he received the mysteries of Esoteric Buddhism from Hui-kuo (746–805) of the Ch'ing-lung (Green Dragon) temple. At that time, thanks to the liberal policies of the T'ang monarchs, Manichaeism, Nestorian Christianity, and Zoroastrianism were tolerated, alongside Confucianism, Taoism, and Buddhism. Kūkai enjoyed the colorful cosmopolitan atmosphere of Ch'ang-an, where he stayed on, after the death of his master Hui-kuo, and studied Sanskrit and other subjects.[22] After collecting the scriptures and the liturgical ornaments of Esoteric Buddhism, Kūkai returned to Japan in 806. Just before leaving China, he left a poem to his fellow student, Acharya I-ts'ao:

> *Studying the same doctrine*
> *Under one master (Hui-kuo),*
> *You and I are friends.*
> *See yonder white mists*
> *Floating in the air*
> *On the way back to the peaks.*
> *This parting may be our last meeting in this life.*
> *Not just in a dream,*
> *But in our deep thought,*
> *Let us meet again*
> *Hereafter.*[23]

By the time Kūkai returned to Japan, his senior contemporary Saichō or Dengyō Daishi (762–822), who had studied the T'ien-t'ai Buddhism in China, managed to secure imperial recognition for the Tendai school with its monastic center at Mt. Hiei. But the Emperor Kammu died in the third month of 806, shortly before Kūkai's return. The Emperor Heizei (reigned, 806–809) succeeded and, distrustful of his own brother, Prince Iyo, forced him to take poison. Kūkai, whose uncle Ato Ōtari was Prince Iyo's tutor, decided to remain in Kyūshū, even though he presented to the court the list of scriptures, ornaments, and art objects which he had brought home from China. It was only in the tenth month of 807 that Kūkai was officially permitted to report in person to the court in Kyōto. Even though Kūkai had a reputation as a man of broad and up-to-date Chinese learning, he did not receive encouragement from the Emperor Heizei in his religious activities. During this period a friendship developed between Saichō and Kūkai.

The picture changed considerably under the Emperor Saga (reigned 809–23), for he patronized Kūkai not only as a man of letters but also as the leading patriarch. In this connection, it might be noted that in sharp contrast to Saichō who stressed the basic incompatibility between the Tendai system and the old established Buddhist schools of Nara, Kūkai presented the Esoteric Vehicle (Shingon school) as the fufilment of all other Buddhist schools without rejecting their validity. Thus, in 810 Kūkai secured a key position at the Tōdai-ji of Nara, and began to propagate Esoteric Buddhism from within the framework of the established schools of Buddhism. In the same year, Prince Takaoka, the former heir-apparent who had been deprived of his succession right because he was implicated in a court intrigue, took priestly vows and became Kūkai's disciple. Meanwhile, Kūkai and Saichō were estranged and the latter left for the Eastern province for an extended evangelistic campaign. In 816 Kūkai was given a charter to establish his monastic center at Mt. Kōya. After the death of Saichō in 822, Kūkai became an unrivaled religious figure in Japan. In the following year, Kūkai was appointed as Abbott of the Tō-ji (Eastern Temple) in Kyōto which came to be known as the temple for the protection of the nation (*Kyō-ō-gokoku-no-tera*).

Kūkai's popularity and influence continued to increase under the reigns of the Emperors Junna (reigned, 823–32) and Nimmyō (reigned, 832–50). He was asked to offer prayers for rain during the drought in 824 and again in 827, and to celebrate the votive service for the protection of the throne in 826. In return, the court showered him with honors and favors. In 828, Kūkai founded a private school, called Shugei-shuchi-in, for the purpose of offering general education. The educational principles of the school were stated by Kūkai as follows: 'The rise and decline of any institution depends ultimately on the personnel, and the rise and decline of any person depends basically on the teaching'.[24] That is to say, the purpose of this school was training for leadership, both secular and religious, and thus it offered a broad curriculum including the teachings of the Confucian, Taoist, and Buddhist systems. He was convinced that the healthy growth of religion presupposed a cultured society, and vice versa.

Kūkai spent the last few years of his life consolidating the organizational structure of the Shingon school and explicating its doctrines. We are told that in 834 he wandered on Mt. Kōya and chose the spot where he would be buried. His affection for Mt. Kōya was well expressed by one of his earlier poems:

Within the quiet forest,
Alone in the straw-thatched but,
So early in the morning
I hear the sound of a bird.
    It sings of the Triple Treasure,
    The Bu-pō-sō [Buddha, Dharma, and Samgha].
The bird has a voice for singing,
A man has a mind for thinking,
The voice and mind,
The cloud and the stream,
Express the Buddha-wisdom.[25]

On the twenty-first day of the third month of 835, Kūkai's colorful life came to an end. In 921, the posthumous title of Kōbō Daishi (the Great Master for the Propagation of the Dharma) was conferred upon him by the court.

Kūkai, the saviour

The transformation of the image of Kūkai from that of a Master to one of a Saviour is a complex problem. A historian of religions, however, is reminded of the fact that deification of saintly figures is a fairly common phenomenon in various religious traditions. In all such cases the personalities and teachings of men in question may differ greatly, but the 'forms' of their biographies as they develop over the years seem to follow an amazingly similar pattern. This is what Martin Dibelius calls the law of sacred biography. According to this law, there is usually a stereotyped notion of a holy man, whose life is marked by a series of supernatural events. His birth is accompanied by miraculous elements, and he proclaims his future calling in his youth. He seems to know ahead of time what kind of death is awaiting him, and often such a person is believed to have overcome physical death one way or the other.[26] On all these accounts, the case of Kūkai follows this general pattern of sacred biography. However, we are here concerned with what particular factors were involved in the deification of Kūkai. In so doing, we will have to deal with the two most important aspects of the problem, namely, (1) Kūkai's own claim of what he was, and (2) how he came to be remembered by his disciples and followers.

1. It is well-nigh impossible to examine the voluminous writings of Kūkai in the limited space of this essay, nor can we assess Kūkai's own self-understanding solely on the basis of his written works. On the other hand, it is not our purpose to evaluate his contributions to many areas of art and culture, even though it is clear that he was endowed with unusual talents and abilities along these lines. Rather, our modest aim is to ascertain his basic approach to religion. This, we realize, is in itself a hazardous undertaking. Kūkai's deeds, techings, and writings are full of existential contradictions. Nevertheless, it is safe to state that Kūkai throughout his life was concerned with a certain type of religious knowledge and concentrated his attention upon the nature of a reality which can be known only by immediate experience and continued contemplation.[27] This may account for the fact that brilliant though he was as a student Kūkai was not satisfied in his youth with the purely academic training of the university and became a hermit. At least judging from the *Sangō-shiiki* (Indications of the teachings of three religions), Kūkai's fundamental question was not primarily an intellectual inquiry into the truth values of Confucianism, Taoism, and Buddhism. He was converted to Buddhism precisely because it presented not only metaphysics and ethics but also a concrete path which promised the certainty of enlightenment. This conviction led him to undergo austere physical disciplines in the mountains while at the same time he continued his intellectual endeavor under learned monks. Eventually he found the answer to his soteriological quest in Esoteric (Shingon) Buddhism.

Sir Charles Eliot once stated that it was not easy to determine 'how far Shingon as we see it in Japan, is the system which Kōbō Daishi learnt in China and how far it is a reconstruction due to himself'.[28] While this question can be argued either way, we are inclined to feel that Shingon Buddhism in Japan developed primarily out of Kūkai's own religious search in spite of the fact that he appropriated the philosophical, cultic and ecclesiastical framework of the traditional Esoteric Buddhism which he studied in China. In this sense, we might rightly regard him as the 'founder' of Shingon Buddhism in Japan and not simply its 'transmitter'. Granting that this observation is an oversimplification, let us now proceed to depict the essential characteristics of Kūkai's religion from this point of view.

Briefly stated, Kūkai's religion was based on three epistemological components: (a) *shōtoku* or *shōgu* (the intuitive function of the mind that enables it to determine moral choices); (b) *shūtoku* (knowledge acquired by learning and experience); and (c) *shinkō* (faith which gives certitude).[29] It was Kūkai's considered opinion that man's intuitive reason is usually hindered by bestial desires. The first step then in the religious life is to overcome those desires and to purify one's mind so that one will be able to make moral decisions. Secondly, religious life requires a continuous training of mind and body by following the ethical and religious teachings of sages and saints. However, in the final analysis one receives the certainty of enlightenment or salvation only by faith. In Kūkai's own case, his ethical and religious pilgrimage culminated in his encounter with the *Dainichi-kyō* (the Great Sun Sutra) which he accepted in faith as the direct teachings of the Great Sun Buddha (Mahāvairocana). Although Kūkai acknowledged the value as Exoteric (public) or relative truths of all the ethical and religious teachings he had received prior to his experience of *metanoia*, he considered them basically to be *prepaeratio* for the Esoteric (secret) truth preached by Mahāvairocana.

The qualitative difference between the Exoteric and Esoteric vehicles was elaborated in Kūkai's major writings, especially in *Benkemmitsu-nikyōron* (Treatise on two teachings–public and secret), the *Jūjūshin-ron* (Treatise on ten stages of spiritual growth), and the *Hizōhōyaku* (The jewel key to the store of mysteries). In all these works Kūkai quotes passages from the Indian and Chinese literature of Esoteric Buddhism to prove that the *dharmakāya* (the truth-body of Buddha), which according to Exoteric teachings is formless and colorless, is no other than Mahāvairocana and that he has body and continuously preaches the Law. His main argument is that the Exoteric teachings were given by Sākyamuni who could not teach the highest truth because he had to adapt himself to the level of his general hearers, whereas Esoteric teaching is the Law understood secretly by Buddha and given to select disciples, like familiar conversation among relatives. These arguments are couched in philosophical language, but they are to be understood as Kūkai's basic affirmation of faith. His 'fideist' principle comes through most clearly in his assertion that one who follows the Exoteric teachings must spend hundreds of thousands of years in discipline for the attainment of Nirvāṇa, whereas one who follows the Esoteric vehicle can attain Buddhahood during his lifetime in his own physical body (*sokushin-jōbutsu*).[30]

The principle of *sokushin-jōbutsu* (attaining Buddhahood in one's body) may be regarded as the final synthesis of the intellectual and practical dimensions of Kūkai's religious pilgrimage. Actually this doctrine is not explicitly taught in the two leading scriptures which Kūkai refers to as his sources – the *Mahāvairocana Sūtra* and the *Vajraśekhara Sūtra*. There is every reason to believe that Kūkai depended on the *Ta-jih Ching Su* (Commentary on the *Mahāvairocana Sūtra*) by I-hsing (683–727) which contains this novel doctrine, even though Kūkai did not credit this commentary with it.[31] More important probably is the fact that *sokushin-jōbutsu* was a logical goal of Kūkai's practical discipline considered as a search for miraculous power. Kūkai, be it remembered, was a child of an age which took seriously the existence of numerous spirits, both malevolent and benevolent, and even many orthodox Buddhists of his time were awed by the example of En-no-Shōkaku, the seventh century *gyōja* (austerity man) and the reputed pioneer of the shamanistic Buddhists (*ubasoku*). He was believed to have acquired superhuman power by exercise of the magic formulas (*dhāraṇi*) of the *Mahāmāyūri-vidyārājnī* (*Kujaku-myōō-ju*).[32] Kūkai himself admits, according to the *Yuigō*, that his initial interest in Buddhism was aroused when a certain monk gave him the *Kokuzō-gumonji-hō* (Rules spoken by the Buddha for seeking to hear and keep the *dhāraṇi* of the most excellent heart, by means of which the Bodhisattva Ākāśagarbha is able to fulfill all wishes).[33] It prescribes, among other things, the *goshin-shuin* (Symbolic gestures for protecting one's body) which give a person who practices them 'the protection of all Buddhas and of Ākāśagarbha. They also obliterate all crime, purify the body and heart, increase felicity and wealth, and drive away all demons and piśācas (vampires).'[34] Thus, following the examples of the shamanistic Buddhists, many of whom were reputed to be wonder workers, Kūkai underwent many years of austere training in order to acquire supernatural power by practicing the *Kokuzō-gumonji-hō*. It was the *Dainichi-kyō* (*Mahāvairocana Sūtra*) that gave theoretical basis for Kūkai's practical attempt to acquire miraculous powers (*siddhi*),[35] and it was this magico-soteriological aspect of Esoteric Buddhism that he pursued during his study in China. There he received from Hui-kuo not only the deeper meaning of the scriptures but also the fivefold baptism, instructions on the Three Mysteries, and the Sanskrit formulas both for the Womb and Diamond Maṇḍalas. Upon his return to Japan, Kūkai attempted to synthesize doctrinal and practical approaches to enlightenment, on the basis of his experience of religious life, and out of this attempt came the principle of *sokushin-jōbutsu*.

The foregoing makes it clear that *sokushin-jōbutsu* was not merely a doctrinal formula for Kūkai. He was convinced that anybody properly trained and initiated into the mystery of the Esoteric vehicle can acquire miraculous powers and actualize the Buddhahood which is implicit within him. Kūkai never tired of advocating the benefit of his soteriological path by his lucid writings, eloquent preaching, exquisite art, as well as by practical demonstration of his miraculous powers. Moreover, following in the footsteps of his mentor, the great shamanistic Buddhist Gyōgi, Kūkai travelled widely initiating charitable activities such as the construction of reservoirs and canals for irrigation, the planting of trees, and the healing of the sick. He also shared with Gyōgi a conciliatory attitude toward Shintō deities, thus strengthening the trend toward the Buddhist-Shintō coexistence which came to be known in later years as Ryōbu-Shintō.

2. As we turn to the discussion of how Kūkai came to be remembered by his disciples and followers, we must bear in mind that the tendency to deify religious founders and saintly figures has been unusually strong in Japan. This is due in part to the fact that the Japanese people, not satisfied with worship of intangible deities believed to reside in another realm, tended to

give absolute devotion to certain charismatic persons and outstanding religious leaders who were closer to them.[36] For example, less than a century after the death of Prince Shōtoku in 621, he came to be regarded as an incarnation of Kannon, the Lord of Mercy. According to a legendary account, people revered the seventh-century wonder worker, En-no-Shōkaku, believing that he was able to control even deities and ghosts by his magic spells. Also, the *Shoku-Nihongi* (Chronicles of Japan, Continued) tells us that Gyōgi (670–749) was actually worshipped by the masses and was called a Bosatsu (bodhisattva) during his lifetime.[37] In all these cases, who these men actually were and what they did became less important than what their followers believed they were and did.[38] That is to say, the memories of these men came to be reconstructed by the soteriological yearnings of their pious followers. Furthermore, in their loving adoration of these deified figures these followers tended to demand and keep alive more and more apocryphal and hagiographical accounts of the supposedly historic memories of these men.

It is readily understandable that the memory of Kūkai, one of the most colorful and charismatic figures in the religious history of Japan, underwent the inevitable process of deification after his death. It is important to note that the two biographies mentioned earlier – the *Kūkai-sōzu-den* (The biography of Abbott Kūkai) and the *Zō-Daisōjō-Kūkai-wajō-denki* (The biography of Archbishop Kūkai) – portray essentially the human figure of Kūkai, the Master. Of the four editions of the *Yuigō* (The last instructions) mentioned earlier, the two earlier editions, presumably written very shortly after Kūkai's death, present him as a human being, albeit an unusually great one. The two later editions of the *Yuigō*, however, give accounts of a markedly deified Kūkai. His death scene is modeled after that of Gautama. Kūkai is said to have proclaimed himself to be a legitimate object of adoration and worship on the part of his faithful. Furthermore, according to these later accounts, Kūkai declared that after he entered trance – which by implication is different from ordinary death – he would be with Maitreya (Miroku) in Tushita Heaven until such time as he would return to this earth with Maitreya. The assurance of his second coming even had a tone of mild warning to the effect that while in Tushita Heaven he would be watching closely the behavior of the faithful, and that those lax in their devotion to him would have reason to be sorry.[39]

Once these deified accounts of Kūkai were accepted by pious tradition, his human figure receded into the background. In this connection, we noted earlier that the belief that Kūkai was the reincarnation of Amoghavajra was instrumental in the development of the theory that Kūkai was born on the fifteenth day of the sixth month of 774, which was the day of Amoghavajra's death. In the course of time a large number of highly embroidered biographies' of Kūkai have come into existence.[40] Although space does 'not permit us even to list the important legends about him cited in these works, we might briefly discuss the deified image of Kūkai in terms of three main motifs of the religious heritage of the Japanese.

(a) The first important motif is preoccupation with the 'here and now' of the phenomenal world. This does not imply that the Japanese have not been aware of the existence of other realms of existence. Indeed, the ancient Shintō myths mention the threefold structure of the world (the heavenly, the earthly and the nether regions) and Buddhism taught the existence of many grades of heavens and hells. Nevertheless, the 'world of meaning' of the Japanese has always been grounded primarily in this world. To put it in religious language, this world is the center of the cosmos and is the very arena of salvation, however this term may be interpreted. It also means that religion is inseparable from the family, community and socio-political order of the nation. It is therefore not without reason that the 'classical figures' of Japanese religious history were not necessarily men of deep spiritual insight but more likely were outstanding men of practical ability who exerted lasting influence on ecclesiastical, philanthropic, cultural or national affairs. In popular legends Prince Shōtoku is regarded as a sort of counterpart to King Solomon, endowed with unusual wisdom and compassion.[41] The fame of Gyōgi was greatly enhanced by his reputation as a great philanthropist, and he was also credited with the first census ever taken in Japan.

Admittedly, it is beyond the competence of a historian of religions to determine the authenticity of many of the legendary accounts that have developed around the life of Kūkai. It is worth noting, however, that the popular image of Kūkai is consonant with the tradition of the 'classical figures' of the Japanese religious history. For example, his name connotes in the minds of many Japanese a man of great brilliance, an accomplished linguist, a talented painter, sculptor, calligrapher, and a gifted poet and prose writer. We are told that when he accompanied the Japanese ambassador to

China, it was Kūkai who impressed the Chinese officials with his mastery of written Chinese. When he called on Hui-kuo, this eminent master of the Esoteric vehicle welcomed the young Japanese monk by saying 'until you came there was no one to whom I could transmit the teachings'. After his death, Hui-kuo told Kūkai in a dream: 'If I am reborn in Japan, this time I will be your disciple'. Kūkai was not only successful in everything he undertook in China, but his achievements after his return to Japan were very impressive. He is credited with having introduced the study of Sanskrit, perfected the two kinds of Japanese alphabet, *Katakana* and *Hiragana*, and originated the *Yamato-e* (Japanese style painting). His reputed ability to use five brushes simultaneously in painting is reminiscent of a superhuman performance of Prince Shōtoku in another domain. His philanthropic activities matched only those of the celebrated Gyōgi. Kūkai's tender love toward his mother is regarded a model of filial piety, and his services to the court make him a paragon of loyalty. Needless to say, Kūkai's notion of *sokushin-jōbutsu* (acquiring Buddhahood in this life) had a great appeal to his followers who were nurtured in the tradition which regarded this world as the very arena of salvation.

(b) The second motif of the religious heritage of the Japanese, which is closely related to the first, is its apprehension of life as concentric circles, not as a series of separate domains. This motif may be illustrated by the principle of *saisei-itchi* (unity of religion and government) or by the tradition of the inseparability of art and religion. To be sure, historical developments in Japan resulted in the gradual stratification of society and the departmentalization of life, but the Japanese have never lost the insight that various acitvities of life, despite their apparent contradictions, share an inherent mid-point.[42] This view of life fostered, in religion as much as in art and philosophy, emphasis on the harmony of contrasts and a rejection of sharp dichotomies between sacred and profane, good and evil, or phenomenal and noumenal.[43] It also accounts for the traditional Japanese preoccupation with aesthetics at the expense of ethics and metaphsics, and it explains, at least in part, the magico-soteriological accent of Japanese piety.

In a real sense, the image of Kūkai as it has come to be remembered by pious tradition is a personification of the traditional religious apprehension of the Japanese. He himself was nurtured in this tradition, and he had unusual competence in various fields of human activities. Throughout his life he endeavored to harmonize religion and art, philosophy and literature, Buddhism and other religious and semi-religious systems, and the spiritual and cultural life of the nation. It was no sheer accident that Kūkai was attracted, among all schools of Buddhism, to the cosmo-theism of the Esoteric vehicle which regards the whole universe as the body of the Great Sun Buddha (Mahāvairocana). Kūkai was no doubt impressed by the comprehensive nature of the Esoteric doctrinal system which offered a cosmological, physical, and psychological analysis in terms of the six elements (five material elements plus one mental element, i.e., consciousness), but he never attempted to teach the Esoteric vehicle only as a system of doctrine. Thus, in the Shōrai-mokuroku he suggests that the Esoteric doctrines are so profound that they cannot be understood without the help of painting. 'The various attitudes and mudras of the holy images all have their source in Buddha's love, and one may attain Buddhahood at sight of them. Thus the secrets of the sūtras and commentaries can be depicted in art, and the essential truths of the esoteric teaching are all set forth therein... Art is what reveals to us the state of perfection.'[44] Kūkai in presenting religion as art represented the central core of Japanese piety, and in this he may be rightly regarded as a paradigmatic figure of Japanese religious history.

(c) The third important motif of Japanese religious heritage is its tendency to depend on the charismatic qualities of religious leaders as efficacious ingredients for salvation of man. Indeed, throughout the history of Japan some of the charismatic holy man have been regarded as *de facto* saviours to whom the faithful paid homage and adoration. This motif originated in pre-Buddhist Shintō tradition, as Eliot aptly observes, and it was subsequently amplified by Buddhist piety. 'Buddhist and Shintoist ideas thus coalesced and the title of Bodhisattva was conferred on departed Emperors and statesmen – on those, for instance, who are described as Hachiman, the patron of soldiers, and Tenjin, the God of Calligraphy, and even on so recent a personage as Ieyasu.'[45] In this respect, the case of Kūkai was one of the most spectacular examples of the homologizing of Shintō and Buddhist saviour motifs.[46]

The deified figure of Kūkai was, as noted earlier, a composite of the many components and stereotypes regarding charismatic persons and saviour images that had been sanctioned and preserved in the communal reservoir of Japanese folk piety. That is to say, the soteriological yearning of the faithful consciously or unconsciously found in the life, teaching and deeds of Kūkai many of the admirable qualities of Prince Shōtoku, En-no-Shōkaku, Gyōgi and others. While we have no way of ascertaining whether Kūkai believed himself to be more than a Master of the Esoteric vehicle or not, it is conceivable that his teaching of the attainability of Buddhahood in this life, his beliefs in the potency of *mantra* and *dhāraṇī* as well as in miracles and divine oracles given in dreams, and his claim to the mastery of *siddhi*, contributed to the creation of a spiritual aura around his own personality. It was most assuredly Kūkai's intention to dedicate his learning, skills and miraculous power solely to the purpose of presenting Esoteric Buddhism as the most effective vehicle of salvation for the people. But in the eyes of his followers it was Kūkai himself who became the vehicle of salvation or the saviour, and with this twist his words and deeds took on new soteriological significance.

One of the most attractive forms of adoration paid to the deified Kūkai is a religious ballad called 'Namu-Daishi' (Hail to Daishi).[47] It tells the life of Kūkai as remembered in the popular fancy. For example, according to this ballad, when Kūkai was in the palace for a religious discussion, his body suddenly assumed the appearance of Mahāvairocana. 'The Divine Light (Kōmyō) streamed out from him, and the whole company, overawed and trembling, fell to the ground and worshipped him' (Verse 31). The ballad, echoing the pious belief that Kūkai did not really die but only entered a deep meditative trance (nyūjō) and that his body is uncorrupted in his tomb, awaiting the coming of the future Buddha, Maitreya, goes on to say that: 'Eighty years after his decease, an Imperial Messenger opened the gate of his sepulchre. His hair, they found, had grown long upon his head; they shaved it off and gave him a change of garments' (Verse 57). Later, 'when Shinnyu, the Imperial Messenger to the Temple in which our great sage is worshipped, was unable to see the face of the Sage, the Sage himself guided the worshipper's hand to touch his knee' (Verse 59). Understandably, the chanting of these verses in corporate worship or during pilgrimages to the holy mountain of Kōya had stirring and cumulative effects on the faithful, and they in turn kept alive the sacred tradition of Kūkai or Kōbō Daishi, who embodied within him the numinous glory of the Great Sun Buddha (Mahāvairocana).

Equally significant was the development of various legends that associate Kūkai with the Shintō tradition. According to one legend, the goddess of

Mt. Kōya, Nifutsu-hime, donated the mountain to Kūkai when he was looking for a place to establish his monastic center. The ballad, 'Namu Daishi', puts it more dramatically: 'In the mountainous districts of the province of Kii, two dogs, one white and one black, and a hunter, came to show him the way...' (Verse 35). 'Then Nifutsu appeared, the god of that place [Kōya], and offered him that place until the coming of Maitreya, in order that the land might be blessed by him [Kōbō]' (Verse 36). According to another account, when Kūkai was appointed as the chief abbott of the Tōji, which was called the Temple for the protection of the nation, a Shintō kami of food and fertility, Inari, appeared at the gate of the temple and told Kūkai: 'Together, you and I, we will protect this nation'.[48] In many districts, including places where Kūkai could not possibly have visited, there are many legends about what Kūkai did during his lifetime in those places. Popular among them are stories about wells or springs which were believed to have been discovered by Kūkai.[49] These legends provided powerful incentives for the formation of a devotional association based on belief in Kōbō Daishi called the Daishi-kō.[50] It is widely held that Kōbō Daishi in disguise walks with pilgrims or that he visits villages on the night of the winter solstice.[51]

As stated at the outset of this essay, the deification of saintly figures, a common phenomenon in many religious traditions, is an intriguing and fascinating problem to the student of *Religionswissenschaft*. We are inclined to hold that one meaningful way to study this phenomenon is to study some of the 'classical figures', in the sense that Joachim Wach used this category. Kūkai or Kōbō Daishi is such a paradigmatic figure in the history of Japanese religion, and a study of his sacred biography will enable us to understand not only the life and teaching of this remarkable Master but also the characteristics of the Saviour motif in the religious heritage of the Japanese.

Notes

This essay has previously appeared in *Studies of Esoteric Buddhism and Tantrism*, edited by Koyasan University, 1965.

1. George B. Sansom, *Japan, A Short Cultural History* (London, 1946), p. 230.
2. 'Der Begriff des Klassischen in der Religionsgeschichte', in *Quantulacunque*, in honor of Kirsopp Lake (London, 1937), pp. 87–97. English translation is included in Joachim Wach, *Types of Religious Experience* (Chicago, 1951), pp. 48–57.

3. See Mori Kanshō, *Sangō-shiiki kōgi* (An exposition on the *Sangō-shiiki*) (Kōyasan, 1941).
4. English translation of a portion of this document is included in Tsunoda, Ryūsaku *et. al.* (Comps.), *Sources of Japanese Tradition* (New York, 1958), pp. 144–147.
5. According to some scholars, the author was Shinshō. Both Shinzei and Shinshō were Kūkai's immediate disciples. Whether or not this biography was written in 835 as the tradition claims is debatable. It is safe to assume, however, that this biographical account was written before 857 when the title of Dai-sōjō (Archbishop) was conferred upon Kūkai posthumously.
6. The third work, the *Daisōzu-Kūkai-den* (The biography of the Great Abbitt Kūkai) was compiled in 869. It contains very little relevant materials, however.
7. See Kōyama, Taiban, 'Kōbō Daishi ni tsuite', Shūkyō Kenkyū, III, No. 9 (1918), pp. 71–76. He points out that one of the texts, known as the *Kōyasan-Ezu-no-maki* (The pictorial volume of Mt. Kōya) includes the description of Mt. Kōya which was taken from the diary of Shinzen dated 875, this in spite of the fact that the *Yuigō* was supposed to be written in 835, immediately following Kūkai's death. Katsuno, Ryūshin, *Hiei-zan to Kōya-san* (Mt. Hiei and Mt. Kōya) (Tokyo, 1959), p. 116, tells us that such leading Shingon scholars as Gonda Raifu (1846–1934), Katō Seishin (1872–1956), and Tomita Kōjun (1875–1955) rejected Kūkai's direct authorship of the *Yuigō*.
8. This theory was first advocated by a famous Shingon prelate, Raiyu (1226–1304) and came to be widely accepted as early as the thirteenth and fourteenth centuries, as evidenced by the reference to it in the *Jinnō-shōtō-ki* (The records of the legitimate succession of the divine sovereigns) by Kitabatake Chikafusa (1293–1354).
9. Kūkai's mother's name, Tamayori, literally means 'The one in whom the *tama* (spirit) of the *kami* dwells (yori or yoru)'. It was a name often given to a shamanic diviner *(Miko)*. See Yanagita, Kunio, *Imōto no Chikara* (Power of the Sister) (Tokyo, 1953), p. 66.
10. There were two divisions of the Saegi family. According to traditional genealogy, one division was traced to the Emperor Keikō and the other to Ótomo Muroya. The former had settled in Harima (present Hyōgo prefecture), while the latter, to which Kūkai belonged, had settled on Shikoku island. Again, according to a legendary account, Kūkai's family is traced to Ame-no-oshihiko-no-mikoto, the son of Takamimusubi-no-mikoto of the mythological pantheon. Ame-no-oshihikono-mikoto's descendant, Michi-no-omi-no-mikoto, was closely associated with the legendary first emperor Jimmu in Japanese mythology. Michi-no-omi-no-mikoto's descendant, Takechi-no-mikoto, was supposed to have accompanied the expedition of Prince Yamato-takeru against the northern barbarians and was later given land on Shikoku island. Takechi-no-mikoto's son, Muroya, was a minister in the court; and Muroya's son, Mimono, and grandson, Yamatoko, both became governors of Sanuki province in Shikoku island. Ōtomo Yamatoko's son was given the family name of Saegi, and his descendants served as governor for four generations. In 646, according to the Taika Reform edict, the position of governor *(kunikko* or *kuni-no-miyatsuko)* was discontinued,

and many of the local officials who lost their posts moved to the capital and were given minor government positions.

11. According to one genealogical account, Kūkai had an older brother, Suzuki-maro. Kūkai's older sister, Chiye, was married to a Shintō priest of Taki-no-miya; their son was Chisen. Kūkai's youngest brother's son was Shinzen. His relation to the Tendai prelate, Enchin (814–91), posthumously called Chishō Daishi, is not certain. According to one theory, Enchin was the son of Wake Iyenari and his wife, who was Kūkai's younger sister. However, according to the Tendai source, Enchin's mother was Kūkai's niece.
12. Prince Shōtoku was undoubtedly aware of a multi-religious policy which was adopted by the first Sui emperor, Wen-ti. On the latter, see Arthur F. Wright, 'The Formation of Sui Ideology, 581–604', in John K. Fairbank (ed.), *Chinese Thought and Institutions* (Chicago, 1957), pp. 71–104.
13. On the government Buddhist policies during the second half of the seventh century, see Futaba, Kenkō, *Kodai Bukkyō-shisōshi kenkyū* (A study of early Japanese Buddhism) (Kyoto, 1962), pp. 23–301.
14 This educational system was more or less kept intact with only minor modifications until the middle of the nineteenth century.
15. Langdon Warner, *The Enduring Art of Japan* (Cambridge, 1952), p. 6. My italics.
16. See J. M. Kitagawa, 'Kaiser und Schamane in Japan', *Antaios*, Band II, No. 6 (März, 1961), pp. 552–566.
17. See Inouye, Kaoru, *Nihon kodai no seiji to shūkyō* (Politics and religion in ancient Japan) (Tokyo, 1961), pp. 202–209.
18. This movement was called the Shizen-chi-shū or the 'Nature wisdom school'. Even such leading priests of the Hossō school as Jinyei, Shōgo, and Gomyō were known to have frequented the Hiso Temple.
19. We have dispensed with Kūkai's secular names to avoid unnecessary complications.
20. As stated earlier, the *Snagō-shiiki* may be regarded as the record of Kūkai's conversion to Buddhism. His conversion took place when he was somewhere between twelve and twenty, but the exact date cannot be ascertained, because different sources give different accounts on this score.
21. One of Kūkai's kinsmen, Saegi Imaemishi, was a confidante of Prince Sawara, the younger brother of the Emperor Kammu and his heir-apparent. Because of a certain intrigue, Prince Sawara was banished in 785 to the island of Awaji, and Saegi Imaemishi also lost his position in the court. This turn of events might have influenced the young Kūkai. Subsequently, Kūkai's uncle, Ato Ōtari, also lost his position when Prince Iyo was banished from the court.
22. It is interesting to note that Kūkai's Sanskrit instructor, Prajna, an Indian monk, is said to have worked with Adam, a Syrian Christian monk, on the translation of the *Shatparamita-sutra* from a Mongolian text. See I-Tsing, *A Record of the Buddhist Religion as Practiced in India and the Malay Archipelago*. trans. J. Takakusu (Oxford, 1896), p. 224.
23. Beatrice Lane Suzuki, 'Poems by Kōbō-daishi', *The Eastern Buddhist*, V (1931), p. 312.

24. Quoted in Kaneko, Daiyei, *Dengyo Kōbō to Nihon Bunka* (Tokyo, 1940), p. 46.
25. Beatrice Lane Suzuki, *op. cit.*, p. 312.
26. Martin Dibelius, *Die Formgeschichte des Evangeliums* (Tübingen, 1919), English translation by Bertram L. Woolf, *From Tradition to Gospel* (New York, 1935), pp 108–109.
27. On this problem of knowledge, see F. S. C. Northrop, *The Meeting of East and West* (New York, 1946), pp. 315–317.
28. Sir Charles Eliot, *Japanese Buddhism* (London, 1935), p. 340.
29. See Kambayashi, Ryūjō, *Kōbō Daishi no shisō to shūkyō* (Tokyo, 1931), pp. 2–11.
30. It must be noted, however, that some scholars, including the late Shimaji Daito, have questioned the authenticity of Kūkai's authorship of the *Sokushin-jōbutsu-gi* (Principles of becoming Buddha with one's physical body).
31. See Kambayashi, *op. cit.*, pp. 264–272. Kambayashi feels that Kukai's references to two portions of the *Mahāvairocana Sūtra*, as the scriptural basis for his soteriology, is far-fetched. He also examines Kukai's quotations from the *Vajrasekhara Sūtra* and finds only a suggestion concerning *bodhicitta* but no explicit statement about *sokushin-jōbutsu*. Kambayashi therefore concludes that this doctrine existed in the mind of Subhākarasinha (637–735), who translated the *Mahāvairocana Sūtra* into Chinese, in rudimentary form but was expounded more fully by his pupil, I-hsing. Kukai must have known I-hsing's commentary and read its meaning into the *Mahāvairocana Sūtra*.
32. *Nanjiō Catalogue*, Nos. 306–311.
33. *Nanjiō Catalogue*, No. 501. It is to be noted that Kokuzo (literally, Womb of the Ether or Space), the patron bodhisattva of Kukai, was believed to be the counterpart of Jizo (Womb of the Earth, Kshitigarbha), the source of abundant blessings of the earth. The *Kokuzō-gumonji-hō* was based on a section of the *Vajrasekhara Sūtra* called the 'Joju-issaigi-bon' (Chapter on all the meanings of *siddhi*).
34. M. W. de Visser, *The Bodhisattva Akāsagarbha (Kokuzō) in China and Japan* (Amsterdam, 1931), p. 41. This Mudra 'consists in raising the right hand, and pinching the middle finger with thumb as if pinching incense. The second joint of the middle finger must be bent, its first joint and the point must be straight. After having made this mudra he must place it on the crown of his head and recite the formula once; then place it on his right and left shoulders, heart and throat, each time with one incantation' (*Ibid.*, p. 40).
35. On the meaning of *siddhi*, see Mircea Eliade, *Yoga: Immortality and Freedom*, trans. Willard R. Trask (New York, 1958), pp. 85–90.
36. See Nakamura, Hajime *Tōyōjin no shii hōhō*, II (Tokyo, 1948), pp. 114–140; English translation, *The Ways of Thinking of Eastern Peoples* (Tokyo, 1960), pp. 355–377.
37. See Hori, Ichiro, *Waga-kuni minkan-shinkō-shi no kenkyū*, I (Tokyo, 1955), pp. 299–300.
38. For a modern example of such a process, see Frank Werfel, *The Song of Bernadette* (New York, 1941), p. 109. Hyacinthe de Lafite, the skeptic, makes a classic remark regarding the authenticity of the vision of Bernadette. He says: 'I find that all you

gentlemen miss the essential point. The true problem is offered not so much by the little visionary as by the great crowd that follows her. . . .'

39. See Kōyama, Taiban, *op. cit.*, pp. 71–76.
40. See Katsuno, Ryūshin, *op. cit.*, pp. 118–121.
41. We are told that he was able to listen to ten different law suits simultaneously.
42. Incidentally, this is exactly the kind of insight which was advocated by G. van der Leeuw. In his *Sacred and Profane Beauty: The Holy in Art*, trans. David E. Green (New York, 1963), p. 34, he says: 'We consider the question of religious dance, because after a few decades we have once again recognized the value of the dance as an expression of art and life, and because we recognize that all values must have a connection with the highest and most comprehensive value known to religion.'
43. See my article, 'Japanese Philosophy', in *Encyclopaedia Britannica*, 8th edition.
44. This translation was taken from Tsunoda *et. al.*, *op. cit.*, p. 142.
45. Eliot, *op. cit.*, p. 183. On the process of deification of Suguwara Michizane, who shortly after his death came to be known as Temma-daijizai-Tenjin, see Watsuji, Tetsurō, *Nihon rinri-shisō-shi*, I (Tokyo, 1927), pp. 232–236.
46. On the Shintō and Folk religious background of this problem, see Hori, Ichirō, 'On the Concept of Hijiri (Holy-man)', *Numen*, V, No .2 (April, 1958), pp. 128–160, and *ibid.*, V, No. 3 (September, 1958), pp. 199–232. On the saviour motif in Buddhism, see Edward Conze, 'Buddhist Saviours', in S. G. F. Brandon (ed.), *The Saviour God*, presented to Edwin Oliver James (Manchester, 1963), pp. 67–82.
47. See Arthur Lloyd, *The Creed of Half Japan* (London, 1911), pp. 243–258. I follow Lloyd's translation in this article.
48. Regarding the legend of Inari and Kūkai, see Kondō, Yoshihiro, *Kodai-shinkō-kenkyu* (Tokyo, 1963), pp. 37–130. It is Kondō's opinion that the legend that associates Inari and Kūkai began to receive wide acceptance during the middle of the Kamakura period.
49. See Yanagita, Kunio (gen. ed.), *Minzokugaku-jiten* (Tokyo, 1951), pp. 24–25 and 198–199.
50. *Ibid.*, pp. 340–341. There are three kinds of *Daishi-kō*. One of them is connected with Shōtoku Taishi (Prince Shōtoku). The second is connected with Kōbō Daishi. The third is strictly an ancient peasant cult which venerated the Taishi (oldest son) of the *kami* who is believed to visit the village between the harvest and the new year. It is to be noted that in the folk tradition these three, especially the latter two, are confused in the minds of people.
51. *Ibid.*, p. 398.

WILLIAM LA FLEUR

The Death and 'Lives' of the Poet-Monk Saigyō

The Genesis of a Buddhist Sacred Biography

The Japanese poet Saigyō (1118–1190) has often been referred to as one of 'Japan's Three Poets' [*Nihon no san shijin*,] that is, as one who must be included in the trinity of the best poets of a people whose pursuit of verse and affection for poets is extraordinary.[1] Modern critics may have at times questioned this evaluation of Saigyō, but they have not doubted that the verse of this medieval monk has been for centuries one of the best known, memorized, and studied in Japan. Of even greater significance is the fact that Saigyō's verse has always been seen as having an inextricable connection with the style and story of his life. Since he was a warrior in the elegant court of Heian Japan who gave up this career to become a Buddhist monk who traveled widely and resided in nature in order to record his experiences of nature in his poetry, the story of his life has had a continuing fascination for Japanese in every stratum of society. He has long been regarded as medieval Japan's Buddhist nature poet *par excellence*. His life, or episodes in it, became the subject of local lore, of later art forms such as Nō and Kabuki, and of fiction in modern times.[2]

However, we also know that he became the subject of biographical representation at a very early date – within less than a century after his death in 1190. For instance, the recently discovered *Towazugatari* of Lady Nijō (1258–), the personal reminiscences of this courtesan of emperors, includes her mention of a scroll which she had seen at the age of nine.[3] She claims to have been deeply impressed with the scroll which pictorially presented the life and travels of Saigyō and included a number of his verses. Lady Nijō, herself a poet, tells us that the effect upon her own life of Saigyō's example was great; the impression it made remained with her so that after years of love and anguish with emperors and other court figures, she decided to emulate Saigyō and to become a Buddhist nun. According to Lady Nijō, therefore, a representation of Saigyō's life existed by the year 1267 or seventy-seven years after his death. Also from her we learn that his life story was employed as an effective religious and didactic model by this time.

Probably the first 'Life' of Saigyō was of the type which Lady Nijō saw. That is, it was an *emaki* or 'painted [picture] scroll', a popular medium for historical romance and biography in medieval Japan. In this medium the narrative unrolls along with the scroll, and it is virtually 'stereoscopic' in its side by side presentation of the written narrative and painted scenes of the life or events recounted. Still extant are portions of what is called the *Saigyō Monogatari Ekotoba*[4] or 'The Story of Saigyō in Pictures and Words', perhaps the same seen by Lady Nijō, since it seems to have been composed sometime in the middle of the Kamakura period (1192–1333).

Slightly later but still within the Kamakura period the paintings and words were divided and a separate work, the *Saigyō Monogatari* or 'Life-story of Saigyō' was composed.[5] This, an anonymous writing, is extant as a whole. It therefore lends itself to my purpose here of studying the structure of a typical sacred biography of Saigyō. The bulk of the *Saigyō Monogatari* – which, for the sake of convenience will usually be referred to as the 'Life' in what follows – is comprised of verse of Saigyō linked to his location in one place or another during his many and widely-ranging peregrinations. However, I am not here concerned to deal with either the poetry as poetry or with the journeys of Saigyō. Rather, I wish to focus on how the biographer structured the 'Life' on the basis of what he knew and did not know about the life of his subject.

My principal claim, however, is that the structuring of Saigyō's life did not originate in the mind of the biographer at all. I wish to show that he merely extended and made more overt a structure intended by his subject, Saigyō himself. That is, in this case the structure was received initially from information which could be inferred from the poems of Saigyō, who, it would seem, had to some degree *self-structured* his life. In my view the biographer did not so much give pattern to what, since it was a life rather than a 'Life', was irregular, incoherent, and incongruous. Instead, he was sensitive to and expanded upon a structure internalized and intended by his subject.

Even if Saigyō himself intended the pattern which his later biographer employed, this pattern was already an adaptation of something he received from the Buddhist tradition rather than a structure original with the poet. To a certain extent Saigyō seems to have conceived of his own life on the model of that of Śākyamuni Buddha. The writer of the 'Life' correctly apprehended this fact and then extended the model by creating certain seemingly fictive episodes in his subject's life, episodes which strengthened the nexus between the founder of Buddhism and the twelfth century Japanese poet-monk. Therefore, in studying the sacred biography of Saigyō we cannot merely compare the life – what we know from contemporaneous materials and from the colophons of Saigyō's own poems – with the 'Life', the *Saigyō Monogatari*. The situation is more complex than this. At least three components must be considered: the life of Buddha, the life of Saigyō, and the *Saigyō Monogatari*. In what follows I wish to look at the interplay of these components in order to suggest the genesis of the *Saigyō Monogatari* as a sacred biography. But also the particularity of Saigyō is of crucial importance, since he modeled his own life after that of the Buddha, but did so while giving expression to his own particular vision of Buddhist truth, namely, the identification of the Buddhist absolute, the Tathāgata, with the world of nature. Both the underlying structure and the particularity of Saigyō's understanding deserve attention in what follows.

Since the writer of the *Saigyō Monogatari* seems to have pushed the Saigyō-Śākyamuni nexus from the occasion of Saigyō's death, where his materials gave him a basis for it, to much earlier points in the poet's life, points where there were no such materials, it seems reasonable here to follow his method. That is, I will examine the life and the 'Life' in an order which reverses the progression in which the life was lived and the 'Life' is presented. The principle of interpretation becomes evident in events surrounding the death of Saigyō. In many ways, the death of Saigyō seems to have been a prime mover behind the creation of a hagiographic tradition concerning him.

To begin, then, at the ending, it is evident that Saigyō's immediate contemporaries saw his death as significant. And this, in turn, seems to have prompted them to view his life, too, as significant and as capable of being exemplary. That is, after noticing the significance of his death they noticed a pattern he himself had given it. Their evidence for this pattern was the extraordinary way in which Saigyō predicted or willed his death, and also the unusual way in which the themes and principal values of his life and verse were encapsulated and harmonized in his death.

After Saigyō died in 1190, a poem he had written a few years earlier came immediately to the minds of those who knew him and his verse. The poem begins with '*negawaku wa*', a phrase which is the personal opening of what is at the same time a prayer, a wish, and a vow that is willed. The verse and my translation of it are as follows:[6]

negawaku wa	Let it be exactly
hana no moto nite	Under blossoms of the spring
haru shinamu	That the death occurs –
sono kisaragi no	At that second month's midpoint
mochizuki no koro	When the moon's completely full.

The key word in the poem is the easily overlooked *sono* in the fourth line; it is a demonstrative adjective which simply means 'that'. But here it modifies 'second month's midpoint when the moon is completely full', and as such, points away from the year of composition. It points toward that time in the ancient past when, according to received Buddhist tradition, Śākyamuni was said to have entered into final nirvana and died. That is, the Great Extinction was believed to have occurred on the fifteenth of the second month of the lunar calendar.

In this verse Saigyō is looking ahead as well as backward in time. Specifically, he is making a prayer, vow, and prediction that his own death be at precisely the same time of the year. The date in antiquity is identified with one in the near future and Saigyō wills, in this way, to die on the same day as Buddha had. The fact that he *did* die as predicted, some two or three years later, appears to have launched the hagiographic tradition concerning him. The fact that he 'missed' by one day, dying on the sixteenth rather than the fifteenth, was scarcely significant since he had simply wanted to die in the middle of the month under the full moon; the moon of the morning of the sixteenth was seen as the same moon of the evening of the fifteenth.

Suddenly Saigyō's contemporaries saw his death as a *significant* one, significant not only because it seemed to demonstrate a general charismatic quality in his person, but also because within Buddhism the capacity to will a peaceful death rather than succumb to death is of special value. Fellow poets and priests saw in this evidence of an extraordinary life and an unusual man. Kawata Jun writes: 'His contemporaries marvelled at the fact that Saigyō died in the middle of the second [lunar] month totally in accord with his own poem'.[7] Having recognized meaning in the death, they began increasingly to see meaning and structure in the life as well. Within a short time his poetry also leaped into prominence – so much so that ninety-four of his poems were included in the next great imperial collection of poetry, the *Shinkokinshū* (The New Collection of Ancient and Modern Times) of 1206, more in number than the poems of any other poet.

In addition to the religious charisma demonstrated by Saigyō's volitional designation of his own death date, a positive link between the poet and the founder was established. It was on the date of the Great Extinction that Saigyō too wished to die; this made his own extinction on that date also 'great'. It would seem that something of the charisma of Śākyamuni was understood to have been present in the life of Saigyō. In death the founder and the poet were in some sense alike; it is no surprise, then, that he who wrote the 'Life' pursued the likeness and suggested the identification even when he had no support from extant materials. Saigyō himself had seemed to offer the 'Life of Buddha' as the structuring principle to the biographer. The quoted poem made that quite clear.

To return to the immediate contemporaries of Saigyō, we see in their comments that they understood the poem not only as evidence of a nexus between the poet and the Buddha, but also as an encapsulation of the aims, values, and orientation of the poet. The poem expressed, to them, the particularity of Saigyō's vision of the essence of Buddhism. For instance, the great Tendai abbot Jien (1155?–1225), himself a major poet of the period, in his *Jūgyokushū* took special notice of this poem by Saigyō, stating that it was one of two of Saigyō's verses which he held in highest esteem, and went on to say that the coordination of the death vow and the actual occurrence was something 'rare in these days of the degenerate Dharma'.[8] The poet Fujiwara Teika, in his *Jūigusō* (1216), also noted the correspondence between the prediction and the fact.[9] In the text of Fujiwara Shunzei's *Chōshū Eisō*, originally composed in 1178, an interpolation was added later which sees special significance in the fact that the blossoms of the cherry tree had been celebrated by Saigyō throughout his life; the poem is seen as typifying and embodying the major theme of Saigyō's life.[10]

If we ask what, from this perspective, are the features of the poem that make it an encapsulation of the life-long concerns of Saigyō, we must locate these features in the degree to which the poem attributes religious value and meaning to the phenomena of nature, including the cherry blossom and the moon. The verse is remarkable in this respect. It alludes – by means of the demonstrative *sono* – to the death of the Buddha, but it really focusses attention on spring, the blossoms of the cherry tree, and the moon which waxes to perfection and fullness. We have the impression that Saigyō unites the death of Buddha as an event in the cycle of the founder's life with an event in the cycle of nature. The correspondences and assimilations are so finely attuned that we sense Saigyō's suggestion not only of a *coincidentia in tempore* between himself and Śākyamuni, but also of an ontological identification between natural phenomena and the Tathāgata.[11] The moment of perfect enlightenment or perfect fullness is demonstrated in what happens to the moon and the blossoms in the middle of the second lunar month; for Saigyō this event in nature *is* the perfect nirvana and the Great Extinction, inasmuch as the moon becomes completely enlightened and the flowers are perfectly opened. The poet wishes to be present in the midst of them at that moment so that he, in his own moment of enlightenment and extinction, might emulate them and be united with them as they begin to fade and die.

Nature creates a bridge between the twelfth-century poet and the founder of Buddhism, but not in the usual instrumental sense. It does so because nature, in Saigyō's world of value, *is* the Tathāgata. In an earlier poem he had written:[12]

hana sakishi	I saw in Yoshino's
tsuru no hayashi no	Billows of blossoms that far-off
sono kami o	Time of Great Passing
yoshino no yama no	When the śāla trees around Him
kumo ni mishi kana	Suddenly turned as white as storks.

My translation of this verse, admittedly, makes overt some aspects which are more covertly presented in the original. But the interesting feature of this poem is the presence again of the adjective *sono;* here as in the other verse it undoubtedly refers to the time of Śākyamuni's death. The phrase *tsuru no hayashi* makes this certain; it is a poetic way of referring to the śāla trees which, according to legend, turned white when the Buddha entered final nirvana. In Saigyō's day the phrase was a perfectly opaque metonymy for representing this event, although the phrase literally means 'the crane grove' or 'the stork grove', and employs the whiteness of the bird [*tsuru*] to indicate the whiteness of the trees. Even though the poetic image is complex, the reference to Buddha's great extinction is unmistakable in the verse.

In this verse, too, the temporal distance between the founder and the poet is eliminated by the latter's presence in the midst of natural phenomena, specifically the blossoming cherry trees on Mount Yoshino. Standing as he is in the midst of the billows – more literally, 'clouds' – of blossoms there, the poet is mystically projected into the time and scene of Śākyamuni's passing. He claims to 'have seen' [*mishi*] 'that time' [*sono kami o*]. The mediator of the experience was the blossoms in which he stood. Unlike the verse analysed above, this verse, composed earlier than the other, is one in which Saigyō does not yet coordinate his own death with that of the Buddha.

To summarize the discussion thus far, I would emphasize the following points. An identification with the Buddha is clearly suggested in Saigyō's poem which wills that the dates of their deaths correspond. This fact, and the almost preternatural way in which the vow was fulfilled, suggested to Saigyō's contemporaries that his death was significant. But this implied that his life too had extraordinary meaning. They did not yet overtly elaborate on the Saigyō/Śākyamuni nexus; instead they concentrated upon the meaningfulness of the life as one in which the man and his own verse were a single harmony. Implicit in their comments is the suggestion that there might be something paradigmatic about Saigyō's life itself, just as in his death he seemed to be following the paradigm of the Buddha. A life so modeled upon the great paradigmatic life might itself serve as a model for others.

The writing of the sacred biographies of Saigyō in the Kamakura period is, in my opinion, a slightly later age's response to this. Since it had been suggested that the life was significant, 'Lives' came to be written. The structure employed for this writing lay close at hand; it had been adumbrated in Saigyō's own verse. The assimilation of the life of Saigyō to that of Buddha was a logical consequence of information received by the biographers. Therefore, the *Saigyō Monogatari* elaborates upon it, makes it certain, and fixes it in the minds of readers who like Lady Nijō might use Saigyō's life as represented in the 'Life' as a model for a Buddhist vocation.

In the *Saigyō Monogatari* the first major suggestion of the Saigyō/Buddha tie occurs in the depiction of Saigyō's own *shukke* or 'departure from the household [life]'. It is here that the 'Life' seems to depart most radically and significantly from what would appear to have been the available resources of the biographer. From historical documents of the period, diaries of his contemporaries and the colophons attached to his own verses, we know that Saigyō's secular name had been Norikiyo and that he was a member of the Sato family, a family whose members for generations had been imperial guards. Norikiyo, the young man who would be the monk known as Saigyō, was a skilled archer, a horseman, and a poet of some promise in the court of Emperor Toba. For a reason which we cannot positively identify, at age twenty-three he petitioned Emperor Toba for permission to leave the service of the court to become a Buddhist monk. This was eventually granted and he took leave of the capital and, perhaps, of a wife and child, to begin his life as a monk and poet in the midst of nature.[13]

Yet, it is precisely here that the 'Life' becomes most explicit and detailed. Having presented the young man as one who was drawn into moods of melancholy while in nature, it tells us that Norikiyo [Saigyō] began to think of leaving the secular life of the court. In this he was joined by a kinsman named Noriyasu, but they knew of the emperor's resistance to the idea of losing their services in his court. One day Norikiyo and Noriyasu had decided to make the break and had agreed to meet the following morning. They went then to their respective homes. The next day Norikiyo went to his kinsman's home. There he met the following scene:

"At the gate there was noise made by many people there. Inside [the house] too could be heard a number of voices crying in sorrow: 'During the night the master of the house [Noriyasu] died!' When [Norikiyo] heard the laments and sorrowful cries of [Noriyasu's] nineteen year old wife and eighty year old mother, complete gloom settled into his own mind and he thought of [life as nothing but] a flickering flame faced by a gale of wind, as a drop of water floating on a lotus, and as a dream within a dream."[14]

In the *Saigyō Monogatari* these analogies become the occasion for the introduction of a number of Saigyō's own poems, poems which celebrate the evanescence of all natural things and of the life of man as well. Through these poems – some of which, such as the one immediately below, are pre-*shukke*, and some of which are much later in composition – we gain the impression of Norikiyo [Saigyō] as one who had been positively drawn towards 'leaving the household' by the power and beauty of nature. The natural world 'invites' him to do so. For instance, the following verse is cited at this point in the narrative:[15]

sora in naru	A man with his mind
kokoro wa haru no	At one with the sky-void steps
kasumi nite	Into a spring mist
yo ni araji tomo	And begins to wonder if he might
omoitatsu kana	Have stepped out of the world.

Here in some sense 'the world' is equivalent to secular and household life. The young poet is presented as one who is positively drawn to nature.

But the 'Life' goes on. The young poet, having seen the suddenness with which death came to his kinsman, makes his decision to 'leave the household [life]' or *shukke*. When he takes official leave of his family – here taken to be a wife and daughter[16] – the following scene unfolds:

"Having made a petition to the Three Jewels [The Buddha, The Dharma, and The Samgha] to the effect that nothing whatsoever obstruct his departure from the household that very evening, Norikiyo went home. Just as he arrived there his four-year-old daughter, who was exactly at an age which would have made it very difficult to leave her behind, came out onto the veranda to greet him. 'Father, I'm so happy you are home', she said, while taking a tight grasp on the sleeves [of his kimono]. His eyes filled with tears and he thought to himself: "It is precisely *this* that is meant by the phrase 'the world's ties and fetters'." But he kicked his daughter down off the veranda to the ground and then, preventing the sound of her sad cries from entering his ears, went inside the house."[17]

His decision to leave that very night is unshakable. He spends the night telling his wife, who is in tears, of his decision. Then he makes his departure. The *shukke*, very literally, has been accomplished.

What is interesting is that the writer of the *Saigyō Monogatari* has introduced material which would not only fascinate readers of his work, but would also give concrete dramatization of a phrase often found in Saigyō's verse, the phrase *yo o suteru* or 'casting away the world'. Saigyō's poems show that he had considerable difficulty ridding himself of the 'world' and secular life, but the biographer has introduced material to demonstrate concretely why the break was so difficult to make.

Most interesting is the fact that this introduced material establishes a certain connection between Saigyō and Śākyamuni. For, *mutatis mutandis*, Saigyō's life here recapitulates events in the life of Buddhism's founder. That is, at this crucial juncture in his life, the commencement of his career as a wandering monk, the life of the young poet is so presented that the paradigm of Śākyamuni is refracted in and through it. The differences and nuances are such that the underlying structural similarity is not at all effaced.

Specifically, the introduction of the episode of Norikiyo's [Saigyō's] totally unanticipated confrontation with the death of his kinsman is obviously meant to fit the story of Śākyamuni's confrontation with a corpse. According to the received biography of the Buddha, he, having led a sheltered life in his father's palace, one day saw, for the first time in his life, a corpse outside the palace.[18] This event, when combined with his seeing an aged man, a sick man, and a holy man, generated the future Buddha's decision to leave the palace and his life as a householder. Over the objections of Śuddhodana, his father, he left and began his search for nirvana.

In the story of Saigyō's decision to leave the household, the corpse seen is that of Noriyasu. As a parallel to the figure of King Śuddhodana, the Emperor Toba is present; it is he who, although not literally the young poet's father, is the controlling figure whose permission to leave secular pursuits and a career is difficult to obtain. The emperor resists the loss of his warrior as Śuddhodana had resisted the jettisoning of a secular career by his own son.

But in addition there is the figure of the child, the focal point of the melodramatic scene on the night of Saigyō's departure from the household. In the received biography of the Buddha, a son, Rahula, had just been born, and this was what made his decision to leave home the excruciating one it was. In the case of Norikiyo [Saigyō] it is not a son but a daughter, one who we are told 'was exactly at an age which would have made it very difficult to leave her behind'. But Norikiyo, like Śākyamuni, overcomes the most binding of fetters, and realizes his goal, namely, leaving home on *the very night* which he had determined would be the end of secular life.

The structural similarity is striking; each figure and personality has an equivalent. The corpse of Noriyasu functions like the one Śākyamuni had seen on the street, the confrontation with which caused him, too, to reflect upon the impermanence of all things. King Śuddhodana has his counterpart in the figure of Emperor Toba who functions in the background as a restraint upon a precipitous relinquishment of a secular career in the court. Rahula the son is assimilated to the young daughter of Norikiyo; each is the child who makes the leaving of the householder's life almost unbearable. Given this cast of equivalent personalities, it becomes very evident that the Buddha-to-be's counterpart is Norikiyo himself. The structure would be so obvious to readers of the *Saigyō Monogatari* that the identifications need not have been explicitly made. The fabric of the 'Life of Saigyō' is sufficiently sheer so that behind it can be seen hanging the received 'Life of Buddha' the model used in its making. Since Saigyō's 'Life' is itself intended to serve others as an exemplar, it implicitly invites readers – especially those who wish to have the vocation of a Buddhist poet – to adopt its basic pattern in weaving the designs of their own lives. Each successive layer has its own particularity but is diaphanous, so that through it the others can be recognized. Because Śākyamuni's life is the first in the series, all subsequent lives, more in the foreground and more indigenously Japanese, still follow his basic pattern and are understood, therefore, to be Buddhist.

But what constitutes the particularity and specifically Japanese quality of the *Saigyō Monogatari* in comparison with the model of Śākyamuni? The answer is, I believe, the presentation of Saigyō as someone who not only takes an increasingly negative stance with respect to the secular world and its multiple illusions but also as someone *positively drawn* into the natural world. Before his *shukke* the young poet is presented as engaging in reverie in natural surroundings and the biographer employs Saigyō's own verses, some of which were composed at a much later date, to suggest that his subject was drawn into nature as though it were the ultimate *mysterium fascinans*. For instance, the poem telling of his feeling of having 'left the world' when he stepped into a spring mist is employed for this reason. The ecstasy on this occasion is literal; is acts on the young poet to draw him into taking a permanent stance outside the secular world.

For this reason I have the impression that the episode of the confrontation with the corpse of Noriyasu, while very important for establishing the Śākyamuni/Saigyō nexus early in the narrative, is simply the occasion or catalyst for the young poet's *shukke;* the underlying *cause* is elsewhere and is, simply, his total enchantment with nature and his compelling desire to be totally at one with it. In fact, the truth of impermanence is learned by

Saigyō from nature – all things are a flickering flame faced by a gale of wind, a drop of water on a lotus, etc. – and for him the confrontation with his kinsman's corpse is nothing more than the final establishment of the truth of impermanence (*anitya* in Sanskrit; *mujō* in Japanese) in his mind.

Thus, the pre-*shukke* Norikiyo and the post-*shukke* Saigyō are alike inasmuch as the truth of Buddhism is learned from nature and nature itself is the Truth. Saigyō's total corpus of verse celebrates the natural world as the locus and source of religious realization. One has the impression from reading his verse that for Saigyō every cherry tree, every willow, and every sprig of plum blossoms is in some way identified with the *pipalla* or 'Tree of Englightenment' under which Śākyamuni gained the realization he had been seeking.

This, the particularity of Saigyō's vision of Buddhist truth and obviously the basic concern of his life, is not lost by the writer of his 'Life'. The bulk of the work is devoted to an account of the poet's journeys, his taking up residence in nature, and his composition of poems when inspired by natural phenomena. The skill of the biographer lies in his employment of the episodes of Saigyō's confrontation with the corpse and of his taking leave of his family to strengthen the correlation between the poet and the founder of Buddhism. But in making this assimilation he does not obscure the particularity of Saigyō as one who was primarily propelled into a Buddhist vocation because of his love of nature.

The central portion of the *Saigyō Monogatari* presents his wanderings and his poems. In this portion no attempt is made to see a parallel between the poet and the Buddha, but this is probably because the nexus between the two has been already established by the presentation of his leaving secular life and beginning a career as a monk, and is assumed to be implicit from that point on. The parallel is, of course, made explicit once again in the portrayal of Saigyō's death, but in this instance the assimilation of Saigyō to the Buddha is established already by the poem which wills the correspondence of death dates; the biographer, as we shall see below, articulates the nexus which Saigyō himself had intimated.

Near the conclusion of the *Saigyō Monogatari* is a portion of the work which is especially interesting because in it the biographer appears to be weaving together both materials from the life of his subject and multiple themes and motifs from his subject's poetry. He assumes that whatever appears in the verse has been somehow 'lived' by Saigyō and can, therefore, be understood not only as a theme of the literature but also as a datum of the life. This portion concretely demonstrates the technique of Saigyō's biographer. He presents the verse and the life as being in the closest possible union. The summary, therefore, reveals his method and serves, in addition, as a compendium of the whole biography at a place close to the biography's end. It is as follows:

"[Saigyō] ... had lived in grottoes in distant mountains, had purified his mind through contemplation of the [paradisal] Pond of the Eight Perfections, had continually sought the Land of Peace and Rest, had pilgrimaged on foot through many provinces, had practised austerities in mountains and forests, and had encouraged others in their chanting of the Lotus Sutra, the Prajñāpāramitās, the Shingon, and the Nembutsu. He had kept in mind the truth that all sentient beings will be reborn in the Pure Land, had so frequently wept tears of compassion that they fell on the sleeves of his clerical robe, had worn a robe colored by the 'dye' of endurance, had concealed within himself a deep longing to go West-ward, and for more than fifty years had dreamt of himself being with and like flowers rather than with and like mankind. Within a single night and day he had experienced 840,000,000 passions and had felt repentent for them all. He had composed verse of thirty-one syllables. As a Buddhist discipline, he had observed water as it runs from east to west and had seen this as indicating the way to the Western Paradise. He had seen the flowers of the spring and the maple-leaves of autumn enticed off their branches by the wind. Both the [receding] cry of the cicada in summer and the [melting] snow of winter had been observed by him as teachers of the impermanence of things. From his own life he had removed all those occasions in which the mind becomes unsettled. When he had reached eighty years of age and when the 'snow' of great age was on his head – piled as if on a mountain – he was able within himself to quiet the 'waves of the four seas'. At that time, even though he still had strength within himself for further pilgrimages, he went instead to the vicinity of Sōrin Temple on Mount Higashi. There he tied together grasses in order to make a hermitage for himself. While there he was as if in a state of *satori;* he did not sleep at all but sat and watched the rising sun for three successive days. There in the temple's garden he waited for the blossoming of the cherry-trees. Since he had vowed to die during the night after the fifteenth of the second month – that is, during the night of Śākyamuni's entry into final nirvana – and since he had composed the following:

> *Let it be exactly*
> *Under blossoms of the spring*
> *That the death occurs –*
> *At that second month's midpoint,*
> *When the moon's completely full.*

It happened that on the fifteenth, exactly in the middle of the second month in the ninth year *(sic.)* of the Kenkyū era – precisely according to his wish – he, completely sound in his mind and under the falling blossoms, went to the West [-ern Paradise]. It is said that on his face there was a smile of ecstasy."[19]

There are a number of interesting features in this portion of the narrative. Certainly here it is made obvious that Saigyō and Śākyamuni are alike in their deaths. All the particulars of Saigyō's death, including his meeting it under blossoms, are understood to have actually happened; that is, the biographer goes beyond the coincidence of dates and, with what appears to be no documentary evidence, makes Saigyō's death totally exemplary – final nirvana greeted in a state of satori under the blossoming of cherry trees.

Of interest also is that this section employs almost throughout diction 'lifted' from Saigyō's own verse. Motifs such as the walking pilgrimages, the tears of compassion, the hued robe, the cries of the cicada in summer, and the tying together of the grasses to make a hermitage are favorite themes and phrases in the verse of the poet-monk. But the biographer has woven them all together and has seen them not as 'motifs' but as actions and experiences in the life of his subject. He sees the poet's diction as derived from his action; the poems are expressive of the life and the life of the poems.

This point requires more attention below, but first it is necessary to look at the thread of Pure Land doctrine and symbolism that runs through this section of the *Saigyō Monogatari.* Here, Saigyō is unmistakably linked to the Jōdo or Pure Land of Buddhism, whereas in his own verse the Jōdo themes, while certainly present, are not nearly as important as they are made to seem in the above portion of the narrative.[20] In part, this is undoubtedly because after the teachings of Hōnen (1133–1212) and Shinran (1173–1262) were widely promulgated, the Pure Land and True Pure Land schools gained prominence in Japanese religious and cultural life which they had not yet had during Saigyō's life.[21] But of greater interest is the fact that Saigyō's Buddhist name, composed of the Chinese characters meaning 'west' [*sai*] and 'to go' [*gyō*] are taken very far here by the biographer; the entire passage is one of orientation – or, more correctly, 'occidentation'– and Saigyō is presented as one whose very name is indicative of his pursuit of the Western Paradise.[22] Throughout the earlier portions of the *Saigyō Monogatari* the poet-monk is pictured as someone belonging to, and relating himself to, virtually every important school of Buddhism in Japan at the time.[23] But in this final summarizing section he is presented as unmistakably in quest of the Western Paradise.

Aside from this Jōdo orientation of the final portion of the narrative, the presentation of Saigyō as one whose life was intimately coordinated with his verse is of primary importance. Diction and action are viewed as inhering in one another. This, a basic implication of the *Saigyō Monogatari's* summary statement, was again intended by the poet himself rather than invented by his biographer. The judgment that the life and work were bound together is shared by some modern scholars. Although he does not discuss the matter in relationship to the biographer's intimation of the same point, the critic Kubota Shōichirō has seen significance in the extraordinary number of Saigyō's poems which bear the simple headnote '*dai shirazu*' or 'topic unspecified'.[24] To Kubota this means that Saigyō, in contrast to the tradition of court poetry out of which he came, was a poet who preferred to compose verses in relationship to his own experiences rather than on prescribed topics and themes. Saigyō must be seen as essentially different from the court poets of the time who, while in their homes or places in the capital, composed verses on topics *(dai)* such as wisteria, cherry blossoms, or travel. Saigyō did, on occasion, write poems on specified *dai*, but generally he seems to have avoided such a separation of experience and composition. He was, in fact, implicitly critical of the court poets' assumption that they could write nature poetry without being directly in nature. Such a criticism is implied in the following verse:[25]

yama fukaku	By imagining
sakoso kokoro wa	These mountain depths, men might think
kayou tomo	They've come and gone here;
sumade aware wa	But, not living here themselves,
shiran mono kawa	Can they know what pathos is?

The unification of verse and life was, therefore, not only implied by the later *Saigyō Monogatari* but also was seemingly intended by Saigyō himself. It would appear that Saigyō himself assumed that life should have the pattern of a poem and that the poem should be an epiphany of the life. For this reason he coordinated his life to an unusual degree.

Therefore, later generations saw him as a man who practised poetry as a basically religious vocation, as a man in pursuit of poetry as a 'Way'. They viewed Saigyō as someone in *kadō*, the way, path, or *tao* [*dō*] of poetry *[ka]*. Even though he himself did not use the term 'kadō', it seemed to later generations that Saigyō was an exemplar of one whose composition of verse was essentially the pursuit of a religious vocation.[26]

The biographers of his life were of crucial importance in establishing this view. The writing of the 'Life' ensured that later generations would see that Saigyō's life was an exemplary model. Even if development of the model necessitated some engineering of 'fits' between particular verses and particular experiences, the intention of the biographer seems to have been the presentation of a life and a body of verse that are mutually illuminating.

When the life of an individual and subsequent sacred biographies of him are compared it is quite often assumed that the structuring of the life is the work of the biographer. It is presupposed that the real life must have been irregular, unstructured, and perhaps even internally incongruous to a great extent and that the biographer imposed upon his materials a pattern and thematic congruity. I have no reason to doubt that this is often the case. I have suggested here, however, that the sacred biographer of Saigyō's life did not invent the structure for his work, but rather accepted a structure which was intended by his subject. Saigyō himself suggested implicitly that his life was in some way modeled on that of Śākyamuni and Saigyō himself made a correlation between his experiences and his writing. Since his daily interest was focussed on the patterning of words, it is not surprising that he also gave attention to the pattern of his life. The writer of the *Saigyō Monogatari* took the intended structure, sharpened and extended it, and transmitted the intention of both the life and the verse to subsequent generations.

NOTES

1. The other two poets in this triad are Hitomaro (fl. ca. 680–700) and Bashō (1644–94).
2. The representations of the figure of Saigyō are many. Significant examples are the Nō dramas *Saigyō Zakura* and *Eguchi*, and a novella, *Futsuka Monogatari*, by the modern author Kōda Rohan.
3. Lady Nijō writes of having seen the Saigyō scroll and then comments: 'I have envied Saigyō's life ever since, and although I could never endure a life of ascetic hardship, I wished that I could at least renounce this life and wander wherever my feet might lead me, learning to empathize with the dew under the blossoms and to express the resentment of the scattering autumn leaves, and make out of this a record of my travels that might live on after my death.' Karen Brazell, trans., *The Confessions of Lady Nijō* (New York: Doubleday Anchor, 1973), p. 52. Reproductions of extant paintings of the *Saigyō Monogatari Emaki* are found in volume 11 of the series *Nihon Emaki Mono Zenshū* [English Title: *Japanese Scroll Paintings*] (Tokyo: Kadokawa Shoten, 1958).
4. The text of this work is reprinted in *Zoku Gunshoruiju*, Vol. 32 A (Tokyo: Zoku Gunshoruiju Kanseikai, 1900), pp. 347–374.
5. The text of the *Saigyō Monogatari* which I have used throughout is reprinted in *Zoku Gunshoruiju*, Vol. 32 A, pp. 375–419. Another medieval biography of Saigyō is the *Saigyō Isshōzōshi [The Book of Saigyō's Whole Life]*, which is reprinted in *Shiseki Shūkan*, Vol. 12 (Tokyo: Kindō Shuppan, 1937), pp. 118–161.
6. Saigyō, *Sankashū*, poem number 88. In citing Saigyō's, verses I have used the texts and numberings of Itō Yoshio, ed., *Nihon Koten Zensho* edition of the *Sankashū*, Vol. 78 (Tokyo: Asahi Shimbunsha, 1946).
7. Kawata Jun, *Saigyō no Den to Uta* [*Saigyō's Life and Verse*] (Tokyo: Sōkansha, 1943), p. 275.
8. As quoted Kawata Jun, *Saigyō Kenkyū Roku* [*Record of Saigyō Research*] (Osaka: Sōgasnha, 1939), pp. 130–131. The reference to the rarity of this phenomenon in the "days of latter – or degenerate – dharma" is characteristic of Jien's view of history; see Charles Hilton Hambrick, *Gukanshō: A Religious View of Japanese History* (Doctoral dissertation, University of Chicago, 1971). Jien uses an earlier Buddhist name, En'i, to refer to Saigyō. Saigyō seems to have used this name rather early in his career as a monk.
9. See Kawata Jun, *Saigyō Kenkyū Roku*, p. 132.
10. See *Ibid.*, pp. 129–130.
11. See my 'Saigyō and the Religious Value of Nature', *History of Religions*, Vol. 13, no. 2 (November, 1973), pp. 93–128, and Vol. 13, no. 3 (February, 1974), pp. 227–248.
12. *Sankashū*, number 2186.
13. For a fuller account of the life of Saigyō as it can be reconstructed from documents of the time, see my 'Saigyō the Priest and his Poetry of Reclusion: a Buddhist Valoriza-

tion of Nature in Twelfth Century Japan' (Doctoral dissertation, University of Chicago, 1973), Chap. 2.

14. *Saigyō Monogatari*, p. 379.
15. *Ibid.*, p. 380. This poem is number 786 in the *Sankashū.*
16. The significant feature of this is that reliable materials from the period give no mention of a wife or of a daughter. Nor do they refer to a kinsman named Noriyasu, or either of the episodes which the *Saigyō Monogatari* provides in rich detail. The *Sompibumyaku [Lineage of the Higher and Lower Nobility]*, a usually reliable genealogical record of the time, lists a son, Ryūshō, as the sole scion of Saigyō. See *Sompibumyaku*, Vol. 62 of the *Kokushi Taikei* series (Tokyo: Yoshikawa Kōbunkan, 1961), p. 391. This is intersting, especially because there was a poet-monk named Ryūshō (?–1206) who might have been Saigyō's son, perhaps by a 'common law' wife.
17. *Saigyō Monogatari*, p. 381.
18. The entire sequence of four 'confrontations' – with an aged man, sick man, dead man, and holy man – need not be provided; the sight of the dead man is taken as representative, since it is the most intense of the four.
19. *Saigyō Monogatari*, pp. 417–418. Modern literary historians place Saigyō's death in the year 1190, the *first* year of the Kenkyō era.
20. Although Saigyō at times sees his own name, the phenomenon of going in a westward direction, and the Western Paradise, as conceptually interrelated (for instance, in his exchange of verses with Horikawa no Tsubone, *Sankashū*, numbers 925 and 926) his religious affiliation seems to have been more generalized than the *Saigyō Monogatari* makes it out to be in the summary statement translated here. Kubota Shōichirō sees an early and continuing influence of Shingon Buddhism on Saigyō, insofar as he was oriented toward any specific school. I share this opinion. See Kubota Shōichirō, *Saigyō no Kenkyū A* [*Study of Saigyō*] (Tokyo: Tōkyōdō Shuppan, 1961), p. 417.
21. This prominence and popularity were not without persecution. Hōnen was banished from Kyoto in 1207 and in 1227 his disciples were banished from the capital. See Joseph M. Kitagawa, *Religion in Japanese History* (New York and London: Columbia University Press, 1966), pp. 111 ff.
22. It is possible that Jien's use of the name 'En'i' for the monk-poet rather than the widely accepted name 'Saigyō' is indicative of the Tendai abbot's reluctance to see the poet 'appropriated' by the followers of Pure Land. See note 8 above.
23. For instance, Saigyō is represented on page 389 of the *Saigyō Monogatari* as not simply 'practicing austerities in the depths of the mountains' [*shugyō*] but as doing *zazen* or 'Zen sitting' in the depths of the mountains. Whereas in Saigyō's century the great impact of Zen had not yet been made on Japan from China, by the time of the writing of the *Saigyō Monogatari* Zen had an important place in the religious life of the Japanese. The specificity of the 'Life', in contrast to the more generalized 'austerities' referred to by Saigyō himself, is an index to influence of the new religious movements that grew soon after the poet's death. The *Saigyō Monogatari*, in my opi-

nion, presents Saigyō as a somewhat "ecumenical" figure but gives decided preference to Pure Land motifs and symbols in its final, summarizing section.

24. Kubota Shōichirō, *Saigyō no Kenkyū*, p. 753.
25. *Sankashū*, number 2161.
26. See Ishizu Jundō, 'Shunzei to Saigyō ni okeru 'Michi'-teki Shikō' [The 'Way'-Type of Aspiration in Shunzei and Saigyō], *Kokugo to Kokubungaku* [The (Japanese) National Language and Literature] 17 (1940), pp. 64–70.

JAMES H. FOARD

15

The Loneliness of Matsuo Bashō

In 1918, Akutagawa Ryūnosuke, one of the leading Japanese writers of this century, wrote a miniature piece of historical fiction called 'Karenoshō' ('Notes on Withered Fields').[1] It described the death of Matsuo Bashō (1644–1694), greatest of all haiku poets and one of the giants of Japan's cultural heritage, whose most famous verses can today be quoted by virtually every Japanese. One of those verses, reputed to be his last, gave the title to Akutagawa's short work:

Tabi ni yande	Ill on a journey,
Yume wa kar eno o	My dreams over withered fields
Kake maguru	Meander.
(KNBZ, 327)[2]	

In his work, Akutagawa described how Bashō's disciples sincerely grieved on the occasion of his death, but grieved over the loss of their master. While they were so occupied, Bashō, the man, passed quietly away, alone in the midst of his disciples.

For over two hundred years before Akutagawa wrote this, the master Bashō had been the object of a cult which was inseparable but distinct from his literary legacy. As Bashō's school of haiku, the *Shōmon*, quickly became orthodox, the memories and practices of this cult spread through haiku circles all over Japan. The memories were of a wandering sage who found truth by communion with nature through poetry. The practices were of two kinds: (1) an annual worship of Bashō by groups of poets, and (2) the imitation of Bashō's wandering life by certain extraordinary individuals.

The clearest evidence of the worship of Bashō is the conferral of *shingo* or 'kami names' upon him.[3] The first conferral came one hundred years after his death, in 1793, when the chief of the Shinto headquarters (the *Jingi Haku*) entrusted a haiku group from Kyūshu to enshrine Bashō as Tōsei Reishin.[4] This granting of *shingo*, however, only confirmed and added dignity to ceremonies already existing throughout the country. Of greatest importance was the observation of the anniversary of Bashō's death (the twelfth of the tenth month), a normal practice for the commemoration of an ancestor or sectarian leader, probably begun the first year after Bashō's death by his disciples. This worship not only reaffirmed the ideal of a man who had achieved fulfillment through haiku, but also bound the haiku group to common loyalties by offering thanks to Bashō for his poetic legacy. The name of the annual ceremony eventually became *Shigureki*, or 'Early Winter Rain Commemoration', after an appropriate haiku 'season word' (*kigo*.)

A record of such a ceremony near Nagoya in 1793 has come down to us in some detail.[5] It tells the story of a local poet called Bokuzan who, in honor of the hundredth anniversary of Bashō's death, was touring all the gatherings of poets being held for the occasion. Arriving at a place called Shimogō, he found people who had preserved a musical instrument (*chiku*) and a portable writing desk (*oi*,) which they said were left by Bashō on one of his travels. Bokuzan also learned that a cedar reputedly planted by Bashō had recently blown down and was being used as a ridgepole in a woodshed. As he had been disappointed in the statues of Bashō he had seen on his tour, Bokuzan, purifying himself beforehand, took five or six feet of this wood and carved a statue of Bashō, setting it up in a special hall or *zodō*. Three years later there was a celebration of 'the opening of the eyes' (*kaigen*, of Buddhist origin) of this statue, a practice normally used in the dedication of a sacred image. This ceremony involved all of the major poets of the area, and the list of its food, incense, flowers, music and other components is truly staggering. The most famous participant on this occasion was Shirō (or Biwaen, 1742–1812), whose close identification of Bashō with nature, such that Bashō was even present in the rain, can be seen in the following verse composed at one such anniversary:

Yo ni furuwa	Falling on the world,
Sara ni Bashō no	Afresh – Bashō's
Shigure kana.[6]	Early winter rain (*shigure*).

Besides these formal occasions, the cult of Bashō worship also centered informally on places where he had written famous verses, often marked with memorial stones (*kubi*)[7], and upon Bashō memorial mounds (*tsuka*).[8] Such mounds were built very early in Bashō's family temple, at Edo, and in Mino province, but were soon widespread.[9] We find the great Shinto scholar, Motoori Norinaga (1730–1801), writing before a statue of Bashō:

Futari nake	Master of whom
Okina nari keri	There is no equal;
Kono michi ni	The master who
Okina to ieba	Walked this road
Kono okina nite.[10]	Was this one alone.

Only a few people actually imitated Bashō's wandering life; the most important among them was Kobayashi Issa (1763–1827). Parallel to what we will see in Bashō's biography, Issa's separation from the normal fabric of life led to his pursuit of intimacy with nature through haiku. His mother died when he was an infant and he was raised partly by his grandmother. Upon his grandmother's death, he was sent by a cruel stepmother to Edo where he studied haiku. After his father's death, Issa had a long struggle for his inheritance which prevented him from living at home. For years he wandered and was finally able to settle and marry, but his wife and four children all died in a short time. He remarried again only shortly before his death.

This tragic life drove Issa to spend more years on the road than Bashō and to write forty thousand verses compared to Bashō's one thousand. Issa's substitution of nature for family shows itself in his companionship with all living things. Instead of dissolving his self into an impersonal world as Bashō did, he personalized the rest of the world. He talked to bugs and frogs and wrote several sentimental verses identifying himself with motherless birds. His use of Bashō as a model comes across most clearly in the following verse:

Basho sama	Nibbling at
No sune o kajitte	Master Bashō's shins –
Yūsuzumi.[11]	The cool of the evening.

'Nibbling at Master Bashō's shins' refers to his copying Bashō. That his image of Bashō was of a sage in harmony with nature is shown by the following, written for that annual Bashō commemoration day:

Ikinaki ya	The old master's commemoration –
Kari mo heiwa na	The geese, too, seem
Narabi sama.[12]	To be mumbling together.

It might not be too rash to call Bashō a founder, then, of a small cult of poets who looked back to him as a wandering sage of nature, to be annually worshipped and occasionally imitated.

The biography and the man

Bashō's cultic position was broken, however, by Masaoka Shiki (1867–1902). On the two hundredth anniversary of Bashō's death in 1893, he published a short attack on Bashō idolatry. Among his irreverent lines, we find:

"The two hundred years commemoration is the two hundred years commemoration – last year was the one hundred and ninety ninth and next year will be the two hundred and first – what's different about this one? Like all the others there is this clamor of, oh, building a shrine, and wow, setting a memorial stone. And in the end the little benefit which falls on these people is just showing their red tongues while facing a portrait in the alcove, smilingly extending their gratitude to Matsuo Daimyōshin (a *shingo* for Bashō), while he obliviously says nothing."[13]

Shiki's attack made possible a more critical appraisal by Akutagawa Ryūnosuke who, along with his 'Karenoshō' mentioned above, wrote two other works on Bashō entitled 'Bashō Zakki' and 'Zoku Bashō Zakki' ('Notes on Bashō' and 'Continued Notes on Bashō'). In the former, he wrote about Bashō's great passion as a poet which seemed to contradict his image as a man who renounced the mundane world, and continued:

"If we must call such passion in a world renouncing man a contradiction, then a contradiction it is. But even if it is so, doesn't this bear witness to Bashō's genius? [. . .] I love the contradiction of Bashō's not truly becoming a world renouncer. At the same time, I love the greatness of that contradiction."[14]

After two hundred years of cultic memory of the master, Akutagawa was suggesting that Bashō, the man, lived in contradiction with the life ideal associated with him as master.[15] Although I disagree with many of Akutagawa's observations, Bashō's life as shown through his poetry does show such a contradiction. More importantly, the difference between the life ideal remembered by the cult and the historical life of Bashō cannot be ascribed solely to enhancements within the cultic memory. Instead, this difference, as we shall see, had its roots in Bashō's life. As Akutagawa suggested, he lived the disparity of an ideal and a real life, a disparity which after his death grew into that between the cultic memory and the historical man. Most ironic of all, his initial success with his ideal led to his having an 'official identity'[16] as a poetic master, and this 'official identity', more than anything else, prevented him from living out his ideal.

The ideal, religious life which the cult remembered sprang from Bashō's own visions and attainments. While he attained such a life, however, he could not sustain it, and his achievement only served to create the mode of his own failure. But with the 'charismatic hunger of mankind',[17] his disciples, devoured his attainments, and for them and the tradition which followed them, Bashō was a master. It was this master of a religious life whom they mourned in Akutagawa's sketch, and who was remembered by tradition, but it was the man who failed to sustain that very life who lay dying.

In *Young Man Luther*, Erik Erikson has written about a man whose solution for the problems of his own life became a solution for those of his age.[18] With Bashō, we find a man whose solution for his own life became a model for a much smaller although definite tradition, but whose own life digressed from that solution, leaving him isolated from, and occasionally even bitter towards, the very life ideal which he had developed.

In becoming the master of an original haiku religious life, Bashō succeeded in discovering a world of meaning from which he later became isolated, but from which he could not escape in life, death, or even after death. His later isolation was tragically ironic, because it was precisely to overcome a sense of isolation and loneliness that he had attempted a new religious discovery. Instead, he found simply another, more profound context from which to become isolated once again.

This isolation was expressed by Bashō as loneliness, a loneliness which passed through different stages in his life. In the following pages we will be examining these stages of Bashō's life by seeing his efforts to overcome loneliness and isolation and to envelop himself, through poetry, in a meaningful, supportive world. We will not find any cataclysmic encounter with the transcendent, nor should we expect to. Bashō understood his possible religious success as providing a fulfilling life by creating a place for him in a sympathetic and immanently sacred universe. Religious failure, conversely, was synonymous with isolation from any such meaningful context. As will be discussed below, this religious goal was rooted in forces which shaped the Japanese personality of the Tokugawa period.

We will examine Bashō's efforts to create his role in a meaningful context in the three following steps. First, we will look at his early life, before his poetic wanderings. Secondly, we will consider the period when Bashō attempted to live the wandering religious ideal, culminating in his masterpiece, *Oku no Hosomichi (The Narrow Road to the Deep North)*. Thirdly, we will look at his failure to sustain this ideal, his return to loneliness, and his attempts to create a new ideal, which were cut short by his death.

Throughout this discussion I rely mainly on the evidence provided by Bashō's haiku. Bashō wrote only about one thousand of these short verses, plus many linked verses (*renku*), short prose works, and critical commentaries. It may appear that I am making too much out of these slivers of poetry, but, as will become apparent below, Bashō staked his life on them. While providing us only with tidbits concerning his early life (for which I will have to rely on a general knowledge of the times), these poems became his technique for relating himself to a meaningful world. Hence they show his efforts to overcome isolation and to discover his true self.[19]

Bashō's early life: The crisis of isolation

Bashō was born after the basic social structures of the Tokugawa Period (1600–1867) had been laid down, and was a young man during or shortly after the original intellectual ferment regarding the values which were to dominate the age.[20] While little is known about his early life, everything we do know suggests that he began a typical, lower-ranking samurai existence. The ultimate source of meaning for such an existence was sacred devotion to parents and lord because of a sense of enormous debt to each. While this is not the occasion to discuss Tokugawa values, we can assume with good reason that particularistic and sacred social duties shaped young Bashō's world of meaning.[21] He was born in 1644 in the province of Iga, southeast of Kyoto, the son of a samurai who was reduced to farming in peacetime.[22] In due course, Bashō entered the service of Tōdō Yoshitada, a young member of the manorial household only two years his senior, and assumed the staunch samurai name of Matsuo Munefusa.

Both Matsuo Munefusa and Tōdō Yoshitada engaged in haiku composition as a kind of elegant pastime, but what was later to be genius was at this stage only cleverness. In this period Bashō was under the influence of the haiku school called Teimon, with its elegant wit, double entendre, and juxtaposition of classical themes.[23] While not without moments of sensitivity,[24] Bashō chose such subjects as women's names, striking but often hackneyed beauties of nature, social occasions, and times of the year.

The comfortable, and by all indications satisfying, fabric of Bashō's world was suddenly torn open by the premature death of his friend and lord, Yoshitada, in 1666. Yoshitada's younger brother took over the family and Bashō resigned from service, forsaking forever his samurai status. As only these bare facts are known, there has been no lack of speculation about intrigues which could have led to his resignation. Professor Ueda's suggestion that he just did not fit into the circle surrounding his new lord is the least spectacular and the most probable.[25]

But we can be certain that, whether as cause or result, Bashō's leaving service involved a loss of that supportive context of social relationships grounded in Neo-Confucian and traditional Japanese values, which gave meaning to the life of a young samurai. In leaving his position, Bashō burned that bridge to fulfillment and began searching for a new world of meaning, though he may not yet have been aware of the search.

Details of his life immediately after Yoshitada's death are unclear. Living close to Kyoto, it is unthinkable that he would not have visited this cultural center, but we do not know if he studied or worked there.[26] There is no evidence that he then thought of being a professional poet, but a few of his poems were published in local collections, and this undoubtedly gave him new confidence.[27] Finally, in 1672, he published his own book, *Kai Oi* (*The Seashell Game*), in which he paired haiku, including his own, and passed a series of judgements upon them. From this we can guess that Bashō's departure from samurai service led him to improve what was formerly an avocation. Later that year, he left Iga for Edo with some ambition which must have included haiku.

The city of Edo to which Bashō migrated in 1672 was soon to reach a population of one million.[28] Along with Osaka, it was the capital of a new kind of city culture, one of sophistication and gay, but refined pleasure. Bashō was probably attracted to Edo by a vision of opportunity, stimulation and adventure. Instead, he had to struggle for a few years to establish his reputation, working perhaps in some clerical capacity, and writing under the name of Tōsei.[29]

Having become a city man with ambition to become a professional poet, Bashō progressed rapidly in style. Two stylistic developments were prerequisites for the religious life of haiku he was later to adopt, although at this time they were strictly literary changes. The first was an expansion of his subject matter to include the commonplace and even lower sides of life. The stimulus for this development came from the Danrin school, which often applied classical allusions to mundane or even wild contexts.[30] A rather extreme extension of subject matter can be found in the following:

Yuku kumo ya	Passing clouds-
Ino no kakebari	Like a stray dog relieving himself,
Mura shigure	Scattered showers.
(KNBZ,19)	

The second and later stylistic development was Bashō's simpler poetic goal of setting an image for emotional impact alone, an image which would grow into an entire scene planted in the reader's mind. As Bashō began concentrating more on emotional impact, rather than on wit and double entendre, the range of sensibility in his poems expanded greatly, often into solemn or even eerie moods. The most famous poem of this type, generally considered a breakthrough, is:

Kare eda ni	On a withered branch
Karasu no tomari keri	A crow settles;
Aki no kure	Autumn dusk.
(KNBZ, 38)	

Besides showing Bashō's new capacity for somber moods, this poem sets a scene which expands in the reader's mind. It also uses an important technical device, the comparison of the crow and the night settling. Later, he will use such internal comparisons to great effect.

Together with this new maturity of style, Bashō attained, by the end of the 1670s, the recognition and position he sought in coming to Edo. The year 1680 seems to mark his emergence as a professional teacher. In that year he published the first collection of his disciples' poems. More importantly, his disciples provided him with a small hut which had formerly belonged to the Shogun's fish warden. In the garden by the hut, they planted a banana tree, an exotic plant in Japan, which is called *bashō* in Japanese. From this, the hut's occupant took his new and lasting professional name.[31]

By 1680, then, Bashō had a new name and new status. He had joined the bustling new city culture and had risen to a comfortable, respectable, and creative role within it. There are a number of poems which show his ease and comfort in this new position, including the following:

Haru tatsu ya	Spring comes –
Shinnen furuki	At the New Year
Kome goshō	Five pecks of rice left
(KNBZ, 44)	(from the old).[32]

We find him also enjoying the refined pleasures of the capital:

Hana ni yadori	Lodging under the blossoms,
Hentanshi to	Although I must call myself
Mizukara iedomo	'Mr. Bottle'.
(KNBZ, 37)	

At this point it might seem that Bashō's essential biography is over. He has achieved success and enjoyment and is flexing and developing his technical muscles. In the midst of this, however, we find a definite opposing strain of loneliness, one which may have begun as poetic fashion, but which crescendoed into painful isolation by 1684. In 1680, Bashō was already writing poems which objectively set lonely scenes at his hut, and by the following year he expressed his sense of loneliness symbolically:

Bashō no waki shite	The banana plant in the gale;
Tarai ni ame o	A night listening to rain
Kikuyo kana	Drip in a tub
(KNBZ, 48)	

He also expressed himself directly, writing:

"I'm lonely towards the moon; lonely towards myself; lonely towards my lack of skill. I want to answer that I'm lonely, but there is no one who will ask. Only in loneliness, loneliness –"

Wabite sume	Live in loneliness;
Tsukiwabasai ga	The moon-lonely one
Naracha uta	With his gruel song.
(KNBZ, 48)	

The winter after he wrote that verse, he wrote:

Ro no koe nami o utte	The sound of oars striking the waves,
Harawata kōru	My bowels chill;
Ya ya namida	Tears in the night.
(KNBZ, 49)	

His verses suggest only two reasons why he felt this way. The first is found in two New Year's poems in which he contrasts his own solitude with the family gaiety surrounding him:

Kure kurete	The year ends, dusk settles,
Mochi o kodama no	The echo of rice cakes being pounded –
Wabine kana	I go to bed alone.
(KNBZ, 50)	

Gan jitsu ya	New Year's –
Omoeba sabishi	When I remember, I'm lonely,
Aki no kure	As in an autumn evening.
(KNBZ, 58)	

The second explanation for his loneliness lies in four poems which show his sense of not having achieved anything. The first is symbolic of grasping for something and getting hurt instead. The others are more explicit.

Gu ni kuraku *Ibara o tsukamu* *Hotaru kana* (KNBZ, 41)	Foolishly in the dark, Grabbing a thorn – Firefly!
Hototogisu *Ima wa haikaishi* *Naki yo kana* (KNBZ, 59)	Cuckoo, Now is a world Without a haiku master.[33]
Tsuki jūyokka *Koyoi sanjūkyū* *No warabe* (KNBZ, 52)	The moon of the fourteenth day, This night, a thirty-nine year old Child.[34]
Aware kiku ya *Kono mi wa moto no* *Furugashiwa* (KNBZ, 58)	Hearing hail – I am just the same as I was, Like that old oak.

This sense of separation from social and family life, and the realization of not having changed or accomplished anything, were really two sides of the same crisis. Upon his withdrawal from samurai life, Bashō had lost that supportive, sacred context of social relations which could have offered him a fulfilling life. He did not resolve this problem directly, but pursued an ambitious career as a professional poet and teacher in the only place where this was possible, the open, bustling city of Edo. This career and its delights consumed his attention for several years, but when he reached a high level of success, its allure had run its course. Only at this point did he face his basic problem, that of the loss of a fulfilling social nexus. A sense of isolation, and hence for a Japanese of his times, a sense of meaninglessness in life, began to haunt him. For this reason, we find poems not only about loneliness, but also about an unchanged, unfulfilled life. By this time, however, Bashō had greatly expanded his poetic range in both subject matter and emotional content. When he finally faced the existential problem brought on by that fundamental loss of a meaningful social nexus, he was well armed.

Two accidental events forced his hand. The first was the burning of his home in 1682. Then, just when it was rebuilt, he received news of his mother's death in Iga (his father had died when he was twelve). Her death must have deepened his loneliness even more, for his efforts to discover a meaningful context for his life in that eventful year of 1684 were closely entwined with an understanding of his loss of that primary sacred context of Tokugawa life, the family. We have already seen him call himself a child. In one of the first passages in the diary of that year, he identifies himself with an abandoned child. Most importantly, his efforts to find fulfillment in a meaningful context began on a trip back to Iga, ostensibly to pay homage to his mother and to visit his family.[35]

In the fall of 1684, then, Bashō began to pursue a new life, one which he hoped would overcome the loneliness that had settled upon him. We must suspend our narrative a bit to look closely at what he was trying to do.

The haiku religious life

First, we must briefly examine the historical sources of Bashō's religious life style, that of religious pilgrimage and the recluse tradition, and look at the new religious understandings and poetic techniques which Bashō developed within that life style.

We can better understand Bashō's travelling life style by finding its sources in the Japanese traditions of pilgrimage and of recluses and wanderers. Joseph M. Kitagawa lists three types of pilgrimage in Japan: (1) pilgrimage to sacred mountains; (2) pilgrimage to shrines or temples associated with certain divinities; and (3) pilgrimage based on faith in certain charismatic holy men.[36] The second type does not concern our discussion of Bashō as much as the first and third. The first type was generally, but not necessarily, a group activity under the supervision of a guide and involved the acquisition of personal soteriological power. Certain places such as Kumano and Yoshino, furthermore, were said to be a foretaste of Amida's Pure Land. This factor, says Kitagawa, 'gives strong impetus to pilgrims to seek the religious meaning of life within the realm of phenomenal existence'.[37] The third type relied on the saving power which had been actualized in a real human being. Such a holy person 'shares every step of the earthly pilgrim'.[38] From this, we can observe that pilgrimage in Japan led to discovery of the sacred in the phenomenal world of nature, tradition-laden mountains or other sites, or in the imitation of the life of an historical individual. We note the immanent accessibility of the sacred as it is indistinguishable from the fabric of a positive, fulfilling world, especially as it carries the mark of a powerful tradition.

We might also note two further aspects of Japanese pilgrimage. First, it was not necessary that everything connected with a pilgrimage be religious. A pilgrimage often involved seeing relatives, simple sightseeing, sampling famous foods, and so on.[39] Secondly, it was a practice well suited to religious syncretism, for one travelled from shrine to temple to famous landmark, partaking of a veritable supermarket of deities and traditions.

The evidence that Bashō did, indeed, combine this prevalent mode of religious pilgrimage with his poetic life is strong. Rather than travelling randomly, Bashō visited many places behind which stood long, most often literary, traditions. Perhaps the clearest example of the importance of tradition in such places is found in *Sarashina Kikō* (1688), in which Bashō says that he was somewhat disappointed with the mountain itself, but when he thought of the old crone abandoned there according to a long literary tradition, he was filled with emotion.[40] His trips to these places often took on a style of pilgrimage, a pilgrimage to visit a place of traditional power and to walk where poets of the past walked and to see what they saw. Two travel diaries in particular record such pilgrimages. *Sarashina Kikō* was mentioned above. *Kashima Kikō* (1687) records a pilgrimage to a Shinto shrine, characteristically undertaken to see the moon famous in literature. Bashō visited the popular pilgrimage sites as well. Particularly interesting to a student of religion is his account of his trip to Mount Haguro, a center for a sect of mountain priests called *Shugendō* which is still a popular pilgrimage site.[41] Bashō even dressed as a pilgrim, shaving his head, carrying a staff, and wearing simple, monkish robes.[42]

A second historical source of Bashō's style of life, which merges with Kitagawa's third type of pilgrimage, is represented by the poetic recluses and wandering priests of the past whom Bashō admired. In *Oku no Hosomichi*, for example, he refers to Saigyō, a twelfth century *waka* poet, to Gyōgi, an archetypical wandering priest from the Nara Period, and to other such figures. Instead of following in their footsteps over particular pilgrimage trails, he identified with their wandering and reclusive life in general, but he did emphasize places associated with them, such as Saigyō's willow.[43] While borrowing important components of his life style from these models, Bashō used a much wider range of subject matter, derived from his Danrin heritage, than these earlier poets knew. This new freedom of range was not incidental to Bashō's religious life, as we shall see.

In summarizing Bashō's life style in relation to these historical precedent of pilgrimage and the recluse or wandering life, we can say that he combined the two, extending both motifs into wider and more inclusive areas. Rather than merely following routes prescribed by a tradition (although he did so on occasions), Bashō also travelled to other places of literary and historical importance. Eventually, he treated virtually everything as partaking of an immanent sacrality conferred by the past, often seeking an ancient tradition or classical allusion in the commonest things. While not neglecting several tradition-laden paths, then, Bashō became a pilgrim in an entire world of immanent sacrality. He found himself in a sacred context wherever he went, thus pushing the wandering life into new areas of the country and new subjects of concern.

Bashō's poetry, in both its technique and goals, was well suited to the content of this expanded pilgrim's life. In every step of his travels, Bashō attempted to find some overriding aesthetic meaning in the moment and place of which he was a part. This aesthetic perception was informed by a sensibility for the sum of the many disparate elements in each of such places and moments. Such a sensibility affected his poetic technique, leading him to use methods for getting these disparate elements into his poems. Often this took the form of bringing together different senses, or in some cases, ascribing the adjective appropriate for one sense to another. A heron's screech, for example, is white above the dark sea. A more technical device, common to haiku generally, is the use of *kireji*, or 'cutting words'. These are short, semantically meaningless syllables which cut off one line from the other two, thereby bringing together, without any predicated explanation, two elements of a given moment or place.

One element which must always be present in a haiku is the *kigo*, or 'season word'. This will be a reference to a natural phenomenon or an adjective like 'cold', which places the haiku in some season. The *kigo* seems to be the clearest manifestation of the haiku postulate that time, rather than being homogenous, consists of different moments, each with its own particular aesthetic content.

It is the task of the poet to perceive this content and give it expression and form. If he is honest in this task, he will be willing to use virtually anything as a subject, a characteristic which sets haiku, and Bashō's in particular, apart from other Japanese poetry. Bashō brings even horse urine and lice into his poems. Furthermore, such a sensibility to the sum of particular moments necessitates a certain ambiguity, which Bashō called *shiori*, or 'flexibility'. It is often difficult to define the object of the aesthetic emotion generated by a haiku of Bashō, even a haiku of one image. We might even say that his images are transparent, rather than opaque, and that through them we receive a satisfying aesthetic sense of all that surrounds and stands behind the haiku.

With this understanding of his poetry, we can see why it was coupled with the diary form. The diary structure permitted Bashō to turn his journeys into a series of rhythms and reverberations of these aesthetic sentiments. In his later diaries, he achieved a balanced interaction between the prose and the poetry, such that the prose set the elements of a scene or moment, the central aesthetic sense of which was illuminated by the flash of a haiku.

Since such an ambiguous aesthetic sense of the moment included the poet as part of that moment, we can understand how poetry could relieve Bashō's isolation. Central to this relief was the dissolution of his own emotions into these impersonal aesthetic senses of the world around him.[44] A striking example is his poem at the grave of a beloved disciple:

Tsuka mo ugoke	Shake, o tomb,
Waga naku koe wa	My crying voice
Aki no kaze	Is the autumn wind.
(KNBZ, 191)	

Here we can see his grief becoming part of the total moment of a chilly autumn day. More typical, however, are the haiku in which the poet is not directly mentioned. With these, one is struck by Bashō's uncanny ability to write an objective poem in which his presence is still strongly sensed. This ability to enter into the things around him he called *hosomi*, or 'slenderness'.[45] From all of this, we can see how Bashō was striving to use his poetry to go beyond his personal emotions or even poetic sentiments. He tried to discover through his poetic creativity an impersonal meaning in each place and moment of his travels.[46]

This tuning of himself to aesthetic senses of particular times and places could have been a powerful antidote for the anguished isolation Bashō was feeling by the middle of 1684. I am not suggesting that he simply tried to create a mock family or a close social nexus by this new use of haiku. I am suggesting, however, that Bashō, from the time he left Iga, had a latent thirst for a sense of belonging, of fulfilling participation in an immanently sacred context, and that this desire had roots in the early shaping of his personality. Because of its continuity in his personality, this thirst remained even when he could ignore it during his early poetic career, and could eventually be satisfied by a source different from that which had originally shaped it. In general, Bashō's case confirms a suggestion by Albert Craig that one interpretation of the Japanese love of nature 'would be to see the Japanese ability to melt into nature as akin to the ability to melt into the social group. The openness and sensitivity to subtle cues in the group mood that the group member can miss only at his peril may be similar to the receptivity toward nature and the willingness to let it flow in on the self.'[47]

One further point about this haiku religious life should be made before we return to our narrative. It may seem that this life dissolves the self, making it dependent upon the vicissitudes of the environment without its own individual continuity. We miss that sense of a person discovering his identity and 'making the environment adapt to him'.[48] Our objections might very well be culture bound, however, for we have no background in the extraordinary claims made upon Japanese individuals by their social situation, claims which tend to produce a different type of self, or 'non-self'.[49] This cultural difference leads to judgments upon the West as well, as in the remark by Mishima Yukio that 'Americans sometimes tend to over-exist. ... The Japanese, nurtured as they are on Buddhism, have the curious conviction that existence is a transitory and basically unessential phenomenon, a shifting process which changes with each moment, a relative state as opposed to nothingness.'[50] Whether this is entirely a Buddhist legacy is debatable, but it should restrain us from looking for a strong, continuous ego, stamping its impression on the world.

THE WANDERING POET

Bashō pursued the travelling life of haiku from the fall of 1684 through 1692, a period of over eight years. During that time, he produced five major travel diaries.[51] While we cannot go into the details of even one of these works, I would like to outline briefly his development within this new life by looking at the first and the last, *Nozarashi Kikō* and his masterpiece, *Oku no Hosomichi.*

In 1684, Bashō took his first trip for strictly poetic purposes to his home in Iga and to some famous areas in that part of Japan. The records of this trip became *Nozarashi Kikō (Secords of a Weather Exposed Skeleton).* This trip and its diary represent only the first, alternately hasty and halting, steps in Bashō's new life of travel. In the beginning, he jumped too much into the part, striking a pose rather than finding an identity:

Nozarashi o	A weather-exposed skeleton
Kokori ni kaze no	On my mind, the wind
Shimumi kana	Piercing my body.
(NKBT, 36)	

In a later part of the diary, Bashō, perhaps feeling a bit foolish for overdoing it, wrote:

"Upon setting out from the Musashi Plain, I had resolved to become a 'weather exposed skeleton'."

Shinimo senu	I am hardly dead
Tabine no hate yo	As a result of my lodging by the road;
Aki no kure	Autumn's close.
(NKBT, 40)	

Despite such initial posturing, Bashō was able to experience and express virtually all the necessary components of his new calling. In the first section of the diary, he senses a separation from his unfulfilling Edo life, but only by a return to what can no longer be a real home. This loss of his old home is expressed in a brief but powerful section in which he cries over strands of his mother's white hair. Most of the diary, however, shows him beginning to work out that new style of life which would replace both his old home and Edo. One of the first poems concerns Saigyō, and a substantial section of the diary centers on the pilgrimage center of Yoshino, a mountain upon which Saigyō had once lived. Towards the end of the diary, there are a number of poems which show Bashō's comfort in his new travelling life:

Iza tomo no	Let's go together
Hogumi kurawau	Eating wheat
Kusa makura	With grass for our pillows.
(NKBT, 43)	

In all, Bashō took great strides in *Nozarashi Kikō* but he still had far to go. Technically, his diary structure broke down completely, the prose serving only to name the place of each poem. His occasional dependence on, rather than use of, classical allusions gives a contrived flavor to some poems, and there are too many verses connected with the stock situations of parting and on people's names. Still, Bashō obviously increased his ability for spontaneous and imaginative observation, so important for his success as a wandering poet:

Akebono ya	Dawn –
Shirauo shiroki	The whitefish; whiteness
Koto issun	Of one inch.
(NKBT, 41)	

These mixed literary achievements reflect the partiality of Bashō's first attempt as a wandering poet. By relying on his mere cleverness of former times, he demonstrated that he had not yet reached the point of using haiku to completely inform his life of the impersonal meaning of each time and place. Still, he had turned his back on his unfulfilling life in Edo, confirmed the loss his old home, worked out the basic components of his new life style

– those borrowed from pilgrimage and the tradition of wanderers – and he had found a new identity into which he could grow.[52] Later, he was to write:

Tabibito to	'Traveler'
Waga no yobaren	I will be called,
Hatsu shigure	First autumn shower.
(NKBT, 52)	

In order to show his growth, we will skip over a great deal of time to 1689. This was the year of his longest journey, in which he produced his masterpiece, *Oku no Hosomichi (The Narrow Road to the Deep North)*. Beginning in the spring, he went over fifteen hundred miles though the most rustic, wild and occasionally dangerous part of old Japan, the northwest section of Honshū. Although only six months were included in the diary itself, he was away from Edo for two and a half years, this time with no destination, unless we can say that the whole trip was a destination. Above all, *Oku no Hosomichi* reveals a man who is 'aware of so much – his memory and imagination swell with associations of the past – and his rapid movements of mind and heart from the high or sublime to the low reveal a very wide-eyed, knowing man'.[53] We are convinced that he has attained final release from isolation and receives sustenance from the impersonal pulse of the world. His identification of his departure from friends with the impersonal flow of a departing spring can be seen in the following passage. By the last line of the haiku, Bashō images the impersonal nature of his emotions as tears within the sea:

"At Senjū, I got off the boat, and my heart swelled all the more at the thought of beginning so long a journey. At this dream-like separation of paths, my eyes filled with tears of parting –"

Yuku haru ya	Spring departs –
Tori naki uo no	Birds cry; fishes' eyes
Me wa namida	Fill with tears.
(NKBT, 70–71)	

When he perfectly flowed with such impersonal sensibilities he made loneliness the most important of these sensibilities, rather than rejecting it. His term for this impersonal loneliness was *sabi*, a term with its own long history in Japanese criticism, which derived from the word *sabishii*, or 'lonely'.[54] *Sabi* cannot be equated, however, with the loneliness Bashō felt in Edo in the early 1680s. His loneliness at that time had been the loneliness of an isolated man. *Sabi*, however, is the impersonal, aesthetic sense of loneliness he *shared* with the ever changing world of nature within which he travelled. *Sabi*, then, expressed the seeming paradox of an aesthetic sense of loneliness discovered in the universe, within which Bashō could find refuge from the very different loneliness of isolation.

Bashō was at the summit of his powers on this trip, and he composed verses which would stand as some of the most powerful haiku ever written:

Shizukasa ya[55] *Iwa ni shimiru* *Semi no koe* (NKBT, 87)	Silence – Penetrating the rocks A cicada's cry.
Araumi ya *Sado no yokotau* *Amanogawa* (NKBT, 91)	Violent sea – Stretching towards Sado Island The Milky Way

His blending of prose and poetry into the pulsating sweep of *Oku no Hosomichi* resulted in perhaps the greatest of such travel diaries. In his life of constant travel, participating in ever changing time and the eternity of common life and nature, all enveloped within an aura of impersonal *sabi*, Bashō had overcome his isolation by wrapping himself in a world of meaning so vast that only a person of his literary genius could have attained or even reached for it. Driven as he was to using his extraordinary powers to their utmost, his *Oku no Hosomichi* became more than a personal document; it became a literary event which has ever since been regarded as one of the pinnacles of Japanese literary history. At the same time, it recorded the attainment of a religious ideal of wandering communion with nature. Precisely because it was recorded in *Oku no Hosomichi* and other works of 1684 and after, this was an ideal which would survive Bashō after death, absorbing his name and memory.

The ultimate loneliness: The disparity of master and man

After completing his *Oku no Hosomichi* trip, Bashō spent 1690 and 1691 around Kyoto and Iga. During this time, he continued to write a great deal, still dominated by his sense of *sabi*. In the summer months of those two years he spent considerable time in solitary huts, first by Lake Biwa and then overlooking Kyoto. This last stay was particularly noteworthy as he produced, not a record of a trip, but a normal diary, the *Saga Nikki* (*Saga Diary*). Also in 1691, he and his disciples compiled the collection known as *Sarumino* (*The Monkey's Raincoat*), which was prefaced by an apology for being too colorful in previous works and offered an appeal for *sabi*. All of this indicates that Bashō was satisfied in his perfection of both his life and poetry within the ideal of *sabi* for some time after the *Oku no Hosomichi* trip.

In 1692, he returned to the Edo he had left in 1689. Once again, he was set up in a hut with banana plants and seems to have been comfortable there, writing at the end of a long prose piece:

Bashō-ba o	Banana leaves
Hashira ni kakemu	Hung by the pillar,
Io no tsuki	The moon at my hut.
(KNBZ, 268)	

This complacency did not last, however. Through his achievements in poetic wandering, culminating in *Oku no Hosomichi*, Bashō had become famous and was swamped with visitors. In a letter at the end of 1692, Bashō told a potential caller that he was busy on the eleventh, twelfth, fourteenth, fifteenth and sixteenth, and asked if he could come on the thirteenth or the eighteenth.[56] In addition, he began caring for an invalid nephew named Yūshi, who died in the spring of 1693,[57] as well as a nun named Jutei and her children. She may have been Bashō's mistress in his youth.

Bashō's fame and success were entangling him in social and familial relations which were totally incompatible with his wandering, *sabi* life. Most distracting of all, perhaps, were the constant meetings for composition at his hut of disciples who came from all over the country.[58] Along with these increasing entanglements we find a growing sullenness creeping into Bashō's poems:

Samidare ya	Constant rain –
Kaiko wazurau	The silkworms are sick
Kuwa no hata	In the mulberry fields.
(KNBZ, 66)	

Bashō had come full circle. He had originally come to grips with the problem of isolation with nothing short of a massive achievement of wandering communion with nature, an achievement so great that he found the role of a sought-after spiritual and haiku leader thrust upon him. As this role ripped open again the immanently sacred fabric in which he had clothed himself, Bashō's *sabi*-filled world became simply another, more profound context from which he suffered longing isolation.

His first response was to rebel against his 'official identity' by simply locking out the world from mid-July to mid-August of 1693. He expressed his feelings at this time in a relatively long *haibun*, or prose piece ending with a haiku.[59] In it, he shows he is slipping into impending old age, but with numerous senseless things still pulling at his mind and heart. With an overall tone of desperation, he describes how even an artist can cling to the perfection of his art, earn a living, and drown without escape in the sewer of the mundane world. As time becomes short, he feels he is being drawn into useless talk and meddling in other people's lives. He wants to discipline himself and writes:

Asagao ya	Morning glory –
Hiru wa jō orosu	At midday a lock is clamped
Mon no kaki	On the gate of my yard.
(NKBT, 209)	

At first he thought that merely cutting himself off from people would permit him to appreciate the morning glory and find the intimacy with nature which he had found in *Oku no Hosomichi*. Eventually, however, he must have discovered that enforced seclusion was not sufficient to return him to his earlier, *sabi*-filled world, but only led to confinement and further isolation. He ended his lock-out with the following poem, incredible for the famed 'nature poet':

Asagao ya	The morning glory –
Kore mo mata waga	This, too, is no longer
Tomo narazu	My friend.
(KNBZ, 286)	

Caught between his new 'official identity' as a haiku master and his inability to return to his earlier life of *sabi* precisely because he had achieved so much, Bashō became severely embittered. We find the same sense of having accomplished nothing which had gripped him in the early 1680s in the following poem:

Toshi toshi ya	Years and years –
Saru ni kisetaru	The monkey keeps wearing
Saru no men	A monkey's mask.
(KNBZ, 276)	

There was nothing to do but try again. Developing his life of *sabi* had taken eight years. This time he had only a few months to live, and so we have only the beginning threads of the new context in which he was trying to wrap himself. Instead of *sabi*, the aesthetic term he emphasized was *karumi*, or 'lightness'.[60] This referred to a sympathetic and often humorous reflection of the lives of common people and everyday social life. From this we can suspect Bashō was taking the attitude that, if he could not escape his 'official identity' of haiku master, he would turn his poetic powers to that new, social life. Through haiku, he would try to find among the human beings who surrounded him a new sacred context of sympathetic communion in which to envelop himself. Due to his early death, we cannot know any more. Poems produced in this period include:

Kuratsubo ni	On the horse's pack
Kobōzu noruya	The little kid sits –
Daikon hiki	Radish pulling.
(KNBZ, 292)	

With this new poetic attitude, Bashō set out on a journey back to Iga, as he had done before when trying to pull his life together in a new fashion.

He may have even desired to go as far as the southern tip of Japan. In contrast to his gate shutting of the previous year, it appears that he met freely with people. He was even able to write occasional poems showing remarkable serenity:

Shiragiku no	A white chrysanthemum,
Me ni tatete miru	Holding my eyes – staring,
Chiri no nashi	Not a speck of dust.
(KNBZ, 325)	

At the same time, however, Bashō was writing more poems showing a sense of unfinished business, of wanting to keep going in the face of old age and death:

Kono aki wa	This autumn,
Nande toshiyoru	Somehow I'm getting older;
Kumo no tori	Into the clouds, a bird.
(KNBZ, 324)	

Kono michi ya	This road
Yuku hito nashi ni	Which no one travels,
Aki no kure	The autumn dusk.[61]
(KNBZ, 324)	

These same sentiments of being alone and wanting to keep going are found even in his death poem quoted at the beginning of this essay. His road, however, was cut short by his chronic intestinal problem near Osaka in 1694, his fiftieth year. While his disciples surrounded their master, the man Bashō died, having failed to complete his reconciliation with that role they had thrust upon him.[62]

This last period of Bashō's life had brought on his ultimate loneliness. This time his loneliness arose not through isolation from the intimate sacrality of a social nexus, but through his isolation from the *sabi*-filled world of meaning he had discovered through poetry on his travels. For his disciples, however, he had become a master, having opened up the possibility of this new world of meaning for others who could perfect their haiku along his path. Ironically, Bashō's isolation from his world of *sabi* was in large part due to his becoming their 'master'. In his very lifetime, then, there was a disparity between Bashō, the master of a haiku world of meaning, and Bashō, the man unable to fulfill that role, who became isolated from his own of meaning. After his death, however, the image of him as master lived on while the lonely man was forgotten, at least until that image of master was broken. The disparity of master and man in life grew into the disparity of a cultic memory and an historical man. Bashō's ultimate loneliness, then, reflects an isolation from his own legacy.

One of the important contributions the study of personalities can make to an understanding of religious traditions is the investigation of the relationships of historical individuals to the sacred life ideals remembered by traditions. The case of Bashō suggests that the impact of a personality upon the establishment of a life ideal for a tradition does not necessarily reflect the successful living of that ideal by the founder. Nor can the difference between the life ideal remembered by the tradition and the historical life of the founder necessarily be ascribed solely to the enhancements, fantasies, confusions, and so forth, of later followers. Instead, as in the case of Bashō and the haiku life ideal, the very disparity between the life ideal seen by a tradition in its founder, and his actual life, may itself have roots in the vicissitudes of that original personality.

NOTES

1. *Akutagawa Ryūnosuke Zenshū* (Tokyo: Iwanami Shoten, 1934–1935), II, pp. 105–120.
2. 'KNBZ' followed by a number refers to the page number in Volume XXX of *Koten Nihon Bungaku Zenshū* (Tokyo: Chikuma Shobō, 1961), the source for the poems in this essay.
   'NKBT' refers to Volume XLVI of *Nihon Koten Bungaku Taikei* (Tokyo: Iwanami Shoten, 1959), the source for the prose passages and poems from the diaries.
3. 'Kami', of course, are the Japanese deities never severely separated from the world of humans.
4. Tōsei was one of Bashō's professional names. 'Reishin' means literally 'spirit deity'. Other names given, including the first one by the court, were: Hana no Moto Myōshin (Bright Deity Under the Blossoms), Shōfu Shūshi (Religious Teacher of the Correct Style), and Hion Myōshin (Bright Deity of the Jumping Sound, after Bashō's most famous haiku on the sound of a frog jumping into an old pond). For these names and

their occasions, see Abe Kimio, *Matsuo Bashō* (Tokyo: Yoshikawa Kōbunkan, 1961), pp. 232–233, and the *Nihon Bungaku Daijiten* (Tokyo: Shinchōsha, 1951), VI, pp. 48–49.

5. This information, with an original text, can be found in Ishida Motonosuke, *Haibungaku Ronkō* (Kyoto: Yōtokusha, 1944), pp. 219–222.
6. From 'Biwaen Kushū', in the *Nihon Haishū Taikei* (Tokyo: Nihon Haishū *Kankō Kai*, 1927), XIV, p. 504.
7. See Abe Kimio, *Matsuo Bashō*, p. 228.
8. These mounds, perhaps deriving from beliefs in kami descending upon mountains, were a traditional means of enshrining a deity in Japanese folk belief. There is evidence that Shingon hijiri and wandering yamabushi also used mounds as altars. See Otsuka Minzoku Gakkai, *Nihon Minzoku Jiten* (Tokyo: Kōbundo, 1972), p. 459.
9. See Abe Kimio, pp. 227–228; *Bungaku Jiten* VI, p. 48; and especially Ishida, pp. 233–240.
10. Quoted in Abe Kimio, p. 232.
11. *Nihon Haishū Taikei*, XII, p. 74.
12. *Ibid.*, p. 226.
13. *Shiki Zenshū* (Tokyo: Kaizōsha, 1930), VI, pp. 131–132.
14. *Akūtagawa Ryūnosuke Zenshū*, VI, p. 310.
15. In reviewing this extremely brief history of the image of Bashō, we can see the force of individual personalities in the shaping of the direction of that history. Those haiku poets who gathered annually around their statues of Bashō must have felt the pressures for group solidarity and belonging, which have been so strong in Japan, and were also drawn to a man whom they thought had found fulfillment in haiku. It will soon be apparent that there were circumstances in Issa's life which were like Bashō's. Shiki demanded an individual expression under the influence of Western thought, an idea which undercut the importance of Bashō. Akutagawa was profoundly interested in the integration of life and art, even killing himself as a supreme artistic act. This led to his fascination with Bashō, a man in whom he saw the disparity of artistic ideals and actual life.
16. Erik Erikson, *Young Man Luther* (New York: W. W. Norton, 1958), p. 54.
17. *Ibid.*, p. 16.
18. *Ibid.*, p. 74.
19. See Yamamoto Tadaichi, 'Bashō Bungaku no Shūkyō Sei', *Bukkyō Bungaku Kenkyū*, ed. Bukkyō Bungaku Kenkyū Kai (Tokyo: Hōzokan, 1964), II, pp. 248, 251–253.
20. Cf. Hayashi Ranzan (1583–1657); Nakae Tōju (1608–1648); Yamazaki Ansai (1618–1682); Yamaga Sokō (1622–1685).
21. A thorough, although controversial, discussion of Tokugawa values is Robert Bellah, *Tokugawa Religion* (Glencoe, Illinois: The Free Press, 1957).
22. Makoto Ueda, *Matsuo Bashō* (New York: Twayne Publishers, 1970), p. 20. See also the more detailed genealogical information in Abe Kimio, pp. 3–10.
23. This school was founded by Teitoku (d. 1653). See Harold Henderson, *An Introduction to Haiku* (New York: Doubleday and Co., 1958), pp. 11–13.

24. See, for example, his poem for the parents of a dead infant, beginning 'Shiore fusu ya (KNBZ, 8).
25. For this, and the speculations of others as well, see Ueda, p. 21.
26. Later he was to claim to have desired at times to be a scholar or hold an official post, and these statements may refer to this period. See Ueda, p. 22.
27. See Abe Kimio, pp. 27–29, for these early successes.
28. George Sansom, *A History of Japan, 1615–1867* (Stanford: Stanford University Press, 1963), p. 114.
29. See Ueda, p. 23. From his poems, there is no indication that he was anything but a willing participant in city culture at this time. This contradicts an often held opinion that he was somehow separated from that gay life, as is suggested from an analysis overly based on class in Hirosue Tamotsu, *Genroku Bungaku Kenkyū* (Tokyo: Tokyo Daigaku Shuppan Sha, 1955), pp. 17–27.
30. This school was founded by Sōin (d. 1682). See Henderson, pp. 13–14. The 'scattered showers' verse is not strictly Danrin, but shows definite Danrin influence on Bashō.
31. For a discussion of the allusions involved in this name, see Donald H. Shively, 'Bashō – The Man and the Plant', *Harvard Journal of Asiatic Studies*, XVI (1953), pp. 146–161.
32. This poem was in reference to the gourd in which disciples donated rice.
31. The cuckoo was an important poetic bird about which even a poetic hack should have been able to write a poem.
34. A man was said to be fully grown at forty. The moon, of course, is full on the fifteenth day. Even so, it is strange that he should refer to himself as a child.
35. Donald Keene points out that if Bashō were moved according to formal filial piety, he should have left earlier to be in time for the memorial service. See his 'Bashō's Journey of 1684', in his *Landscapes and Portraits* (Tokyo and Palo Alto: Kodansha International, Ltd., 1971), pp. 94–103. This article is also in *Asia Major*, VII (1959), pp. 131–144.
36. Joseph M. Kitagawa, 'Three Types of Pilgrimage in Japan', *Studies in Mysticism and Religion Presented to Gershom G. Scholem*, ed. E. E. Urbak, et. al. (Jerusalem: Magnes Press, 1967), pp. 155–164.
37. *Ibid.*, p. 164.
38. *Ibid.*, p. 164.
39. Cf. Victor Turner, 'The Center Out There: The Pilgrim's Goal', *History of Religions*, XII, 3 (February, 1973), especially pp. 204–205, where he speaks of the pilgrim's path as 'increasingly sacralized at one level and increasingly secularized at another'. Also of interest is his observation (p. 207 and elsewhere) that the pilgrim moves from particularistic to universal bonds, such as 'brother'. We will find Bashō doing this to an extraordinary degree as he has no particularistic bonds to return to.
40. Donald Keene, 'Bashō's Journey to Sarashina', in his *Landscapes and Portraits*, p. 124. This article is also available in *Transactions of the Asiatic Society of Japan*, third series, V (Dec., 1957), pp. 56–83.
41. See H. Byron Earhart, *A Religious Study of the Mount Haguro Sect of Shugendō* (Tokyo: Sophia University Press, 1970).

42. His self-description is in *Nozarashi Kikō* (NKBT, 58).
43. NKBT, 75.
44. This discussion of technique and the idea of impersonality owes a heavy debt to Makoto Ueda, *Literary and Art Theories in Japan* (Cleveland: Western Reserve University Press, 1967), pp. 145–172. Yamamoto, pp. 257–259, describes Bashō's participation in *mujōkan*, or 'transitoriness', in somewhat similar fashion.
45. See Ueda, *Literary and Art Theories*, p. 156. Also, Nippon Gakujutsu Shinkōkai, *Haikai and Haiku* (Tokyo, 1958), pp. XIX and XVII.
46. While it is true that Bashō revised many of his works, at no time did this seem to lessen the importance of experiencing everything he tried to express, and composing on the spot.
47. Albert Craig, 'Introduction: Perspectives on Personality in Japanese History', *Personality in Japanese History*, ed. Albert Craig and Donald Shively (Berkeley: University of California Press, 1970), p. 23.
48. Erikson, *Young Man Luther*, p. 100.
49. Craig, 'Introduction', p. 17.
50. Quoted in Craig, p. 18.
51. Bashō, *Nozarashi Kikō* (*Records of a Weather Exposed Skeleton*, 1684–1685, dates reflecting the time of the trip).
    –, *Kashima Kikō* (*A Visit to Kashima Shrine*, 1687).
    –, *Oi no Kobumi* (*Records of a Travel Worn Satchel*, 1687–1688).
    –, *Sarashina Kikō* (*A Visit to Sarashina Village*, 1688).
    –, *Oku no Hosomichi* (*The Narrow Road to the Deep North*, 1689).
    The translations of these titles are borrowed from those in Nobuyuki Yuasa's *The Narrow Road to the Deep North and Other Travel Sketches* (Middlesex: Penguin Books, 1966). In addition to travel diaries, Bashō continued to write other haiku, *renku*, and short sketches called *haibun*.
52. Several poems from this period have Buddhist overtones, but are most often composed in temple settings and can be seen as being simply appropriate to the place in which Bashō found himself. There is no evidence that Bashō had more than a very general popular understanding of Buddhism, filtered through his reading of ancient literature and Nō drama. He would draw upon this understanding during visits to famous Buddhist temples, but only as part of his general concern with historical and literary background in every place he went. At one point in *Nozarashi Kikō*, he seems irritated when he cannot get into the Ise Shrine because he is mistaken for a Buddhist priest. Bashō had briefly flirted with Zen in Edo under a master named Buccho. This priest, however, moved away in 1682, and, while Bashō remained fond of him, it is impossible to think that he practiced Zen for more than the shortest period of time.
53. Earl Miner, *Japanese Poetic Diaries* (Berkeley and Los Angeles: University of California Press, 1969), p. 45. Here, too, is the suggestion of the whole trip as a destination.
54. Ueda, *Literary and Art Theories*, pp. 149 ff.
55. One version of this begins, 'Sabishisa ya', or 'loneliness'. See NKBZ, 182.
56. Quoted in Abe Kimio, p. 189.

57. *Ibid.*, pp. 15–16.
58. *Ibid.*, pp. 186 ff.
59. *Heikan no Setsu* (NKBT, 208–209).
60. See Ueda, *Literary and Art Theories*, pp. 165 ff., and Nippon Gakujutsu Shinkōkai, *Hakai and Haiku*, p. xx.
61. Ueda, in *Matsuo Bashō*, p. 61, notes that this was written at the peak of his fame, while he was surrounded by disciples.
62. I suspect that Kyōrai, Bashō's truest disciple, did not take many students because he realized what had happened to his master.

DONALD CAPPS

16

Lincoln's Martyrdom

A Study of Exemplary Mythic Patterns

The relationship of the historical personality to the myths which attach to him has been of longstanding interest to historians of religion. The study of this relationship contributes to our general understanding of the complex interaction of history and myth in the evolution of religious traditions. Religious traditions are rooted in historical actuality and religious leaders are therefore compelling insofar as they communicate their historical presence to other men. On the other hand, the presence or charismatic power of such leaders is seldom adequately expressed by simply attesting to the fact that they once lived and dwelt among the people. Myths are required to locate the fact of their existence within a rich, inspiring context of meaning.

Oftentimes, myths successfully locate the 'life' within the context of a preexisting model or paradigm.[1] Jesus is perceived as the new Adam, the new Moses, the new Abraham. Whether or not Jesus himself considered his life to be the mirroring of these well-established paradigms, his followers and supporters believed it necessary to interpret his life in terms of these primitive mythical models. His own life, in turn, may itself become an exemplary model, worthy of emulation because it has demonstrated its affinity with traditional models. Mircea Eliade captures the dual thrust of this relation of individual lives to exemplary models when he observes:

"One of the chief characteristics of the myth [...] is the creation of exemplary models for a whole society. In this, moreover, we recognize a very general human tendency; namely, to hold up one life-history as a paradigm and turn a historical personage into an archetype. [...] As Gide has rightly observed, Goethe was highly conscious of a mission to lead a life that would be exemplary for the rest of humanity. In all that he did he was trying to *create an example*. In his own life he, in his turn, was imitating, if not the lives of the gods and mythical heroes, at least their behavior. As Paul Valéry wrote in 1932: 'He represents for us, *gentlemen of the human race*, one of our best attempts to render ourselves like gods'."[2]

Now, obviously, the relation between the actual life of the historical personage and the mythical exemplar or biographical myth never admits a perfect fit. Yet followers of the historical personage have a vital stake in their belief that he truly fits the exemplary model. And since the exemplary model has already achieved widespread currency within the given religious tradition, it is more likely that the life of the historical personage will be adjusted to coincide with the model than that the model will be revised to fit the life.[3] There is nothing in these adjustments to imply deliberate deception or conscious distortion. It simply means that the model provides the basis for the selective evaluation of the life. Usually, therefore, the highly idiosyncratic aspects of the leader's life and personality are muted or entirely eliminated, and those aspects which coincide with the exemplary model are retained and even highlighted. Again, as Eliade tells us: "To repeat, the historical character of the persons [. . .] is not in question. But their historicity does not long resist the corrosive action of mythicization. The historical event in itself, however important, does not remain in the popular memory, nor does its recollection kindle the poetic imagination save insofar as the particular historical event closely approaches a mythical model."[4] Eliade then observes that sometimes, though very rarely, an investigator has opportunity to observe the actual transformation of an event into myth.

This 'reduction' of the life to its exemplary model is probably the most typical way in which historical personages come to be related to the myths which attach to them. However, there is an extremely important variation on this typical pattern, one which allows for greater ingenuity and synthesizing skills on the part of those responsible for interpreting the life in terms of longstanding traditions. This variation occurs when the historical personage is believed to have fused in his own life two or more exemplary patterns. This fusion is especially remarkable when it involves two patterns previously considered incompatible. For example, the two patterns may have originated in an earlier split in the religious tradition which the historical personage is now understood to have reconciled; or the two patterns may represent types of religious authority (e.g. prophetic vs. priestly roles) which the historical personage is now understood to have synthesized in his own religious leadership. But, whatever the precise nature of this fusion of two or more exemplary models, the historical personage is understood to be, in some sense, the very embodiment of these exemplary patterns. Hence, his life exemplifies a new image of man in which two or more seemingly incompatible life-models are shown to be reconcilable, perhaps even complementary.[5]

The life-history of Abraham Lincoln constitutes for the historian of religion an extremely fertile ground for investigation of these issues. Like Goethe, Lincoln has come to be understood both as the embodiment of traditional exemplary models and as an exemplar which gentlemen of the human race may profitably emulate. In addition, Lincoln has been understood by his 'followers' to have fused two previosuly exemplary models, these models having been considered irreconcilable by their respective constituencies. And, finally, we are fortunate to be able to observe in Lincoln's martyrdom the transformation of the event into myth. Indeed, the argument which I want to develop in this discussion of Lincoln's paradigmatic death is that the event of his martyrdom was the catalyst for the fusion of two exemplary models previously believed irreconcilable. Thus, while prior to his martyrdom Lincoln was considered by some to be the very embodiment of one exemplary model and by others of the opposing exemplary model, his martyrdom achieved the reconciliation of these two mythological patterns. Thus, the martyrdom was that critical event which was transformed into myth, namely, the myth of his reconciliation of two exemplary models.

Representative man and folk hero: Two exemplary models

One of the most prominent uses of exemplary models in popular responses to Lincoln is to be found in Lincoln biography. I shall center attention on this biographical tradition, recognizing that there have been similar efforts to locate Lincoln within the context of these exemplary models in poetry, drama, historical novels and religious sermons.

A limited number of biographies of Lincoln predate his death. The first were published shortly after his nomination for the Presidency in 1860; but these, being essentially campaign biographies, were sketchy and evidenced limited investigation into the details of Lincoln's life. Thus, with the exception of these campaign biographies and William M. Thayer's widely read *The Pioneer Boy*, published in 1863, Lincoln biography consists entirely of works written after his death. After his death, however, biography of Lincoln flourished and continued unabated until the turn of the century.

During this thirty-five year period, there appeared such major biographies as J. G. Holland's *Life of Abraham Lincoln* (1865); Ward H. Lamon's *Life of Abraham Lincoln* (1872); William H. Herndon and Jesse W. Weik's *Herndon's Lincoln* (1888); John G. Nicolay and John Hay's *Abraham Lincoln: A History* (1890); John T. Morse, Jr.'s *Abraham Lincoln* (1893); Ida M. Tarbell's *The Life of Abraham Lincoln* (1895); and Norman Hapgood's *Abraham Lincoln: The Man of the People* (1899).[6]

After this initial flowering, Lincoln biography was again revived with the publication of another spate of biographies beginning in 1817. In this second group of biographies were such major works as Lord Charnwood's *Abraham Lincoln* (1917); Nathaniel Wright Stephenson's *Lincoln* (1922); William E. Barton's *The Life of Abraham Lincoln* (1925); Carl Sandburg's *Abraham Lincoln: The Prairie Years* (1926); Albert J. Beveridge's *Abraham Lincoln* (1928); L. Pierce Clark's *Lincoln: A Psycho-Biography* (1933); and Carl Sandburg's *Abraham Lincoln: The War Years* (1939). This second wave of Lincoln biography was accompanied by two major studies of earlier Lincoln myths, including the mythical assumptions of the first period of Lincoln biography. These two studies, Lloyd Lewis' *Myths After Lincoln* (1929) and Roy P. Basler's *The Lincoln Legend: A Study in Changing Conceptions* (1935), were not entirely unique in recognizing that the earlier biographies were shaped according to then prevailing mythical patterns, for the earlier biographers leveled the charge of mythicization at the door of other biographers. But these two studies constituted the first effort in Lincoln scholarship to recognize that all earlier biographies of Lincoln were shaped by myth. Thus, William Herndon's self-congratulatory observation to his collaborator, 'Why, Lamon, if you and I had not told the exact truth about Lincoln, he would have been a myth in a hundred years after 1865', does not persuade Lewis and Basler that certain biographers in the early period succeeded in providing a 'realistic' portrait of Lincoln. Rather, to these Lincoln scholars, all early biography of Lincoln was profoundly mythical; the problem, then, was not to distinguish realistic from mythical biographies but to identify the mythical patterns which shaped the various life-histories. Similarly, the biographers writing in this second period evidence less preoccupation with the necessity of avoiding myth.

Before we discuss these mythical patterns, however, we should note that the event of Lincoln's martyrdom was the major contributing factor in the mythicizing of his life-history. As the Lincoln scholar, Richard N. Current, observes: 'If Booth *had* missed, our knowledge of Lincoln undoubtedly would be much clearer than it is, much less clouded by mystery and myth. The awful fact of the assassination falls between us and the man [...] Lincoln's whole life tends to become obscured by the circumstances of his death.'[7] Historians acknowledge that, given his role as President in a time of Civil War, some degree of mythicization was perhaps inevitable. Yet, they also point out that the nation's spontaneous grief-reaction to Lincoln's death was so overwhelming that the mythic imagination generated by this emotional outpouring would not be denied. David Donald, Civil War historian, captures the emotional tenor of these troubled times: 'The times and events of the Civil War had made a great popular leader necessary. There had been the emotional strain of war, the taut peril of defeat, the thrill of battles won, the release of peace. Then had come the calamitous, disastrous assassination. The people's grief was immediate and it was immense [...] Mourning intesified grief. The trappings of death – the black-draped catafalque, the silent train that moved by a circuitous route over the land, the white-robed choirs that wailed a dirge, the crepe-veiled women, the stone-faced men – made Lincoln's passing seem even more calamitous. Over a million persons took a last sad look at the face in the casket and went away treasuring an unforgettable memory.'[8]

Th first wave of biographies was not unaffected by this emotional response to Lincoln's death. Indeed, as I now want to show, their mythicizing endeavors bore a remarkable similarity to the mourning ritual itself. For, if the funeral train as it circled its way westward united a grieving populace, the biographies began to effect a similar unification on the mythic level. More precisely, they began to unite two seemingly incompatible exemplary patterns – the 'representative man' of the East and the 'frontier hero' of the West. Lincoln, through his tragic death, came to be recognized as the embodiment of both exemplary models. Without the tragic, untimely death, there would have been efforts to identify him with one or the other exemplary pattern. Indeed, such efforts were underway prior to his death. But, in the wake of the assassination, biographers sensed theirs to be a more profound responsibility, namely, to demonstrate that the life of Lincoln exemplified a new image of man. Lincoln was larger-than-life because he, alone, had embodied the two exemplary patterns which other men had, at best, embodied singly. The event of Lincoln's martyrdom inspired more than effusive adulation; in addition, this spontaneous outpouring of grief gave rise to an enduring moral purpose, the mythmaker's task of depicting Lincoln's embodiment of the two exemplary patterns which had most shaped the nation's sense of its heroic dimensions: the Western folk hero and the Eastern representative man.

David Donald points out that Lincoln biography of the early period (1865–1900) has manifested two opposing schools of tradition. One is the Eastern perspective based on the literary tradition of the representative man (following George Washington and Christ) and the other is the Western folk tradition based on the biographical pattern of the folk hero[9]. Now, Donald does not explore the historiographical bases for the myth of the representative man, but it is evident that the foundations for this view were laid by major New England historians of the early 19th Century. As another historian, David Levin, indicates, the major historians of that period (Bancroft, Prescott, Motley and Parkman) were romantics who shared a special interest in heroes, especially in men and women who exemplified Emerson's 'representative man'.[10]

Levin isolates two dominant heroic characteristics in these historians' view of the representative man – naturalness and loftiness. As a *natural* man, he has an underlying simplicity, a moderate amount of passion which expresses itself in warm emotions, a quick sympathy, a delicately balanced sensibility and a natural eloquence which enables him to establish a deep rapport with the people. On the other hand, he has a *loftiness* of spirit a sense of detachment, of responding to 'a necessary law of his being' which informs actions which might otherwise be taken to be prompted by mere personal ambition. Above all, he is a man whose loftiness expresses itself in visible suffering for the whole nation. With sublime patience and constancy, he endures the depths of personal despair and even the misunderstanding of his people in order to accomplish the common good.

Significantly, Emerson himself recognized Lincoln to be an exemplar of his 'representative man'. In the wake of Lincoln's death, Emerson described Lincoln as 'the true history of the American people in his time. Step by step he walked before them; slow with their slowness, quickening his march by theirs, the true representative of this continent; an entirely public man; father of his country.'[11] As representative man, Lincoln met the requirement that he participate deeply in human affairs, in the lives of the people. As Emerson himself put it, 'The constitutency determines the role of the representative. He is not only representative, but participant. [...] Man, made of the dust of the world, does not forget his origin. [...]' On the other hand, Lincoln was more than participant in human affairs, the natural man. He was also lofty. Or, as Emerson expressed it, 'I count him a great man who inhabits a higher sphere of thought, into which other men rise with labor and difficulty; he has but to open his eyes to see things in a true light and in large relations, whilst they must make painful corrections and keep a vigilant eye on many sources of error'.[12] In short, Lincoln was that rare man who combined in one being both simplicity and loftiness. He was a man who had not lost touch with his natural origins but who, at the same time, inhabited a higher sphere of thought than other men.

Probably the most concise literary effort to capture Lincoln's embodiment of the representative man image – his naturalness and loftiness – is a sonnet by George W. Bell entitled 'The Nation's Seer'. Published in 1913, the poem views the naturalness and loftiness of Lincoln as counterpoints; his loftiness is the more remarkable in a man of profound simplicity:

The tall and stately pine-tree rears aloft
Its needle-pointed vestments bears its sway,
As prophet o'er a wilderness, and oft
Tells to the ear attuned, of storms that play.

So rose Lincoln to his lonely view
Above the hill tops springing from the plain;
Then saw he far beyond, and through and through,
As earth contact thrilled messages of pain.

A man, our very own, to earth so near,
So simple in his heartfelt tenderness,
Yet with a vision, piercing heights, a seer,

Tracing the storm clouds and the war's duress.
Seems human life a vain and worthless thing
Attuned by Lincoln to love's deathless spring?[13]

This sonnet reads almost as a paraphrase of Emerson's description of the representative man. Lincoln is a man who is close to us, simple in his heartfelt tenderness. At the same time, he is a man who rises to the hilltops and, from this heightened vantage point, sees far beyond what normal men can see.

But poets were not the only literary scholars to view Lincoln as representative man. At the turn of the century, a new kind of scholar had arrived on the scene. These were not Lincoln scholars per se, but were, instead, scholars interested in discerning the common characteristics of great men throughout the centuries. Their books usually consisted of essays, each of which attempted to isolate the 'greatness' of such heroic figures as Christ, Buddha, Goethe, Napoleon, Cromwell, Bismarck and Washington. Some considered Thomas Carlyle's lectures on 'Hero-Worship' their spiritual heritage, and it is interesting to note that Emerson wrote *Representative Men* (which also consists of a collection of essays on great men, including Plato, Montaigne, Shakespeare, Napoleon and Goethe) as a consequence of his correspondence with Carlyle regarding the lectures on 'Hero-Worship'. In any case, one such essayist who offered a portrait of Lincoln, J. N. Larned, depicted him in representative man terms. In stressing the loftiness of Lincoln's character, Larned describes him as one who stood 'like a firm, strong pillar in the midst of the swaying tempest of that uncertain time, for a tottering nation and a shaken cause to hold themselves fast by [. . .].' But Larned is convinced that Lincoln's loftiness was the effect of his deep simplicity: 'And, yet, from what simplicity of nature that influential strength of the man had come! Here, in truth, was the final secret of it. He had kept his nature as it was given him. He was so little a world-made man – so very much a God-made man. The child had grown into the man – not the man out of the child. That rare kind of growth must preserve the best fibre and elasticity of being. It must have helped to produce the quaint, homely humor which some people mistook strangely for clowniness and levity.'[14]

The literary writings of Bell, Larned and others in the early 20th Century clearly indicate that Lincoln as 'representative man' was by then firmly established. Through the Eastern biographical tradition, Lincoln could now take his rightful place in the pantheon of great moral and spiritual leaders – not only other political leaders like Napoleon, Bismarck, Cromwell and Washington, but also such paradigmatic spiritual personages as Plato, Buddha and even Christ himself. One suspects perhaps that Lincoln would have found his inclusion in this formidable company somewhat amusing. And yet, as Basler points out, Lincoln was not adverse to comparing himself to the prophet Moses, who would not live to see the promised land, and Christ, who suffered his agonies in the garden of Gethsemane before his final triumph. Thus, Lincoln himself was evidently conscious of his 'loftiness' as expressed in visible suffering for the whole nation. And, as we shall note shortly, it was precisely this aspect of the exemplary pattern of the representative man which articulated with his untimely death.

As we turn to the second biographical tradition, we enter the world of 'clowniness and levity' which Larned especially deplored. According to David Donald's description, the frontier hero for these biographers was the story teller, the shrewd bargainer, the chaste wooer, the henpecked husband, the man of great physical prowess and the anti-cleric. Thus, Lincoln was portrayed as a great spinner of yarns; as the country lawyer who eschewed fine legal reasoning in favor of shrewd common-sense; as the chaste and honorable wooer of Ann Rutledge, forbearing to plead his own cause until it seemed certain her fiance would not return to claim her; as the wrestling champion of New Salem and the indefatigable splitter of rails; and as the deeply religious man who preferred to avoid the formalities of church-going. Lincoln as 'frontier hero' originated in the West and was more truly folkloristic than the Eastern tradition of the representative man. As Donald points out: 'The grotesque hero – the Gargantua or the Till Eulenspiegel – is one of the oldest and most familiar patterns in folk literature. In America the type had been already exemplified by such favorites as Davy Crockett, Mike Fink, and Paul Bunyan. Of a like cut was the myth of Lincoln as frontier hero. [. . .] He was Old Abe, a Westerner, and his long flapping arms were not the wings of an angel.'[15]

Significantly, this Western tradition in Lincoln biography emerged as a reaction against the Eastern representative man model. Herndon, fearful that Lincoln's life would be entirely enveloped in myth if the Easterners had their way, determined to present a 'realistic' Lincoln which his former neighbors in southern Illinois would recognize. Thus, Herndon interviewed these Illinoisans, many of whom were only too willing to spin a yarn about the local boy who made good. Nor was Herndon unusually discriminating in sifting his materials. It was Herndon who first publicized the story of Ann Rutledge, a large measure of fancy mixed with a small kernel of fact, and who depicted Mary Todd as the shrewish wife whom Lincoln ought never to have married. Herndon also portrayed Lincoln as an infidel.

Herndon's work was roundly castigated. Leaders of the Republican party thought it demeaned their leader.[16] The general reading public wondered what was to be gained from painting Lincoln's origins in such earthy light. Herndon's argument, that he wanted to show how one man rose from 'putrid, stagnant' origins to the 'topmost round of the ladder', was not compelling. As the daughter of his collaborator, Dorothy Lamon Teillard, complained of this general reaction: 'It was thought his fame would suffer if all the ugly facts were known. But it was prompted in part also by the timid and the conventional cowardly notion that opinions of the time about social standing, about education, and about religion would somehow suffer if all his experiences and opinions were frankly told. [...]'[17] This general reaction to Herndon's work does not obviate the fact that the frontier hero tradition made its mark. The story of Ann Rutledge was hardly demeaning to Lincoln. Indeed, it captured the imagination of a nation ambivalent about Lincoln's widow. Also, the frontier emphasis on Lincoln's physical prowess, especially as it centered around his rail-splitting activities (and not his wrestling matches), was symbolic of the continuing strength which he had infused into the Republican party.

Yet, in spite of these obvious survivals of the frontier hero tradition, it has been argued that this tradition did not fare nearly as well as the Eastern tradition as the movement toward the fusion of these two traditions took hold. The subordination of the Western tradition was evident, it is argued, in efforts to render that tradition more genteel. Witness Larned's preference of 'quaint, homely humor' over 'clowniness and levity'. Later, 'homely humor' would give way to 'cryptic mirth'. As Basler describes this fusion of the two traditions: "Thus the wilderness hero has remained somewhat a local legend confined to the Lincoln country. The drinking, cock-fighting, rough-and-tumble hero, 'the big buck of the lick' who dared anyone to 'come on and whet his horns', the lover of broad humor – such a hero was worthy idolatry on the frontier, perhaps, but not in New England. Hence New England made its own Lincoln which it was able to a certain extent to foist upon the Lincoln country. And as the spiritual picture grew, the reminiscences became more and more in keeping with it. What there is of the frontier hero in the great Lincoln of poetry and fiction, is spiritualized and hallowed by the simple process of omission, emphasis, and invention, *which has so largely biased even the biographical accounts.*"[18] Here, Basler recognizes the fusion of the two traditions, but believes that the frontier hero tradition was necessarily shortchanged as the spiritualizing process ran its course. David Donald makes a similar point when he describes the fusion of the two traditions, though he makes a greater case for a reciprocal give-and-take. Thus, he notices that "By the centennial year of Lincoln's birth the frontier stories that had been considered gamy and rough by an earlier generation had been accepted as typical Lincolnisms; and on the other side, the harshness of the Herndonian outlines was smoothed by the acceptance of many traits from the idealized Lincoln. The result was a 'composite American ideal', whose 'appeal is stronger than that of other heroes because on him converge so many dear traditions'."[19]

Here, then, we come to the very crux of the issue. There is no question that the Eastern tradition of the representative man influenced Lincoln biography from the beginning. Uncertainty arises, however, when Lincoln scholars attempt to assess the role of the Western frontier tradition as the two traditions become merged. Was the Western tradition so thoroughly spiritualized that its unique contribution to the Lincoln myth was effectively lost? Did the Eastern tradition so dominate the mythicization of Lincoln that it admitted only those aspects of the frontier hero model that were already consistent with the model of the representative man? Basler and Donald attempt to answer this question by adducing those aspects of the frontier hero model which were 'spiritualized' in the fusion of the two traditions. Following this procedure, the Western model would necessarily appear to have fared badly in the fusion process, if only because it had far more to lose as the life-history of Lincoln became 'spiritualized'.

Now, on the basis of our earlier discussion of the manner in which life-history becomes mythicized, there is every reason to agree with Basler that the Lincoln life-history became spiritualized. The real question, then, is whether the frontier hero pattern was the mere victim of this spiritualization process, or whether it may actually have played a major role in this very process. We can gain a handle on this question by considering the possible effect of Lincoln's martyrdom in the transformation of the frontier hero model. Can we realistically expect that, after Lincoln's tragic death, the frontier hero could any longer be considered a merely comic figure a la

Crockett, Fink and Bunyan? In my judgment, the frontier hero myth underwent considerable transformation in the years following Lincoln's death, a transformation which is evident in biographers' efforts to come to terms with his frontier years. The martyrdom forced them to consider what there was about his frontier beginnings which enabled Lincoln to rise far above the essentially ludicrous folk hero, and especially whether there was some profoundly tragic element in frontier life which prepared Lincoln for the tragedies to come. Thus, it was not simply a matter of the frontier hero pattern being incorporated into the Eastern myth of the representative man and thereby spiritualized. Rather, the frontier hero pattern was itself undergoing certain transformations as a consequence of Lincoln's tragic death, and it was this transformed frontier hero which came to be fused with the Eastern model. We might say, therefore, that aspects of Herndon's portrayal of Lincoln were rejected from the composite heroic image not merely because they were inconsistent with the Eastern model, but because they had become incompatible with the frontier hero pattern as Lincoln's martyrdom had transformed it. Or perhaps behind his earthy realism, Herndon was struggling to articulate the tragic dimension of frontier society; there are elements of this tragic sense in his account of the death of Ann Rutledge.

To substantiate this line of argument, we need to turn to the biographies themselves, and then develop a more adequate description of the frontier hero as transformed by Lincoln's untimely death. Our discussion of the biographies will center on their understanding of the 'simple beginnings' from which Lincoln rose to greatness. Our attempt to describe the frontier hero myth as Lincoln transformed it will focus on Lincoln's image as Father Abraham. Since both are extremely large and complexly related problems, our consideration of each will be relatively brief. My primary concern here is not to fully substantiate this reconstruction of Donald's analysis of the biographical traditions, but to show how the martyrdom event itself played a formative role in the fusion of two seemingly incompatible exemplary patterns. As a consequence of the martyrdom, the two patterns were no longer so obviously incompatible. The frontier vision of Lincoln as not only the chaste wooer and the henpecked husband but also, and more fundamentally, the frontiersman's Father Abraham, had much to do with overcoming this incompatibility.

MARTYRDOM AND THE TRANSFORMATION OF THE FRONTIER HERO

As Wilhelm Dilthey and other have pointed out, the primary task confronting the biographer is that of depicting the 'unity' of a life. Lincoln represented an extremely difficult challenge in this regard because there seemed to be an unbridgable gulf between his simple beginnings and his later years of greatness. His biographers found this the most vexing problem they encountered and they solved it in various ways. Nicolay and Hay brought Lincoln's past into keeping with his later years. Morse pointed to some unspecified quality 'which made Lincoln, as a young man, not much superior to his coarse surroundings' but which, 'ripening and expanding rapidly and grandly with maturing years and a greater circle of humanity, made him what he was in later life'. Morse concluded that 'It is through this quality that we get continuity in him; without it we cannot evade the insoluble problem of two men – two lives – one following the other with no visible link of connection between them'.[20] Hapgood offered the theory that conflicting tendencies could reside in the same individual, such that Lincoln might 'reach as high as the saints in one direction and as high as Rabelais in another'.[21] He might be 'the prairie male as well as the sage and martyr, the deft politican as well as the generous statesman'. This position, however, has generally led those who hold it to remark on the essentially enigmatic quality of Lincoln. Thus, Richard N. Current's more recent exemplification of this theory bears the title *The Lincoln Nobody Knows*.

These early efforts to 'get continuity' in Lincoln were not altogether unsuccessful. However, the second wave of biographers did not consider the problem solved in the earlier wave for they also addressed the same problem. Charnwood attacked the problem by reducing the gap between the early and later Lincoln. Lincoln, he suggests, was neither a spiritual genius nor a low clown of tricky mind, but a consistently quiet man who bent his powers to the vindication of certain principles. David Donald appears to subscribe to this approach when he notices that, after all, the common elements in the Eastern representative man and the Western frontier hero would portray Lincoln as having all the decent qualities of civilized man: patience, tolerance, humor, sympathy, kindliness and sagacity. Hence, Lincoln is neither the great genius nor the Rabelaisian clown but a man of enduring civilized decency. Carl Sandburg, another biographer of the second wave, would not reduce the gap between Lincoln's simplicity and loftiness by denying to Lincoln these heightened expressions of greatness and commonness. Rather, he suggests that the problem has been the biographers' efforts to derive Lincoln's greatness from his simple surroundings. He proposes that Lincoln's simplicity and greatness were cut from the same piece of cloth. The environment which made Lincoln a simple man also made him the great man. This view requires Sandburg to depict a frontier environment of unique complexity, one capable of producing a man of similar complexity; hence, the prairie assumes 'epic' proportions consistent with the epic of Lincoln himself. Thus, the frontier environment is itself the basis of continuity in Lincoln; there one finds simplicity and greatness intermingled.

Now, it should be evident from even this extremely brief synopsis of Lincoln biographies that the problem of 'continuity' in Lincoln's life-history was inseparable from mythical concerns. How a biographer addressed the problem had much to do with the implicit exemplary pattern which informed the narrative. While these patterns could not prescribe the actual solution which the biographer developed in struggling with this problem, they did inform the general perspective from which he addressed the life. Identifying the 'sources' or 'roots' of Lincoln's subsequent greatness was the biographer's primary task, and the two exemplary patterns provided him general guidelines for approaching this task. On the one hand, the Eastern model of the representative man understood the 'sources' of Lincoln's greatness to be in some sense 'inherited'. As Larned has it: 'And, yet, from what simplicity of nature that influential strength of the man had come! Here, in truth, was the final secret of it. He had kept his nature as it was given him. He was so little a world-made man – so very much a God-made man.' In contrast, the Western model of the frontier hero considered the sources of Lincoln's greatness to be largely environmental. Lincoln was not possessed of a 'simplicity of nature'. Rather, he was raised in simple surroundings, in a frontier setting with its own carefully constructed image of the ideal frontier man. The dominant traits of the frontier man are social – they involve wooing, bargaining, conviviality and the like. In contrast, the representative man is strangely untouched by specific environments. His simplicity, his rootedness in human life, derives from the fact of his being 'made of the dust of the world'. In contrast to this rather imprecise depiction of the great man's social roots, the Western biographer provides vivid descriptions of the surroundings in which the frontier hero rises to maturity.

These contrasting understandings of Lincoln's simplicity are difficult to reconcile. However, biographers have recognized the critical importance of reconciling these two perspectives on the sources of Lincoln's greatness. This is a considerably more fundamental biographical task than that of reconciling the two perspectives at the level of biographical traits. For, as Basler and Donald point out, the latter problem can be handled by omitting traits which are at variance with the composite American ideal to which both traditions point. The task of 'getting continuity' in the Lincoln life-history presents a more difficult problem. Where, indeed, are the sources of Lincoln's greatness? Is greatness inherited or acquired? This problem, which is usually taken to be scientific in nature, is profoundly rooted in mythic structures – in the exemplary patterns which came to inform biographical understandings of Lincoln's life-history. However he resolves this problem for himself, the Lincoln biographer considers it to be the single most important issue which he must address if he wants to penetrate the Lincoln enigma.

Now, concerning the fusion of the Eastern model of the representative man and the Western model of the frontier hero: The biographical tradition, taken as a whole, accepts the view that Lincoln's simplicity – the basis of his greatness – was at once 'natural' and 'social'. As a natural man, he possessed warm emotions, a quick sympathy, a delicately balanced sensibility and a natural eloquence. As a 'social' man, he was a spinner of yarns, a shrewd bargainer, a chaste wooer, a henpecked husband, a man of great physical prowess, an opponent of organized religion. In short, he possessed the 'simplicity' of both the representative man and the frontier hero. In this mixture of natural and social sensitivities, the biographical tradition discerns the roots of his future greatness. Thus, at the level of the 'sources' of Lincoln's greatness, the biographical tradition finds it possible to fuse the two exemplary models.

On the other hand, it is not enough that the biographical tradition effects the fusion of the two patterns only at the level of 'sources' of greatness. For an adequate fusion to occur, there ought also to be a similar fusion at the level of his 'achievement' of greatness. Here we encounter a difficulty if we view the frontier hero model in its untransformed state (i.e., as Donald depicts it). For, the model of the representative man has incorporated the level of the achievement of greatness in its notion of 'loftiness'. The lofty man, elevated through the agency of his naturalness, is characterized by his endurance of the depths of personal despair and even the misunderstandings of his people in order to accomplish the common good. He is a man whose loftiness best expresses itself in visible suffering for his people. The fact that the loftiness theme plays heavily on the notion of suffering is important, for it supports the claim of biographers that Lincoln's embodiment of such loftiness could not, in the wake of his martyrdom, be seriously challenged. Hence, his loftiness is predicated on the view that his simplicity was enhanced or purified in the event of his martyrdom.

When we turn to the frontier model, we find no corresponding level of the 'achievement' of greatness. The characteristics of the frontier hero constitute 'sources' of greatness, but there is no provision within the model for the frontier hero to actually rise to greatness. No characteristic in Donald's depiction of the model corresponds to the loftiness of the representative man. The absence of such provision leads necessarily to the view that the characteristics of the frontier hero may be sources of greatness, but the life of the frontier hero must somehow be transcended if one is to achieve greatness. It is little wonder, therefore, that with this description of the frontier hero, the Western exemplary pattern has been considered subordinate to the Eastern pattern.

However, I have been contending that the model of the frontier hero underwent a transformation through the agency of Lincoln's martyrdom. Now we are in a position to see that this transformation took precisely the form of making provision for the achievement of greatness. Lincoln, in his role as national leader but especially through his martyrdom, became a truly 'great' frontier hero. It remains for us to discern the character of this achievement of greatness.

The answer is relatively simple. The sources of Lincoln's greatness were, according to the frontier hero model, essentially social. We should expect, then, that the frontier myth would express his achievement of greatness in social terms. If so, what the frontier model lacks in Donald's description is the hero as father – Father Abraham. Concerning sociality at the community level, the original model includes the spinner of yarns, the shrewd bargainer, the combatant, the eschewer of institutional religion; and at the domestic level, it includes the chaste wooer and henpecked husband. The father role is notoriously absent. And yet, as Basler points out,

Exemplary patterns of greatness

REPRESENTATIVE MAN	FRONTIER HERO
Sources Natural simplicity	*Sources* Social simplicity
The intervening event:	Lincoln's martyrdom
Achievement Loftiness: The image of the Martyred Christ	*Achievement* Consolation: The image of Father Abraham

this image of 'Father Abraham' was a great source of personal consolation as the nation mourned Lincoln's death: 'Lincoln as he walks at midnight is the symbol of all ideals of democratic humanity, but he is also the tender memory in apparition of the beloved personal saint, the folk Father Abraham. It was thus, in the Middle Ages that saints were said to have appeared at times of extreme exigency to cool the torturing fire, turn aside the below, or snatch the helpless out of trouble.'[22] In Father Abraham, the folk tradition had a suffering hero comparable to the Eastern image of the martyred Christ, but more accessible, more unabashedly domestic. Basler describes this image of Father Abraham as that of 'a kindly, pleasant old man with a humorous smile which often fades into a look of sadness. He is forever enshrined in popular memory dressed in black, with tall hat and black shawl. The touch of earthiness is never in the picture drawn with loving fancy. He is never thought of as having any personal interest or ambition. It is only as the guardian angel of his children that he overlooks the vast arena of war and sadly smiles as the blood sinks into the thirsty sand. He bears his own burden uncomplainingly and gladly seeks to lighten the burden of others. His sad, plain features are simply glorious in their reflection of benignity, devotion, and a wisdom passing that of earth.'[23] Thus, 'Father Abraham' came to be incorporated into the exemplary model of the frontier hero. And, because it was such an all-enveloping image, it is accurate to say that it transformed the whole.

Conclusion

Exemplary patterns such as those of the representative man and the frontier hero are not easily transformed. As we noted earlier, the great tendency is toward the omission of those characteristics of the historical personage which do not fit the exemplary pattern. This is not to say that Lincoln's life was left untouched by the exemplary patterns. Obviously, aspects of his life were played down and various adjustments in the life-history were made as biographers began to fuse Eastern and Western exemplary models. However, the image of Father Abraham is a striking addition to the exemplary model and therefore there must have been an intense need in frontier America for a mythic element of this nature. A thorough investigation into the spontaneous emergence of the Father Abraham image is well beyond the scope of our present discussion. On the other hand, Erik H. Erikson provides an important clue as to its emergence in his assessment of frontier America. Erikson notes that we have in America, as epitomized by the late 19th Century frontier, 'an ingenious arrangement which diffuses the father ideal'. He goes on: 'The boy's male ideal is rarely attached to his father, as lived with in daily life. It is usually an uncle or friend of the family, if not his grandfather, as presented to him (often unconsciously) by his mother. The grandfather, a powerful and powerfully driven man [. . .] sought new and challenging engineering tasks in widely separated regions. When the initial challenge was met, he handed the task over to others, and moved on. [. . .] His sons could not keep pace with him and were left as respectable settlers by the wayside; only his daughter was and looked like him. Her very masculine identification, however, did not permit her to take a husband as strong as her powerful father. She married what seemed, in comparison, a weak but safe man and settled down. In many ways, however, she talks like the grandfather. She does not know how she persistently belittles the sedentary father and decries the family's lack of mobility, geographic and social. Thus she establishes in the boy a conflict between the sedentary habits which she insists on, and the reckless habits she dares him to develop. [. . .] it is as if these boys were balancing on a tightrope. Only if they are stronger than or different from the real father will they live up to their secret ideals, or indeed, to their mother's expectations; but only if they somehow demonstrate that they are weaker than the omnipotent father (or grandfather) image of their childhood will they be free of anxiety.'[24]

If Erikson's analysis is accurate, it is probably not accidental that the model of the frontier hero lacked the father ideal. Perhaps under normal conditions it was possible to identify as heroes those who resented the domestic roles of husband and father. But the tragic implications of this omission of the father ideal were probably always just below the surface. In times of severe social stress, the need became great for a hero capable of embodying a father ideal which was stronger than the weak, sedentary father but less reckless and unapproachable than the omnipotent grandfather. In Abraham Lincoln, the nation found not only the namesake but also the exemplar of the strong but faithful father of the nation Israel.

For a balanced treatment of the exemplary patterns of East and West, we would need to center attention on the Christological myths of the representative man, especially on Lincoln's mythic role as martyred victim. However, the image of Father Abraham is distinguished for its restorative quality: 'He bears his own burden uncomplainingly and gladly seeks to lighten the burden of others'. Hence, this image is perhaps most exemplary of the Lincoln myth itself, for it was that very myth which followed the divisive acts of war with words of fatherly consolation.

NOTES

1. For an interesting discussion based on Karl Jaspers' notion of the 'paradigmatic individual', see Antonio S. Cua's 'Morality and the Paradigmatic Individuals', *American Philosophical Quarterly*, vol. 6, no. 4 (October 1969), pp. 324–329.
2. Mircea Eliade, *Myths, Dreams, and Mysteries*, trans. Philip Mairet (New York: Harper Torchbooks, 1967), pp. 32–33. My italics.
3. For an extremely interesting example of such an adjustment, see Kenelm O. L. Burridge, *Mambu: A Melanesian Millenium* (London: Methuen and Company, Ltd., 1960).
4. Mircea Eliade, *Cosmos and History*, trans. Willard R. Trask (New York: Harper Torchbooks, 1959), p. 42.
5. Arthur F. Wright addressed this problem in his essay 'Sui Yang-Ti: Personality and Stereotype' in Arthur F. Wright, ed., *Confucianism and Chinese Civilization* (New York: Atheneum, 1965). Wright points out: 'It would be too much to say that the elite and popular images of Yang-ti fused into a single myth, but it is certain that the two images, influencing each other, have drawn closer together during the thirteen centuries since the death of Yang-ti'. P. 186.
6. A useful summary of the major Lincoln biographies written prior to 1935 may be found in Roy P. Basler's *The Lincoln Legend: A Study in Changing Conceptions* (New York: Octagon Books, 1969), pp. 8–34.

7. Richard N. Current, *The Lincoln Nobody Knows* (New York: Hill and Wang, 1958), pp. 272–273.
8. David Donald, *Lincoln Reconsidered: Essays on the Civil War Era*, 2nd. rev. ed. (New York: Vintage Books, 1961), pp. 145–146.
9. *Ibid.*, p. 148.
10. David Levin, *History as Romantic Art* (Stanford: Stanford University Press, 1959), p. IX.
11. Ralph Waldo Emerson, quoted in Carl Sandburg, *Abraham Lincoln: The War Years* (New York: Dell Publishing Company, 1959), pp. 882–883.
12. Ralph Waldo Emerson, 'The Uses of Great Men' in *Representative Men: Seven Lectures* (New York: AMS Press, 1968), pp. 3–35.
13. See Roy P. Basler, p. 198.
14. J. N. Larned, *A Study of Greatness in Men* (Boston: Houghton, Mifflin Company, 1911), pp. 300–301. Another famous essayist in this tradition, Gamaliel Bradford, chose not to write an essay on Lincoln. However, his reasons for not doing so are suggestive. As Roy P. Basler points out: "Bradford, who splendidly interpreted in his 'psychographies' so many American heroes, never attempted a portrait of Lincoln. I have checked his numerous comments on Lincoln scattered through several volumes. Together with this work [*The Haunted Biographer*, which consists of "dialogues of the dead" between the spirit of Lincoln and those of Shakespeare, Lamb, Twain, Moody and John Wilkes Booth] they indicate an interest that is profound, and at the same time, an amount of uncertainty that is not common to Bradford's work as a whole. It is interesting to speculate that for the great 'psychographer' as for so many Lincoln biographers, Lincoln was too complex a soul. To quote Bradford's own phrase, "He still smiles and remains impenetrable." Pp. 50–51.
15. David Donald, p. 154.
16. There is a parallel here with Arthur F. Wright's study of Sui Yang-ti, *op. cit.* Wright points out that popular anecdotes and tales were drawn upon by the political leaders insofar as these were consistent with an accepted historical version of a given event in the life of Sui Yang-ti.
17. Quoted by Roy P. Basler, p. 10.
18. *Ibid.*, p. 147. My italics.
19. David Donald, pp. 162–163.
20. Quoted by Basler, p. 15. Donald comments on Morse in his essay 'The Folklore Lincoln', *op. cit.*, p. 162.
21. Quoted by Basler, p. 18.
22. Roy P. Basler, p. 200.
23. *Ibid.*, pp. 125–126. The reader's attention is also drawn to certain significant parallels between this description of Father Abraham and aspects of the Saint Nicholas myth. Cf. Adriaan D. de Groot, *Saint Nicholas: A Pyschoanalytic Study of His History and Myth* (The Hague, Paris: Mouton; New York: Basic Books, Inc., 1965).
24. Erik H. Erikson, *Childhood and Society*, rev. ed. (New York: W. W. Norton and Company, 1963), pp. 312–313.

Bibliography

1. Lives of founders

1 AMBEDKAR, Bhimrao Ramji. *The Buddha and His Dhamma*. Ahmednagar: People's Education Society, 1957.

2 AŚVAGHOSA. *The Fo-sho-hing-tsun-king. A Life of Buddha*, trans. Sanskrit to Chinese by Dharmaraksha, A. D. 420; Chinese to English by Samuel Beal. Oxford: The Clarendon Press, 1883.

3 BAREAU, André. *Recherches sur la biographie du Bouddha dans les Sutrapitaka et les Vinayapiṭaka anciens: De la quête de l'èveil à la conversion de Sériputra et de Maudgalyayana*. Paris: Ecole Française d'Extrême-Orient, 1963.

4 BARTHELEMY-SAINT-HILAIRE, Jules. *Life and Legend of Buddha*, trans. Laura Ensor. Calçutta: Susil Gupta, 1957.

5 *The Buddha and His Religion*, trans. Laura Ensor. London: G. Routledge and Sons, 1895.

6 BIGANDET, Paul. *The Life and Legend of the Gaudama, the Buddha of the Burmese*, 2 vols., 3rd ed. London: Trubner, 1880.

7 CSOMA, Sándor. *The Life and Teachings of Buddha*. Calcutta: Susil Gupta, 1957.

8 DATTA, Manamatha Nath. *Buddha: His Life, His Teachings, His Order*. Calcutta: The Society for the Resuscitation of Indian Literature, 1901.

9 DEV, Govinda Chandra. *Buddha, the Humanist*. Dacca: Paramount Publishers, 1969.

10 DUTT, Sukumar. *The Buddha and Five After-Centuries*. London: Luzac, 1957.

11 FOUCHER, Alfred. *The Life of the Buddha according to the Ancient Texts and Monuments of India*, trans. Simone Boas. Middletown, Connecticut: Wesleyan University Press, 1963.

12 GOUR, Sir Hari Singh. *The Spirit of Buddhism, Being an Examination – Analytical – Explanatory and Critical of the Life of the Founder of Buddhism: Religion and Philosophy, its Influence* . . . etc. London: Luzac, 1929.

13 LAMOTTE, Etienne. *Histoire du Boudhis meindien des origines à l'ère Saka*. Louvain: Institut Orientaliste, 1958.

14 LUBAC, Henri de. *Aspects of Buddhism*, trans, George Lamb. New York: Sheed and Ward, 1954.

15 OLDENBERG, Hermann. *Buddha: His Life, Doctrine, His Order*, trans. William Hoey. London: Williams and Norgate, 1882.

16 ROCKHILL, William W., trans. *The Life of the Buddha and the Early History of His Order*. London: Kegan Paul, Trench, Trubner, & Co., 1884.

17 SENART, Emile Charles-Marie. *Essai sur la légende du Bouddha, son caractère et ses origines*, 2nd ed. rev. Paris: E. Leroux, 1882.

Mani

18 PUECH, Henri. *Le Manichéisme: son fondateur, sa doctrine*. Paris: Civilisations du Sud (SAEP), 1949.

19 WIDENGREN, Geo. *Mani and Manichaeism*, trans. C. Kessler. London: Weidenfelt and Nicholson, 1965.

Muhammed

20 ANDRAE, Tor. *Mohammed, the Man and His Faith*. New York: Scribners, 1936.

21 BENGALEE, Mutiur Rahman. *The Life of Muhammad*. Chicago: The Moslem Sunrise Press, 1941.

22 BLACHEVE, Régis. *Le Problème de Mahomet. Essai de biographie critique du fondateur de l'Islam*. Paris: Presses Universitaires de France, 1952.

23 BODLEY, Ronald V. C. *The Messenger: The Life of Mohammed*. Garden City, New York: Doubleday and Company, 1946.

24 BUSH, George (Reverend). *The Life of Mohammed, Founder of the Religion of Islam and of the Empire of the Saracens*. New York: J. & J. Harper, 1832.

25 DERMENGHEM, Emile. *The Life of Mahomet*, trans. A. Yorke. London: G. Routledge & Sons, 1930.

26 ESSAD, Bey. *Mohammed: A Biography*, trans. H. L. Ripperger. New York, Toronto: Longmans, Green and Company, 1936.

27 GAGNIER, Jean. *La Vie de Mahomet. Traduite et compilée de l'Alcoran, des traditions authentiques de la Sonna, et des meilleurs auteurs arabes*. Amsterdam: Wetsteins and Smith, 1732.

28 GLUBB, Sir John Bagot (Glubb Pasha). *The Life and Times of Muhammed*. New York: Stein and Day, 1970.

29 GUILLAUME, Alfred. *New Light on the Life of Muhammed*. Manchester: Manchester University Press, 1960.

30 HAKEEM, F. R. *Life of Muhammed*. London: Oxford University Press, 1961.

31 IRVING, Washington. *Life of Mahomet*. NewYork: E. P. Dutton and Company, 1911.

32 IBN ISHAQ. *The Life of Muhammed*, trans. A. Guillaume. London: Oxford University Press, 1955.

33 AL-KUSHANI. *Commentary on Ibn Hisham's Biography of Muhammed according to Abn Dzarr's Mss. in Berlin, Constantinople and The Escorial ...*, ed. Paul Bronnle. Cairo: F. Diemer, 1911.

34 MUIR, Sir William. *The Life of Mohammad from Original Sources*, new and

revised by T. H. Weir. Edinburgh: J. Grant, 1923. First edition: *The Life of Mahommad and History of Islam, to the Era of the Hegira.* London: Smith, Elder & Company, 1961.
35 WATT, William Montgomery. *Muhammed at Mecca.* Oxford: Clarendon Press, 1953.
36 ——— *Muhammed at Medina.* Oxford: Clarendon Press, 1956.
37 ——— *Muhammed: Prophet and Statesman.* London: Oxford Press, 1961.
38 ——— *Muslim Intellectual: A Study of al-Ghazali.* Edinburgh: University Press, 1963.
39 WIDENGREN, Geo. *The Ascension of the Apostle and the Heavenly Book.* Uppsala: Lundequistska Bokhandeln, 1950.
40 ——— *Muhammed, the Apostle of God, and His Ascension.* Uppsala: Lundequistska Bokhandeln, 1955.

Jesus: Biography and Lives

41 ABBOTT, Lyman. *A Life Christ Founded on the Four Gospels, and Illustrated by Reference to the Manners, Customs, Religious Beliefs, and Political Institutions of His Times*, 2nd. ed. New York: Harper & Brothers, 1882.
42 ARON, Robert. *Jesus of Nazareth, the Hidden Years*, trans. F. Frenaye. London: H. Hamilton, 1962.
43 BACON, Benjamin Wismer. *Jesus, the Son of God.* New York: H. Holt and Co., 1930.
44 BALLOU, Robert Oleson. *The Other Jesus: A Narrative Based on Apocryphal Stories not included in the Bible.* Garden City, N. Y.: Doubleday, 1972.
45 BARTON, Bruce. *The Man Nobody Knows: A Discovery of Jesus.* Indianapolis: The Bobbs-Merrill Company, 1925.
46 BARTON, G. Aaron. *Jesus of Nazareth: A Biography.* New York: The Macmillan Co., 1922.
47 BEECHER, Henry Ward. *The Life of Jesus the Christ.* New York: Bromfield & Co., 1891.
48 BERGUER, Georges. *Some Aspects of the Life of Jesus from the Psychological and Psycho-analytic Point of View*, trans. Eleanor Stimson Brooks and Van Wyck Brooks. New York: Harcourt, Brace & Co., 1923.
49 BLACKBURN, William Maxwell. *The Holy Child, or, The Early Years of Our Lord Jesus Christ.* Philadelphia: Presbyterian Board of Publications, c. 1860.
50 BOSWORTH, Edward I. *Studies in the Life of Jesus Christ.* New York: n.p., 1924.
51 BOTAW, Clyde W. *The Gospels and Contemporary Biographies in the Greco-Roman World.* Philadelphia: Fortress Press, 1970.
52 BRADEN, Charles S. *Jesus Compared: A Study of Jesus and Other Great Founders of Religions.* Englewood Cliffs, New Jersey: Prentice-Hall, 1957.

53 BRANDON, Samuel G. F. *Jesus and the Zealots*. Manchester: Manchester University Press, 1967.
54 BURTON, Ernest DeWitt. *The life of Christ: An Aid to Historical Study and A Condensed Commentary on the Gospels*. Chicago: University of Chicago Press, 1904.
55 CADOUX, Cecil John. *The Life of Jesus*. West Drayton: Penguin Books, 1948.
56 CASE, Shirley Jackson. *Jesus. A New Biography*. New York: Greenwood Press, 1968.
57 COFFIN, Henry Sloane. *The Portraits of Jesus Christ in the New Testament*. New York: Macmillan, 1926.
58 COQUILL, Frank Brooks. *Jesus the Patriot*. Boston: The Christopher Publishing House, 1928.
59 DANIEL-ROPS, Henry. *The Life of Our Lord*, trans. J. R. Fosler (vol. 68 of the Twentieth Century Encyclopedia of Catholicism), 1st. ed. New York: Hawthorn Books, 1964.
60 DUNCAN, George Simpson. *Jesus, Son of Man. Studies Contributory to a Modern Portrait*. Lincoln: Nisbet, 1948.
61 ERSKINE, John. *The Human Life of Jesus*. New York: William Morrow and Co., 1945.
62 FARRAR, Frederic William. *The Life of Christ*. New York: E. P. Dutton & Co., 1874.
63 FARRELL, Walter. *Only Son*. New York: Sheed and Ward, 1953.
64 FLUSSER, David Gustav. *Jesus*, trans. R. Watts. New York: Herder and Herder, 1969.
65 FOSDICK, Harry Emerson. *The Man from Nazareth as His Contemporaries saw Him*. New York: Harper, 1949.
66 FRANK, Henry. *Jesus, A Modern Study*. New York: Greenberg, 1930.
67 GOGUEL, Maurice. *The Life of Jesus*, trans. Olive Wyon. New York: Macmillan Company, 1944.
68 GOODSPEED, Egar Johnson. *A Life of Jesus*. New York: Harper, 1950.
69 GORE, Charles. *Jesus of Nazareth*. New York: H. Holt & Company, 1929.
70 HALL, Granville Stanley. *Jesus, the Christ, in the Light of Psychology*. Garden City, New York: Doubleday, Page & Co., 1917.
71 HANNA, William. *The Life of Our Lord*, 6 vols. New York: R. Carter & Brothers, 1970–71. 1st pub. as *Our Lord's Life on Earth*, 6 vols. Edinburgh: Edmonston & Douglas, 1878.
72 KLAUSNER, Joseph. *Jesus of Nazareth: His Life, Times and Teachings*, trans. H. Danby. New York: The Maimonides Co., 1925.
73 LAUBNACH, Frank Charles, ed. *The Autobiography of Jesus*. New York: Harper & Row, 1962.
74 MURRY, John M. *Jesus, Man of Genius*. New York, London: Harper & Brothers, 1926.

75 OWEN, George Earle. *A Study of Recent Biographies of Jesus*. A. M. Thesis, University of Chicago, 1938.
76 PASCAL, Blaise. *Short Life of Christ*, trans. Cailliet and Blankenagel. Princeton: Princeton Theological Seminary, 1950.
77 RAVEN, Charles E., and Eleanor. *The Life and Teaching of Jesus Christ*. Cambridge: The University Press, 1933.
78 RENAN, Ernest. *Vie de Jésus*. 61st Edition, Paris: C. Lévy, 1921; Pb. 1965. Also *The Life of Jesus*. New York: Modern Library, 1955.
79 RHEES, Rush. *The Life of Jesus of Nazareth. A Study*. New York: Charles Scribner's, 1906.
80 SCHLEIERMACHER, Friedrich E. D. *Das Leben Jesu*. Berlin: G. Reimer, 1864.
81 SCHOEN, Max. *The Man Jesus Was*. New York: Knopf, 1950.
82 SCHONFIELD, Hugh Joseph. *Jesus. A Biography*. London: Duckworth, 1939.
83 ——— *The Passover Plot: New Light on the History of Jesus*. London: Hutchinson, 1965.
84 SCHWEITZER, Albert. *The Mystery of the Kingdom of God: The Secret of Jesus' Messiahship and Passion*, trans. Walter Lowie. New York: Macmillan, 1950.
85 SEELEY, Sir John R. *Ecce Homo: A Survey of the Life and Work of Jesus Christ*. London: J. M. Dent, 1907.
86 SHEEN, Fulton John. *Life of Christ*. New York: McGraw-Hill, 1958.
87 STEINMAN, Jean. *The Life of Jesus*, trans. P. Green. Boston: Little Brown, 1963.
88 TAYLOR, Jeremy. *The Great Exemplar: Or, the Life of Our Ever-Blessed Saviour Jesus Christ*. New York: R. Carter & Brothers, 1859.
89 TAYLOR, Vincent. *The Life and Ministry of Jesus*. London: Macmillan, 1954.
90 TORREY, Reuben Archer. *The Real Christ: The Christ of Actual Historic Fact as Distinguished from the Christ of Man's Dreams and Fancies and Imaginings*. ... London: Pickering & Inglis, 1966.
91 VOGT, Joseph, et al. *Jesus in His Time*, ed. Hans Jurgen Schultz, trans. B. Watchorn. Philadelphia: Fortress Press, 1971.
92 WILLIAM, Franz Michel. *The Life of Jesus Christ in the Land of Israel and among its People*. St Louis and London: B. Herder, 1954.
93 ZIOLKOWSKI, Theodore. *Fictional Transfigurations of Jesus*. Princeton: Princeton University Press, 1972.

Jesus: Studies in the Quest for the Historical Jesus

94 BRAATEN, Carl E. *The Historical Jesus and the Kerygmatic Christ: Essays on the New Quest of the Historical Jesus*, trans. and ed. Roya Harrisville. New York: Abingdon Press, 1964.
95 FUCHS, Ernst. *Studies of the Historical Jesus*, trans. A. Scobie. Naperville, Illinois: A. R. Allenson, 1964.

96 GLOVER, Terrot Reaveley. *The Jesus of History*. New York: Association Press, 1917.

97 HAHN, Ferdinand; W. LOHFF; and G. BORNKAMM. *Die Frage nach dem historischen Jesus*. Göttingen: Vandenhoeck & Ruprecht, 1966.

98 JEREMIAS, Joachim. *The Problem of the Historical Jesus*, trans. Norman Perrin. Philadelphia: Fortress Press, 1964.

99 KAHLER, Martin. *The So-called Historical Jesus and the Historic, Biblical Christ*, trans. Carl E. Bratten. Philadelphia: Fortress Press, 1964.

100 KECK, Leander E. *A Future for the Historical Jesus, The Place of Jesus' Preaching and Theology*. Nashville: Abingdon, 1971.

101 KITTEL, Gerhard. *Der 'historische Jesus'*. Berlin: Furche Verlag, 1932.

102 LÉON-DUFOUR, Xavier. *The Gospels and the Jesus of History*, trans. and ed. J. McHugh. New York: Desclee, 1968.

103 MCARTHUR, Harvey K., ed. *The Quest through the Centuries: The Search for the Historical Jesus*. Philadelphia: Fortress Press, 1966.

104 MCCOWN, Chester C. *The Search for the Real Jesus: A Century of Historical Study*. New York: C. Scribner's Sons, 1940.

105 MACKINNON, James. *The Historic Jesus*. London, New York: Longmans, Green & Co., 1931.

106 MICHL, Johann. *Fragen um Jesus: Antworten aus historischer Sicht*. Luzern, Munchen: Rex-Verlag, 1967.

107 MORE, Paul E. *The Christ of the New Testament*. New York: Greenwood Press, 1969.

108 MUSSNER, Franz. *The Historical Jesus in the Gospel of St. John*, trans. W. J. O'Hara. New York: Herder and Herder, 1967.

109 OLMSTEAD, Albert Ten Eyck. *Jesus in the Light of History*. New York: C. Scribner's Sons, 1942.

110 OTTO, Rudolf. *Leben und Wirken Jesu nach historisch-kritischer Auffassung*. Göttingen: Vandenhoeck & Ruprecht, 1902. Trans. as *The Life and Ministry of Jesus according to the Historical Method*. Chicago: Open Court, 1908.

111 PIEPENBRING, Charles. *The Historical Jesus*, trans. L. A. Clare. New York: Macmillan Co., 1924.

112 ROBINSON, James M. *A New Quest of the Historical Jesus* (Studies in Biblical Theology, No. 25). Naperville, Illinois: A. R. Allenson, 1959.

113 SCHLESINGER, Max (Rabbi of Albany). *The Historical Jesus of Nazareth*. New York: C. P. Somerby, 1876.

114 SCHWEITZER, Albert. *The Quest of the Historical Jesus: A Critical Study of its Progress from Reimarus to Wrede*, trans. W. Montgomery. London: A. & C. Black, 1910.

115 SLENNCZKA, Reinhard. *Geschichlichkeit und Personsein Jesu Christi: Studien zur Christologischen Problematik der historischen Jesusfrage*. Göttingen: Vandenhoek & Ruprecht, 1967.

116 STRACHAN, Robert H. *The Historic Jesus in the New Testament.* London: Student Christian Movement Press, 1931.
117 STRAUSS, David F. *The Life of Jesus Critically Examined*, ed. P. C. Hodgson; trans. of 4th German edtn. by G. Eliot. Philadelphia: Fortress Press, 1972.
118 WORSLEY, Frederick William. *The Apocalypse of Jesus: Being a Step in the Search for the Historical Christ.* London: J. J. Bennett, 1912.
119 WREDE, William. *Das Messiasgeheimnis in den Evangelien: Zugleich ein Beitrag zum Verständnis des Markusevangeliums.* Göttingen: Vandenhoeck & Ruprecht, 1901. Trans. as *The Messianic Secret*, by J. C. G. Greig. Cambridge, England: J. Clarke, 1971.

2. LIVES AND LEGENDS OF SAINTS

120 BLOOM, Alfred. 'The Life of Shinran Shonin'. *Numen*, Vol. 15, No. 1, pp. 62 ff.
121 BROWN, Paul Alonzo. *The Development of the Legend of Thomas Becket.* Philadelphia: University of Pennsylvania Press, 1930.
122 DELEHAYE, Hippolyte. *The Legends of the Saints*, trans. Donald Attwater. New York: Fordham University Press, 1962.
123 DERMENGHEM, Emile. *Le culte des saints dans l'Islam maghrebin*, 5th ed. Paris: Gallimard, 1954.
124 DUCKETT, Eleanor Shipley. *The Wandering Saints of the Early Middle Ages.* London: Collins, 1959.
125 ——— *Anglo-Saxon Saints and Scholars.* New York: Macmillan, 1947.
126 FARĪD, al-Dīn 'Attar. *Muslim Saints and Mystics: Episodes from the 'Memorial of the Saints'*, trans. A. J. Arberry. Chicago: University of Chicago Press, 1966.
127 GHURYE, G. S. *Indian Sadhus.* Bombay: Popular Book Depot, 1953.
128 HODGES, George. *Saints and Heroes to the End of the Middle Ages.* Freeport, New York: Books for Libraries Press, 1967.
129 HURWITZ, Leon. 'Chih-i'. *Mélanges Chinois et Bouddhique*, Vol. 12, Bruges, 1963.
130 HUTTON, William Holden. *The Influence of Christianity upon National Character, Illustrated by the Lives and Legends of the English Saints.* London: W. Gardner, Darton, and Company, 1903.
131 ICHIRŌ, Hori. 'On the Concept of Hijiri (Holy Man)'. *Numen*, Vol. 5, No. 2 (April, 1958), pp. 128–160; and, *Ibid.*, Vol. 5, No. 3 (September, 1958), pp. 199–232.
132 JACOBUS DE VARAGINE. *The Golden Legend; or, Lives of the Saints, as Englished by William Caxton.* London: J. M. Dent and Company, 1900. Trans. and adapted G. Ryan and H. Ripperger, London, New York: Longmans, Green, 1941.
133 JONES, Charles William. *Saints' Lives and Chronicles in Early England; together*

with first English translations of the oldest life of Pope St. Gregory the Great by a monk of Whitby, and the life of St. Guthlac of Crowland by Felix. Ithaca: Cornell University Press, 1947.

134 MAHADEVAN, Telliyavaram M. P. *Sankaracharya.* New Delhi: National Book Trust, 1968.

135 ——— *Ten Saints of India.* Bombay: n.p., 1965.

136 ——— ed. *Seminar on Indian Saints.* Madras: n.p., 1960.

137 MECKLIN, John M. *The Passing of the Saint: A Study of a Cultural Type.* Chicago: University of Chicago Press, 1941.

138 MICHELET, Jules. *The Life of Joan of Arc by J. Michelet, and Other Biographies* n.p.: Spencer Press, c. 1937. (Includes Mahomet by E. Gibbon; Luther by C. K. J. Bunsen; Frederick the Great by T. B. Macaulay; Cromwell by A. Lamartine.)

139 TATTWANANDA, Swami. *The Saints of India.* Calcutta: Nirmalendu Bikash Sen Gupta, 1960.

140 WHITE, Helen Constance. *Tudor Books of Saints and Martyrs.* Madison: University of Wisconsin Press, 1963.

141 WIDENGREN, Geo. *Literary and Psychological Aspects of the Hebrew Prophets.* Uppsala: Lundequistska Bokhandeln, 1948.

142 WINTERBOTTOM, Michael, ed. *Three Lives of English Saints.* Toronto: Pontifical Institute of Medieval Studies, 1972.

143 WORDSWORTH, Christopher. *Ecclesiastical Biography: or, Lives of Eminent Men, Connected with the History of Religion in England*, 6 vols. London: Rivington, 1810.

144 WRIGHT, Arthur F. 'Biography and Hagiography: Huei-chiao's Lives of Eminent Monks'. In *Silver Jubilee Volume*, Kyoto University: Kyoto Daigaku Jimbun Kagaku Kenkyujo, pp. 383–443.

3. SAVIORS, HEROES, AND DIVINE PERSONAGES

145 BRANDON, Samuel G. F., ed. *The Saviour God.* Manchester: Manchester University Press, 1963.

146 ELIADE, Mircea. *Shamanism: Archaic Techniques of Ecstasy*, trans. Willard Trask. New York: Bollingen Foundation, 1964.

147 FESTUGIÉRE, André-Jean. 'Popular Piety'. In *Personal Religion among the Greeks.* Berkeley: University of California Press, 1954, pp. 85–104.

148 HADAS, Moses; and Morton SMITH. *Heroes and Gods: Spiritual Biographies in Antiquity.* Freeport, New York: Books for Libraries Press, 1970.

149 HUNTER, Henry. *Sacred Biography, or, The History of the Patriarchs, to which is added, the History of Deborah, Ruth, and Hannah.* Philadelphia: J. J. Woodward, 1836.

150 RAGLAN, Lord. *The Hero: A Study in Tradition, Myth, and Drama.* New York: Oxford University Press, 1937.
151 RANK, Otto. *The Myth of the Birth of the Hero*, ed. P. Freund. New York: Vintage Books, 1959.
152 SCHOLEM, Gershom. *Sabbatai Sevi: The Mystical Messiah, 1626–1676.* Princeton: Princeton University Press, 1973.

4. REFORMERS, RULERS, AND OTHER RELIGIOUS LEADERS

153 ALGER, Horatio. *Abraham Lincoln, the Backwoods Boy; or, How a Young Railsplitter became President.* New York: J. R. Anderson and H. S. Allen, 1883.
154 ANESAKI, Masaharu. *Nichiren, the Buddhist Prophet.* Cambridge: Harvard University Press, 1916.
155 ARENDT, Hannah. *Men in Dark Times.* New York: Harcourt, Brace and World, 1955.
156 BASLER, Roy P. *The Lincoln Legend: A Study in Changing Conceptions.* New York: Octagon Books, 1969.
157 CARLETON, William. 'A New Look at Woodrow Wilson'. *Virginia Quarterly Review*, Vol. 38 (1962), pp. 545–566.
158 CORBIN, Henry. *Creative Imagination in the Sufism of Ibn 'Arabi*, trans. R. Manheim. Princeton: Princeton University Press, 1969.
159 GEERTZ, Clifford. *Islam Observed: Religious Development in Morocco and Indonesia.* New Haven: Yale University Press, 1968.
160 KAHN, Harold. *Monarchy in the Emperor's Eyes: Image and Reality in the Ch'ien-Lung Reign.* Cambridge: Harvard University Press, 1971.
161 LINK, Arthur. 'The Biography of Tao-an'. *T'oung Pao*, Vol. 46 (1958), pp. 1–48.
162 LIU, James T. C. 'An Early Sung Reformer: Fan Chung-Yen'. In *Chinese Thought and Institutions*, ed. John Fairbank, Chicago: University of Chicago Press, 1957.
163 MASSIGNON, Louis. *Akhbar al-Hallāj.* Paris: J. Vrin, 1957.
164 PIERCE, David C. 'Jonathan Edwards and the "New Sense" of Glory'. *The New England Quarterly*, Vol. 41, No. 1 (March, 1968), pp. 82–95.
165 SMITH, Lacey Baldwin. *Henry VIII: The Mask of Royalty.* Boston: Houghton Mifflin Co., 1971.
166 WERBLOWSKI, R. J. Zwi. *Joseph Karo, Lawyer and Mystic.* London: Oxford University Press, 1962.
167 WRIGHT, Arthur F.; and Denis TWITCHETT, eds. *Confucian Personalities.* Stanford, California: Stanford University Press, 1962.
168 ——— 'Sui Yang-ti: Personality and Stereotype'. In *Confucianism and Chinese Civilization.* New York: Atheneum, 1965, pp. 158–187.

5. Social scientific studies of religious individuals

Psychological studies

169 Bainton, Roland H. 'Psychiatry and History: An Examination of Erikson's *Young Man Luther*'. *Religion in Life* (Winter, 1971), pp. 450–478.

170 Beck, Samuel J. 'Abraham, Kierkegaard: Either, Or'. *The Yale Review*, Vol. 62, No. 1 (Autumn, 1972), pp. 59–75.

171 Binion, Rudolph. *Frau Lou: Nietzsche's Wayward Disciple*. Princeton: Princeton University Press, 1968.

172 Bodkin, Maud. *Archetypal Patterns in Poetry: Psychological Studies of Imagination*. London: Oxford University Press, 1963.

173 ——— *Studies of Type-Images in Poetry, Religion, and Philosophy*. London, New York: Oxford University Press, 1951.

174 Bradford, Gamaliel. *Biography and the Human Heart*. Boston and New York: Houghton Mifflin Co., 1932.

175 ——— *A Naturalist of Souls: Studies in Psychography*. Port Washington, New York: Kennikat Press, 1926.

176 ——— *Saints and Sinners*. Boston and New York: Houghton Mifflin Co., 1932.

177 Bushman, Richard L. 'Jonathan Edwards and Puritan Consciousness'. *Journal for the Scientific Study of Religion*, Vol. 5, No. 3 (Fall, 1966), pp. 383–396.

178 ——— 'Jonathan Edwards as Great Man: Identity, Conversion and Leadership in the Great Awakening'. *Soundings*, Vol. 52, No. 1 (Spring, 1969), pp. 15–46.

179 ——— 'On the Uses of Psychology: Conflict and Conciliation in Benjamin Franklin'. *History and Theory*, Vol. 5, pp. 225–240.

180 Campbell, Joseph. *The Hero with a Thousand Faces*. Princeton: Princeton University Press (Bollingen Series), 1949.

181 Capps, Donald. 'John Henry Newman: A Study of Vocational Identity'. *Journal for the Scientific Study of Religion*, Vol. 9, No. 1 (Spring, 1970), pp. 33–51.

182 ——— 'Orestes Brownson: The Psychology of Religious Affiliation'. *Journal for the Scientific Study of Religion*, Vol. 7, No. 2 (1968), pp. 197–209.

183 Clark, L. Pierce. *Lincoln: A Psycho-biography*. New York: Charles Scribners Sons, 1933.

184 Dittes, James E. 'Continuities between the Life and Thought of Augustine'. *Journal for the Scientific Study of Religion*, Vol. 5, No. 1, pp. 130–140.

185 Dodd, C. H. 'The Mind of Paul: A Psychological Approach'. *Bulletin of the John Rylands Library* (The Manchester University Press), Vol. 17 (1933), pp. 91–105.

186 Dodds, E. R. 'Augustine's *Confessions:* A Study of Spiritual Maladjustment'. *The Hibbert Journal*, Vol. 26 (1927–1928), pp. 457–473.

187 EISSLER, K. R. *Goethe: A Psychoanalytic Study, 1775–1786*, 2 vols. Detroit: Wayne State University Press, 1963.

188 ERIKSON, Erik H. *Gandhi's Truth: On the Origins of Militant Nonviolence*. New York: W. W. Norton, 1969.

189 ——— 'The Legend of Hitler's Childhood'. In *Childhood and Society*, 2nd rev. ed. New York: W. W. Norton, 1963, pp. 326–358.

190 ——— 'The Legend of Maxim Gorky's Youth'. In *Ibid.*, pp. 359–402.

191 ——— 'On the Nature of Psychohistorical Evidence: In Search of Gandhi'. *Daedalus*, Vol. 97 (Summer, 1968), pp. 695–730.

192 ——— *Young Man Luther*. New York: W. W. Norton, 1958.

193 ——— 'The Founders: Jeffersonian Action and Faith'. In *Dimensions of a New Identity*. New York: W. W. Norton, 1974, pp. 9–60.

194 ERIKSON, Joan M. 'Nothing to Fear: Notes on the Life of Eleanor Roosevelt'. *Daedalus*, Vol. 93, No. 2 (Spring, 1964), pp. 781–801.

195 FEUER, Lewis S. 'Anxiety and Philosophy: The Case of Descartes'. *The American Imago*, Vol. 20, No. 4 (Winter, 1963), pp. 411–449.

196 ——— 'The Conversion of Karl Marx's Father'. *The Jewish Journal of Sociology*, Vol. 14, No. 2 (December, 1972), pp. 149–166.

197 ——— 'The Dream of Benedict de Spinoza'. *The American Imago*, Vol. 14, No. 3 (Fall, 1957), pp. 225–242.

198 ——— 'God, Guilt, and Logic: The Psychological Basis of the Ontological Argument'. *Inquiry*, Vol. 11 (1968), pp. 257–281.

199 ——— 'Lawless Sensations and Categorical Defenses: The Unconscious Sources of Kant's Philosophy'. In *Psychoanalysis and Philosophy*, ed. M. Lazerowitz and C. Hanly, New York: 1970.

200 GEORGE, Alexander and Juliette. *Woodrow Wilson and Colonel House: A Personality Study*. New York: Dover, 1964.

201 GROOT, Adriaan D. de. *Saint Nicholas: A Psychoanalytic Study of His History and Myth*. The Hague: Mouton; New York: Basic Books, 1965.

202 HITSCHMANN, Edward. *Great Men: Psychoanalytic Studies*. New York: International Universities Press, 1956.

203 JAMES, William. *The Varieties of Religious Experience*. New York: A Mentor Book, 1958.

204 JUNG, Carl G. 'The Psychology of the Child Archetype'. In *Essays on a Science of Mythology*, by C. G. Jung and C. Kerényi. Princeton: Princeton University Press, 1959, pp. 70–100.

205 KIELL, Norman. *Psychological Studies of Famous Americans: The Civil War Era*. New York: Twayne Publishers, 1964.

206 KRETSCHMER, Ernst. *The Psychology of Men of Genius*, trans. R. B. Cattell. London: Kegan Paul, Trench, Trubner and Company, 1931.

207 KRIS, Ernst. 'A Psychological Study of the Role of Tradition in Ancient Biographies'. In *Psychoanalytic Explorations in Art*. New York: Schocken Books, 1964, pp. 64–84.

208 KUNZLI, Arnold. *Karl Marx: Eine Psychographie*. Vienna: Europa Verlag, 1966.
209 LIFTON, Robert Jay. 'Protean Man'. *Partisan Review*, Vol. 35, No. 1 (Winter, 1968), pp. 13–27.
210 LUBIN, Albert J. *Stranger on the Earth: A Psychological Biography of Vincent van Gogh*. New York: Holt, Rinehart and Winston, 1972.
211 MITZMAN, Arthur. *The Iron Cage: An Historical Interpretation of Max Weber*. New York: Knopf, 1969.
212 SCHNEIDERMAN, Leo. "Ramakrishna: Personality and Social Factors in the Growth of a Religious Movement". *Journal for the Scientific Study of Religion*, Vol. 8, No. 1 (Spring, 1969), pp. 60–71.
213 SHORE, Miles F. "Henry VIII and the Crisis of Generativity". *The Journal of Interdisciplinary History*, Vol. 2, No. 4 (Spring, 1972), pp. 359–390.
214 WARD, Aileen. *John Keats: The Making of a Poet*. New York: The Viking Press, 1963.

Anthropological and Sociological Studies

215 BARTON, Roy F. *Autobiographies of Three Pagans in the Philippines*. New York: University Books, 1963.
216 BURRIDGE, Kenelm O. *Mambu: A Melanesian Millenium*. London: Methuen Press, 1960.
217 DOLLARD, John. *Criteria for the Life History*. New Haven: Yale University Press, 1935.
218 DYK, Walter. *Son of Old Man Hat: A Navaho Autobiography Recorded by W. Dyk*. New York: Harcourt, Brace, 1938.
219 HANDELMAN, Don. 'The Development of a Washo Shaman'. *Ethnology*, Vol. 6, No. 4 (October, 1967), pp. 444–464.
220 LEWIS, Oscar. *The Children of Sanchez: Autobiography of a Mexican Family*. New York: Random House, 1961.
221 RADIN, Paul. *Crashing Thunder: The Autobiography of a Winnebago Indian*. New York: D. Appleton and Co., 1926.
222 SIMMONS, Leo. *Sun Chief: The Autobiography of a Hopi Indian*. New Haven: Yale University Press, 1942.
223 TOZZLER, Alfred M. 'Biography and Biology'. In C. Kluckhohn and H. Murray, eds., *Personality in Nature, Society and Culture*. New York: Alfred A. Knopf, 1948, pp. 144–157.
224 TURNER, Victor. 'Hidalgo: History as Social Drama'. In *Dramas, Fields, and Metaphors*. Ithaca, London: Cornell University Press, 1974, pp. 98–155.
225 WACH, Joachim. 'Types of Religious Authority'. In *Sociology of Religion*. Chicago: University of Chicago Press, 1944, pp. 331–374.

6. Comparative biographical studies

226 Carlyle, Thomas. *Oh Heroes, Hero-Worship and the Heroic in History.* London: E. P. Dutton, 1908.
227 Emerson, Ralph Waldo. *Representative Men.* Boston: Phillips, Sampson and Company, 1850.
228 Jaspers, Karl. *The Great Philosophers*, ed. H. Arendt, trans. R. Mannheim. New York: Harcourt, Brace, and World, 1962. (Paradigmatic Individuals: Socrates, Buddha, Confucius, Jesus.)
229 ——— *Philosophy*, Volume II, trans. E. B. Ashton. Chicago: University of Chicago Press, 1970 (pp. 343–359, especially 352–353 on personal greatness and types of great figures).
230 ——— *Three Essays: Leonardo, Descartes, Max Weber*, trans. R. Mannheim. New York: Harcourt, Brace and World, 1964.
231 Larned, J. N. *A Study of Greatness in Men.* Boston: Houghton Mifflin Company, 1911.
232 Lewis, Richard W. B. *The American Adam: Innocence, Tragedy, and Tradition in the Nineteenth Century.* Chicago: University of Chicago (Phoenix) Press, 1959.
233 Macmurray, John, ed. *Some Makers of the Modern Spirit (A Symposium).* London: Methuen, 1933.
234 Muzzey, David S. *Spiritual Heroes: A Study of Some of the World's Prophets.* New York: Doubleday, Page, and Company, 1902.
235 Sorokin, Pitirim A. *Altruistic Love: A Study of American 'Good Neighbors' and Christian Saints.* Boston: Beacon Press, 1950.
236 Strachey, Giles Lytton. *Biographical Essays.* New York: Harcourt, Brace, 1949.
237 Turck, Herman. *The Man of Genius.* Berlin: Wilhelm Barngraher Verlag. 1914.

7. General works in biography and autobiography

238 Allport, Gordon W. *The Use of Personal Documents in Psychological Science.* New York: Social Science Research Council Bulletin No. 49, 1942.
239 Berry, Thomas E., ed. *The Biographer's Craft.* New York: Odyssey Press, 1967.
240 Bowen, Catherine Drinker. *Biographer: The Craft and the Calling.* Boston: Little Brown, 1969.
241 Ebner, Dean. *Autobiography in Seventeenth Century England: Theology and the Self.* The Hague: Mouton, 1971.
242 Edel, Leon. *Literary Biography.* London: R. Hart-Davis, 1957.

243 KLUCKHOHN, Clyde. *The Use of Personal Documents in Anthropology*. New York: Social Science Research Council Bulletin No. 55, 1945.
244 LANGNESS, Lewis L. *The Life History in Anthropological Science*. New York: Holt, Rinehart & Winston, 1965.
245 MCCLENDON, James. 'Biography as Theology' *Commonweal*, XXI (Fall, 1971), pp. 415-430.
246 MISCH, George. *A History of Autobiography in Antiquity*, trans. with author by E. W. Dickes. London: Routledge and Paul, 1965.
247 MOMIGLIANO, Arnold. *The development of Greek Biography*. Cambridge: Harvard University Press, 1971.
248 MORRIS, John N. *Versions of the Self: Studies in English Autobiography from John Bunyan to John Stuart Mill*. New York: Basic Books, 1966.
249 NICOLSON, Hon. Harold G. *The Development of English Biography*. New York: Harcourt, Brace, 1928.
250 OLNEY, James. *Metaphors of Self: The Meaning of Autobiography*. Princeton: Princeton University Press, 1972.
251 O'NEILL, Edward H. *A History of American Biography, 1800–1935*. Philadelphia: University of Pennsylvania Press, 1935.
252 SAYRE, Robert F. *The Examined Self: Benjamin Franklin, Henry Adams, Henry James*. Princeton: Princeton University Press, 1964.
253 SHEA, Daniel B. *Spiritual Autobiography in Early America*. Princeton: Princeton University Press, 1968.
254 WATKINS, Owen C. *The Puritan Experience: Studies in Spiritual Autobiography*. New York: Schocken Books, 1972.

8. AUTHOR'S INDEX TO THE BIBLIOGRAPHY

The numbers refer to the numbers in the bibliography)

Index of Proper Names